Post-Authoritarian Cultures
*Spain and Latin America's
Southern Cone*

HISPANIC ISSUES • VOLUME 35

Post-Authoritarian Cultures
*Spain and Latin America's
Southern Cone*

Luis Martín-Estudillo

AND

Roberto Ampuero

EDITORS

Vanderbilt University Press
NASHVILLE, TENNESSEE
2008

© 2008 Vanderbilt University Press
All rights reserved
First Edition 2008

This book is printed on acid-free paper.
Manufactured in the United States of America

The editors gratefully acknowledge assistance
from the College of Liberal Arts
and the Department of Spanish and Portuguese Studies
at the University of Minnesota.

*The complete list of volumes in the
Hispanic Issues series begins on page 275.*

Library of Congress Cataloging-in-Publication Data

Post-authoritarian cultures : Spain and Latin America's Southern Cone
/ Luis Martín-Estudillo and Roberto Ampuero, editors. — 1st ed.
   p. cm. — (Hispanic issues ; 35)
 Includes bibliographical references and index.
 ISBN 978-0-8265-1604-6 (cloth : alk. paper)
 ISBN 978-0-8265-1605-3 (pbk. : alk. paper)
 1. Democratization—Southern Cone of South America.
 2. Democratization—Spain. 3. Art—Political aspects—Southern Cone
of South America. 4. Art—Political aspects—Spain. 5. Politics and
literature—Southern Cone of South America. 6. Politics and
literature—Spain. 7. Popular culture—Southern Cone of South
America. 8. Popular culture—Spain. 9. Latin American literature—
20th century—History and criticism. 10. Spanish literature—20th
century—History and criticism.
 I. Martín-Estudillo, Luis. II. Ampuero, Roberto, 1953–
 F2217.P67 2008
 306.098—dc22
 2008015544

HISPANIC ISSUES

Nicholas Spadaccini
Editor-in-Chief

Antonio Ramos-Gascón and Jenaro Talens
General Editors

Nelsy Echávez-Solano and Luis Martín-Estudillo
Associate Editors

Eric Dickey and Kelly McDonough
Assistant Editors

Advisory Board/Editorial Board
Rolena Adorno (Yale University)
Román de la Campa (Unversity of Pennsylvania)
David Castillo (University at Buffalo)
Jaime Concha (University of California, San Diego)
Tom Conley (Harvard University)
William Eggington (Johns Hopkins University)
Brad Epps (Harvard University)
Eduardo Forastieri-Braschi (Universidad de Puerto Rico, Río Piedras)
*Ana Forcinito (University of Minnesota)
David W. Foster (Arizona State University)
Edward Friedman (Vanderbilt University)
Wlad Godzich (University of California, Santa Cruz)
Antonio Gómez-Moriana (Université de Montréal)
Hans Ulrich Gumbrecht (Stanford University)
*Carol A. Klee (University of Minnesota)
Eukene Lacarra Lanz (Universidad del País Vasco)
Tom Lewis (University of Iowa)
Jorge Lozano (Universidad Complutense de Madrid)
Walter D. Mignolo (Duke University)
*Louise Mirrer (The New-York Historical Society)
Mabel Moraña (Washington University in St. Louis)
Alberto Moreiras (University of Aberdeen)
Bradley Nelson (Concordia University)
Michael Nerlich (Université Blaise Pascal)
Miguel Tamen (Universidade de Lisboa)
Teresa Vilarós (University of Aberdeen)
Iris M. Zavala (UNESCO, Barcelona)
Santos Zunzunegui (Universidad del País Vasco)

In memoriam
René Jara (1941–2007)
Scholar, mentor, friend.

Contents

Introduction:
Consent and Its Discontents
Luis Martín-Estudillo and Roberto Ampuero   xi

PART I
Contesting Power, Forging Commitment

1   Democratic Culture and Transition in Chile
Jorge Edwards   3

2   Writing from the Margins of the Chilean Miracle: Diamela Eltit and the Aesthetics and Politics of the Transition
Juliet Lynd   12

3   The Riders Get off the Horse: David Viñas and the Demise of the Authoritarian Argentine Military
Hans-Otto Dill   34

4   A Journey through the Desert: Trends of Commitment in Contemporary Spanish Poetry
Luis Bagué Quílez   58

PART II
Interrogating Memories

5   Testimonial Narratives in the Argentine Post-Dictatorship: Survivors, Witnesses, and the Reconstruction of the Past
Ana Forcinito   77

6   *Tejanos*: The Uruguayan Transition Beyond
Gustavo A. Remedi   99

7   Dancing with Destruction: Pop Music
    during the Spanish Transition
    Antonio Méndez-Rubio   122

8   Popular Filmic Narratives and the Spanish Transition
    Germán Labrador Méndez   144

PART III
Looking In/Looking Out: Negotiating Identities

9   Staged Ethnicity, Acted Modernity: Identity and Gender
    Representations in Spanish Visual Culture (1968–2005)
    Estrella de Diego   175

10 Creating a New Cohesive National Discourse in Spain
    after Franco
    Carsten Humlebæk   196

11 Intellectuals, Queer Culture, and Post-Military Argentina
    David William Foster   218

12 Some Notes on International Influences on Transition
    Processes in the Southern Cone
    Heinrich Sassenfeld   233

    Afterword
    David William Foster   249

    Contributors   255

    Index   261

◆ Introduction:
Consensus and Its Discontents

Luis Martín-Estudillo and Roberto Ampuero

In Argentina, Chile, Uruguay, and Spain there is still a debate about whether or not the complex processes that have been called "transitions to democracy" have ended. The growing insistence on the elaboration of historical judgments on those periods, as well as other recent relevant events—such as the death of Chilean dictator Augusto Pinochet or the trials of military officials in Argentina—may be a sign of their completion. But one could also mention elements of continuity which point to the currency of social and political tensions associated with the dictatorial heritage of those nations. Witness the Uruguayan initiative to reinterpret a piece of legislation known as "impunity law," or the vibrant debates about so-called "historical memory" which are currently on various nations' agendas. This would indicate that they also face the potential impossibility of completing the process, which would express itself in the never-ending conflicts between retelling the past and deleting it, or between justice and impunity. It is equally difficult to assign starting dates to transitions, especially when they are not defined as strictly political events. Operating with a relative autonomy from the government, cultural production in the above-mentioned countries often anticipated the kind of change and opening associated with the recovery (or reinvention) of democratic freedoms. Thus, the cultural sphere has proven to be a significant locus of debate and agency, as proponents of different (and often conflicting) ways of dealing with the past and imagining the future contributed there to numerous civic projects. In this sense, it might be productive to recall Erich Auerbach's notion of *Retardierung* as it helps to understand how art, and especially literature, allows for the possibility to explore history in depth by "slowing down" events and focusing on crucial aspects through aesthetic and intellectual lenses. This volume of *Hispanic Issues* analyzes the role of intellectuals and artists in the creation of postauthoritarian orders, while this Introduction tries to cast light on how opposing stances of acceptance and defiance of those orders were configured. While the scope of the problem (which articulates something as vast as *culture* in four different countries) prompts us to desist from the start from trying to reach encompassing conclusions, we believe that it is possible to advance some notions that are common to these processes.

One of the main differences between the genesis of the dictatorship in Spain and those of the Southern Cone lies in the character of the conflicts which led to them. While in Spain there was a war involving a confrontation mainly between two regular armies, supported by their respective international allies, in the Southern Cone this situation was lacking, even if the military of Argentina and Chile sought to impose their version of such a war. Southern Cone regular armies operated within the Doctrine of National Security dictated by the Pentagon within the political frame of the Cold War, launching systematic repression against political parties, civic movements, and scattered armed groups which had advocated armed struggle under the inspiration of the Cuban Revolution, whose leaders offered moral and technical support. The asymmetrical military clash between antagonistic forces signaled the dirtiest wars ever directed against civilians in Latin America. Once in power, the armies closed congress, exercised control over the police, the press and the judiciary, and imposed a state of emergency to exert repression without legal limits. Hans-Otto Dill's essay in this volume deals with several novels by Argentine author David Viñas and offers an analysis of an "insider's" view of the military. Dill elaborates on the worldview and resentment of the Argentinean military regarding civil society, and also provides us a key for understanding the logic of its repression of wide sectors of the nation's population. How this brutal repression and authoritarian control of the public realm affected demands for justice and memory and negotiated different forms of oblivion during the democratic transition is a subject that various other essays included in this volume explore in an oblique way.

The character of a transition is also determined by how a dictatorship ends. In Spain, the ruling metonymy of General Francisco Franco's natural death while still in power tends to overshadow the severely conflictive reality of those years, when the regime was still imprisoning, torturing and even killing its citizens for political reasons. Thus, it must be pointed out that while the State slowly dismantled its own authoritarian structures, the result was not a situation of *tabula rasa* in which all participants in the emerging democracy had equal opportunities regarding the construction of a new model of society. The hegemonic narrative of a "model transition" that has been presented from above for years has recently begun to be contested in the mainstream media by people such as political scientist Vicenç Navarro, who argues that:

> En Alemania y en Italia, el nazismo y el fascismo fueron derrotados. En España, sin embargo, el franquismo no lo fue. El estado franquista fue adaptándose a una nueva realidad resultado de una presión nacional e internacional. Las estructuras dirigentes de aquel Estado se percataron de la necesidad de cambiarlo para ir adaptándolo a un nuevo proceso que, junto con las izquierdas—todavía débiles debido a la enorme represión sufrida durante la dictadura—, elaboró el sistema democrático. Es probable que a la vista de esta falta de equilibrio de fuerzas entre derechas e izquierdas, en las que las primeras tenían muchos más poderes que las segundas, no hubiera otra forma de realizar la transición que aquella en la que se hizo. Pero me parece un error hacer de esta situación una virtud y llamarla modélica. (201–2)

> (In Germany and in Italy, Nazism and Fascism were defeated. However, Francoism was never defeated in Spain. The Francoist State adapted itself to a new reality due to national and international pressures. Its rulers realized the need to change it in order to adapt it to a new process which, along with the Left (still weakened by the great repression suffered during the dictatorship), elaborated the democratic system. It is probable that a lack of balance of power between the right and the left, with the former having much more power than the latter, there was no other way to make the transition than how it was actually done. But it seems to me that it is a mistake to consider this situation a virtue and call it a model.)

The transition was partly an exercise in conscious oblivion by the elites, which avoided open and far-reaching debates on the dictatorship in order to not instrumentalize the past politically out of fear of social instability, as Carsten Humlebæk shows in his essay in this volume. Humlebæk looks at the ways in which the Spanish democracy relates to its immediate past (the preceding authoritarian regime and the events which brought it to power) in order to analyze the discourses of continuity and rupture which have conformed to the new order. One could also argue that the politics of silence practiced then constituted a covert instrumentalization of the past, although one carried out by omission, and that the consequences of not confronting the nature and oppressive practices of Franco's regime continue to have an impact on the nation, as Humlebæk points out. Humlebæk also calls attention to the idealized (and manipulative) notion of consent that has dominated Spain's political scene since the constitutional processes: "To strive for consensus," he writes, "was seen as a fundamental characteristic of a real democrat, whereas not to strive for consensus was equaled with being Francoist." This kind of sacralization of agreement is still a major force in Spain's political and cultural debates, in which discrepancy and criticism are often regarded as a sort of violence against the common good rather than as an essential ingredient of democracy. We will retake this point later.

The military defeat of Argentina in the Falkland/Malvinas war was the crucial factor which ignited the political transition there. The country fell in a deep economic and political crisis, the military rule was questioned by the great majority of the nation, and the aftermath of the defeat deeply affected the self-esteem of Argentineans. In *The Art of Transition: Latin American Culture and Neoliberal Crisis*, Francine Masiello sees a crucial—and historically determined—difference between Argentinean and Chilean literary approaches to their respective realities. According to her, Argentinean artists and writers seek to recuperate "a totalizing story" to tell the fate of their nation, while micro-narratives tend to predominate among Chileans. We suggest that the basic difference traced by Masiello in this regard is determined by the specificity of the different national transitions. While the collapse of the military rule in a defeated and economically ruined Argentina allowed artists and writers to project a utopian macro-recit not restrained by massive concessions, the Chilean transition, founded on political concessions towards a still strong dictatorship (one which was relatively successful in macroeconomic terms), did not offer much room for grand alternative recits. The restrained present and future of the country exerted an influence on rather individual and fragmented narratives, which functioned in the interstices of its "transición pactada" (accorded transition) and later its "democracia de los acuerdos" (democracy of agreements) between the military and its supporters, on the one hand, and the democratic opposition, on the other. In the case of Chile, the manifestations and demands of the democratic movement, led by an alliance of personalities and parties of the political center, the left and the democratic right, succeeded in imposing the new order. However, the Pinochet regime was defeated by the *Concertación por la Democracia* (Coalition for Democracy) on the political field, but not on the economic one. Moreover, while the political leadership of the dictatorship was defeated, the military as such was not. Chile's transition to democracy was born in the cradle of compromise between democratic forces and dictatorship. The political system was questioned, but not the essence of the neo-liberal model imposed by Pinochet.

This compromise has determined the philosophy of the Chilean transition, clearly expressed in the 1990s by President Patricio Aylwin, who stressed "prudencia" ("prudence") and "avanzar en la medida de lo posible" ("to advance as it becomes possible to do so"). This vision has determined the rhythm, character and depth of the transition, as well as the role and structure of culture in the process. Since the return of democracy, Chile has been one of the Latin American states (if not the major one) which spends the most on cultural activities such as financing artists, writers and essayists, funding scholarships, conferences and tours of "national" cultural delegations, or by appointing artists and writers as diplomats (Antonio Skarmeta, Diamela Eltit, Carlos Franz, among other authors). However, this cooptation of intellectuals has not always succeeded. For instance, during the 1990s, acclaimed novelist Luis Sepúlveda publicly conditioned the acceptance of a position as diplomat in Germany to the previous liberation of "all political prisoners in Chile."

Such official cultural strategy shows similarities with the one exercised by Spanish governments at both the central and regional levels. Even if the times following Franco's dictatorship were marked by dynamics of change and what amounted to an explosion of freedom, it should not be assumed that Spain's cultural space was characterized necessarily by projects with emancipatory ideals. What might have appeared at first sight as progressive, upon closer examination often reveals its conservative or even reactionary values. Such would be the case of many of the manifestations of the so-called *movida* of the early-1980s or many individualistic young writers and artists emerging in the 1990s. In both cases, a recurrent rhetoric of sexual liberation and generalized hedonism often concealed a remarkable complicity with the status quo. More critical projects were in the meantime shunned by an artistic/intellectual mainstream which focused more or less openly on the glorification of banality or on the direct search of support from central and regional governmental institutions.

The motivations of those apparently art-loving institutions can be traced in Estrella de Diego's essay in this volume. De Diego analyzes the continuities in, and alternatives to, government-supported strategies of representation of Spain as a "modern" nation from the final years of Francoism until today. The efforts in creating a corporate image of the country for local as well as international consumption have oscillated between the emphasis on ethnic stereotypes and incursions in international trends both in low- and high-brow cultural products.

More often than not, official support went to artists who could offer an image which was "modern" or "international" and, at the same time, included sufficient elements of *Spanishness* which could be identified as such by the dominant culture—the economic and political centers of the West—whose acceptance and/or approval governmental institutions sought. Thus, more political (and therefore conflictive) artistic projects were left aside, even if they were usually more in tune with contemporary practices, as were those dealing from a conceptual standpoint with issues of gender or colonialism. De Diego connects the problematics of (self)identity which have been reemerging since the times of the dictatorship with the changing face of a society which has rapidly become multiethnic due to large waves of immigrants from Latin America and Northern Africa. This phenomenon has been observed and invoked by new artists to contest and subvert traditional notions of Spanish identity.

Some of the works of art examined by De Diego remind us that the spectacularized recovery of liberties tends to hide the reality of the incorporation of these nations to the simulacra of civic and personal emancipation common to postindustrial societies. A citizenry who is rarely the protagonist and effective subject of political agendas becomes compacted into a mass of consumers seeking material prosperity and relegates or ignores communitarian goals. In the meantime, the State abdicates its regulatory powers in order to please international capital, which often decides many aspects linked to the fate of these societies from positions of growing invisibility. Politics becomes aestheticized: the spectacle of the political prevents the questioning of authoritarian legacies and guarantees an economy of democratic power which is based on the mediatic representational value of its actors and their projects. These dynamics are often supported from cultural initiatives that, far from contesting them, maintain their regressive social tendencies, as they complacently reproduce the power structures postulated from above.

Even before the formal end of the dictatorship there were, of course, spaces of freedom and criticism which contested those tendencies, and many of them can be found in cultural circuits which have often been overlooked by studies of transition processes, as is the case with the musical scene, whose broad symbolic influence cannot be understated. Antonio Méndez Rubio (in this volume) deals with the "musical memory" of the Spanish transition, a period whose recovery he sees as the nostalgic cover-up for an expected societal rupture which did not materialize. The contestatory message of many Spanish bands which emerged not long after Franco's death became tamed as a result of their marketed "hyper-visibility," as the democracy imposed its "homogeneous or normalizing imperative." Other bands, on the contrary, expressed their discontent with the new order's *doxa* without alienating themselves from the media that ensure a wide audience (among which they found many agreeing ears).

It seems pertinent to add that a few songwriters (akin to the Bob Dylan model in the U.S.) had an essential role in the expression and broad diffusion of political messages during these processes of transition. Songs by artists such as José Antonio Labordeta and Raimon in Spain, Víctor Jara and Violeta Parra in Chile, Mercedes Sosa in Argentina, or Daniel Viglietti in Uruguay became anthems for those struggling for political freedoms. One of them, the Catalan Lluís Llach, has recently argued that "la transición española fue posible porque muchas capas de la sociedad la hicieron antes en la calle. Los políticos siempre han ido a remolque de la sociedad civil. La legislación también" (in Ribas 159) (the Spanish transition was made possible by the many layers of society which had already acted it out in the street. Politicians have always lagged behind civil society, and so has the law). It should be noted that although some of their earlier music was deprived of political strength, as democracy was established and a feeling of disenchantment grew among the population, its current appeal is not only of a nostalgic kind. Thus, one of Llach's songs, "L'estaca" (The Pole), originally meant as protest against Franco (who was metaphorized in a rotten pole which would finally break if everybody joined the push) later became recodified by some sectors of Catalan nationalism into a protest against centralism.

In a sense, protest songwriting occupied the space which the *poesía social*, a dominant trend in Spanish poetry during the middle years of the dictatorship, sought to have. While those poets (Blas de Otero, Gabriel Celaya and Gloria Fuertes among them) sought to deliver a critical message on social issues and thus awake the consciousness of their fellow citizens, the traditionally limited impact of the genre could not be surpassed by its colloquial diction and popular themes. Luis Bagué (in this volume) analyzes the main trends of contemporary Spanish poetry in connection to their post-1975 socio-cultural context, underscoring the different attitudes which poets had vis-à-vis the changing political climate of the nation's post-authoritarian order and an international intellectual sphere shaken by the irruption of postmodernism. The aestheticism of the *Novísimos* or generation of 1968, whose projects were dominant in the early transition years, found a response in the realist/figurative currents which emerged in the beginning of the 1980s. The latter, and most especially those related to what has been called "poetry of experience," showed an intense preoccupation with the possibility of an accessible and committed literature working in favor of ideas of civic equality, although from a highly individualistic perspective. One could argue, however, that a more semantically open poetry does not necessarily mean a more democratic one, in the sense that its unchallenging language might end up reproducing the prevailing discourses in a society still marked by inequalities.

Thus, social injustice and political conflict are still important issues in these societies, even if they seem to have disappeared from the most visible cultural agendas. The left's consuming efforts of self-promotion and its disdain for history have cooperated with secular conservative efforts to suppress valuable traditions which could help imagining new alternatives for societies which are, still now, far from offering dignity to many of their members. Amnesia was part of the price some progressive forces had to pay for pragmatism and, eventually, power. It brought along a waste of critical resources which lay in a rich tradition of dissidence and heterodoxy going back centuries, as Juan Goytisolo and Eduardo Subirats have pointed out. The reasons for this kind of ellipsis can be found in the sacralization of a notion of consensus which is scarcely democratic, as it tends to silence those "eccentric" voices which defy the rampant uniformization of society and culture. As Goytisolo writes, "Nada mejor para la sociedad civil que el libre debate de ideas y desacuerdo fértil fuera del recinto de las ideologías" (396) ("nothing is better for civil society than a free exchange of ideas and a fertile dissent outside the closed space of ideologies").

Few people are in a better position to reflect about the role of culture in transitions to democracy than Jorge Edwards. In his double condition as a man of letters (author of an oeuvre recognized with Chile's National Prize of Literature and the Cervantes Prize) and a former ambassador for the democratic government of *Concertación por la Democracia*, Edwards played a key role in the opposition against Pinochet as president of the Permanent Committee for the Defense of Free Speech. In his essay in this volume, Edwards stresses the broad character of the alliance of intellectuals of different generations, ideological bent and religious stripes in the fight for democracy. In his view, "Chilean exceptionality" rests not only on the economic reforms and liberalization of the market, but also on the existence of a solid civil society prior to the dictatorship. His essay offers a panoramic view of the role of Chilean intellectuals in the transition. Edwards explores how the Chilean revolutionary process was inserted—with or without the knowledge of their actors—into a Cold War context in which the main actors were the United States and the Soviet Union. Moreover, the political pressure exerted on the dictatorship, and the subsequent democratic process in Chile, were not only the product of national social forces which fought for freedom, but the result of the international solidarity and pressure of progressive forces in the United States and Europe (see Heinrich Sassenfeld in this volume, who also pays attention to the role of foreign support for democracy in Argentina). An exploration of the international political climate which developed around "Chile's case" would further highlight the relativity of the concept of "Chilean exceptionalism" mentioned by Edwards, whose essay also mentions some of the factors which contributed to the recovery of democracy in Chile beyond the strictly political realm: from activities linked to theaters and the Catholic Church, to the role of opposition publications and intellectuals.

Juliet Lynd's essay (in this volume) also explores the role of intellectuals in the political transition in Chile, focusing on two of Diamela Eltit's novels (*Lumpérica* and *Mano de obra*). According to Lynd, both novels were written from the margins of society and represent marginalized sectors of society. They also criticize the market-oriented politics of Pinochet's dictatorship (1973–90) as well as those of the democratic governments which followed it, thus continuing an order which "reduce(s) bodies to a monetary value and put them up for sale." In this sense, Eltit can be counted among the vast majority of Chilean writers who supported the struggle against the dictatorship, and who now criticize the logic and social consequences of neoliberalism and free market which dominate the current Chilean democracy. Eltit's practice of writing from the margins in a society in transition to democracy questions the dynamics of literary production and reception, the Chilean macroeconomic model of the past twenty years, and the influence that the editorial market exerts over writers and artists. One could argue, however, that due to their highly cryptic style, both novels are rather elitist, inasmuch as they appeal only to a narrow circle of readers in Chile and elsewhere. The essay explores the complex articulation that both works establish in relation to popular resistance towards the State and towards the logic of the neoliberal free market.

Eltit's "marginal condition" might be nuanced even more if one were to consider the novelist's close relationship with the governments of the *Concertación*, which includes her experience as a diplomat, and her position within Chile's elite, due in part to her partnership to a distinguished ambassador, minister, political party leader and international consultant. Such facts invite to reflect on the possibilities and limits of literary representation of the marginalized from the perspective of literary elites entangled with political power. Another question, in this case of a moral nature, emerges in this context when Lynd cites the case of Eltit exposing "*Lumpérica* to a brothel on Maipú Street in Santiago, where she cuts and burns her arms and reads selections of her as yet unpublished book to an audience of prostitutes, transvestites, clients, vagabonds, and a few accompanying artists, filming the performance." One wonders about the implications of the use of such an audience and the kind of reception elicited by her message and, consequently, about the "implicit reader" for a work such as *Lumpérica*. Is it someone among the marginalized citizens whom the novelist seeks to represent, or a public who will consume and reflect upon such performances in the "lettered city" of artistic and academic circles?

A figure like Eltit and her work open questions about the nature of the participation of artists and writers in public political debates, whose traditional model (after figures such as Zola or Sartre) lost its former relevance in the countries dealt with in this volume soon after the reestablishment of democracy. Haunted by the post-utopian disenchantment of stabilized democracies, most academics deserted the public arena, renouncing their role of public intellectuals and limiting their activities to university classrooms and professional venues. The vacuum that they left in the media was covered in many cases by technicians or polemicists who are often unable or unwilling to connect the most pressing issues to wider historical problematics. It is still possible, however, to find contributions by some established authors who operate with a certain degree of autonomy.

One of the most distinguished among such contestatory voices has been precisely Juan Goytisolo. Since the 1950s, Goytisolo has been the author of an extremely coherent series of fiction and essayistic writings whose main tenet is an unfathomable critique of Western—and especially Spanish—culture. Working always from the margins (as a political exile during Franco's dictatorship, as a gay person, and for some years now also as an engaged resident of Morocco), he is an uncomfortably independent figure for people at both ends of the political spectrum. From different venues, he has denounced the silence of a majority of intellectuals who have become image-adoring servers of the capital. Goytisolo has also been the author of an oeuvre which bridges past and present and East and West through a fruitful reading of the classics. As it has been pointed out earlier in this Introduction, he is particularly concerned about the lack of variety within, and dialogue between, proponents of different discourses. Nevertheless, the generalized negativity of his poignant critique does not equal pessimism, as he believes in the power of arts and letters to overcome moments of uncertainty: "la cultura sobrevive a menudo a los cataclismos más destructores y busca y encuentra en tiempos de crisis sus propias respuestas. La imaginación opuesta a todo dogmatismo y el conocimiento de la historia y sus ciclos nos permiten abrigar alguna esperanza" (409) ("culture often survives the most destructive cataclysms and seeks and finds its own answers in times of crises. An imagination opposed to all kinds of dogmatism, and knowledge of history and its cycles make it possible to have some hope").

In his essay in this volume, David William Foster explores the work of three Argentinean intellectuals (Sebreli, Perlongher and Gorbato) whose positions have connections with some of Goytisolo's. Foster stresses that Jews, women and homosexuals were singled out for special persecution by the military government during the period of 1976–1983, and explains why those groups were granted special recognition of individual rights during the redemocratization. He also reminds us that during the 1970s and 1980s, conservative dictatorships were as homophobic as the Cuban Revolution and leftist activists, suggesting that the roots of intolerance in Latin America are much older than depicted by traditional political analysis. Furthermore, Foster establishes a difference between academic and non-academic intellectuals, and between texts produced under "deep commitment" and others under "great objectivity," something which may open the discussion about the role of marginal voices in relation to hegemonic discourses.

The kind of historical consciousness vindicated by Goytisolo is closely connected to one of the issues which have gained most relevance in current discussions on transitions from authoritarian rule: that of memory and oblivion. It is a major topic in the collective agendas due to its ambivalent function, being both a strategy for keeping remembrance alive and an instrument invoked by those willing to bring closure to the darkest hours of their nations' contemporary histories. From a literary point of view, we face some risks when we explore these subjects. The first has to do with an assumption shared by some writers and academics who believe that the fragmentary memory from marginal and subaltern groups expresses itself mainly through written texts. But these texts are usually the instrument of hegemonic or totalitarian forces in a given society. Marginal and popular groups in Latin America have usually constructed memory first through witnesses' oral accounts, popular songs, musicalized political poetry and street theater.

However, such constructions require a cultural structure which is usually damaged after years of authoritarian rule. Gustavo Remedi's essay in this volume suggests that the social and cultural changes imposed by the neo-liberal model in Uruguay have been so deep that some expressions, including the formerly influential traditional theater, have been unable to represent the new, fragmented reality of that country. *Tejanos*, the fresh alternative to established drama which he analyzes, is based mainly on the cooperation and interaction of diverse groups of citizens who represent and/or create distant realities which would never connect due to the fragmentation of their society. This kind of interaction puts forth a new identity and agency, and allows for the exploration of neo-liberalism's impact on the impoverished middle and lower classes, as well as on exiles. *Tejanos* is their attempt at articulating a new voice and a viewpoint of their own, especially in a context in which the most influential intellectuals were repressed and forced to leave the country, losing contact with their nation's different social spheres. Such disconnect can last longer than the authoritarian regime for economic reasons which, as in the case of Uruguay, prevent the return of exiles. Remedi's essay dialogues with Lynd's on the question of progressive intellectuals' ability to represent and project artistically the interests of the popular classes without patronizing them. They also touch on the issue of the popular classes' self-representation, their artistic and political agencies, and their influence. *Tejanos*, also called "frontier theater," offers a unique way of confronting such issues and a concrete and productive alternative to the so-called organic intellectuals during different stages of political resistance.

Due to the fear latent in a given society in transition from a recent authoritarian past, and the complex and expensive distribution system of books, memory expressed in written texts takes a long time to find its way, and expressions such as the one studied by Remedi offer an alternative for analysis and commemoration. Another issue related to the function of memory in these processes is connected to the role of the intellectual, who selects and mediates the testimonial stories and/or articulates them fictionally: is s/he able to speak on behalf of the voiceless, and where does her/his authority come from? One relative surprise for progressive Latin American political movements after the dictatorships was the cancellation of the concept of the intellectual as the personification of a vanguard who represents popular interests and sensibility. "Memory" novels move, therefore, in the tension between the criticism from conservatives who question the veracity of political witnesses, and progressives who problematize the legitimacy of intellectuals as voices of the people.

In her essay in this volume, Ana Forcinito explores two crucial aspects of the recovery of historical memory after the redemocratization process in Argentina, which started in 1983. The first one is the impossibility for the victims of human right abuses to rebuild a gap-free version of the past. The second is related to their necessity of rebuilding a counter-official version of history based on collective (but fragmentary and often vague) memories. This process does not take place only in the sphere of political debate, but also in that of symbolic production, and especially in novels, memoirs and testimonial writing. In *Pasos bajo el agua* (Steps under Water, 1987) by Alicia Kozameh, and *Una sola muerte numerosa* (A Single, Numberless Death, 1997) by Nora Strejilevich, Forcinito looks for narrative strategies exerted to recover memories that hegemonic interests and history have tried to marginalize and delete. This oppositional strategy aims to erode official history, to correct the asymmetry of discourses about the dictatorial past, and to avoid the second and definitive vanishing of the missing ones, the "desaparecidos" (being their first disappearance physical, and the second one in the discursive dimension). It can be argued that supporters of dictatorships in the Southern Cone tried to keep exerting control over signifiers (disappeared bodies) in democracy. Thus, by withholding the signifier, they intended to eliminate the signified (the political meaning of disappeared bodies). On their part, democratic groups, by demanding the recovery of the bodies, stress the meaning of the disappearances, and contribute as well to a growing awareness of human rights. One group stopped the circulation of people using repressive methods, and afterwards they tried to avoid the circulation of their meaning. The other one supports the circulation of a new meaning in order to recover the bodies.

To some extent, Forcinito's text dialogues with Edward Said's *Reflections on Exile*: "the study of literature is not abstract but is set irrecusably and unarguably within a culture whose historical situation influences, if it does not determine, a great deal of what we say and do" (xxxi). Although the democratic process started in Argentina in 1983, the history of impunity began with the Full Stop and Due Obedience Laws, and the Laws of Pardon of 1989 and 1990. The aim of the dominant sectors in Argentina was and is to establish social amnesia rather than cultivating social memory. Thus, they push for the legal obliteration of those who can speak on behalf of the "desaparecidos." Forcinito states that under these repressive circumstances progressive intellectuals prioritize the recollection of testimonies of former political detainees, which are "connected with the constitution of the disappeared as a figure that could no longer be ignored in the redemocratization process."

A character in J.M. Coetzee's novel *Elizabeth Costello* says: "Nevertheless, there is something miraculous about the past that the future lacks. What is miraculous about the past is that we have succeeded—God knows how—in making thousands and millions of individual fictions created by individual human beings, lock well enough into one another to give us what looks like a common past, a shared story" (38). Forcinito's essay shows that these individual fictions actually never miraculously "lock" as a whole, but stay in a permanent interaction, plethoric of contradictions, tensions, marginations, deletions and oblivion. The capital aim of this process is to achieve a hegemonic view about the past. As Said stresses in his essay about memory and exile, "it is what one remembers of the past and how one remembers it that determines how one sees the future" (xxxv).

In Spain, several civic groups have recently advocated for a "Historical Memory Act," a piece of legislation which would seek to give moral and symbolic recognition to the victims of Francisco Franco's regime and to establish parameters for the commemoration of some of the most conflictive episodes of Spain's recent history, beginning with the Second Republic (1931-1936). The need to revisit those events comes from what is now perceived as a faulty transition to democracy, one which was conducted by a political elite which was unable or unwilling to confront problems of historical justice. A sign of the current impact of these issues beyond the circles of professional historians has been the significance of what has been called "the obituaries war": a recent mediatic confrontation of the two sides which fought the Civil War, this time expressed in the form of paid newspaper advertising which featured explicit tributes to friends and family members who had been killed during the war or the subsequent repression carried out by Francisco Franco's authoritarian regime.

There are also numerous works of fiction published within the last five years which deal with the effects that the fratricidal conflict and its aftermath had on individuals whose stories were obliterated by the wind of History or by political convenience (if they can be separated at all). One could mention Javier Cercas's *Soldados de Salamina* (Soldiers of Salamis), Rafael Chirbes's *La larga marcha* (The Long March), Almudena Grandes's *El corazón helado* (The Frozen Heart), or Javier Marías's *Tu rostro mañana I: Fiebre y lanza* (Your Face Tomorrow, Volume I: Fever and Spear). These narratives convey a variety of literary strategies to offer a vision of history from the perspective of the defeated. Thus, they prioritize a recreation of the voices of those who had been condemned to silence by the long monologue of Francoism and also problematize the subsequent political decision to "forget" the past, a choice allegedly made in order to avoid conflicts which could jeopardize the newly established democracy. The novel has been the genre in which these ideas have had a greater echo. In contrast, the presence/absence of the Spanish transition to democracy either as a background or main theme in filmic manifestations is analyzed by Germán Labrador in this volume. Labrador studies the production of visual media (film and television) dealing with Spain's recent history in a complex and counter-hegemonic way, one which could facilitate public debates on the period. Such films inform a narrative which contests the lack of debates on memory at the institutional level.

What stands out from these novels and films is the need to recover and protect the memories of those who had them silenced not only by the dictatorship's apparatus, but also by the elites of the democratic system which, for the most part, thought that it was convenient to ignore a long history of crimes and oppression. The post-dictatorship establishment, initially derived directly from the Francoist political class, opted to ratify a status quo by which those responsible for atrocities such as the ones described in some of these and other texts would die untouched by justice, just as the dictator did. A great number of works of art and literature created and publicized during the last few years have contributed to the establishment of debates on the importance of remembering, or better, of commemorating: to remember along with others.

This collective effort seems to be transcending the shallow presentness which characterized Spain's precipitated run to high modernity and in a sense concealed the legacy of silence left by the dictatorship. The triumphal assertions of some historians and the majority of the political class, who claim that the Spanish transition was a model process whose principles could serve as an example for (re)emerging democracies in Latin America and Eastern Europe, have been increasingly contested during the last few years. As a political arrangement, it was produced mainly from above, and it did not provide closure to important issues. Consequently, it set a symbolic system which was far from satisfactory for many and consolidated a post-authoritarian social sphere marked by oblivion.

One aspect of the debate which still remains open in Spain as well as in Latin America is the one related to the permanence of the transitional moment already in the recovered democracy. In Chile this issue has been the subject of harsh discussions between those who think that there are still authoritarian enclaves in the democratic system (namely, in the Constitution), and those who affirm that the transition ended with the recovery of full civil power over the military. In this sense, Edwards stresses that the main question for Chilean intellectuals today is if the state "has deep, solid roots, if they are somehow anchored in our intellectual and ethical consciousness." This crucial question addresses the issue of the relationship between the development of a civil society, and the influence exerted over that process by intellectuals. It is the historical tension between the "lettered city" and politicians.

However, the dictatorships' brutal repression against political parties and trade unions, the emergence of broad political and civil coalitions formed to fight for democracy and human rights, the increase of consumerism, and the collapse of the communist states in Eastern Europe, all contributed to a lessening of the traditional importance of politics in the Southern Cone at the end of the 1980s. As in Spain, during the 1980s and 1990s there was a transversal explosion of sexual liberation and consumption of drugs and alcohol. A kind of historical optimism developed as the new democratic systems seemed able to fulfill the historical expectations of broad sectors of the population. This was accompanied in the 1990s by a period when the Argentinean, Chilean and

Uruguayan economies thrived, although such a "miracle" was in fact a macroeconomic phenomenon which kept the historically marginalized on the margins.

At the same time, young novelists such as Argentina's César Aira and Ricardo Fresán, and Chile's Gonzalo Contreras, Jaime Collyer, Alberto Fuguet, Ana María del Río and Marcela Serrano conquered book sales rankings and were widely read by a population used to censorship or self-censorship. Interestingly enough, their stories did not talk about political heroes, workers, or strikes, but rather about young people in a modern, internationalized, democratic and hedonistic society. Those narratives did not project ideal moral characters. Rather, they focused on isolated, egotistical and cynical individuals of the middle class, who tried to experience life in all its dimensions. A kind of cosmopolitan present, and not the recent national past, became increasingly relevant: a pop-culture "reality" imported from the United States and the United Kingdom through music, films and literature was enthroned as "the real thing." Amnesia was not a conscious choice, but the result of a democracy founded in compromise and the internationalization (or "Americanization") of culture.

Those who called attention to the region's conflictive recent past were not always highly considered. Only years later, at the end of the nineties, national history, biographies and autobiographies of influential individuals, artists and intellectuals became fashionable. But politics did not recover its centrality in terms of social prestige. On the contrary; political corruption and mismanagement, and the feeling that under the new democracy "we all get more of the same," led to the generalized perception of a greater distance from traditional politicians and increased disillusionment, skepticism, and individualism. That marked the birth of societies characterized by decreasing solidarity, and also of recits which could only narrate in fragments a growingly fragmented reality.

The complexity of the social and cultural post-authoritarian scenarios in the countries dealt with in this volume has been rather simplified by the master narratives of their recent past. The most pervasive landscapes of the periods known as transitions from authoritarian rule to democracy were mapped out by a set of institutions (governments, media, academia) whose combined narratives are still—in the best cases—necessarily incomplete. They often silence the experiences of collectives such as women, expatriates, underground youth movements or workers' unions, who offered alternatives to the type of order instituted from above after the demise of the respective dictatorships. The official transitional accounts have also tended to suppress the concessions granted to authoritarian elements by democratic establishments as a way to ensure the viability of the processes, an option which has often meant the assumption of old practices within the new regimes. Those individuals advancing alternatives to, or various forms of criticism of such practices, often find their arguments overlooked by the advocates of a widespread notion of consent who, under the pretext of the frailty of the regained liberties, have tended to favor uniformity of thought and depolitization of society. Nevertheless, the symbolic production of (and on) these historical moments can help to shape and codetermine the social interpretation of the authoritarian regimes as well as the subsequent transitional processes, even though the nature of its relation to factuality remains still a heated topic, especially among postmodernists. This issue underscores the importance of art and literature in the articulation of post-authoritarian identities and historical memories, reopening the old debate about the relation between creative imagination and reality and the capacity of the former to "reflect," "denote," or "deform" political contexts and thus to function as a counter-discourse to institutionalized consensus.

Works Cited

Coetzee, J.M. *Elizabeth Costello. Eight Lessons.* London: Secker and Warburg, 1999.
Goytisolo, Juan. *Pájaro que ensucia su propio nido.* Barcelona: Galaxia Gutenberg, 2001.
Masiello, Francine. *The Art of Transition: Latin American Culture and Neoliberal Crisis.* Durham/London: Duke University Press, 2001.
Navarro, Vicenç. *Bienestar insuficiente, democracia incompleta. Sobre lo que no se habla en nuestro país.* Madrid: Anagrama, 2002.
Ribas, José. *Los 70 a destajo. Ajoblanco y libertad.* Barcelona: RBA, 2007.
Said, Edward. *Reflections on Exile and Other Essays.* Cambridge, Massachusetts: Harvard University Press, 2002.
Subirats, Eduardo. *Memoria y exilio: revisiones de las culturas hispánicas.* Madrid: Losada, 2003.

Part I
Contesting Power, Forging Commitment

1

Democratic Culture and Transition in Chile

Jorge Edwards

(Translated by Anna Guercio)

When discussing the Chilean democratic tradition in the years prior to the military coup d'etat, many understood this tradition to be a highly fragile one, having suffered dramatic interruptions, in 1891 for example, when a rebellion by Congress's conservative majority, in alliance with the navy, toppled the constitutional govermentment of President Balmaceda, or during the instability of the 1920s, which culminated in the dictatorship of General Carlos Ibáñez del Campo between 1927 and 1931. In any case, for most of its history, independent Chile has enjoyed relative political stability, putting it in stark contrast with the rest of Latin America and with Spain itself. This is why Argentinian general José de San Martín, in a letter to a Chilean friend from his exile in the north of France, could say that Chile was the only country that "knew how to be a republic and speak Spanish at the same time." The pronouncement, as you can see, implicated Spain and the Spanish-speaking republics of North, South, and Central America. The question that many Chileans have often asked themselves, above all those in the cultural sector and in the social and political sciences, is whether this stable republican condition, linked to what some early twentieth-century essayists called "Estado en forma," has deep, solid roots, if they're somehow anchored in our intellectual and ethical consciousness, or if it's all been simply a historic mirage. That is to say, we ask ourselves if our old democratic pride, the product of what has been referred to as the "Chilean exception," was truly warranted or really just an oasis, a ceasefire, almost an accident, in the middle of an enormous desert patrolled by either barbaric warlords or by vaguely learned ones. The coup by General Augusto Pinochet, followed immediately by institutional collapse and repression charactered precisely by such barbaric ferocity, was, among other things, an intellectual scandal, the spectacular fall of all manner of illusions and widely held myths, foremost among them the myth that Chile possesses a strictly "professional" military, one utterly subject to the primacy of civil power.

The myths of Chilean democracy, like all myths, have had their variations, their conflicting versions and inversions. To a large extent, the country's civil society, from the center to the right, constructed the legal scaffolding and foresaw all the legal maneuvers needed to justify that coup d'etat. This work was carried out within the context of the Cold War, and it was precisely the Cold War phenomenon that pushed Chilean politics out of its purely national and local coordinates. The narrow electoral victory of Salvador Allende put an end, perhaps forever, to the remote, naive country where nothing, according to wide-spread belief, ever happened. After those elections the first Sunday of September, 1970, in Chile, in the country were nothing ever happened, everything began happening—internal and international conspiracies; interventions, one, by the CIA, and the other by the world's leftist fringe—and I have now come to believe that the intellectuals, at least in those first moments, found themselves disoriented, adrift, without direction or a clear frame of reference. What happened among us was not—and was very far from being—the October Revolution, or the Chinese communists' Grand March, or the arrival of a group of bearded guerillas in Santiago. It was an electoral process like all those prior, a civic colloquium with which we were well-acquainted, intimately familiar since infancy, with a winner, moreover, who secured only 37 percent of the votes cast, but nevertheless, based on political circumstances that some thought lucky and others perverse, that mediocre outcome at the ballot boxes, incredible as it may seem, had profound revolutionary consequences. The country with groundhog dreams, as nineteenth-century historian and essayist Benjamín Vicuña Mackenna liked to call it, suffered a rude awakening. Not everyone immediately grasped the dangers of these circumstances, but I've now reached the conclusion that the principal actors, all along the political spectrum, had grasped them indeed. I was then director of the Chilean embassy in Lima, and I had to travel to Santiago in October, a month and a half after the elections and a few weeks before the presidential transfer of power. I've quoted more than once the first thing that Pablo Neruda said to me when I went to visit him one morning at his house in the foothills of San Cristóbal, in the northern region of Santiago. Remember that Neruda, up until nine months prior, had been a candidate for the communist party presidential nomination, revealing that his personal perspective and political outlook were not merely that of a lyric poet dedicated to the exclusive contemplation of the clouds or his own belly button. So then, I climbed up to his library, located in the highest part of the house, and one of the first things that the poet said to me, after hello, was: "I see only black." Nothing could have been clearer: the intuition of a lyric poet who had, after decades, entered the political arena, pointed to imminent danger. It strikes me, even when I don't recall the exact words, that he detected an extreme polarization, a feeling of hatred and war in the air.

Later, on a different occasion with Neruda and some of his friends, I exchanged impressions with Luis Corvalán, then secretary general of the Chilean communists, and he told me something that worked out to more or less the same thing: "It's far more difficult to be in the government than to oppose it." And, above all, we might add now, more difficult for them, for those orthodox communists, who sought to exercise a moderating influence and who, after the fall of the Unidad Popular, were probably the most persecuted and beaten. All of this stems from one essential fact: the Cold War, which we had been accustomed to viewing as a conflict more or less removed from us, a drama played out on other stages, had arrived abruptly, dramatically, and relatively unexpected on our shores. In those same days of October, 1970, I met with Salvador Allende, then president-elect, in his modest home on Guardia Vieja Street in the Santiago neighborhood of Providencia. I came away with the strong impression of a man intensely worried, harried, not yet prepared to adopt a clearly defined code of conduct. For example, the following day he was obliged to attend a rally in the Plaza Victoria in Valparaíso and there were rumors circulating of a planned attempt on his life. "But, I said, as president-elect, I cannot go into hiding. I must take the risk and show my face." Two or there days after that conversation, when I was already back in Lima, there came the kidnapping attempt followed by the assassination of General René Schneider, the army's Commander in Chief, an event that revealed that all the apprehension, all the fear, was absolutely justified. In a few short weeks, the Chilean political climate had taken a radical, irreversible turn. While the left struggled to organize its defense despite scarce resources and evident internal divisions, the far right conspired shamelessly, aided by the government of Richard Nixon and his adviser, Henry Kissenger.

In the midst of this climate of latent civil war, it seems to me that the intellectual class, certain exceptions aside, did not possess a unified voice. There was a great deal of internal debate and it would be absurd to suggest that there was a united front of intellectuals, writers, and artists, such as existed, for example, in republican Spain. The difference was fundamental: Spanish intellectuals had been united since the outbreak of war. In Chile, on the other hand, there had been a tense period of waiting, accompanied by frequent, aborted attempts at various revolutions, but the possibility of war seemed less and less likely. It has been pointed out a few times that the process of Allendeism began with a serious crisis of the Cuban intellectual world, highly symptomatic and influential throughout Latin America. Poet Heberto Padilla's imprisonment and his subsequent, terrible self-indictment, obviously prepared and orchestrated by Cuban security organizations, was an unsettling occurence and provoked all sorts of distrust and guardedness. Allendeism, unlike Castroism, did not begin its march with the enthusiastic support of Spanish-language poets, philosophers, and artists. There was a dominant note of reserve, even if it was not made entirely explicit. Cuba's dogmatic excesses, seen even by those who would have preferred not to, must have had a substantial impact, although neither declared nor well-studied, on the Chile of the Unidad Popular. After the military coup d'etat of September 1973, the political consciousness of cultured people would have had to readjust, to be brought up to speed, to relearn the feeling of modern democracy, before they could participate powerfully, enthusiastically, imaginatively, in Chile's transition.

Today I can see a prehistory, an era of weak germination—incipient, sparse—followed by a more defined, solid history. There is a period of catacombs and another of emergence in the air. I'm reminded of meetings in the choir house at the University of Chile, directed by Mario Baeza, of the exchange of books that might be considered dissident, of conversations in church yards, of one or another public reading. In the Plaza of Mulato Gil de Castro, in Lastarria Street, Nicanor Parra read some of his "jokes to disorient the poetry police." This would have been in the early 1980s. Parra belonged to that well-defined species of writer that had felt uncomfortable, relatively marginalized, during the three years of the Unidad Popular, but afterward he had morphed, gradually, not from the first, into an increasingly resolute critic of the military leaders. So then, the poet responsible for *Poems and Antipoems*, at a predetermined moment in his long reading at the Plaza, announced from the podium that he would read a censored sonnet. He approached the microphone and held his tongue for the approximate length of time it would take to read fourteen ten-syllable lines. When he finished, there came an eruption of laughter and applause. The poet, a consummate actor, had considered well his effect. On another occasion, during a two day conference attended by sociologists, historians, and writers, he read a legal writ regarding freedom of expression. It was a revolutionary text, intensely provocative, and seemed like it must have been written just a few hours prior. Then he offered some historic background: the text was dated 1817 or 18, signed by General Bernardo O'Higgins, and it referenced the newborn republic's founding degree regarding freedom of the press. At the very same time, modern day soldiers, under the superior command of Augusto Pinochet Ugarte, had march in tribute before the statue of Bernardo O'Higgins in the Alameda. At that time, there was no one in Chile who could have prohibited the reading of one of his classic decrees.

In those days, you could attend performances by the Teatro Ictus, with Nissim Sharim and Delfina Guzmán in the leads, which took up the issue of Chilean dictatorship without hesitation or minced words. These were little theaters, fresh catacombs, and their symbol, the drawing of a fish, an "ictus," doubtless alluded to this, as well as giving name to the group. After each show, the first christians would take the stairs on Merced up to the street, inspired, charged up against the authoritarian system. I am certain it was not in vain, that those intellectuals and artists exerted influence over the collective conscience, but it all took time, a fairly long ripening process and a lot of patience. The young people, who aren't always so good at waiting, began to adopt risker modes of defiance, and their parents, while often in agreement with them, were forced to ask and then beg that they exercise more caution in the face of the authoritarian monster.

It was in those early years that there came to be something called the parliament of columnists. In a move born of opportunism, of the desire to attract more readers, of everything that was going on, the "establishment" press made space available for the publication of opinion columns against the dictatorship. And little by little, opposition magazines and papers rose up, finding their way through legal loopholes: Hoy, Fortín Mapocho, Apsi, Análisis. The dissident columnists' work was carried out in secret, but proved a substantial force in eroding the dictatorship's theoretical underpinnings, based as they were on primitive anti-communism and the Cold War. We should now begin to study the extent to which the collapse of the eastern block, the fall of the Berlin Wall, contributed to the growing feeling in Chile that right-wing dictatorship was outdated, utterly unnecessary. To some extent, the critiques of "modern socialism" and those of extreme right-wing Pinochetism converged. It strikes me as no coincidence that certain similar types of books coming from Eastern European writers found exceptional success with Chilean readers during the eighties: works, for example, by Milan Kundera or Vaclav Havel. Their messages were transparent and the Chilean reader grasped and internalized them immediately. In other words, local circumstance facilitated swift schooling in the grand themes and dilemmas of contemporary world politics.

It seems to me that the Catholic Church played a fundamental role in these developments, and that the intellectuals, in some tacit way, frequently allied themselves with it. The Vicaría de la Solidaridad, for example, together with the Vicaría de la Juventud, created safe spaces for victims of human rights violations, but also for dialogue, controversy, and free contemplation. The Mensaje Magazine's monthly editorial and layout meetings, held in their offices on Almirante Barroso Street, just south of Santiago, provided another forum for broad discussion and exchange. Intellectuals of different generations and the most diverse ideological and religious stripes collaborated on the magazine and—via book reviews, commentary on public affairs, essays on philosophy or the social sciences—illuminated the road toward democracy reclaimed. At those meetings, theory and practice came together. On the eve of the Referendum, when a resounding *no* triumphed over Pinochetism, the extent of the information that reached even the most marginalized populations, unions, and parrishes of Santiago and the surrounding provinces was, frankly, remarkable. To have been on the board of editors in those moments is an unforgettable experience of the highest intellectual, ethical, and political order.

Here I am reminded of Matilde Urrutia, Pablo Neruda's widow, and of Francisco Coloane, the outstanding speaker who throughout his long life presided over the Chilean communist party, over masses and religious ceremonies whose political content, whose confrontational stance toward the dictatorship, was readily apparent. The Catedral Metropolitana was one of these sensitive spots. Listening to a sermon with the evangelical theme of charity, justice, or social solidarity, listening to protest songs at the foot of the high altar, and then walking out into a Plaza de Armas guarded by the regime's police—armed to the teeth—was an experience both unforgettable and difficult to describe. Those who stepped from inside in half-light, singing the Hymn of Joy, and the forces that were arrayed before the church door, with their helmets, their shields, their spears, brought to mind immediately, without further reflection, early Christians and Roman centurions. Even though many of these supposed Christians belonged to agnostic, secular belief-systems. There was an overriding emotion and conviction. No one could imagine, after attending one of those collective liturgies, that the dictatorship's days were not numbered.

And in fact, the final days of Pinochetism were rapidly approaching. The call for a referendum, provided for by the dictatorship's very own legal workings and reluctantly accepted by the regime, proved a decisive moment. On the Committee for Free Elections, an important, clear-thinking initiative started by branches of the Democracia Cristiana (Christian Democracy), there were fourteen members conscripted from various sectors of the democratic opposition, without excluding the odd representative from what we might call the liberal right. Also on the Committee was a small but active group of intellectuals and church officials. They did not preach that *no* as though it were fundamentalist propaganda, but rather sought to convince people to enroll on the electoral registers and to vote without fear, secure in the knowledge that the secrecy of their vote would be maintained and that there would be no danger of reprisals. At the beginning, the campaign adopted a fairly discreet tone and low profile, as if the very participants doubted their ability to bring down the regime at the polls. But there came about a curious phenomenon of collective contagion, separate from the opposition leaders' work with their electoral base. Even the communist party, which had at the outset been in favor of abstention, in the end succumbed and directed its militants to enroll and vote *no*. The appearance every day of that *no* for fifteen minutes on the screens of official television channels took on an air of conviction, a spark, a vigor that those long military years had crushed. It was a collective creation, a stage set by thousands, and the electoral result landed a conclusive blow. The days of the Referendum and the ones following reached unique levels of tension and drama. It seems certain that General Augusto Pinochet sought to reverse the damage through some obscure maneuver, the details of which remain unclear even today. But then came the grave warnings from Washington and the international community. And when General Mathei, at midnight on the day of the tally, declared to the press that the result for him was clear, that the *no* had triumphed, we felt that the transition must be unstoppable.

There can be no doubt that novels, poems, political and sociological essays, opinion columns, forums, and seminars influenced all aspects of the process. I recall receiving a slip of paper during a book fair at the Parque Forestal, in which poet Enrique Lihn asked me to hurry down and help get him out of the police station on Santo Domingo Street, where he had been taken by carabineros, Chile's uniformed police, on the charge of public disturbances. These disturbances consisted of having read fragments from his book, *El Paseo Ahumada*, while dressed and made up as his fictional "Gerardo de Pompier," the epitome of the anachronistic artist, a character directly inherited from the modernism of Rubén Darío (end of the nineteenth century), on Ahumada Street, right in the center of Santiago, which has now been turned into a pedestrian walkway. In spite of his deliberate use of anachronism, the poems alluded to the current reality of the dictatorial regime. Curiously enough, the two of us had wound up at the very same police station forty years earlier, detained by a pair of night shift carabineros, charged with disturbances after leaving a party at the University of Chile's School of Dance. Worried now, I walked down the street to the detention center, and found that the poet had already been freed. But it is very much possible that each one of those exploits of literary life, those "disturbances" that accumulated day by day, influenced the climate that would determine the defeat of the dictatorship by referendum.

I'll conclude with a personal testimony. From the moment I assumed the role of president of the Permanent Committee for the Defense of Free Speech, I found myself more censored than ever and in the most varied ways. One day I received a call from an official at the University of Santiago who told me that a planned and already publicized conference of mine about the city novel would have to be canceled on account of scheduling conflicts. But the vice-chancellor sent his thanks and word that a check for my honorarium was nonetheless prepared. If I do not hold the conference, I responded, naturally I will not accept the honorarium. Alarmed, the official told me that this would be an offense to the vice-chancellor. What ever shall we do!, I responded, and cut off this strange conversation.

A short time later, customs authorities blocked the arrival of a new edition of my book *Persona non grata*, recently reissued by Seix Barral. The book had been censored by the Junta when it was first published, in the early months of 1974, and then liberated in 1978. Facing a customs ban, several lawyer friends and I appealed for protection, a legal maneuver incorporated into the Chilean legal system by Pinochet's 1980 constitution. I remember the instance and the closing arguments in one of the rooms of the Supreme Court of Justice, in the presence of Nicanor Parra, José Donoso, and Antonio Avaria, Cristián Huneeus and Enrique Lafourcade, as well as several other colleagues. It was a solemn and fascinating occasion, a vibrant, impassioned public defense of the freedom to write and to publish. The court rejected the appeal, but the military government, via a speech that Pinochet made out in the provinces, declared that the authorizing procedures regarding books had been repealed. Chileans had the right to read whatever they wished. If the books ran contrary to the law and public order, this would have to be cleared up by the tribunals. It was a partial success, and a demonstration that applying both internal and external pressures could yield results. Several international Pen organizations, as well as the members of a British group linked to Amnesty International and called the Index on Censorship, had sent an authentic flood of letters to that day's minister of the Interior. Since then, many banned books have been allowed into Chile, including books by the enormously popular Isabel Allende.

It seems to me now, from the perspective of thirty or so years, that the existence in Chile of a relatively enlightened civil society and of a group of writers, economists, and politicians that dared to raise their voices and who felt ever greater determination, greater power, was one of the decisive elements in the change that came about: one of the keys. There were others, of course, and up until now their history has only been half-written. Brought together, they would form a variegated, heterogenous mosaic of opinions, and perhaps we might thereby come closer to an encompassing historical truth.

◆ 2

Writing from the Margins of the Chilean Miracle: Diamela Eltit and the Aesthetics and Politics of the Transition

Juliet Lynd

Author, professor, public intellectual and former performance artist Diamela Eltit has consistently been a voice of critique of the official discourse of the state, be it Pinochet's military regime or the democratic governments that have followed. Her work reveals a suspicion of the rhetoric of the Transition, with its attendant illusions of egalitarianism and its adherence to the myth that the junta created an "economic miracle" out of the chaos of the Allende years.[1] She suggests that Chile's new neoliberal democracy is ill equipped if not altogether unwilling to resolve the pressing social issues that persist as economic and cultural forms of domination. Eltit's resistance to Pinochet's rule and participation in redemocratization movements was carried out principally from within the (highly politicized) artistic realm, although she did participate in the politics of Patricio Aylwin's Transition government by serving as cultural attaché to Mexico from 1990–1993, thereby extending her support of transition efforts from within the system. Nonetheless, her post-dictatorship novels and essays reveal a profound unease with redemocratized Chile in general, and the objects of critique set forth in her earlier works in particular: the violence of the state, the stupefying lull of consumerism, the unchecked power of the private sector, the subjection of women to repressive gender codes, the suppression of indigenous cultures, and the exclusion of the poor from public life persist unabated throughout the so-called Transition.

Eltit's narrative subversions of the powers that structure both dictatorship and postdictatorship cultures insist upon the continuities in Chilean social life that undermine the discourse of the official Transition from dictatorship to democracy and point to the residual traces of authoritarian power and the multiple—political, economic and social—legacies of the Pinochet years. This is not to suggest that the real historical changes of contemporary Chile are lost within the trajectory of the author's work, but democratic Chile is represented as a system under which brutal mechanisms of oppression thrive—through, for example, the suppression of the maternal and the displacement of the poor (problems originating pre-Transition, obviously)—and within which opposition is impossible. Furthermore, her nonfiction work points consistently to the 1973 *golpe* as a historic rupture and the defining moment of Chile's democracy as well as its recent dictatorship, positing that the failures of democracy have less to do with the residual traces of authoritarian enclaves in the government than with the limits of a system determined to actively continue to yield power to the economic elites.[2]

Eltit's devastating critique of contemporary Chile does not constitute an opposition to democracy per se. Her work, by representing the ruinous effects of neoliberal economic policy on the marginalized and underrepresented, stakes out a position for the literary text as a space in which to further the ideals of democracy. An analysis of her cryptic engagement with Chile's Transition and historical shifts will reveal in her work an aesthetic that forges a representation of the changing configurations of the dynamics of power over public space, and explores the complexities of art's strategic positing of solidarity with the marginalized as a utopian impossibility, but nonetheless a necessary project. While the "difficulty" of her texts seems to invite attacks not only of hermeticism, but also of elitism, her work nonetheless reveals a careful interrogation, however problematic, of injustices perpetuated by the contemporary political and cultural context. Before continuing with an analysis of her work—specifically her first novel, *Lumpérica* (1983), and her most recent *Mano de obra* (2002)—it will be worthwhile to situate her *oeuvre* within the political parameters of these larger theoretical questions that have surrounded literary and artistic production in postcoup Chile.

Idelbar Avelar, in his interpretation of Eltit's treatment of Chile's political transitions, productively reads her novels as mourning-work, literary expressions of grieving over the defeat of the left: a mourning of the human losses of the physical and psychological repression carried out by the regime, but also of the effective dismantling of utopian discourse that accompanied the "epochal shift" from state to market authority, brought about symbolically to South America on September 11, 1973. He convincingly argues that this mourning is more acute and more profound in the post-dictatorship period, when the regime has retreated from the center of power yet the social ills that once fueled utopian revolutionary discourse remain intact, only now without a guiding narrative promising resolution. Indeed, the concept of mourning has been a dominant one in the critique of contemporary Latin American literature,[3] and certainly Eltit's work reveals the traumas of a society recently brutalized.

Nevertheless, her novels have never fully bought into a utopian teleology, leftist or otherwise; her concern for the multiple layers of control and exclusion via the doubling and tripling of the standard "identity politics" tropes of class, race, and gender has always functioned to deconstruct any guiding narrative of redemption. Less than the mourning of a loss, one finds a bitter critique of the false sense of coherency provided by any ideology, from the right or the left. Eltit's critique of the Transition is realized through a narrative positioning of marginalized subjectivities, as both presence and absence: presence by way of the text's reminders of the exclusionary forces of neoliberal economic policy, absence because the text refuses to speak for an other. So despite the increased sense of futility that characterizes postdictatorship culture, the urgency of writing in, from and about the margins remains a constant. Deconstructing binaristic configurations of power is the writer's literary weapon with which to destabilize, at least within the space of the novel, the discourses of Transition and the neoliberal global order.

Although clearly different forms of "marginalization" function to differentiate and control subjects (by way of class, gender, race, ethnicity and so forth) in unique ways, and neither the processes nor the experiences are necessarily the same, the broad term is useful for discussing the engagement of her literary and performative texts with various peripheral identities. Firstly, because her texts engage these different forms of marginalization (of gender, of race, of ethnicity, of class) to expose the networks of power that operate simultaneously on the subject. But also her fragmented, poetic narratives divest language of its centralizing function, a characteristic that earns her the label "postmodern" and situates her within Chile's neo-, and later post-, avant-garde.[4] Marginality, therefore, constitutes a range of positions from which to begin the interminable project of deconstructing discursive power in its multiple manifestations through language. This literary-artistic practice provides the cultural diagnoses and analyses of interstices of power, allowing a reading of her work that is beyond mourning in its refusal of nostalgia (for the past, for coherency of subjectivity) and in its unwavering commitment to challenge contemporary forms of control, both discursive and literal.

Literature, therefore, continues to function after dictatorship as a site of critique and a location from which to refuse to accept a social order of compromise and tolerance fostered by the democratic regime and its rhetorical promises that free-market laws attract global capital and will bring Chile a brighter future and heal the wounds of the past. Eltit, in her essay "La compra, la venta," has underscored the importance of reserving a role for literature within the public sphere of democracy as space from which to check these political decisions of the state. She condemns the uncritical euphoria surrounding the publishing boom of the so-called New Chilean Narrative[5] for its overriding complicity with Chile's neoliberal economic program. The obvious complexities of literature's relationship to the market notwithstanding, she insists upon the need to resist determining the value of cultural products in terms of the laws of supply and demand. By suggesting that such laws constitute a dominant logic—and not a "natural law"—she points out that within a pluralist democracy, there ought to be a space from which to critique that logic. Making the additional point that the literary text must compete for an audience that is constantly barraged by the mass-media—a culture industry which favors and benefits from free-market policies—she argues for support of a literary practice that fosters a different mode of reading, one that values texts that take on the complexities of difference and pluralism, one that tackles the questions of collective memory in an amnesiac society built to sustain itself through the acquisition of consumer goods.[6] Eltit maintains that such a space for resistance to and interrogation of any dominant logic of contemporary society can be found in the realm of literary aesthetics:

> [L]a pregunta básica, por estratégica, continúa siendo para mí la interrogación al sistema neoliberal y cómo los productores literarios: críticos, escritores, teóricos pueden abrir una pequeña brecha que paralice lo monolítico de los poderes dominantes para establecer, aunque sea en los bordes del sistema, una especificidad literaria. ("La compra" 27)
>
> (The basic question, because it is a strategic one, is still for me the interrogation of the neoliberal system and how the producers of literature: critics, writers, theoreticians, can open a small breach that paralyzes the monolithic-ness of the dominant powers in order to establish, even if it is son the edges of the system, a literary specificity.)

She thus sets an ethical standard for literature to deterritorialize, to borrow language from Gilles Deleuze and Felix Guattari, to critique from within, to make the reading of literature a space from which to see the contradictory and problematic logics upon which the state's version of free-market politics rests.[7] The specific challenge is thus to question the cultural consequences of a consumerism that appears inextricably entangled in the compromises of the Transition governments, which forgive the crimes of the past that were the original price of laying the groundwork for this particular incorporation into the global economy, and which perpetuate those same economic policies and their hierarchizing and silencing mechanisms.

Eltit's entire *oeuvre* can be and has been read as a social critique of post-coup Chile, beginning with her early participation in CADA (Colectivo de Acciones de Arte)[8] and her first novel, *Lumpérica*, both of which have been credited with forging new aesthetic modes of resistance to the dictatorship.[9] All of her novels, clearly anchored in the context of post-coup Chile, have been read as engaging discourses of authoritarianism, be it a condemnation of the dictatorship from within or critique of its legacies in the collective memory of the nation. Additionally, critics have noted her overt challenges to the discourses of neoliberalism, especially in *El cuarto mundo* (1988), *Los trabajadores de la muerte* (1998) and *Mano de obra*.[10] Criticism of her work has also focused on the innovative, often daring, representations of gender and sexuality; yet it is fundamental that the feminist dimension of Eltit's work be considered in relation to various processes of discrimination that her work attacks and as part of an overall aesthetic project that posits otherizing as part of the cultural logic of repression.

Eltit's aesthetic responses to her historical circumstances map the legacy of dictatorship within a long history of marginalization on the basis of class, race and gender, and insist on the postvanguard as a uniquely privileged space for articulating cultural critique. These processes can be sent throughout her work; here, an analysis of her first and most recent novels, *Lumpérica* and *Mano de obra*, will exemplify them. Both texts engage the economic discourses of neoliberalism and condemn the human consequences of policies that cheapen the labor force. But whereas *Lumpérica*, a novel protesting dictatorship, invites a reclaiming of the public sphere, in *Mano de obra* there is no public sphere—the public space is that of the supermarket—and the marginalized workers must, if they are to reclaim their humanity, take to the streets. These novels belie the myth of the Chilean miracle, expose the limits of Chile's democracy, and state the urgency of seeking historical solutions.

The Seductive Sign: Submission and Resistance in Diamela Eltit's *Lumpérica*

The story of *Lumpérica* begins with a performance. In Santiago, in 1980, in protest of dictatorial oppression in every realm of life, in the midst of an economic crisis, and in defiance of aesthetic practices whose political commitment avoids self-questioning, Diamela Eltit takes the manuscript of her highly cryptic and non-mimetic novel *Lumpérica* to a brothel on Maipú Street in Santiago, where she cuts and burns her arms and reads selections of her as yet unpublished book to an audience of prostitutes, transvestites, clients, vagabonds, and a few accompanying artists, filming the performance all the while for a work of art that will become known as simply "Maipú."[11] The final text of *Lumpérica* (published in 1983) includes references to the art action at the brothel and consists of a series of ambiguously interconnected performances; a literature-performance hybrid, it questions the limits between literature and performance and between the artistic text and its audience. In the novel, a woman in a public plaza during the dead of the curfew night, illuminated only by a flashing neon sign, constitutes the only discernable narrative thread that connects the disjointed scenes of bodies writhing in ecstasy and in pain, a film crew shooting multiple takes of a woman falling on the plaza, the interrogation of a man who has interrupted this scene, descriptions of torture, and declarations of the multiple functions of writing. Through the fragmented overlapping and the narrative intertwining of these performances, the novel explores at once the inscription of bodies into the new body of law ushered in by the Pinochet regime and the possibilities for resistance *vis a vis* the literary text.

In the first narrative fragments of the principal performance of the novel ("as much a staging as a narrative," notes Jean Franco [*Decline* 180]), a woman called L. Iluminada and an indistinct number of vagrants occupy the public plaza after the fall of curfew and perform ambiguous rituals under the light of a flashing neon sign, "el luminoso" referred to throughout the text as "el luminoso," or "that which gives off light." As if to emphasize the characters' entry into a new era, the first paragraph establishes that the protagonist "ya no relumbre como antaño cuando era contemplada con luz natural" (9). Likewise, the entire conferring of new identities in the opening "baptismal" scene (10) brings about an entry into a "desolada ciudadanía" (10) (desolate citizenry) with religious fervor. "El luminoso" has been identified by Mary Louise Pratt as a "potent image for the authoritarian state: light/power emanating from an unseen source" (160) and by Sara Castro-Klaren as analogous to a torturer (43). Yet "el luminoso" not only suggests the ubiquitous power of dictatorship: the commercial connotations of the neon sign presiding over the ritual scenes of the plaza suggest that it can also be understood as a metaphor for the seductive lure of the market and the privatization of public space. And the text will reiterate that under "esa luz que se vende" (11) *los pálidos* (the vagrants, the "lumpen") enact their strange movements throughout the public place, "Por puro deseo propietarios al venderse al luminoso como mercaderías" (14).

Throughout the text, the neon sign is consistently referred to as "el luminoso," or "that which *actively* gives off light."[12] This at once complements and dominates the name of the protagonist "L. Iluminada," the past participle suggesting that which is *passively* lit up, ambiguously either from an outside source or from within. This name is given to her, no less, by *el luminoso*: "Le ratifica el nombre en dos colores paralelos, el luminoso ampliado sobre el cuerpo escribe L. Iluminada" (10). The "L" is never expanded upon in the text, and remains for the reader only an initial, open to interpretation.[13] But the letter has specific connotations in the context of Pinochet's dictatorship: "L" was the randomly chosen letter stamped on the passports of those individuals fleeing the country to indicate that the bearer was prohibited from returning (Wright and Oñate 171). *El luminosos*'s act of inscription on L. Iluminada's body, then, thus reflects this maneuver of the dictatorship and proscribes the protagonist from the new laws of the nation; the ambiguity of the initial evokes the arbitrariness of the "L"-stamp that marked the regime's absolute power to determine the right to citizenship and to empty the term of its implied right to participation in civic life. Citizenship conferred by *el luminoso* is meaningless.

Yet the *pálidos* are fascinated by the message written for them by the neon sign—"Porque este luminoso que se enciende de noche está construyendo su mensaje para ellos" (11) (Because this light that comes on at night is constructing its message for them), a point which contrasts with the narrator's later observation that the public lampposts have no audience: "y se encienden para nadie los faroles, para nadie este ornamento" (114) (and the lampposts come on for no one, this ornament for no one). So the dictatorship's curfew makes the illumination of public space an empty gesture, the lampposts a mere remnant of a public space not prohibited by curfew. Only the narrator, however, makes this suggestion; L. Iluminada and the vagrants are focused only on the flashing neon sign, attracted to it while it illuminates their bodies "como productos comerciales" (10) (like commercial products). Submission to the seductive sign is rendered all the more transgressively pleasureful, as L. Iluminada and the masses seek frenzied sexual union under the blinking neon light that speaks to them. In stark contrast to the sometimes gleeful, sometimes masochistic rapture of submitting to *el luminoso*, however, the narrator also insists on the degraded state of the *pálidos*: "A ellos, que pudieron brillar de otra manera, están aquí lamiendo la plaza como mercancía de valor incierto" (11) (To them, who might have shone in a different way, they are here licking the plaza like merchandise of uncertain value). The language from these quotes shifts the focus from the dictatorship's encroachments on the freedom to inhabit public space, the right to free expression and the human right to dignity, and the text associates the abuses of civil and human rights with a cold economics—it is very cold in *Lumpérica*'s plaza—that assigns a monetary value to human life and then cheapens it.

The narration of this performance of identity alternates between a condemnation of the subjugation of the *pálidos* and an affirmation of their agency, but their voice goes consistently unheard throughout the text. Here, the narrator shrouds a near celebration of self-renewal in the dark reality of traffic in humans:

> Con sonidos guturales llenan el espacio en una alfabetización virgen que altera las normas de la experiencia. Y así de vencidos en vencedores se convierten, resaltantes en sus tonos morenos, adquiriendo en sus carnes una verdadera dimensión de la belleza. Porque hasta ése podría estar comprometido en la disposición azarosa de los cuerpos. Los mismos que se van preparando para una nueva circulación.
> Aunque no es nada novedoso, el luminoso anuncia que se venden cuerpos.
> Sí, cuerpos se venden en la plaza.
> A un precio no determinado. Es más bien el placer que emanan en lo profundo de su compromiso. Sus palabras caen en el vacío ampliando sus moléculas para petrificar lo eterno de la producción. (13–14)

(They fill the space with guttural sounds in a virgin literacy that alters the norms of experience. And so they are changed from vanquished into conquerors, standing out in their brown tones, acquiring in their flesh a true dimension of beauty. Because even this could be compromised in the hazardous disposition of the bodies. The same ones that are preparing for a new circulation.
Although it's nothing new, the neon sign announces that bodies are for sale.
Yes, bodies are for sale in the plaza.
At an undetermined price. It's rather the pleasure that emanates in the profundity of their compromise. Their words fall in a void broadening their molecules to petrify the eternity of their production.)

A double narrative exists in this fragmentary text: the victorious emergence of the *desamparados* into language, on the one hand, and the loss of these recuperative moments within an economy of power over bodies on the other. If there are points at which the text seems to resist any mechanism that would deny the subjectivity, the language, the voice of the subaltern, that resistance is in turn subjected to the grim assertion that their words are beyond the reader's reach.

In fact, the issue of authorial control over the subjects represented in the narrative, while present throughout the novel, arises forcefully in the powerful performance described in Chapter 5. Titled "Quo Vadis," Latin for "Where are you going?," this section contains a glorious moment in the narrative when, after a series of attempts at communication, the lumpen who have inhabited the plaza accept pieces of chalk from L. Iluminada and write their own questions on the public pavement, under the light, thus acquiring not only a voice, but also the power of the written word—an agency that *el luminoso* had rendered dubious at best. L. Iluminada reads what they have written and basks in the wonder of this event after *los pálidos* first had censured her written question, "dónde vas?" (122) (Where are you going?), etched in chalk on the gray, rain-washed cement of the plaza. *Los pálidos*, who have carefully been watching her and reading her questions (122–23), stand on top of her words and blot them out: "Es evidente que se sienten expulsados hasta los bordes de la plaza como notas al margen. Por eso tapan el rayado. Han comprendido la agresión" (123) (It's clear that they feel expelled to the borders of the plaza like notes on the margin). And they have understood correctly, for L. Iluminada's impulse to write to/for them seems to spring from a disdainful attitude, born of a tired tension between them as they stare at one another, as if to challenge the possibility of genuine communication.

This passage is peppered with references to the interchange of glances and stares between the protagonist and the lumpen inhabiting the plaza. Despite the apparently desired communication, the protagonist eventually "neutraliza su mirada recomponiéndose de la pasajera debilidad de prenderse a esos ojos que ofrecían la ficción de una apuesta fracasada" (121) (neutralizes her gaze, recomposing herself after the passing weakness of getting caught up in those eyes that offered the fiction of a failed bet). The narrator goes on to explain the protagonist's scorn: "Elabora su sonrisa porque ella no los ve más que en su producto comercial y transferible. Circulante material abusado por la extranjería del ojo ajeno a la plaza que no sabrá de los originales estropeados, del abandono de las matrices, que no soportará su segunda impresión" (122)

(She produces her smile because she sees them only in their comercial and transferable product). The vagrants comprehend that she has forcefully sought to ignore the originality of their communion in the plaza and reduce their presence to a literary fiction, their existential questions served up for the use of others. Although she had previously been aware of their oblique gazes "hacia otros paisajes chilenos" (113), she seems to comprehend their defiance only after offering them the chalk, finally allowing them their own right to write, to represent their voice. It is then that L. Iluminada and *los pálidos* all seem to escape, if only momentarily, the reductive relationship established by the tension of desiring gazes and the section concludes that "toda esa plaza al fin pudiera almacenar la tinta para repetir otros escritos" (126) (the entire plaza at last could store the ink to repeat other writings).

Nevertheless, despite this tremendous moment for the protagonist and the vagrants, the reader is not privy to what they have written. Not only do they write in the mutable material of chalk, the text never reveals even one word of their messages. Just as *el luminoso* has no discernable text for the reader to decipher, the questions asked by the vagrants must go unread by the reader, thereby posing a different set of questions as to the desires and demands of the *pálidos* and the narrator's refusal to reveal them. These questions are then framed by the larger question posed by the title of the chapter, Quo Vadis, the interlocutor of which is ambiguous: is it directed from the author or the narrator to the reader? To L. Iluminada? To the occupants of the plaza? To Chile? At one and the same time, the novel celebrates the written expression on the censured public square, establishing the potential for resistance and for renewal of civic life, and underscores the sense of defeat of the "failed bet," the loss of possibility of an easy articulation of solidarity with the poor. If the aforementioned jubilee would suggest a progressive move toward a hopeful future, this interpretation is offset by the utter lack of directionality, temporal or spatial, in this chapter and throughout the novel, a point reiterated by the openness of the novel's ending, though not precluding the possibility of imagining another direction, one not determined by the dehumanizing logic of the market or the controlling objectification of the other in literature determined to speak for—rather than with—the marginalized.

This rather ambiguous conclusion returns to the question of the very function of literature and what its relationship is to the marginalized and to marginalization, and what that relationship can be in this post-coup context of market-oriented politics. On the one hand, the novel writes its own destruction by refusing to satisfy its apparent desire to tell a story, not to mention the reader's presumed desire to read one, to know the answer(s) to the provocative "Quo vadis" question; on the other hand, as Avelar asserts, the fleeting communion in the plaza constitutes "an affirmation of the impossible" (185). To add to Avelar's suggestions that the post-coup novel can no longer engage in utopian narratives of redemption in an era dominated by the authority of the marketplace logic of late capitalism, it can seek out in the politicized terrain of aesthetics a mode of critique not only of any dominant logic but specifically the prevalence of an ideology that would reduce bodies to a monetary value and put them up for sale.

Eltit's work, however, engages not only the question of the place of the literary text in the culture of a market economy; her novels reiterate a parallel between literature and the specific economy of exchange of women's bodies as commodities through the institution of prostitution.[14] In *Lumpérica*, this relationship is established by the text's overt references to the author's 1980 happening staged at the Maipú brothel (a still from the video of the performance showing Eltit's sliced up forearms is included in the "Ensayo general" section, which makes direct references to the cuts). This controversial performance piece involved one of many instances of the author "taking literature to the most marginal of spaces" (Franco, "Going Public" 52). The filming of the performance arguably problematizes the gesture of solidarity with the marginalized subjects of the brothel, objectifying the audience for the sake of an art object (the film) to be consumed elsewhere. However, it certainly questioned the circulation of the literary text and the kinds of reception it can and should receive.

Yet if the apparent attempt by the "Maipú" performance to problematize the relationship between the literary text and the marginalized (or between the artist and his or her obscure object of desire) is undermined by the filming, the novel delves into another layer of critique, and questions the motivations of the filmmaker in the plaza, at the same time that the narrator renders the director's presence ambiguous. While the filming of the "Maipú" performance arguably appropriates and objectifies the audience within the brothel for the speculation of the audience of the film, in the novel the filming of the protagonist's coming together with the lumpen is both problematized by the association of the director with the authoritarian stance of the interrogator (if not the torturer) of other chapters of the novel, and by the very incorporation of the film production within the narrative. Metafiction thus becomes, as Linda Hutcheon would have it, a means of questioning the very bases upon which the text constructs its representations and thereby demands that the reader do the same. The complexities of the literary, and the possibilities of metafiction, and the genre-bending plays with performance place the responsibility for constructing meaning and questioning cultural assumptions with the reader.

In this debut novel, Eltit perpetuates the concerns set forth in her performance work. The performance-novel hybrid demands that cultural production problematize the multiple ways in which individuals are marginalized not only by the dictatorship's policies of controlling bodies by torture and disappearance, but by the control of bodies *vis a vis* the wholesale of the workforce. The complex inter-workings of these powers, both physical and discursive, respond to the horrors of dictatorship and to the shift toward a neoliberal economy in which the "authority of the market" is both omnipresent and impossible to locate. This shift, present not only in Chile but throughout the Americas—as reiterated by the title's play on "luz," "lumpen," "perica" (slang for prostitute) and "América"—is that which will continue to define the post-dictatorship democracy, and will return with a vengeance in Eltit's later novels in which she continues to articulate connections between otherness, power and the perpetuation of economic self-interest by exploring the margins of Chile's so-called economic miracle.

From the Plaza to the Supermarket: *Mano de obra*

Eltit's subsequent works, both before and after the return to democratic rule, explore the status of women and the poor in a society marked by fear, paranoia and a distinctively absent democratic ethos, but her most recent novel, *Mano de obra* (2002), explores the utter degradation of supermarket employees. This novel portrays a series of characters and situations with little narrative movement; the various scenes take place almost claustrophobically in the *súper* or in the home; only at the end do the characters take to the streets. The novel, consistent with Eltit's earlier work, is challenging: it deploys gaps and silences in the narrative to evoke the historical context of the desperate poverty it exposes. This text is at once a denunciation of any claims to Chile's economic success, an appeal for a renewal of solidarity with and among the working class, and a statement of skepticism about that very possibility. However, it poses the novel as a space in which to contemplate the devastating effects of the nation's economic policies, while insisting that any solutions lie in negotiation beyond the space of the literary text.

The first half of the novel is written in the first person singular. The narrator is a supermarket employee in what is described as a Wal-Mart-like superstore, complete with a variety of plastic-wrapped products including food, clothes, toys and appliances; constant announcements of bargains over the loudspeaker; glaring fluorescent lights; ubiquitous surveillance cameras; surreptitious supervisors; customers desperate for the best sale; and apron-clad employees donning nametags and obligatory smiles. Although the narrative is peppered with the distinctly oral register of insults and foul language, the narrator also keenly theorizes the diminution of his own existence. He complains of being ill, an "enfermedad laboral" ("labor sickness"; 50) he calls it, characterized by the utter exhaustion and anonymity of his job. He writes of his own lack of historicity, noting how "[e]l tiempo juega de manera perversa conmigo porque no termina de inscribirse en ninguna parte de mi ser. Sólo está depositado en el super, ocurre en el super" (31) (time plays a perverse game with me because it does not stop inscribing itself on any part of my being. It is just deposited in the supermarket, it occurs in the supermarket). The narrator of this first half of the book reveals nothing of his life or identity beyond the supermarket. He mentions once that the streets outside the store are frightening, but otherwise he describes his existence as entirely defined by the demands of clients, supervisors and the unending streams of products that flow in and out of the store. There is no narrative plot, merely a litany of situations that describe the degraded state of the employee.

The first chapters of the book establish the novel's critical vision of this consumer society by giving the reader a grotesque vision of the supermarket's clients. Children terrorize the employee by destroying displays and throwing tantrums in response to their uncontrollable desires for the products marketed to them. Senior citizens, the "viejos del súper," are picky shoppers—more so than other clients, for they have extraordinarily limited means—and the employee coldly complains of their complaints of deteriorating bodies and existences. Other customers, in their infinite consumer needs, make endless demands on the employee and are quick to denounce him to the supervisor for any inconvenience in their shopping experiences. When this happens, the employee apologizes, "apelando a mi extenso servilismo laboral" (22) (appealing to my extensive labor servitude). At one point he thinks that "Es posible que no merezca que los clientes me traten tan mal" (23) (It is possible that I don't deserve to be badly treated by the clients). But he adds "Pero no lo pienso enteramente. En realidad no. No enteramente" (23) (But I don't think it entirely. In reality no. Not entirely) and he later concludes that he does indeed deserve the poor treatment of the customer (75), for the client is, after all, "el amo [. . .] el tutor absoluto de la mercadería" (75) (the boss [. . .] the absolute guardian of the merchandise). The supervisors are equally cruel, watching his every move, yet the employee writes of his own commitment to this hierarchy, almost bragging of how quickly he mops up the spit on the floor left by the customers so that no manager will slip and fall.

In the final section of this first half of the novel, the employees have been assigned a 24-hour shift to cover a New Year's Eve sales event. The narrator complains of the damage wrought to his feet, but also to his bladder and kidneys as he works twelve, fourteen, sixteen hours with no break and no additional salary. As the clock strikes midnight and fireworks go off in the distance, the narrator states, "Yo celebro mi año (nuevo), mi triunfo. Y mi silencio" (76) (I celebrate my (new) year, my triumph). His triumph is the completion of his obscenely long shift, but the fact that the word "new" is placed in parentheses—a strategy utilized throughout the narrative to disconcerting ends—gives the lines a double reading: he ironically, it would seem, celebrates the year past—and his silence. But he also celebrates the new year, and as the final line in this section suggests, there will be change: "Hay que poner fin a este capítulo" (76) (This chapter must end). What the next chapter will be is left entirely unclear, but the novel punctuates the urgency of bringing an end to the current situation.

The second half of the book is narrated in the first person plural and it tells the story of a group of supermarket employees who pool their resources to share a house and living expenses in order to put together a barely subsistence existence in an impoverished urban neighborhood. Whether or not the narrator is the same employee from the first half is impossible to determine. This narrator speaks of "us" and talks about the group's relationship to the various individuals who share the house, but never does the narrative voice in this half speak in the singular form, so it is not clear if this narrator is another unnamed individual in the house or a disembodied collective voice. Whichever the case, the use of the plural suggests an appealing sense of solidarity that was conspicuously absent from the first narrator's strikingly solitary existence—though the lack of an "I" is also odd and the reader is never quite privy to the full story. In fact, the "nosotros"-narrator makes references to personal experiences beyond the frame of the novel: for instance, "we" know the motivations of Enrique's profound sadness, but the reader does not. Indeed, the reader knows nothing about the individual circumstances of these supermarket employees that seem to have no other family or friends beyond the "we" of the household.

The novel tells the story of the increasingly precarious situation of this group as the supermarket takes ever more drastic measures to reduce costs and increase profits. They are subject to dramatic wage reductions, first extended hours for less pay, and then cuts to their shifts resulting in even less pay. The reason, the narrator explains over and over again, is the seemingly infinite lines of people looking for work. Increased competition for jobs reduces the cost of labor—hence the title: the characters are reduced to their status as objects in a profit formula. We learn of the increasing physical, psychological and emotional deterioration of each of them, as they are individually subjected to various forms of humiliation at their jobs: Isabel must allow the boss to "lamerle el culo," (lick her ass) which she believes makes her a "lameculos" as well; Enrique is demoted, ordered to enthusiastically sell nearly expired cans of fruit at drastically reduced prices; Sonia is banished to the butcher's section, which causes her to stink day in and day out—and one day she chops off her own finger, an offense which earns her another transfer to the seafood section. The group amazingly survives the personnel cuts (until the end of the novel), but they live in terror of being "placed on the lists" of people to be fired, in desperate poverty as their diminishing wages cause them to lose their electricity, their water, and ultimately their humanity. As the narrator explains when the residents join Andrés in his drug habit, "Aspirábamos, sí, sí, para alegrarnos y, por una vez, lograr conversar y reírnos con el afecto, la decencia y la sinceridad que caracteriza a los seres humanos" (167) (We would inhale, yes, yes, to cheer ourselves up and, for once, manage to converse and laugh with all of the affection, decency and sincerity that characterizes human beings).

The narrator constantly speaks of the affection that unites the disparate group (they are unrelated, brought together only by their common employer, the supermarket) and of their collective efforts to support one another: for instance, they take turns caring for the baby of the single mother, Isabel; they allow Gloria to be housewife to all as her particular contribution to the household when she is unable to find other work; they take in an adolescent, Gabriel, despite his character flaws. But despite the solidarity implied by the "nosotros" and the constant references to the group's "cariño," the narrative is peppered with incidents of backstabbing and mistrust. They complain about having to care for the "guagua"; Gloria's role as house maid comes with the responsibility of allowing all of the men to "mount" her, and Gabriel accuses and is accused of betraying the group.

The most dramatic of these incidents of backstabbing, though, comes early on, when Andrés is suspected of organizing a union, which is strictly prohibited. The group is aghast, incredulous that their friend would do such a thing that would jeopardize them all. Gloria turns him in to the supervisor and he is fired before anything more can happen. The final betrayal comes at the end of the novel, when the natural leader of the group, Enrique, has collaborated with the supervisors to "put them on the lists" and have them fired. As the group walks through the streets stunned at what has happened, however, it is the adolescent among them, Gabriel, who emerges as the next leader and declares—to general agreement—that it is time to demand their equality as Chileans and "dar vuelta a la página" (176) (turn the page). This demand for change at the end of the novel comes only when the employees have been pushed to the absolute limit of destitution and degradation, and the declaration—the first reference in the narrative to the nation—is one of rage. Gabriel declares: "vamos a cagar a los maricones que nos miran como si no fuéramos chilenos igual que todos los demás culiados chuchas de su madre. Ya pues huevones, caminen. Caminemos. Demos vuelta a la página" (176) (we are going to fuck up the faggots who look at us as if we weren't Chileans just like all the other sissy motherfuckers. Let's go already, assholes, walk. Let's walk. Let's turn the page). As the reader of *Lumpérica* might ask: Quo vadis?

The struggle between solidarity and solitude that plays out throughout the novel is inscribed in a series of curious chapter headings. The first half of the narrative (the first person singular) is divided into chapters titled with the names of anarchist, communist and socialist newspapers from the early twentieth century and the names of cities and years that witnessed repression against labor organizing: *El despertar de los trabajadores* (Iquique, 1911), *Verba roja* (Santiago, 1918), *Luz y vida* (Antofogasta, 1909), etc. The second half of the novel receives the title of another workers' paper from 1970, *Puro Chile*. These obscure historical references anchor the novel in Chile's long labor history, a dramatic and violent struggle between strong organized movements and bloody repression; the recent coup was only one chapter in a longer story. The second part is also divided into chapters, but *Puro Chile* is the last newspaper title—the rest are references to actions in the narrative, as if to underscore the individual nature of the struggle of the employees in relation to the history of worker organization. The only other reference to Chile is Gabriel's declaration at the end of the novel, so the links to the historical circumstances that have left the workers in such dire straits are up to the reader to put together. The novel rejects both utopian proposals from the left and the current neoliberal doctrine, leaving only a profound longing for— but also a deep skepticism about—the solidarity that might "put an end to this chapter" and "turn the page."

To conclude, Eltit's stark and grotesque portrayal of urban poverty challenges the official narrative of Chile's economic success and shows workers to be utterly marginalized from the political life of the nation. Her disconcerting narrative style challenges the reader to question his or her own relationship to the realities represented in the text. True to Eltit's suggestion that literature constitute a space from which to expose the problems inherent in Chile's neoliberal model and thereby problematize the rhetoric of the transition, her novels can be read as mapping the dispersion of power that marks the post-coup embrace of recent trends in the global economy—that is, not only the transition from dictatorship to democracy but also, and more clearly, of the neoliberal transition from state to market authority. In Eltit's work, this involves a polemical commitment to abstract and challenging aesthetics, as well as a forging of deconstructive critique from a position of solidarity (always interrogated but never lost) with the marginalized. Her work is therefore caught up in the slippery terrain of interpolating the popular into highly intellectualized texts, an issue which has brought her work into conflict with those who would prioritize the value of transparent representation. Eltit's work forges an aesthetics that responds to the shifts in the public and private spheres brought about by an adherence to a neoliberal program that appears to exacerbate the unequal distribution of wealth and it writes the local history of Chile into a broader critique of economic policies common throughout the global economy. Eltit does not offer any solution to these issues; but she poses the literary text as a space for historicizing these circumstances and demanding a new historical transition.

Notes

1. The Pinochet regime, under the guidance of University of Chicago-trained economists (known as *los Chicago Boys*), implemented a radical experiment in neoliberal economic policy. The "structural adjustments" to the economy (also called "shock treatments") involved dramatic reduction of public spending, privatization of government enterprises, new labor laws that weakened workers' rights, and the deregulation of the economy to attract foreign investment. The result has been touted by some as an economic miracle (neoliberal guru Milton Friedman himself coined the phrase), holding Chile up as a model for developing countries worldwide; others have condemned neoliberal policy for deepening the divide between the wealthy and the poor. Although post-Pinochet governments have increased public spending and have succeeding in improving poverty rates, they have fundamentally embraced the neoliberal model. With the recent election of Michelle Bachelet to the presidency, Chile tentatively enters the so-called New Latin American left; it remains to be seen how effectively these emergent leaders will challenge corporate power and foreign interests in the region or the cultural forms of otherizing that benefit them, but certainly they have planted seeds of hope.
2. See, for example, her cleverly titled "Las dos caras de la Moneda" (1997; the English translation would be "The Two Sides of the Coin," though lost is the play on *Moneda*, the name of Chile's presidential palace). In this essay she analyzes the symbolic dimension of the staging of the coup—the dramatic impact of the bombing of the presi-

dential palace—in terms of the irreparable violence that would later be enacted upon the economy, the other *moneda*. Denying Chile's much celebrated "development," Eltit attacks the social violence inherent in the new economy and the stupefying consumerism that currently pervades Chilean culture. This marking of the coup as the transitional moment to define Chile's recent history, however, articulates the defeat associated with the epochal shift ushered in by Pinochet, and effectively rewrites history. The essay can be found in *Emergencias* (17–24).

3. Avelar's seminal book analyzes novels from the Southern Cone and Brazil and reads postdictatorship literature as allegories of precisely this defeat of the left, thus positing the literary text as an appropriate space for a cultural, collective mourning. See also Alberto Moreiras' *Tercer espacio: literatura y duelo*, which examines literature from throughout the continent, throughout the latter half of the twentieth century to consider the ways in which the practice of mourning—of the loss associated with the *in between* space that defines Latin America's postcolonial literature—works toward a new sense of historicity. He suggests that it is the task of mourning to get beyond the impasses of the present, determined largely by the traumas of dictatorship, and reimagine utopianism. See also the collection of essays in *Memoria, duelo y narración: Chile después de Pinochet: literature, cine, sociedad* (Roland Spiller, et. al., eds.).

4. Eltit's work, from her art interventions to her novels, can be considered part of the *avanzada* movement that emerged in Chile in the mid-seventies. The movement shared its outrage at social injustice and its political opposition to the dictatorship with traditional leftist groups, but departed radically on the question of strategies. Rejecting grand narrative utopias, the *avanzada*, Nelly Richard explains, "tried to reformulate the conditions of artistic production through a mechanism, not of the 'representation' of reality, but of its *intervention*, in order to transform the figurative and symbolic web of institutional order in which the Chilean subject was ensnared" (*Margins* 107). Eugenia Brito, crediting the publication of Eltit's first novel with the opening up of a "scene of writing" that forged innovative forms of resistance to the dictatorship, explains the frequent rejection of her work in terms of a tendency (on all sides of the political spectrum) to reject what is truly questioning. She specifically accuses the leftist press of being "muy poco interesada en recepcionar sistema disidente, alguno que no calce con los modos habituales de propagar la ideología impugnadora al sistema militar. Se deseó siempre continuar, en esta prensa, con un tipo de cultura pre-militar, con tópicos favoritos, como el tema de los exiliados, la canción-protesta, el teatro callejero, etc., sin siquiera cuestionar el valor estrictamente literario de estas producciones" (115). And indeed Brito goes on to provide an analysis based on how the literary value of Eltit's work lies precisely in its particular engagement of its context.

5. In the compilation of papers delivered at a conference on the "New Chilean Narrative" (*Nueva narrativa chilena*, edited by Carlos Olivárez), Eltit's contribution ("La compra, la venta" 57–60) stands out as one of the most derisive of the political ambivalence that dominates the recent trend. See also her interview with Walescka Pino-

Ojeda ("Diamela Eltit: el letrado y el *lumpen*") for further discussion of her views on the relationship between literature and market demand.

6. The critique of consumerism as a distraction from the horrors of the human rights abuses committed under the Pinochet regime, and then as symptomatic of a collective amnesia and a personal avoidance of the traumatic past, can be found in a broad range of writers, from sociologist Tomás Moulián (*Chile actual: anatomía de un mito*) to novelist and playwright Marco Antonio de la Parra (*La mala memoria: historia personal de Chile contemporáneo*). The ironic dimension of this cultural symptom is that the behavior (shopping, obsessive acquisition of goods, desire for "First World" status, accruement of debt to satisfy this consumer fetishism) is dependent on the very violence it supposedly avoids in that economic policies designed to attract foreign capital are the same policies that exacerbate poverty to combat inflation and lower the cost of labor.

7. And indeed her novels have been read as such, as shown by Juan Carlos Lértora. See "Diamela Eltit: Hacia una poética de literatura menor," included in the collection of articles that he edited dedicated entirely to Eltit's (pre-1993) *oeuvre*: *Una poética de literatura menor: la narrativa de Diamela Eltit*. All of the articles in some way engage various manifestations of poststructuralist theory to explore the author's manipulation of language to effect a critique of the ordering power of language and "to express another possible community and to forge the means for another consciousness and another sensibility" (Deleuze and Guattari 17). (Several of the articles gathered in *Creación y resistencia: La narrativa de Diamela Eltit 1983–1998*) take up similar concerns, focusing primarily on the novelist's postdictatorship work).

8. This eclectic group of writers (Raúl Zurita and Diamela Eltit), visual artists (Lotty Rosenfeld and Juan Castillo), and a sociologist (Fernando Balcells) declared itself militant and revolutionary, working toward social consciousness-raising and collective liberation through art. The group created a number of happenings in the late seventies and early eighties, including the publicized distribution of milk to the poor ("Para no morir del hambre en el arte"), the tossing of fliers from an airplane over the city proclaiming that "el trabajo de ampliación de los niveles habituales de la vida" is a true work of art ("¡Ay, Sudamérica!"), and the painting of the expression "No +" throughout the city. The latter was spontaneously integrated into popular redemocratization movements, as people added their own endings to the slogan ("no + tortura," "no + hambre," etc.). See Neustadt's *CADA día: la creación de un arte social* for an examination of the art collective's short-lived collaboration and the lasting impact of the group's work on how art, politics and the social are conceived in contemporary Chile.

9. See especially Brito and Richard ("Tres funciones"). Also García Corales.

10. See Francine Masiello. Masiello also observes of *Lumpérica* that Eltit "anticipates the market-run democracy that was to be installed seven years after the publication of her novel" (68). See also Mónica Barrientos as well as Richard's *Residuos y metáforas*.

11. The video recordings of Eltit's performances (by Lotty Rosenfeld) are not commer-

cially available, and my interpretations are based on published descriptions of the happenings. It should be noted that the performance also included washing the street outside the brothel and projecting a video image of herself across the street. For descriptions and analyses of *Maipú*, see Robert Neustadt's *(Con)Fusing Signs* (25–81) and also Nelly Richard's *Margins and Institutions* (especially pages 66–72). See also the Eltit's interviews with Leonidas Morales T. (164–72) and Juan Andrés Piña (234).

12. Ronald Christ (in *E. Luminata*, the English translation of the novel) consistently translates "el luminoso" as "the sign," thereby capturing the poststructuralist spirit of the text by denoting simultaneously the double meaning of sign as signboard *and* the linguistic sense of that which indicates the existence of something else. The translation gives up this play on names, and as Christ himself fully recognizes in the essay that accompanies the translation, any number of specific references to the Chilean context are lost in translation.

13. The pronunciation of the letter, "ele," might read as an amalgam of the masculine "él" (he) and the feminine "ella" (she), thereby questioning the protagonist's markers of gender, or suggesting the androgynous nature of her subjection to the arbitrary power of *el luminoso*.

14. More broadly, several critics have connected Eltit's work with Luce Irigaray's theories on the commodification of women and on desire and the female body. See Castro Klaren (42) and Neustadt (*(Con)fusing Signs* 58–59), as well as Sotomayor's "Tres caricias: una lectura de Luce Irigaray en la narrativa de Diamela Eltit."

Works Cited

Avelar, Idelbar. *The Untimely Present: Postdictatorial Latin American Fiction and the Task of Mourning*. Durham: Duke University Press, 1999.

Barrientos, Mónica. "Vigilancia y fuga en Mano de obra de Diamela Eltit." *Espéculo: Revista de Estudios Literarios* 31 (Nov. 2005–Feb. 2006 Feb): NP (Electronic publication).

Brito, Eugenia. *Campos minados: Literatura post-golpe en Chile*. Santiago: Cuarto Propio, 1990.

Cánovas, Rodrigo. *Novela chilena, nuevas generaciones: el abordaje de los huérfanos*. Santiago: Ediciones Universidad Católica de Chile, 1997.

Castro-Klaren, Sara. "The Literary Body or the Politics of Eros in Lúmperica [sic]." *Indiana Journal of Hispanic Literatures* 1.2 (Spring 1993): 41–51.

Christ, Ronald. "Extravag(r)ant and Un/erring Spirit." *E. Luminata*. Santa Fe, New Mexico: Lumen, 1997. 205–34.

Deleuze, Gilles, and Felix Guattari. *Kafka: Towards a Minor Literature*. Trans. Dana Polan. *Theory and History of Literature* 30. Minneapolis: University of Minnesota Press, 1986.

Eltit, Diamela. *Mano de obra*. Santiago: Seix Barral, 2002.
———. *Emergencias: escritos sobre literatura, arte y política*. Ed. Leonidas Morales Santiago: Planeta Chilena, 2000.
———. "Diamela Eltit: el letrado y el *lumpen*." Interview with Walescka Pino-Ojeda. *Journal of Iberian and Latin American Studies* 5.2 (1999): 23–43.
———. *Conversaciones con Diamela Eltit*. Interviews with Leonidas Morales T. Santiago: Cuarto Propio, 1998.
———. *Los trabajadores de la muerte*. Santiago: Planeta Chilena, 1998.
———. *E. Luminata*. Trans. Ronald Christ. Santa Fe, New Mexico: Lumen, 1997.
———. "Diamela Eltit: escritos sobre un cuerpo." *Conversaciones con la literatura chilena*. Interview with Juan Andrés Piña. Santiago: Los Andes, 1991. 223–54.
———. *El cuarto mundo*. Santiago: Planeta, 1988.
———. *Lumpérica*. Santiago: Las Ediciones del Ornitorrinco, 1983.
Franco, Jean. *The Decline and Fall of the Lettered City: Latin America in the Cold War*. Cambridge: Harvard University Press, 2002.
———. "Going Public: Reinhabiting the Private." *Critical Passions*. Ed. and Intro. Mary Louise Pratt and Kathleen Newman. Durham: Duke University Press, 1999.
García Corales, Guillermo. "La deconstrucción del poder en *Lumpérica*." *Lértora Poética*: 111–25.
Hutcheon, Linda. *The Politics of Postmodernism*. New York: Routledge, 1989.
———. *A Poetics of Postmodernism: History, Theory, Fiction*. New York and London: Routledge, 1988.
Lagos, María Inés, ed. and Intro. *Creación y resistencia: la narrativa de Diamela Eltit 1983–1998*. Nomadías / Serie monográfica. Santiago: Cuarto Propio, 2000.
Lértora, Juan Carlos. "Diamela Eltit: Hacia una poética de literatura menor." *Lértora Poética*. 27–35.
———, ed. *Una poética de literatura menor: la narrativa de Diamela Eltit*. Para Textos. Santiago: Cuarto Propio, 1993.
Masiello, Francine. *The Art of Transition: Latin American Culture and Neoliberal Crisis*. Durham: Duke University Press, 2001.
Moreiras, Alberto. *Tercer espacio: literatura y duelo en América Latina*. Santiago: Universidad Arcis/LOM, 1999.
———. "Postdictadura y reforma del pensamiento." *Revista de Crítica Cultural* 7 (Nov. 1993): 26–35.
Moulián, Tomás. *Chile Actual: anatomía de un mito*. Serie Punto de Fuga. Colección Sin Norte. Santiago: LOM-Arcis, 1997.
Neustadt, Robert. *(Con)fusing Signs and Postmodern Positions*. New York: Garland, 1999.
———. *CADA Día: la creación de un arte social*. Santiago: Cuarto Propio, 2001.
Olea, Raquel. "El cuerpo-mujer. Un recorte de lectura en la narrativa de Diamela Eltit." *Revista Chilena de Literatura* 42 (August 1993): 165–71.

Olivares, Carlos, ed. *Nueva Narrativa Chilena.* Santiago: LOM, 1997.
Parra, Marco Antonio de la. *La mala memoria: historia personal de Chile contemporáneo.* Santiago: Planeta, 1998.
Pratt, Mary Louise. "Overwriting Pinochet: Undoing the Culture of Fear in Chile." *Modern Language Quarterly* 57.2 (1996): 151–63.
Richard, Nelly. *Residuos y metáforas (Ensayos de crítica cultural sobre el Chile de la Transición).* Santiago: Cuarto Propio, 1998.
———. "Tres funciones de escritura: desconstrucción, simulación, hibridación." *Lértora Poética.* 37–51.
———. *Margins and Institutions: Art in Chile Since 1973.* Bilingual edition. Trans. Juan Davila and Paul Foss. Melbourne: Art & Text, 1986.
Sotomayor, Aurea María. "Tres caricias: una lectura de Luce Irigaray en la narrativa de Diamela Eltit." *Modern Language Notes* 115 (2000): 299–322.
Tompkins, Cynthia. "La somatización del neoliberalismo en Mano de obra de Diamela Eltit." *Hispamérica: Revista de Literatura* 33.98 (Aug 2004): 115–23.
Uribe, Olga. "Breves anotaciones sobre las estrategias narrativas en *Lumpérica, Por la patria,* y *El cuarto mundo* de Diamela Eltit." *Hispanic Journal* 16.1 (Spring 1995): 21–37.
Wright, Thomas C., and Rody Oñate. *Flight from Chile: Voices of Exile.* Albuquerque: University of New Mexico Press, 1998.

◆ 3

The Riders Get off the Horse: David Viñas and the Demise of the Authoritarian Argentine Military

Hans-Otto Dill

(Translated by Sara Laschanzky)

With the dictatorship of Rosas in the first half of the nineteenth century and the military *junta* from 1976 to 1982, Argentina experienced the worst two totalitarian military regimes of America. At the same time, and for the same reason, Argentine literature has controversially dedicated itself more and more to the topic of authoritarianism, from Echeverría (*Slaughterhouse*), Mármol (*Amalia*) and Sarmiento (*Facundo*) in the nineteenth century, to Rodolfo Walsh (*Operation Massacre*) and David Viñas (*The Landowners, The Experts, Pack of Hounds* and *Direct Fight*) in the twentieth century. But Viñas's works differ greatly from the anti-authoritarian narrative of both centuries, both the "dictator's novel" as much as a large part of Argentine literature about the 1976–1982 dictatorship: their singularity stems from his focus, which is not on the dictatorship, but rather on the military.

In the military, the generals give the orders. Viñas writes, instead of the "dictator's novel," the "general's novel," as I like to call it. This novelty of focusing on the military has only been seen by Borello and Gutiérrez Haces. Another subtle and brutal narration about the military, comparable to that of Viñas, is José Pablo Feinmann's *El ejército de ceniza* (The Army of Ashes), which reconstructs the civil wars at the end of the 1820s exclusively with soldier protagonists from the regular military, and showing the frequent killings, tortures and slaughtering of the military, with images of the piles of bodies that the author takes from *The landowners* by Viñas.

However, I have doubts concerning Spiller's affirmation that the aforementioned texts about the dictatorship of 1976–1982 are "close to the literary sphere of David Viñas." The victim-victimizer relationship is distinct. The dictatorship narrative is characterized as follows. Themes, mimesis and *écriture* reflect the effects of authoritarianism: violence, torture, death, condemnation, resistance, amnesia, exile, broken identities, uprooting, and despondency (Spiller 7–8). But *death, exile, broken identities,* and *uprooting* are "effects" on the victims—the word "suffering" in the title of Claudia Gilman's work (1991) about *The Paths* (1980) by Jorgelina Loubet seems very well chosen—while Viñas dedicates himself to the *victimizers*, the soldiers of the military with their *arrogance, elitism, brutality, insensitivity, sadism,* and *machismo*. Viñas dramatizes the *military* in its daily functions, in war as in peace, in peace above all; and not during the dictatorship—above all as his incubator and instrument. If Cortázar and Borges show us, according to Borello (55), only the effects of something that is not described, Viñas describes, in my opinion, the causes (the spirit and ideology of the military) of effects (coups and dictatorships) that he does not describe. Also, his journalism and theater are an exhaustive military phenomenology. As an historiographer, in *The Tragic Week* (1966), *Argentine Military and Oligarchy* (1967) and *Indians, Militaries and Borders* (1983), he presents Argentine history as "the victims' drama" (Croce 42), a history more military than civil of the wars of independence, passing from the civil wars and The Conquest of the Desert of the nineteenth century to those of the twentieth century against the village itself.

From birth, Viñas had an intimate knowledge of the military, having been from the ages of twelve to seventeen (from 1941 to 1946) a student of the military school, an institution for the formation of the elite army ("I Know the Monster Inside"), which he had to leave due to both ideological and disciplinary problems. Future dictators Videla and Viola were both his classmates, which explains the ease with which he describes the education in the school of future victimizers and his profound knowledge of the terminology, rituals, and jargon of the teachers and students. Similar experiences had already been thematized by Vargas Llosa, student of a similar establishment, in *The City and the Dogs* (1962). For this reason, Viñas dedicated *The Horseriders* to Vargas Llosa, his great model.

Valle-Inclán *(Banderas the Tyrant)*, Asturias *(Mr. President)*, García Márquez *(Autumn of the Patriarch)*, Carpentier *(The Means of the Method)* and Roa Bastos *(I, the Supreme)*, contemporaries of Viñas, wrote monopersonal biographical works about the misdeeds of heads-of-state who had risen to power by means of fighting. Viñas, however, did not do this. The dictator does not interest him, but instead only the soldier as a personification of the military. One would expect the Chilean narrative of Donoso, Edwards and Teitelboim that was dedicated less to the leadership and more to the military, whereas Viñas puts it into play in more constitutional circumstances. Viñas does not describe the military as a collective group, as a sociologist would, but instead he dramatizes it as a novelist through characters: soldiers, officials, and generals, dissolving the political-historical entity "military" into the personality of the soldier. By thematizing the military and not the dictator, Viñas is probably the only one to adequately resolve the civilization vs. barbarism problem planted by Sarmiento, who was, on one hand, an ardent defender of western democracy, the "civilization," and at the same time a sworn enemy of every type of barbaric dictators, against whom he wrote *Facundo*. On the other hand, he was a self-declared adversary of the Indians and "barbaric" gauchos (contrary to the civilization), and he proclaimed the war of extermination against them a truly barbaric war, entrusted to the Argentine military. Viñas quotes him:

> Puede ser muy injusto exterminar salvajes, sofocar civilizaciones nacientes, conquistar pueblos que están en posesión de terreno privilegiado. Pero gracias a esta injusticia, la América, en lugar de permanecer abandonada a los salvajes, incapaces de progreso, está ocupada hoy por la raza caucásica, la más perfecta, la más inteligente, la más bella, la más progresiva de las que pueblan la tierra. (41)

> (It may be very unfair to exterminate savages, to smother rising civilizations, to conquer towns that are in possession of privileged terrain. But thanks to this injustice, America, instead of remaining abandoned to the savages, incapable of progress, today it is occupied by the Caucasian race, the most perfect, most intelligent, the most beautiful, and the most progressive of the races which inhabit the Earth.)

For this dirty work, which included the overtaking of the indigenous lands, he needed the civilized democracy of a barbaric soldier, of the "Argentine soldier" of the regular military:

> De esta pasta están amasados los soldados argentinos; y es fácil imaginarse lo que hábitos de este género pueden dar en valor y sufrimiento para la guerra. Añádese que desde la infancia están habitados a matar las reses, y que esto los familiariza con el derramamiento de sangre y endurece su corazón contra los gemidos de las víctimas (Sarmiento 30)

(From this dough are kneaded the Argentine soldiers; and it is easy to imagine what inhabitants of this genre can give in value and suffering for the war. Add to that the fact that since infancy they are used to killing the animals, and that this familiarizes them with the bloodshed and hardens their heart against the groaning of the victims.)

Violence and the habit of killing were, by the way, always present in the Argentine armed forces, studied by Viñas as a historian, a virus that could always degenerate into a dictatorship. This barbarity of the military is hidden by the "dictator's novel," which, by focusing on the "barbaric" dictatorial leader, never would have been capable of dramatizing the daily barbarity of the military in a democratic state: Sarmiento's *Facundo* expresses only the opposition civilization and barbarity, hiding his identity. Echeverría, as well as Mármol, in their respective works, characterize not the regular military, but rather the *mazorca*, the secret henchmen of Rosas, as brutal and uncivilized barbarians.

A very subtle, and at the same time brutal narration about the Argentine military, comparable to that of Viñas, has been embarked upon by Feinmann in *The army of ashes* (1986). Feinmann shows the barbarization of the nineteenth-century military, which supposedly defends the "civilization" against the "barbaric" Indians, gauchos and peasants. In an excellent study, Walter Bruno Berg analyzes the almost-identification of the extremes of the Sarmientine binary of civilization and barbarity and its deconstruction by Feinmann. However, upon examination of the *Facundo* pretext and its model civilization-barbarity dichotomy, Berg does not pay any attention to the significant fact that Sarmiento, by describing only the evil of the federalist dictator Rosas and provincial leaders of the "Facundo" type, he omits the evil of the civilized Unitarians. He describes the opposition (formal) and not the identity (dialectic) of both constituents of the binomial.

The fiction works of Viñas never thematize the coups, alluding only to the anti-Yrigoyenista coup of Uriburu in 1930, to the establishment of the Perón regime in 1946, to the anti-Peronist *putsch* of the military in 1955, and to the military dictatorship from 1976 to 1982. He focuses on the role and the phenomenon of the military during democratic periods between dictatorships. Viñas underlines as a particularity of the Argentine military its national role and its subsequent nationalist-military mythology:

"The Military is the previous and the permanent: it precedes the Nation and is the substance of the Nation" (*The Horseriders*, 70). Instead of the history of the Argentine military as a result of the political history of the country written by Viñas the historian, Viñas the novelist writes the political Argentine history as a result of the military history.

The differences between *The Landowners* (1959) and *Direct Fight* (1979) are not due to the historical eras that are described in them, and even less to the changes in focus of the author, but instead are of an artistic-literary and aesthetic nature. They reveal the development of the narrative and linguistic structures in concordance with the great contemporary Latin American literature. There is a world of difference between *The Landowners*—with its lineal and coherent narrative structure, its well-defined characters, its omniscient and unequivocal narrator, its scarce metaphors and the customary language of critical-social realism—and *Direct Fight*—with its cinematographic montage of narrative sequences, its diverse temporary shots, its enormous number of characters, its syntactic and half-oral, half-allusive structures, as well as allusions to its rich cultural background—as if they were two works from two very different authors.

Viñas, considered by the official critics, with reason, as a realist and compromised author, is an author more and more preoccupied with the formal side of his work. Perhaps because of his obsolete political compromise, critics such as Gutiérrez Haces, Croces or Borello erroneously describe him using the names didactic and polemic, which only describe him in his work as a historian and literary critic (Cruz), but not in his works of fiction. Leopoldo Marechal writes about *The Horseriders* (on the book jacket): "The work of Viñas, upon denouncing the fact (of militarism), does not have one bit of demagogy and very little political discussion; it's just that its author, as a craftsman, has proposed to write a novel, or rather a work of art." Spiller places Viñas's works among testimonial literature: "the non-fiction aspect in the tradition of Rodolfo Walsh and David Viñas unites the testimonial with assumptions of the compromised writing of the 1960s and with the realist programmatic" (11).

But while Walsh *is* a non-fictional, testimonial writer, Viñas is a fictional, non-testimonial narrator. Bocchino (163) opposes the fiction of Viñas's *Direct Fight* against the documental texts of Walsh. Spiller is right when he writes about Viñas's realistic strategy. But Viñas does not write the "compromised writing of the 1960s," as the German critic claims, but instead the "American behaviorist realism" from Steinbeck and Hemingway to Capote and Mailer (Borello 55) with structural and linguistic features of avant-gardism (not of neo-avant-gardism) in his mature works. The most significant feature is the subjectivization of the viewpoint, which, instead of the omniscient narrator, is composed of multiple perspectives of characters, therefore achieving a multi-faceted internalization. The homodiegetic narrator unveils to the maximum his own interior life as much as the motivations of the Argentine soldier, its psychology and its personality, still non-existent in his first novel, which focused solely on the political role of the military.

The Landowners (1958): Landlords and the Military

The title of the novel indicates as a protagonist not the military caste, but instead the landowner class. The narrator speaks only briefly of the struggles between them and the sheepshearers and both their social and salary demands—which would have constituted the principal theme of social realism. He does not mention nor denounce the injustices, but rather remains equidistant from both parts, adopting the neutral perspective of the protagonist, Vera, a diplomat and a lawyer. His neutrality emerges from his role as an emissary of Yrigoyen, in charge of obtaining objective information about the conflict and finding an adjustment. He knows little of the political-social situation in this territory and he carries out his investigations without prejudice. The reader almost has to share his homodiegetic point of view. Vera finds a solution, and the landowners and the working class sign an agreement. He leaves for vacation in Chile with his lover, an immigrant teacher from Eastern Europe, who would later become his (pregnant) wife. Upon his return, he is informed of new hostilities between the working class and the wealthy landowners, and the intervention of the military, which brutally pursues the strikers accused of acts of violence without investigating the concrete circumstances or asking for reasons, convinced before hand of the workers' guilt. Their bloody massacres are reminiscent of the misdeeds of the German Nazis in the concentration camps and the killings of the Sarmientine army fifty years earlier between the indigenous groups. The commissary is convinced that the wealthy landowners are the guilty ones for having broken the agreement to fire the farm workers after the annual harvest. He returns to the capital disappointed, without attaining a positive arrangement.

Viñas describes the interdependence between the military and the landowners. Both classes seem to be two faces of the same coin. However, the latter are the ones who rule over the obedient soldiers, carrying out the strongest role, even though in the Patagonia, a region conquered only fifty years earlier, the traditional creole oligarchy which supplies the generals does not even exist. Already the name of its spokesman, Brun-Braun, indicates his Jewish-German origin, from immigrants.

Another connection exists between the military and the liberal-radical government of Yrigoyen, which carries out a politics supported by the working and middle classes, but also maintains an ambiguous position in the conflict. The military—which overthrew Yrigoyen in 1930—never would have carried out its campaign in Patagonia without its consent, or practically his request. Besides, Yrigoyen, through the military, covered many working-class demonstrations in blood in Buenos Aires.

In this first novel, there is little individualization of the farm workers and the soldiers. Among the leaders of the strike, a few individual characters appear, but they are not individualized. One knows nothing of their ancestors, their families, or even their ethnic and racial origins. Besides that, Viñas does not idealize, as the proletarian novel does, the farm workers: he sees them as brutal as the violent soldiers. The social motivation of the conflict does not interest Viñas the novelist, but rather the role of the military in the bloody smothering of the farm workers' strike. There is a noticeable change from *The Landowners*, with a military dependent upon the landowners, to *The Horseriders*, where it becomes so independent that the roles are almost reversed.

The military and the landowners are described from afar, by a narrator close to the protagonist, a character that does not belong to the landowners or the soldiers and beyond that is not even from the region, with his sober and distant, even foreign, look.

The title expresses the anti-romantic sobriety of the political economy: not socio-historical terms (*masters*), nor archaic-poetic (*lords*), but rather *owners*, relating them with property, typical of the materialistic perspective of the author. This is Viñas' most documental novel. He found the historical events in the book by Osvaldo Bayer, *The Avengers of Tragic Patagonia*, illustrated with photographs that could well be the originals of the scenes that are visually evoked by the author. In this book, Braun the landowner also appears, the Brun of the novel. Another documental feature: Viñas' father was, as a judge, a witness in Patagonia of these events. The teacher is the poetization of Viñas's mother,

> una rusa judía y anarquista, que en 1899 llegó como inmigrante desde los pogromos de Odessa ... una heterodoxa en esa especie de Far-south argentino de 1920 ... Osvaldo Bayer habla detalladamente de mi madre en su libro Los vengadores de la Patagonia trágica. La idealiza ... aunque ella no sólo influyó para que mi padre pusiera en libertad a los obreros presos ... sino que lo ayudó a redactar un—insólito en esos años y viniendo de un juez—elogio del anarquismo ... Incluso, los obreros de la FOBA cuando mi madre murió, pusieron una placa en su tumba. ("Ellos allá" 1)

(a Jewish and Anarchist Russian, who in 1899 arrived as an immigrant from the pogroms of Odessa . . . a heterodox in that kind of Far-south of Argentina of 1920 . . . Osvaldo Bayer speaks with detail of my mother in his book *The Avengers of Tragic Patagonia.* He idealizes her . . . even though she not only influenced my father to give freedom to the imprisoned workers . . . but rather that she helped him to draw up—unusual in those years and especially coming from a judge—a praise of Anarchism . . . The workers of the FOBA even put a plaque on her tomb when she died.)

As the new historical novel, Viñas wanted to fill in the gaps of the official history and call attention to the dirty details of an event silenced by the recorded historiography. It evokes, with great sensual and visual force, the tortures and massacres of the captives, the piling up of bodies like mattresses in a furniture store or trash in a dumpster. The officials as well as the common soldiers are of a bestiality that we find only in the dictator Rosas' *mazorca,* described by Echeverría and in the gauchos painted by Sarmiento. Viñas makes the jump from the proletarian novel and the narrative report of the Mansilla type and its sequel (*The Passion of the Nomads,* by María Rosa Lojo) to the novel *about the military,* which differs from the descriptions of the massacres in the social, proletarian and indigenista novel of Alegría (*The World is Wide and Foreign*), Vallejo (*Tungsten*) and Teitelboim (*Son of the Saltpeter*) which, with only the exception of Vargas Llosa (*The War of the End of the World*) do not focus on the military.

The military is not described as an institution with its rituals of a *sui generis* social body, but rather through its instrumental, political role as a weapon of the landowners, who take on the function of the ancient creole aristocracy in Patagonia. This novel, in the realist-naturalist style, is consumed by a homodiegetic focus of the central character. His opinions externalize themselves either in the comments of the extradiegetic narrator or in the dialogues between him and the sheepshearers, the estate owners, the soldiers and the teacher, unveiling their respective mentalities. There are few metaphors, and a lineal structure, as linear as the profile of the people in this book.

The Horseriders (1967): A Military-Family Saga

The most differentiated description, of the military in Latin American literature is found in Viñas's *The Horseriders,* which was awarded a House of Americas award by a jury composed of Julio Cortázar, José Lezama Lima, Leopoldo

Marechal, Mario Monteforte Toledo and Juan Marsé. Viñas wrote this novel in the year of the so-called "Argentine revolution" of 1966, which established a militarized state, both autocratic and bureaucratic, dismantling the unions and the political parties, causing an incurable economic crisis, the contra-terrorism of the urban guerilla and also neoperonism. The same armed forces that had overthrown Perón in 1955 intervened in 1966 to stop the elected Peronist governments, not with the goal, as in 1962, of handing the power to a non-Peronist civilian, "but rather to maintain the soldiers in power in order to activate a different political project, authoritarianism" (Lucena Salmoral 685). This semi-dictatorship ended in 1973 with the re-election of Perón. Given that the motivations and causes of the dictatorships are what interest Viñas most, he does not thematize this, but rather deals with the daily military life under the disguised dictatorship.

With great analytical force, Viñas examines the military as a sociological, political, psychological and mental phenomenon, but always through a literary lens, converting it into a textual fiction, and distancing himself of traditional realism through his complex narrative structure, just as García Márquez did in *One Hundred Years of Solitude*, which also appeared in 1967. The first part of the book deals with the private life of the Godoys, as well as the activities and the way of life of the Argentine soldiers who were linked to this family. The second part deals with *The Ayacucho Operative*, conjoined maneuvers in Peru by the armed forces of some Latin American countries. Three important elements characterize this novel: the saga of the Godoy family, the national myth of the Argentine military and the role of the Military School.

It is a modern saga of the Godoy clan through nearly two centuries of generations; parents, relatives, wives, lovers, brothers and sons, following the examples of *Die Buddenbrooks* by Thomas Mann, *Les Thibaud* by Roger Martin du Gard, or *The Forsyte Saga* by John Galsworthy. Fleeting reminiscences of the nineteenth-century appear about the birth of the Godoy clan, the civil wars and the War of the Triple Alliance against Paraguay, where the mortal action of the aggressive militaries along with the active participation of a Godoy cost this last country more than half of its population. The Godoys subsequently support all of the military coups against democratic regimes, as shown by the memories of old family friends. They are bossy in the troops as well as in the family, where they practice a machista government with their wives, daughters and other female loved ones, who are seen as inferior and subordinate beings, although in a more civilized and less violent manner than that which was practiced by their nineteenth-century ancestors, described in *The Pack of Hounds*. While the sons practice fencing, the women dedicate themselves to poetry and chats with the Bishop. The family follows the lifestyle of the great and rich bureaucracy, with large estates, country homes, trips, calashes, parties, servants and riding areas for their horses.

General Leandro Godoy was a traditional creole soldier, Prussian-like, messianic nationalist, enemy of psychoanalysis, homosexuals, foreigners and immigrants, land owner with many horses, and friend of general Uriburu. He was called by Yrigoyen to suppress the strikers during the "Tragic Week" of 1919, which did not prevent him from happily participating, in 1930, in the *putsch* of Uriburu against Yrigoyen and the subsequent massacres. Godoy and Uriburu objected *manu militari* to elections, democracy and the Peronist populism.

His son Marcelo is the traditional official, ex-exemplary student of the Military School like his father and his brother, self-declared "golpista," guerrilla and active participant in the failed anti-Peronist revolt of 1951 and in the shootings of Peronists after the military coup of 1955 against Perón, rejected by them not on account of his authoritarianism and his demagogy, but for his plebeian, non-oligarchic descendents, and his populist politics. Marcelo is "castrated," or rather not promoted, for having been a "colorado" or an extremist in a failed revolt, and also for having offended general Valeiras by his mother's rejection of Valeiras' daughter as a wife for Marcelo. Having made himself a soldier and nothing more, upon finding no satisfaction in life without a uniform, he commits suicide.

His younger brother Emilio, protagonist of the novel, is an official critic, who, without being very excited about or capable of the military career, successfully assumes it and becomes a colonel. The black sheep of the family is *El Chango*, Leandro's brother, who is a Yrigoyenist, a Peronist and an anti-militarist, for which reason he abandons the military. Leandro and *el Chango* are two very dissimilar brothers, just as Marcelo and Emilio were—one of the many formal parallelisms that the author enjoys. Except for *el Chango* and Emilio, the Godoys exhibit their elitism and the arrogance of the oligarchy, including the mother, who prohibits because of class pride the marriage between Marcelo and the daughter of general Valeiras, so that her grandson would be a descendent of a caretaker of the old, elite landowners.

As a central event, Viñas puts into play *The Ayacucho Operative* in Perú, the ploys of many Latin-American countries to participate in the anti-guerilla fight. The leader of the Argentine detachment, including Emilio Godoy, is general Valeiras, called The Old Man. Valeiras is a traditional soldier like Leandro Godoy. He expresses the spirit of the Argentine army, whose history, since the independence, is alluded to in the novel through the memories of elderly men.

The Old Man expresses the myth of the military in his speech to the soldiers, in conversations with Emilio and in the soliloquies that he trusts to his tape recorder. According to him, the military is the vertebral column of the nation, a guarantee of its independence and its identity. In accordance with that, in all of Viñas's books, and in Argentina more than in other countries, the soldiers consider the military to be a founding element of citizenship.

The second most significant feature of the Argentine military is its elitism, which adds to the classist elitism of the landowner's oligarchy, but is also a completely different thing, not referring to other socially inferior classes, but rather expressing the feeling of superiority of the soldier compared to the civilian. The disdain for the civilians includes the politicians and engenders the fact that they are convinced that the soldiers could substitute them in the government. The third characteristic, as it comes out of the mouth of the general (according to the novelesque construction of the author) is his authoritarian, anti-democratic and anti-liberal attitude:

> Hasta ahora siempre he estado dispuesto a supeditar mi acción profesional a la politica. Con mayor precisión: la actividad castrense a la civil. (pero) el liberalismo . . . debe conceder el voto universal. . . . la subordinación de los militares a la política civil fue siempre nefasta. (282–3)

> (Until now I have always been willing to put my professional action before politics. With greater precision: the military activity before the civil one. (But) liberalism . . . should concede the universal vote . . . the subordination of the soldiers to the civil politics was always disastrous.)

General Uriburu referred, in 1930, to such topics from San Martín with his respect for the liberals of Buenos Aires to "the concessions that had to be done to the politicians." The Old Man reveals himself as an inspired member of the military government of Videla-Galtieri, established six years later, enunciating the ideology that guided the golpistas. He defends the eventual replacement of the civil government by a military one. After having lost the inherited dependency of the creole landowner's oligarchy (the Italian and German last names of the officials signal their immigrant backgrounds), the army could substitute the antique oligarchy and become the ruling and governing force of the country. For this reason, The Old Man complains that the *Operative* had been decided by the politicians and not by the soldiers.

Viñas also awards The Old Man with the function of the director of the Military College, the center of the formation of the Argentine military elite founded by Sarmiento. Leandro, his brother, his sons Marcelo and Emilio, and also The Old Man are (just as Viñas himself) ex-alums of the Military College, having internalized their militarist, anti-democratic, elitist and nationalist principals. The teachers, at the beginning mainly German disciples of Clausewitz—German was the second language of instruction—taught their students the Prussian style of war, instilling in the cadets a spirit of fierce discipline and absolute obedience, the conviction of the superiority of the military, and their full identification with the armed forces.

As we saw, Viñas, instead of great narrations of individual and collective actions—in his texts very few things happen—he focuses on the ideology, the conscience, the psychology and the mentality, the personality, the interior life of the Argentine soldier in his formation and in his active power. In order to impede a trivial reading focused on the actions and acts, he destroys the spatial and temporal "realista" continuum—the Bakhtin chronotype—of the national history and the stories of the characters, upon presenting a montage of texts, speeches and dialogues. For this purpose, he constructs various temporal planes, that of a strict present time contrasted with retrospectives of various eras and many characters, unlike the linearity of his first novel.

In order to present the interior life and ideology of his soldiers, he turns to a narration without an omniscient and homodiegetic narrator, fabricating a text with many speaking subjects with their own diverse, subjective perspectives, a text of the nineteenth-century memories of the grandmother and the many discussions between The Old Man and Emilio and the soliloquy of The Old Man with his tape recorder. The vast cast of characters permits the author to introduce the soldiers of all levels in their mentality through dialogues or interior monologues in the oral Argentine, Buenos Aires and military language that most expresses his manner of thinking and feeling.

Among the many formal resources Viñas uses, he emphasizes the metonym "horse," which already appears in the title. "Horse" is a metonym of the agriculture of the oligarchic landowners and of the traditional means of transportation, preferred as an aristocratic animal by the landowning oligarchy. But, it is also a metonym of the military and of its officials, outside of the rural oligarchy, who always went on horseback. Thus, the strong symbolism of the cavalcades, sometimes signifying the union between the estate-owners and the military. As an aristocratic animal, the horse has, as its counterpart, the mule, metonym of the rural people of the plains. The Godoys, excellent horsemen, always seem to look at the rest of the civilian people from the stamp of the horse, from above, indicating their arrogance against the common people.

Viñas has borrowed the gallant tropology from Carpentier, who had already developed it in *The Lost Steps* (1953) and *The Means of the Method*

(1974) (Dill). "Horse" is a metonym of the traditional military, since the leaders of the wars of independence and the nineteenth-century civil wars. For these landowners and generals, the horse played a prime role, for which they are metonymically named "The Horseriders."

But the horse-riding soldiers do not go on horseback to Peru, but rather are transported with their trucks in planes. Emilio has difficulties in driving a truck with his boss: "I am not sure I am a first-rate driver" (182), to which the general answers: "Realmente usted necesita caballos... Los caballos se han muerto, Godoy, no sueñe. De-fi-ni-tiva-mente liquidados. Nada más que para los desfiles sirven. O para que algunos de ustedes se luzcan en el Hípico" (183) (Honestly you need horses... The horses have died, Godoy, don't dream. Com-plete-ly gone. They aren't good for anything more than parades. Or for some of you who flaunt in the equestrian).

There was "an enormous troop of sorrels that advanced lethargically through a sandy area with fallen necks and very long, limp manes... One hundred, two hundred discolored horses knocked down on the beach." I will discuss this symbolism at the end of my essay.

The Pack of Hounds (1974)

This narration, published two years before the coup against president Isabel Perón and the subsequent military dictatorship from 1976 to 1982, is an historical novel about the war after the dictatorship of Rosas, between Buenos Aires, the port city monopolized by the exterior commerce, guided by Mitre, and the Confederation of the Provinces led by Urquiza, with allusions to the war of the Triple Alliance against Paraguay.

Viñas dramatizes the relationship between a provincial commander and his officials and collaborators, employing the "general" military grade, not permitting, even metaphorically, terms like *dictadorzuelo*, chief, and only a few times "leader." He is not a political ringleader, but rather a general from the line of the military. The novel describes the fight between various militaries of the Argentine provinces among themselves and the successive formation of a united Argentine army, "the great army," if it's at all possible that the country itself unites as well, signaling the predominant role of the military in the unification of the nation. But the term "nation" does not appear, and the words "Argentine" and "Argentina" only a few times. The military reconstructs—*a posteriori* the myth of its national role.

The history almost exclusively between soldiers begins with the end of the "histoire," inverting the chronological succession of the intended real events, with the assassination of the General also named The Old Man, by Colonel Simón "for treason." After, he puts into play, in a retrospective divided into many fragments, the escape of the Colonel persecuted by the henchmen of the troops (the historical model is the fleeing of the assassin of Urquia), which ends in a circus where Simón shows a type of western show, exhibiting his abilities as a horseman, a swordsman and a marksman: after the tragedy, a (folkloric) comedy.

These fragments (*The Pack of Hounds*) alternate with retrospective episodes (*Hypotenuses*) of the military life of Simón and his encounters with "my general," describing the development of his personality and motivating his decision to assassinate the general. The prolypsis direct the attention of the reader who knows the final ending, toward those mental processes that culminate in homicide. Other episodes under the ironic title *Gatherings* are dedicated to the military machismo, describing the regular visits of Colonel Simón to the whorehouse of Miss Encidia, in which he shares with the General the beautiful and expert prostitute Arminia, while the *Castlings* deal with the relationship between Buenos Aires and the general, who does not want to fight anymore, and who retires despite the possibility of a definitive triumph (like Urquiza did after having won a battle against the Buenos Aires military of Mitre). This same general that renounces the war, had earlier cruelly punished the soldiers who refused to fight without being paid. But in his way of thinking, this contradiction does not exist: the soldiers made themselves insubordinate, they did not obey in the manner that they should, and considering blind obedience is the number one rule in all of the militaries of the world, it was essential for their discipline. The episodes entitled *Castlings* show that he did not want to fight anymore either, negotiating instead with Buenos Aires. He has gotten rich enough to make peace. He is assassinated by Simón because he, as many officials of his kind of pre-modern mentality, feels tricked, or rather betrayed by The Old Man, for whom they settle the debts in the customary folkloric manner, by sword fighting.

The description of the violent Buenos Aires soldiers by Simón is true for all of the armed Argentine people of all times: "They slit throats without disgust, even of those who have surrendered. They slit their throats with jagged knives. It's true, yes. They like to do it, not with obligation and without disgust" (149–50). The assassination is described very sensually, almost physiologically, showing the enjoyment of the military in killing, still accustomed to the direct killings in *Direct Fight*, very different from the modern terrorist attacks by computer-guided self-bombs or by long-distance shots.

Motete registers the urbanization (the process of civilizing oneself) of the general, his conversion to a corrupt soldier and a civilized leader with a court imitating that of Napoleon III, which signifies a turn, a change in the evolution of the military as a political institution. The Old Man betrayed the ideals and the objectives of the provinces to maintain their conservatism based on the breeding and exportation of cattle and their independence from Buenos Aires, to conserve their autonomous moral, religious and cultural values, considered "barbaric" by the "civilized" city with its bourgeois progress, a binomial theorized by Mitre's successor, Sarmiento. Simón realizes the Old Man's treason, which was a bribe from the enemy, and the comfortable life that it brings, accumulating precious objects and antiques, which lend him a new reputation of a cultured and civilized person, increasing his riches through the transport and sale of cattle—one thousand pieces transported in rafts through the Paraná river—and more importantly putting electric fences around their new lands with help from a German surveyor, and constructing a small palace instead of the usual rustic estates, for which they retire from the military and the war, wanting to enjoy in peace their new status and "to make the most of . . . everything that was piling up (137) . . . the belly (of the general) is made of Buenos Aires money" (219). His two sons inherit a fortune in order to buy the entire province.

He modernizes the administration of his assets, puts to work a swarm of workers—bureaucrats and his former "non-uniformed escorts," a secretary with an office instead of the traditional foreman, substituted by his son-in-law, known as "the prince." The son-in-law always appears in blue coattails, reminiscent that Sarmiento considered the coattails with a top hat to be the outfit of the civilized bourgeois, instead of the gauchos' attire. The leader transforms himself into a member of the landowner's oligarchy, just as the royal lands come to be property of the national military heroes of the Independence as compensation for their sacrifices in the name of the nation, and not, as one could easily think, that the landowners created the military to defend their interests. In reality, even though he was called The Old Man, it was he who modernized himself, while his assassins defend the obsolete tradition, a society destined to disappear, that does not participate in the newly distributed riches. It is not a coincidence that Simón is a "colonel," one of García Márquez's many colonels who await their pensions as compensation for their merits in the wars.

His legitimate wife and his family still do not carry out the role of the military and landowner families as described in *The Horseriders*. Very important, on the other hand, is his old-leader machismo, which is expressed in a multitude of natural sons and daughters, as well as "godchildren" who belonged to the general's family, just like the many descendants of colonel Aureliano Buendía in *One Hundred Years of Solitude*. Also, through this biological fact, he is the "father" of the province.

This machismo also expresses itself in the general's frequent visits to the whorehouse, always a preferred place by soldiers who were far away from their families, or those who did not have any family. Arminia the prostitute evicts Simón because the general, upon modernizing his love, makes her his lover with her own house, servants, expensive clothes and all classes of luxury, for which the general also flaunts his condition of a member of the nineteenth-century oligarchy with the Parisian lifestyle of the era, and therefore his assassination by Simón has a hint of jealousy in it.

The neighborhood of brothels and barracks, of killing and loving, is underlined by the author through the voice of one of his characters, who even theorizes the identity of love and death, comparing the penetration of the saber in the enemy's body with the penetration of the penis in the woman's body: "To penetrate a woman is the same as to kill . . . To kill the general and to enter you, Rosa . . . Bliss and death is the same, my general!" (156–57). "Killing is like violating a woman" (167b).

Death is a means and an end to the war: "In war, people die and people kill," says the General. Thus in the whole novel there is a worship of weapons, first the knife, and later the rifle with its physical invocation—the weapon as part of the soldier's body—starts and ends the novel. Horse worship is also established, as alluded to in *The Horseriders*, and in fact the entire fleeing of the colonel is played out on a horse: "Yes, I am a horse" (33). The horse also has a sexual connotation. To sleep with Arminia the "mare" is "like mounting a horse." The general shows for the first time, historically, the mounting disdain for human life and the treacherous military punishments: upon ordering execution as a punishment for insubordination on the part of twelve rebel soldiers, he comments: "Soldiers. In our province, people obey." To motivate the execution, he orders the soldiers—who never had the possibility of choosing, but rather an obligation to obey—to choose which comrades are going to be executed—a procedure that was a rule in the Argentine army, to such a degree that the soldiers accept and execute the procedure without protest. In fact, even in *The Landowners* the commander of the army orders an execution of a ringleader of the strikers that they themselves must choose. All of this happens in real life, in both times of war and times of peace, under constitutional regimes, although largely overshot by the military government from 1976–1982 which, because of an attack in the La Plata police station that caused the death of a few police officers, ordered the execution of no less than 55 hostages in different places throughout Argentina.[1]

Direct Fight (1979)

The last novel of Viñas's novels on generals is "of enormous complexity; as complex as the actual Argentine history in recent years" (Gutiérrez Haces 13). It was written during the dictatorship of 1976–1982 in the Spanish exile. It deals with the spiritual germination of the dictatorship as an indirect response to it. The main character is once again in accordance with Viñas' personalistic concept, a *general*, the lieutenant general Mr. Alejandro Cé Clans Mendiburu (El Payo), "of national heroes' last name," a modern soldier, technocrat, and politician. His military plan: to rid, according to the doctrine of National Security, all of Latin America of adversaries, even if it be through dirty wars. His motto: "it doesn't occur to anyone to discuss a shot" (148).

The military has taken over his personality of father, husband, citizen, and landowner, as well as his spirit. In order to "militarize" his body, he exercises daily. He develops, unlike the pragmatic "training" of the *rangers*, a philosophy of the body of a soldier, with *geography, spelling, and theology*. Some of his mottos "ruthless of his own body": "I have a body that obeys me . . . one must give orders to his own body . . . so that one's whole body is converted into a type of regiment . . . To be the boss of my own body." The general participates personally in tortures and scenes similar to gladiator games, where two subordinates mutually mistreat each other in an organized sports duel. It is as if he wanted to complement the training of his body with intellectual and emotional gymnastics as well, upon getting used to the insensitivity in the face of alien suffering, the violence and the brutality of the torturer—who is not called a guerilla, but rather "mastiff" (197)—which explains the killing fury of the soldiers in power.

This barbarization complements the enormous culture of the intellectual in uniform. He reads Clausewitz, but also Marx's *Grundrisse*, Gramsci, and Marcuse, not to satisfy receptive philosophical necessities, but rather only to inform himself about the enemies of the system. The family relationships, which are very oligarchic, show very important changes as a result of the son's and daughter's confessions. The general is convinced of the cohesive role of the family in preserving the oligarchy. He brought up his son Marcelo, from a very young age, in the military and machista spirit. In the first, very drastic long scene he grabs the little boy's testicles on the occasion of his birthday in order to instill in him, as in a conspiring litany, a machista spirit. He sent him to the Military School, where he himself had been educated. He also educates his daughter Mariana in the same military spirit, calling her "little soldier."

Unlike other, earlier novels, his children are even more critical than Emilio or El Chango in the Godoy family toward their father and the military, adopting parricide attitudes and dreaming about killing him. It is remarkable that the son does not follow his father's military career, interrupting the chain that assures the existence of the military oligarchy. This fact signals the dissolution of the oligarchic creole elite (which united militarism, landownership, and machismo through the succession of father to son), and, despite the military dictatorship between 1976 and 1982, marks the end of authoritarianism.[2]

That this novel can be read as a socio-psychological X-ray of an Argentine society ready for the recent dictatorship, the hardest in the history, indicates the speech—the announcement by the mouth of general Manuel Saint-Jean in 1976 of the government military program:

Primero vamos a matar a todos los subversivos, después, a sus colaboradores, después, a los simpatizantes, después, a los indiferentes. Y, por último, a los tímidos. (367)

(First we are going to kill all of the subversives, and after that the collaborators, and then the sympathizers, and then the indifferent. And, finally, the timid.)

Direct Fight also signifies the civil war in the city, the fight of the people in the struggle for survival, between the military and the urban guerilla, creoles and immigrants, men and women. The general rarely appears personally, and, like Asturias's *Mr. President*, acts behind the narration most of the time, influencing the development of the personalities and biographies of the rest of the characters, the people of his *entourage*: his family and the military, both officials and subordinates. Their voices describe the image of the general as much as the mark he has left on them. Technically, Viñas achieves this by the fictional interviews that are done by editor Gregorio Yantorno, nicknamed Goyo, for a magazine that wants to publish them in parts. The novel ends with the closing of the newspaper, censorship, detention, persecution and "disappeared ones," of having to cover one's mouth with their hand (according to the title of the episodes about journalism) and to burn in auto-da-fé the material of the dangerous interviews, precisely because of their criticism of the soldiers. Here, Viñas summarizes his own experiences as a journalist, professionally presenting the game of questions and answers. These interviews also constitute a mixture of distinct individual languages, social and psychologically characteristic of the Buenos Aires citizens under the impact of an imminent military intervention in their lives (whose description was the work of writers like Rodolfo Walsh, Haraldo Conti and other disappeared ones, to whom this book is dedicated).

Thus the narration comes from the narrow sphere of the military theme, presenting Buenos Aires in narrative segments ("Babylon") as a city of immigrants, whose cosmopolitan presence contradicts the nationalist attitude of the soldiers. This Babylonian co-existence, not present in any other metropolis of the world, is also a "direct fight," whose homogenization has been one of the objectives (although not fulfilled) of the "patriotic" soldiers. It is a fiction that reflects the extra-literary reality in the materiality of the language. More than a physical or mental confrontation, it is a linguistic, verbal one, of words that do not have anything to do with one another, of publicity slogans, titles of editorials, commonplaces of the television and the yellow press, of the political indulgence, of the literature, of soldiers and of the communiqués. It is detritus, a waste, and social discourse garbage (Bocchino 164) under the military impact; in my opinion, a montage of fragments, as modern or perhaps more modern than the linguistic fragmentation of his contemporary Piglia. Piglia composed *Artificial Respiration* in 1980, in the middle of the dictatorship. His novel is a mosaic of clandestine, subversive, anti-government and figurative texts by writers who equally wrote in conditions of censorship. Piglia, then, deals allegorically or metaphorically with the situation of the Argentine writer under the censorship of the dictatorship, showing how to write novels in these conditions. A novel not about the military, but about literature; about the author, not the soldier; the victim, not the victimizer; dictatorship, and not democracy. Viñas also addresses unknown texts, but very traditionally, as paratexts (epigraphs), direct quotes, or allusions. Both writers share the feature of prompting through the blanks the cooperation of the reader to fill them according to the recipes of the aesthetics of reception of the Konstanz School and the examples of Borges and Cortázar.

It is a *stream of consciousness* in the style of Joyce's *Ulysses* and Broch's *The Death of Virgil*, and at the same time a syntactic and structurally baroque novel, comparable to Lezama Lima's *Paradise*. It consists almost exclusively—as it deals with personal confessions—of interviews, statements, epigraphs, monologues and dialogues that reveal the attitudes of the Argentine soldier.

The Future of the Argentine Army and of the Military Theme

In later publications, Viñas practically abandons the Argentine army, a central theme of his life: In *Claudia the Convert*, the story of a student of the disappointed province of Buenos Aires, he alludes only vaguely to the military coup. He does not confirm the prediction of María Teresa Gutiérrez Haces, who writes in his book about Viñas that the soldiers are not happy to be merely second-raters of politics, and aspire to regain "the control of a great part of the Latin American political direction." I believe, however, that after the fall of the military regimes of the Southern Cone, Viñas felt that this is no longer an autonomous political and social class.

In the *Ayacucho Operative*, he narrates the incipient military integration of Latin America through the Western European example, where the national armies reduce their importance as a result of the policies of the European Union. With the integration, the symbolism and national mythology of the soldier disappear, and with that the virulence of the myth that the Argentine army is a guarantee of the nation. The *Operative* also gives motive to discussions about the international military situation, the cold war between the USSR and the United States, the wars in Asia and the Near East, abandoning the narrow national frame.

The military that preserves a tradition of authoritarianism through its caste or class existence reproducing itself throughout the generations in clans and families like the Godoys, disappears with the modern civil government. This framework requires soldiers specialized in their profession, who know how to handle weapons and computerized equipment, who have to study engineering and public relations, and who have to appropriate the military and general psychology, no more than strategic and tactic, to order and to obey. Their specialization does not include the political art of governing, which is also a highly specialized activity trusted only to professionals. Only in under-developed societies men like Miranda, Bolivar, Sarmiento or Mitre could be good soldiers and capacitated leaders at the same time. For this reason, the modern-age soldiers failed as leaders, and also the *juntas* in Chile, Argentina and Uruguay, and Banzer in Bolivia. In this sense, Viñas constructs a discussion during the Ayacucho Operative between Emilio, the critical soldier, and general Valeiras about a military government. Emilio says to The Old Man:

> Si todo se viene abajo, lo único que se rescata somos nosotros. Por eso tenemos la obligación de estar preparados para hacernos cargo de todo triunfo. Los elementos transitorios fracasan... de 1930 hasta aquí nos hemos hecho cargo de todo en

varias oportunidades ... en 1930 mi padre y sus amigos creían que eso era fácil y hoy nosotros sabemos que no es así. Y cada vez menos.
-¿Eso? –se frunció el Viejo-. ¿Qué es eso?
-Gobernar, mi general.
-No está demostrado que no sea posible, siempre que haya hombres ...
-Usted dice "posible" y yo digo "fácil", mi general. (73)

(If everything came down, the only thing that would save itself is us. That's why we have the obligation to be prepared to take charge of the entire triumph. The transitory elements fail ... from 1930 until now we have taken charge of everything in various opportunities ... in 1930 my father and his friends believed that that was easy and today we know that it is not. And every time it is harder.
"That?" frowned The Old Man. "What is that?"
"To rule, my general."
"It has not shown to be impossible, as long as there are men ..."
"You say 'possible' and I say 'easy,' my general.)

He almost senses the possible final failure of the military regime in 1982. The future governments no longer depend on the military, but rather on the economy. The Argentine *junta* not only failed as a result of the Falklands/Malvinas war, but also because of its misguided economic politicies of de-industrialization, only in the interest of the oligarchic landowners of the coast, attracting itself for that, and less for the general repudiation of its terrorist regime, the opposition of the business community.

Viñas also registers the change of military paradigm from the obsolete Prussian-German to the modern North-American. So it is said of the North American technician in the *Ayacucho Operative*: "The new trend is already the blonde Harry," and the German-Argentine soldier Schindler says: "... da gusto trabajar con un tipo como este ... porque es como yo, ingeniero" (197) (... it is a pleasure to work with someone like this ... because he is like me, an engineer). Viñas does not allude to the military dependence of the United States, a traditional theme of the left, but rather to the technical aspect of this cooperation.

Instead of the horse, the computer appears. When a technician spoke in *Direct Fight*,

el General lo escuchaba atentamente ... Incluso, se incomodaba cuando alguno de nosotros lo interrumpía a ese hombre:

"Computadora y no un disco rayado de Caruso... hay que oírlo aunque rechine... A un ténico no se lo interrumpe... Cortarle su explicación es tan imbécil como apagar una computadora que nos informa de cifras en contra." (296)

(the general listened attentively to him... He even got uncomfortable when one of us interrupted that man:

"Computer and not a gramophone record of Caruso... one has to hear it even though it squeaks... one doesn't interrupt a technician... To interrupt his explanation is as stupid as turning off a computer that informs us of enemy codes.")

He wants objective information, not ideological, confirming Viñas's assertion: "Hoy, en 1980, son los militares quienes funcionan como sus propios 'intelectuales organicos' en el sistema... la imagen tan fácil (y estereotipada) del 'militar' bruto o 'cabeza de bota' es algo tan periclitado como los bragueros" ("Ellos allá" 15) (Today, in 1980, it is the soldiers who work as their own 'organic intellectuals' in the system... the easy (and stereotyped) image of the brutal 'soldier' or 'airhead' is something as old-fashioned as trusses).

In this context, I interpret the final goodbye to the "horse" metonym in *The Horseriders* as a farewell to the traditional military oligarchy. With the irreversible establishment of a civil society, with democratically-elected leaders, with parliaments, with the horizontal structuring of society in functional groups, among them the military, the army loses its extraordinary statue and its terrible secular influence over the government, the state and the nation. Viñas's work admits, at least, this vision. Faced with the handcrafted literary production of many contemporary writers about the dictatorship, Viñas offers the refreshing reading of an authentic narrator.

Notes

1. They were executed the 10th of November: 8 in La Plata and 8 in Tolosa and City Bell; the 11th: 7 in La Plata: the 12th: 4 in La Plata and 4 in Tolosa: the 13th: 6 in the Las Quintas neighborhood; the 14th: 3 in Punta Lara; the 15th: 5 in Los Hornos; and the 16th: 10 in Arana.
2. Viñas insists on the terrible role of the soldier, without signaling, contrary to his position as a critic and literary historian, the political-economic reasons as fundamental motivations. Moreover, he does not touch on the attitude of the United States on the matter—not yet knowing that, according to the archives, the soldiers followed through

with the coup of 1976 only after Henry Kissinger's expressed consent. Viñas treats it as an internal, technical and professional problem.

Works Cited

Balderston, Daniel (ed.). *Ficción y política. La narrativa argentina durante el proceso militar*. Buenos Aires: Alianza, 1987.
Bamberg, María. *Ella und der Gringo mit den großen Füßen*. Reinbeck bei Hamburg: Rowohlt, 2000.
Barra, María Josefa. "Respiración artificial: retórica y praxis." *La novela argentina de los años 80*. Ed. Roland Spiller. Frankfurt: Vervuert, 1991.
Berg, Walter Bruno. "Civilización hecha cenizas: la presencia de Sarmiento en la novela histórica contemporánea." *La novela argentina de los años 80*. Ed. Roland Spiller. Frankfurt: Vervuert, 1991.
Bocchino, Adriana A. "Textos de cultura/textos de barbarie: *Prensa clandestino* de Rodolfo Walsh. *Cuerpo a cuerpo* de David Viñas." *Iberoromania* 55 (2002): 147–80.
Borello, Rodolfo A. *El peronismo (1943–1955) en la narrativa argentina*. Ottawa: Devehouse Editions, 1991.
Croce, Marcela. *David Viñas. Crítica de la razón polémica. Un intelectual argentino heterodoxo entre contorno y Dios*. Buenos Aires: Suricata, 2005.
Dill, Hans-Otto. "Unter dem Zeichen des Pferdes." *Lateinamerikanisches Wunder und kreolische Sensibilität: Der Erzähler und Essayist Alejo Carpentier*. Hamburg: Verlag Dr. Kovac. 337–50.
Feinmann, José Pablo. *El ejército de ceniza*. Buenos Aires: Legasa, 1986.
Gilman, Claudia. "Historia, poder y poética del padecimiento en las novelas de Andrés Rivera." *La novela argentina de los años 80*. Ed. Roland Spiller. Frankfurt: Vervuert, 1991.
Gutiérrez Haces, María Teresa. *El militar argentino como proyecto literario*. UNAM: México, 1991.
Historia de Iberoamérica. VVAA (coord. Lucena Salmoral, Manuel). Madrid: Cátedra, 1988.
Pagni, Andrea, and Karl Kohut (eds.). *Literatura argentina hoy. De la dictadura a la Democracia*. Frankfurt: Vervuert, 1989.
Rodriguez Monegal, Emir. *Narradores de esta América*. Buenos Aires: Alfa-Argentina, 1974.
Sarmiento, Domingo Faustino. *Facundo*. Buenos Aires, 1948.
Spiller, Roland (ed.). *La novela argentina de los años 80*. Frankfurt: Vervuert, 1991.
Viñas, David. ———. *Menemato y otros suburbios*. Buenos Aires: Adriana Hidalgo editora, 2000.
———. *Prontuario*. Buenos Aires: Planeta del Sur, 1993.
———. *Indios, ejércitos y frontera*. Buenos Aires: Siglo XXI editores, 1983.

———. "Ellos allá, nosotros en la vereda de enfrente." *Sin censura*. Washington / Paris, 1980.
———. *Cuerpo a cuerpo*. Mexico: Siglo XXI editores, 1979.
———. *Jauría*. Buenos Aires: Granica editor, 1974.
———. *Argentina: ejército y oligarquía*. Havana: Casa de las Américas, 1967.
———. *Los hombres de a caballo*. Havana: Casa de las Américas, 1967.
———. *Los dueños de la tierra*. Buenos Aires: Losada, 1959.
Wittmán, Tibor. *Historia de América Latina*. Budapest: Corvina Kiadó, 1980.

◆ 4

A Journey through the Desert: Trends of Commitment in Contemporary Spanish Poetry

Luis Bagué Quílez

A Civilized Transition (1975–1985)

The Spanish transition to democracy triggered a cultural process that led to a new political framework. In this sense, one can delimit a *double transition* which not only modified the previous regime but also removed the preceding aesthetic, literary and artistic models (Buckley). The first democratic period, between 1976 and 1978, justified a complete social change based on the following events: the legalization of the Spanish Communist Party; the victory of the center-right UCD at the general elections in 1977; the creation of the Ministry of Culture; the reestablishment of the *Generalitat Catalana* with Josep Tarradellas as President, and the promulgation of the democratic Constitution in December 1978.

From a cultural perspective, two facts were crucial. One was the appearance of *El País*, a daily newspaper which represented an ideological referent in the early democracy because of the collaboration of writers and journalists from the liberal movement known as *gauche divine*. This paper established an official culture which met the radical, critical thinking of Aranguren, Savater, García Calvo and Sánchez Ferlosio (Fusi 48; Mainer, *De Postguerra* 141). On the other hand, the Nobel Prize won by Vicente Aleixandre in 1977 implied both the acknowledgment of the Generation of 1927 and the validation of the aesthetic canon assumed by the *Novísimos*. In fact, in 1977 several poets of the Generation of 1968 published their selected works, while others tried different styles in their books: *L'espai desert,* by Pere Gimferrer; *Pasar y siete canciones,* by Félix de Azúa, and *Alegoría,* by Jaime Siles (Lanz, *Introducción* 25).

In 1979 a new political period began. The municipal elections showed a favourable outcome for the Socialist Party (PSOE). After that, the resignation of the president Adolfo Suárez (UCD), followed by the failed coup attempt in 1981, developed into the victory of the PSOE in 1982. This new government tried to combine the ideological premises of May'68, with some kind of moderation in its political behavior. As a consequence, the cultural map was defined by Punk skepticism and the New Age's relaxed tendencies. The *Movida Madrileña* of the early 1980s was more a social attitude than an aesthetic option (Bessière 64–65). This movement represented a peculiar urban subculture which was especially reflected in Spanish cinema of that decade, as it is shown in Pedro Almodóvar's early films, or even before, in *Arrebato* (1979), by Iván Zulueta, where drugs played a fundamental role.

The deep socio-political changes of Spanish Transition are related to a wider cultural framework that explains the development of literature between 1975 and 1985. The origin of the new writing can be found in the discussion about Postmodernism. In 1974, Peter Bürger, in his *Theory of the Avant-garde,* defended the importance of Avant-garde as a revolutionary strategy to question the autonomy of arts for the bourgeois society. However, this recovery of Avant-garde culture was an anachronism, even in 1979. In that year, Lyotard published his book about the postmodern condition, and in 1980 Habermas imparted his lecture about the limits of Postmodernism, published later in the volume *The Anti-Aesthetic: Essays on Postmodern Culture* (1983), edited by Hal Foster. Habermas intended to connect the Enlightenment premises with the idea of progress and social freedom (3–15). To do so, he defended modernity as an unfinished project which would regain democratic values; in other words, his defense of modernity implied a defense of democracy (Savater 111–39; Ortiz-Osés 161–67).

In Spain, this "Enlightened Postmodernism" meant the return to a figurative literature, different from the experimentalism of the previous years, like the formalism of Juan Goytisolo or the symbolism of Juan Benet in the novel. For instance, *La verdad sobre el caso Savolta* (1975), by Eduardo Mendoza, combined Avant-garde innovation with a new reading of tradition. Between 1975 and 1982, Spanish poetry went through a similar process with the evolution of the *Novísimos* and the appearance of a new group in 1977 (Prieto de Paula, *Musa* 157–72, and "Poetas" 159–83). Those latter poets rejected the *Novísimos*' cold culturalism through the fusion of art and intimacy. In this sense, it is worth mentioning *Canciones del amor amargo y otros poemas* (1977), by Javier Salvago; *Transparencia indebida* (1977), by Francisco Bejarano; *Primera despedida* (1978), by Fernando Ortiz; *Maneras de estar solo* (1978), by Eloy Sánchez Rosillo; *Clima* (1978), by Andrés Sánchez Robayna; *Mitos* (1979), by Abelardo Linares, and *Las cosas que me acechan* (1979), by Víctor Botas.

At the beginning of the 1980's, young poets began to publish books which already showed an opposition to the aesthetic parameters of the *Novísimos*. Between 1980 and 1982 the first figurative poetry came to existence as a radically different tendency from the previous abstract one, which had broken its links with tradition. Figurative poetry used a colloquial language and was concerned with realism (García Martín).[1] Examples of this tendency can be found in books like *Los devaneos de Erato* (1980), by Ana Rossetti; *Junto al agua* (1980), by Andrés Trapiello; *Y ahora ya eres dueño del puente de Brooklyn* (1980), by Luis García Montero; *Tristia* (1982), by García Montero and Álvaro Salvador; the first version of *Las tradiciones* (1982), by Trapiello; *Muro contra la muerte* (1982), by Juan Lamillar; *Dióscuros* (1982), by Rossetti; *Hiperiónida* (1982), by Aurora Luque; *Paseo de los Tristes* (1982), by Javier Egea, and *Paraíso manuscrito* (1982), by Felipe Benítez Reyes. It was precisely in 1982 when the traces of future Spanish poetry are delimited. In fact, in this year García Montero won the *Adonais* Prize for *El jardín extranjero*, and Amparo Amorós received a mention for *Ludia*. While Amoros's work was the beginning of the *rhetoric of silence* tendency, García Montero's carried out an analysis of intimacy and history related to Habermas's Enlightened Postmodernism.[2]

García Montero was (together with Álvaro Salvador and Javier Egea) the author of the anthology *La otra sentimentalidad* (1983).[3] The *otra sentimentalidad* (different sensibility) was influenced by the Marxist thinking of Juan Carlos Rodríguez and by the cultural milieu of the city of Granada. This aesthetic tendency constituted an amalgam of feelings and collective commitment. It also promoted an approach to Postmodernism which can be defined as *subjective epics* (Mainer, "Con los cuellos" 9; Soria Olmedo 121–26). In contrast with the conformist conception of Postmodernism, the adherents to the *otra sentimentalidad* tendency believed in the historical construction of the individual and advocated for a return to the premises of equality defended by the French Revolution (Rodríguez 41; Salvador 217–20).

"A Federico, con unas violetas," included in *El jardín extranjero* (1983), by Luis García Montero, is a good example of this attitude (García Montero, *El jardín* 91–98). This poem, dedicated to Federico García Lorca, has two main influences. On the one hand, it is inspired by "A Larra, con unas violetas [1837–1937]" (*Las nubes*, 1943), by Luis Cernuda; on the other, it is a free recreation of *Llanto por Ignacio Sánchez Mejías* (1935), by Lorca. García Montero's poem is divided into three parts which combine historical reflection with a tribute to the dead poet. The first part is placed in 1929 and it revises some aspects of *Poeta en Nueva York*: references to Harlem and Columbia University, to the financial crisis, and the recurrent presence of solitude and love. García Montero describes a city full of bridges, wharfs and scaffolds, which reminds us of his *opera prima*: *Y ahora ya eres dueño del Puente de Brooklyn*. From its first line, "A Federico, con unas violetas" is presented as a dialogue between García Montero and an absent addressee (Lorca):

> Has llegado de nuevo. Te esperaba
> para tenderte el brazo perdido de los humos,
> la curva de los muelles, la soledad ajena
> de Columbia University
> y esta ceniza fría
> en los párpados rotos
> de la ciudad sin sueño.

(You arrived again. / I was waiting for you / to offer you the lost arm of smokes, / the curve of the piers, the alien solitude / of Columbia University / and that cold ash / in the sleepless city's / broken eyelids.)

In the second part of the poem, some surrealist images are inserted, as happens in the lines "la sonrisa forzada de una máscara rota" and "el alcohol es la sangre que desnuda los labios." This aesthetic option is also observed in the metric ruptures and in the discursive references. In that fashion, García Montero rewrites "y recuerdo una brisa triste por los olivos," the last line of "Alma ausente," which closes *Llanto por Ignacio Sánchez Mejías*:

> Triste por los olivos,
> mientras Harlem entorna sus ventanas,
> el tiempo es una brisa que ya nadie recuerda.

(Sad about the olive trees, / as Harlem closes its windows, / time is a breeze which nobody remembers.)

At the end of "A Federico, con unas violetas" the poet returns to his present where nothing has changed "después de tantos años y una guerra" in Lorca's Granada, which is evoked by the deictic particle *aquí*. This process allows the two tenses of the poem to be integrated in the same discourse. Thus, García Montero connects both post-war Spanish history with his own history and the language of social poetry with that of the poetry of experience. Furthermore, the ideological perspective of the poem is outlined by its relation to Cernuda's texts dedicated to Lorca: "A un poeta muerto (F.G.L.)" (*Las nubes*) and "Otra vez, con sentimiento" (*Desolación de Quimera*, 1962). In fact, in the last lines García Montero expresses a moral lesson similar to Cernuda's:

> Hoy no puede pesar sobre esta sombra
> un ramo de violetas
> y es dulce así dejarlas
> frescas entre la niebla
> como un rumor de cuerpos que no cesa
> y esta lágrima extraña
> que llamamos historia.

(Today, a bouquet of violets / cannot feel heavy on this shadow / and it is sweet to leave them like this, / fresh among the fog / as an endless rumor of bodies / and that strange teardrop / which is called history.)

Although García Montero insisted on the subject of this poem in later texts—"Larra" (*Las flores del frío*, 1991), "El insomnio de Jovellanos" (*Habitaciones separadas*, 1994), and "Las confesiones de don Quijote" (*La intimidad de la serpiente*, 2003)—"A Federico, con unas violetas" remains as a proof of a time when enthusiasm was still alive.

An Inverted Millenarianism (1986–1991)

Several historical events triggered a general feeling of disappointment after 1986. The end of the *Movida*, the definitive incorporation of Spain in the NATO or its participation in the First Iraq War led to what Mainer called "bankruptcy of the progressive tradition" (Mainer, *De postguerra* 131). The disappearance of the *Movida* meant that the cultural renovation carried out by the younger generation had failed. Besides, the reelection of President Felipe González determined the opposition of some of the parties that had supported him before. In poetry, a clear example of this situation is best represented by the anthology

1917 versos (1987), edited by Vanguardia Obrera, which showed the rebuff to the permanence of Spain in NATO.[4] In this political frame, the university demonstrations in 1986–1987 and the general strike of February 14, 1988 were the outcome of an ideological atmosphere which had replaced the Avant-garde of the *cultura de la movida* by the consumerism of the *cultura del pelotazo* (nepotism and financial speculation).

In this context, any aspiration to any kind of "Enlightened Postmodernism" becomes futile. Instead, Postmodernism is identified with a new cultural trend related to the capitalist systems. For Fredric Jameson, postmodern culture turns art works into merchandise and destroys the lineal continuity of history. It is in this way that Postmodernism is best defined as an *inverted millenarianism*, which can be characterized by the acceptance of the end of ideology, arts or class struggles.

Jameson's pessimism can only be refuted with other proposals seeking a wide description of Postmodernism. Hal Foster points out that Postmodernism was divided into two different tendencies since its origins: the *Postmodernism of reaction*, one which accepted official culture, and the *Postmodernism of resistance*, which rejected it (Foster 1983). In the same direction, concerning the intellectual postmodern sphere, Huyssen differentiates between an eclectic attitude, which renounced to concepts such as history and representation, and a critical attitude, which defended the role of the individual and the importance of interpretation (Huyssen 241). Several authors; however, argue that postmodern reality can be both radical and conservative at the same time. In fact, although Postmodernism rejected the dominant ideology of the system, in practice it did not change the behavior of consumerist society (Eagleton *Illusions*).

In Spanish poetry, the different polemics within Postmodernism became a literary debate. In 1986 and 1987, Spanish poetry was subsumed in a battle between the so-called *poesía de la experiencia* and the *poesía metafísica*.[5] The *poesía de la experiencia* was related to figurative literature and the *otra sentimentalidad* tendency. This movement was inspired by the ideas of Juan de Mairena (Antonio Machado) about the evolution of feelings, by Diderot's paradox of the comedian, and by the dramatic monologue as studied by Robert Langbaum. All these authors conceived poetry as a way of fiction. On the other side, the *poesía metafísica* was determined by several abstract tendencies, like Rimbaud's negativism, Mallarmé's hermetism, or the contribution of the Avant-garde, from Walter Benjamin to André Breton. While "experience" poets defended ideas like normality and utility, metaphysic poets vindicated the romantic notion of inspiration. The difference between both tendencies was connected with the distinction between the *poesía del diálogo*, which proposed a personal reading of the literary tradition, and the *poesía del fragmento*, which questioned the ability of language to represent reality (Lanz, "Joven poesía" 204–5; Prieto de Paula, "Sobre la poesía" 378–79).

Both Jameson's and Foster's theories were soon reflected in Jorge Riechmann's works. Riechmann advocated for a *researching realism*, which led him to discover and modify his relationships with the world around him (Riechmann, *Canciones* 133). This author developed a kind of literature able to embrace several aspects of reality, as an evidence of the interaction between the writer, the reader, and their surrounding situation. In relation to this, Riechmann stated: "Realismo es una actitud, no un estilo" (*Poesía practicable* 34) (realism is an attitude, not a style). He has consequently defined his poetry as a *practicable* one or a *helpful* one, trying to show his concern about his time and its conflicts.

Among his initial texts, it is worth mentioning "Posmodernidad" (*Cuaderno de Berlín*, 1989), where Riechmann makes fun of the *reaction postmodernism* defended by Foster: its scarce interest in cultural matters, its constant publicity content, its *light* thinking, and so forth. In this poem, Riechmann combines elements from realistic poetry and Avant-garde poetry, such as the use of irony ("Ponga un jíbaro en su vida"), the *collage* with one of Brecht's sentences (the revolutionary "cambia el mundo, lo necesita" turns into "*changer la vie*"), and the *post scriptum*, which synthesizes the negative aspects the writer has displayed in the lines above (Riechmann, *Cuaderno* 38):

Una ética de mínimos
con encefalograma plano
Una razón en saldo
por quiebra del negocio
La anhelada revelación
del anhelado agente histórico
capaz de *changer la vie*:
la propaganda comercial

Ponga un jíbaro en su vida

A ratos se me antoja
que la única virtud aún no ambigua
es ser intempestivo

PS Y eso que son connaturalmente las virtudes
desmemoriadas, sedantes, vengativas.

(An ethics of minimums / With a flat EEG, / reasons for sale / due to business failure / the expected revelation / of the expected historical agent / able to changer la vie: / advertisement. // Put a Jibaro in your life // Sometimes I feel / like the only virtue which is not yet ambiguous / is to be startling // P.S. Not bad, considering that virtues are connaturally / forgetful, sedating, revengeful.)

A New Disillusionment (1992–1996)

The year 1992 was considered a symbol of the modernization of Spain and a metaphor of the *Spanish fashion*. The Olympic Games held in Barcelona, the Universal Exhibition in Seville, the celebration of the Fifth Centenary of America's Discovery, and the election of Madrid as the European capital of culture simulated a feeling of success which was far from the actual reality. The funny mascots of the events, Cobi (for the Olympic Games) and Curro (for the Universal Exhibition), hid a political atmosphere characterized by several financial frauds involving relevant people in the public life. This situation triggered a sense of general corruption which contributed to the victory of the PP Party in the European elections (1994) and later on in the General elections (1996). The new government improved the nation's international economical relationships and decreased the amount of unemployment, but it was unable to solve the social problems that the country suffered.

Concerning Postmodernism, it is worth mentioning the expansion of the thinking related to *light* ideology. Two clear examples are the *end of history*, announced by Fukuyama, and the *pensiero debole*, proclaimed by Vattimo and Rovatti. Fukuyama's thesis defended that the fall of the last communist government in Europe (in 1989) meant the triumph of the Western capitalism due to the lack of alternatives to this system. For Fukuyama, the end of history solved the contradictions generated by modern liberalism, since the strong systems it was opposed to (fascism and communism) during the twentieth century had failed. He argued that capitalist democracy was able to survive religious conflicts and nationalisms. However, Fukuyama defined the end of history as a sad period, in which ideology and imagination had lost their sense. In sum, after the fall of the Berlin Wall, the end of history could be interpreted as a new kind of ethnocentrism based on the reduction of human civilization to capitalism.

Far from the conservative thesis of the end of history we find the concept of *pensiero debole*, or weak thought, defined by the Italian philosopher Gianni Vattimo. In his books *Al di là del soggetto* (1981) and *La fine della modernità* (1985), Vattimo claimed that philosophy was in a situation in which it had to choose between renouncing to truth or seeking new, less pretentious reasons to think about current reality. Thus, the *pensiero debole* tried to recover those aspects of philosophy which were able to reflect the values of a world in which metaphysics had lost its importance. Inside the postmodern context, weak thought focused on the analysis of daily experience. Such interest in the ordinary life moved the attention from philosophical expression to literary forms. This movement intended to carry out a reflection on history out of both ancient metaphysics and new postmodern trends. However, weak thought did not always overcome the contradictions derived from its radical skepticism. The abandonment of absolute truths and the lack of a normative program impeded its socio-politic application and paralyzed its desire of transforming reality (Vattimo and Rovatti).

Despite their differences, both the notion of the end of history and weak thought had enormous repercussions in the Spanish literature of that period. The poetry of experience had confronted Postmodernism because of its definition of the poetic subject and its interpretation of the literary tradition. While postmodern tradition seemed to demand an individual in conflict with the world and an ironical re-reading of the tradition, the figurative authors opted for an autobiographical conception of the poetic subject and a respectful attitude for the literary tradition (Cañas 52–53).[6] However, the poetic productions of the 1980s and the 1990s gradually incorporated postmodern elements. In this sense, the important role that the mass media and urban reality had in the new books of poems must be underscored. One could also mention a Postmodernism whose first instantiations used humor to face the end of humanism, the arts, or history. Susan Sontag had already noticed that clearness in the style or simplicity in the message were also ways of objecting to the topics of the interpretation.

The end of history is related to the apocalyptic impulse of what has been called *dirty realism*. It was born in the United States and durimg the early 1980s it became a tendency inside poetry of experience: a prosaic, subjective poetry which combined humor, urban jargon and scatology. In Spain, this movement is best represented by Roger Wolfe, from his first book *Días perdidos en los transportes públicos* (1992). Wolfe's attitude to Postmodernism is synthesized in "Fin de la historia" (*Mensajes en botellas rotas*, 1996). In this poem, Wolfe criticizes the new ways of millenarianism at the end of the twentieth century "ante la supuesta / inminente amenaza / del vacío" (when facing the alleged threat of the void). The author manifests his contempt for sects and tribes which look for arguments within the ontological emptiness (15):

> Pero en cualquier caso
> no es tan mala idea
> que la gente se encierre
> en dogmas y patrañas
> de ese modo.
> Que se encierre
> donde quiera.
> Siempre y cuando arroje
> bien lejos de mí
> y de cualquier parte conocida
> la maldita llave.[7]

(In any case, / it is not a bad idea / for people to lock themselves up / in dogmas and lies / like that. / Let them lock themselves / wherever they please / as long as they throw / the damn key / far away from me / and from anywhere I know.)

Furthermore, the ideas connected to weak thought are also reflected in some other compositions placed between critical intention and ironical distance. This ethical ambiguity is observed for instance in "Treintagenarios" (*Partes de Guerra*, 1994), by Juan Bonilla. In this poem, the generational disappointment is expressed through textual repetitions ("Aquí me veis, viajero"), chaotic enumerations ("ropas, viajes, hadas"), punning ("los partidos / de Sartre lo cambiaron por el sastre") and the mixture of high and colloquial registers. At the end, the writer appropriates the negative aspects used previously to describe the components of his generation, like consumerism, lack of solidarity and ideological conservatism (Bonilla 26–27):

> Aquí me veis, viajero
> de una generación desencantada
> cuyo dios seductor es el dinero
> que hemos gastado en ropas, viajes, hadas.
>
> Las luchas y consignas
> palabras son que anhelan nuestros viejos
> nostálgicos de tanta causa digna
> porque se miran poco en los espejos.

Somos conservadores
según denuncia una revista en boga,
por preferir usar consoladores
al sexo y masticar chicle a la droga.

Aquí me veis, viajero
de una generación que en vano
quiere evitar los aguaceros
pues vino sólo a pasar el verano.

Somos insolidarios
y nos da igual que el mundo sea un desastre
(a fin de cuentas ya los partidarios
de Sartre lo cambiaron por el sastre).

No es por casualidad
que sea época de pocas luces
morales. Vuelve el Dogma o la Verdad
a convencernos con mentiras dulces.

Aquí me veis, viajero
de un tiempo que se pierde en la espesura
del paso y el me da lo mismo . . . pero
nunca fue tan hermosa la basura.[8]

(Here I am, a traveler / who belongs to a disenchanted generation / whose god is the money / we spent in clothes, trips, fairies. // The struggle and the slogans / are words missed by our elders, / who are nostalgic of so many worthy causes / because they rarely look at themselves in the mirror. // According to a trendy magazine, / we are conservatives, / because we prefer dildos to sex / and chewing gum to doing drugs. // Here I am, a traveler / who belongs to a generation / which in vain wants to avoid the rain / as it came just to spend the summer. // We are not altruist / and we do not care about the world being a disaster / (after all, Sartre's followers / prefer his tailor now) // It is not by chance / that these are not morally enlightened times. / Dogma or Truth come back / to convince us with sweet lies. // Here I am, a traveler / of a time getting lost in the jungle / of disengagement and carelessness. . . . / but trash was never so beautiful.)

The ironical tone of these poems, a consequence of political disillusionment, was considered a justification for hedonism. However, the apparent conformism of the poetry of experience hid not only a skeptic position toward reality but also the vindication of intimacy as a way of rebelliousness, out of collective instructions. Despite the important presence of pubs in this poetry, these authors did not drink to forget the surrounding world, but to seek refuge in their own individuality as the only way to salvation.

Landscapes for the Third Millennium (1997–2005)

A new political stage began in 2000 with the new electoral victory of the Partido Popular, which obtained an absolute majority in Parliament. Aznar's government got to balance the Spanish economy with that of the rest of Europe, but his social reforms were scarce—except for the military service abolition, in December 2001. In his last term as a president, José María Aznar made some decisions which increased popular dissatisfaction, like his answer to an environmental catastrophe in the Northern coast, or his support to U.S. President George W. Bush in his invasion of Iraq at the beginning of 2003. The terrorist attack of March 11, 2004, in Madrid, related to Islamist movements and to the Spanish collaboration in Iraq's conflict, contributed to the electoral triumph of the Socialists three days later.

The first years of the third millennium have favored a wider conception of Postmodernism. Although postmodern theory has not lost its importance in the current thinking, some critics have tried to study its genealogy (Anderson) and to offer a summary of its results (Eagleton, *After Theory*). Furthermore, contemporary eclecticism has provided the possibility of a progressive Postmodernism, opposed to the risks of globalization. Thus, postmodern culture raises again the recovery of ideological commitment, either as a productive nihilism (Lucy 96), or as a postmodern realism (Oleza 34–42). Postmodern realism intends to make compatible postmodern philosophy with realistic discourse. To do so, it assimilates some of Postmodernism's features: the reappropriation of tradition, the use of expressive mechanisms from popular culture, the reactivation of the narrative forms or the democratization of beauty. Postmodern realism also defends the return to the individual in order to fuse the language and its referent, the aesthetic elaboration and the everyday life (Scarano "Políticas" 204–5). From this perspective, some writers and intellectuals have used postmodern culture's contradictions to reflect their ideas. For García Montero, if Postmodernism assumes that reality is a simulation, then the author and the reader could choose "el simulacro que más nos interese" (the most convenient simulacrum), including ethic and aesthetic aspects, like the return to representation or the recovery of Enlightenment moral values.

In accordance with this new postmodern atmosphere, the latest Spanish poetry has evolved to positions that express a return to commitment. Like figurative poetry, some trends try to establish different links between the individual and the surrounding world: the ironic, personal view of *critical hiperrealism* (*El día que dejé de leer EL PAÍS*, 1997, by Jorge Riechmann); *dirty realism*'s open-minded approach to collective problems (*Cinco años de cama,* 1998, by Roger Wolfe), or the incorporation of social crises in the author's intimacy (*La semana fantástica,* 1999, by Fernando Beltrán). For all these authors, postmodern realism is considered a *reality effect* which acquires a political purpose when it focuses on the social sphere. From this perspective, it is worth mentioning García Montero's intention to eliminate the limits between public and private life. This kind of realism includes a civil ethics, a conception of the writer and its addressee as standard people, and an interpretation of arts attaching history (García Montero, *Realismo singular*; Scarano, *Luis García* 206–27). These premises are displayed in his collection *La intimidad de la serpiente* (2003), where a postmodern individual struggles with the current ontological emptiness.

In recent Spanish poetry there is also a still weak Avant-garde tendency which seeks a revolutionary purpose through formal experimentation. This process is reflected in the romantic verses of *La tumba de Keats* (1999), by Juan Carlos Mestre; in the social epic *La marcha de 150.000.000* (1994 and 1998), by Enrique Falcón, and in the absence of rhetorical language in *Trasluz* (2002) and *Por más señas* (2005), by Antonio Méndez Rubio.

Since the transition to democracy, Spanish poetry has tried a return to a commitment related to both recent political events and changes in postmodern thought. While García Montero claimed in his first books his desire of *otra sentimentalidad* to confront the democracy's convulsive atmosphere, the generational disappointment triggered both a strong attack to consumerism in Riechmann's case and a seeming conformism hiding personal rebelliousness in the case of the poetry of experience. Although chronological closeness makes it difficult to test its results, during the last decades Spanish poetry has intended to combine a realistic perspective with a plural discourse (Bagué Quílez). Contemporary poetry may have always been a fiction, but after Pessoa an author is definitely condemned to pretend the sorrow that s/he really feels.

Notes

1. García Martín defined the figurative poetry "por analogía con la distinción entre pintura figurativa y pintura no figurativa: todos ellos se encuentran más cerca de Gaya que de Tàpies" (García Martín 1992: 209).
2. Between 1983 and 1985 appeared *El jardín extranjero* (1983) by Luis García Montero; the first version of *Europa* (1983) by Julio Martínez Mesanza; *La vida fácil* (1985) by Andrés Trapiello; *Diario de un poeta recién cansado* (1985) by Jon Juaristi; and *Los vanos mundos* (1985) by Felipe Benítez Reyes (Villena 2000: 27–30).
3. In his study-anthology, *La otra sentimentalidad*, Díaz de Castro included in this trend the following authors: Álvaro Salvador, Javier Egea, Ángeles Mora, Antonio Jiménez Millán, Luis García Montero, Teresa Gómez, Benjamín Prado, and Inmaculada Mengíbar (Díaz de Castro 2003).
4. In 1986, Ángel Muñoz Petisme announced the end of the *Movida* and the inversion of the punk premises developed during the early eighties: "Cuando empecé a tomarme lo de escribir en serio, allá por el 79, la gente de mi edad estaba en otra historia (de broma), se figuraron tribus y estereotipos de moda—naturalmente importada—y no había demasiado espacio para la creatividad [. . .]. Recuerdo que fui de los primeros, en Zaragoza, que salía a la calle de nuevo romántico, de corsario, con cintas en el pelo y pendientes y esas cosas. Ahora todo eso se ha acabado y *hay que tender la ropa al sol*" (in Ilie 1995: 27).
5. Concerning this impact in the literary ambit, Lanz claimed: "En torno a 1986–1987, diversos autores que habían quedado marginados de la tendencia que comenzaba a establecer su dominio, empiezan a publicar una serie de libros (en muchos casos sus primeros libros) que alteran el relato generacional tal como se desarrollaba en aquellos años [. . .], continuando en cierto modo la diversidad de poéticas de los años anteriores" (Lanz 1998: 278). Miguel Casado also accepted these reasons in his article "87 *versus* 78." In his view, 1987 had been a crucial year for the new poetry for three motives: Antonio Gamoneda, one of the masters for the young metaphysics, published *Edad*; Aníbal Núñez, one of the most personal authors of 68, died; and there appeared several books which broke the experience generational discourse, like *Cántico de la erosión* by Jorge Riechmann and *De barro la memoria* by Menchu Gutiérrez (Casado 1994: 6–7).
6. Julia Barella and Anthony L. Geist shared Dionisio Cañas's opinion. The former, after studying the main postmodern stylistic features, concluded: "No creo que pueda hablarse con rigor de una literatura posmoderna en la España de los ochenta, si nos atenemos a las definiciones que los críticos han venido dando del término desde los años cincuenta en Estados Unidos" (Barella 9, n. 5). And, from a very similar perspective, Geist considered: "no quiero decir que toda la poesía que se escribe y publica actualmente en España sea, ni muchísimo menos, posmoderna. Más bien al contrario. Así vemos, por ejemplo, en una misma colección editorial poesía que varía desde el formalismo más clásico hasta la experimentación posestructuralista más radical, pasando por varios estilos netamente vanguardistas" (Geist 147). However, these reasons did

not seem convincing. While Barella proposed a quite simplistic identification between Postmodernism and Avant-garde, the diversity observed by Geist could be considered a reflection of a postmodern *pluralism*.
7. Another poem from the same book ("Ética del cavernícola contemporáneo") showed the emotional disappointment suffered by the author in a different way. In this case, Wolfe defended that the only plausible weapon against social violence was "enquistarse en la zozobra," in other words, to live in scepticism. This acknowledgment did not lead to the *tremendismo* of Dámaso Alonso's *Hijos de la ira*, but to an almost trivial tone: "No hay otra alternativa / más que enquistarse / en la zozobra / cerrar puertas y ventanas / bajar persianas / pinchar a Purcell / desplomarse en la cama / y respirar pausadamente / mientras el mundo / ahí fuera / se destroza" (Wolfe 78).
8. The origin of this kind of discourse is found in poems like "Imagino el infierno" (*El último de la fiesta*, 1987) by Carlos Marzal and "Los convidados de las últimas fiestas" (*Pruebas de autor*, 1989) by Felipe Benítez Reyes. In these compositions, the poets exhibited their existential fatigue through a confession related to "Yo, poeta decadente" by Manuel Machado (*El mal poema*, 1909). Note that Manuel Machado's poem finishes with a corollary synthesizing the *fin de siècle* scepticism: ". . . No sabemos nada. / Todo es conforme y según" (Machado 2000: 205).

Works Cited

Anderson, Perry. *The Origins of Postmodernity*. London and New York: Verso, 1998.
Bagué Quílez, Luis. "Entre clasicismo y vanguardia: el compromiso poético en los autores de los años ochenta." *Anales de Literatura Española* 17 (2004): 11–33.
Barella, Julia (ed.). *Después de la modernidad. Poesía española en sus lenguas literarias*. Barcelona: Anthropos, 1987.
Bessière, Bernard. "El Madrid de la democracia: comportamientos culturales y crisol de creación. Realidades y dudas." *España frente al siglo XXI. Cultura y literatura*. Ed. Samuel Amell. Madrid: Cátedra / Ministerio de Cultura, 1992. 51–75.
Bonilla, Juan. *Partes de guerra*. Valencia: Pre-Textos, 1998.
Buckley, Ramón. *La doble transición. Política y literatura en los años setenta*. Madrid: Siglo XXI, 1996.
Bürger, Peter. *Theory of the Avant-garde*. Minneapolis: University of Minnesota Press, 1984.
Cañas, Dionisio. "El sujeto poético posmoderno." *Ínsula* 512–13 (1989): 52–53.
Casado, Miguel. "87 *versus* 78." *Ínsula* 565 (1994): 6–8.
Díaz de Castro, Francisco (ed.). *La otra sentimentalidad. Estudio y antología*. Sevilla: Fundación José Manuel Lara, 2003.
Eagleton, Terry. *After Theory*. New York: Basic Books, 2003.
———. *The Illusions of Postmodernism*. Oxford: Blackwell, 1996.

Foster, Hal (ed.). *The Anti-Aesthetic: Essays on Postmodern Culture*. Seattle: Bay Press, 1983.
Fukuyama, Francis. *The End of History and the Last Man*. London: Penguin Books, 1992.
Fusi, Juan Pablo. "La cultura de la transición." *Revista de Occidente* 112–13 (1991): 37–64.
García Martín, José Luis. *La poesía figurativa. Crónica parcial de quince años de poesía española*. Sevilla: Renacimiento, 1992.
García Montero, Luis. *El jardín extranjero* preceded by *Poemas de "Tristia."* Madrid: Hiperión, 1999.
———. *Confesiones poéticas*. Granada: Diputación, 1993.
———. *El realismo singular*. Bilbao: Los Libros de Hermes, 1993.
Geist, Anthony L. "Poesía, democracia, posmodernidad: España, 1975–1990." *Del franquismo a la posmodernidad. Cultura española 1975–1990*. Ed. José B. Monleón. Madrid: Akal, 1995. 143–50.
Habermas, Jürgen. "Modernity —An Incomplete Project." *The Anti-Aesthetic: Essays on Postmodern Culture*. Ed. Hal Foster. Seattle: Bay Press, 1983. 3–15.
Huyssen, Andreas. "Cartografía del postmodernismo." *Modernidad y postmodernidad*. Ed. Josep Picó. Madrid: Alianza, 1988. 189–248.
Ilie, Paul. "La cultura posfranquista, 1975–1990: La continuidad dentro de la discontinuidad." *Del franquismo a la posmodernidad. Cultura española 1975–1990*. Ed. José B. Monleón. Madrid: Akal, 1995. 21–39.
Jameson, Fredric. *Postmodernism, or, the Cultural Logic of Late Capitalism*. Durham: Duke University Press, 1991.
Lanz, Juan José. *Introducción al estudio de la generación poética española de 1968*. Bilbao: Universidad del País Vasco, 2000.
———. "La joven poesía española. Notas para una periodización." *Hispanic Review* 66 (1998): 261–87.
———. "La joven poesía española al fin del milenio. Hacia una poética de la postmodernidad." *Letras de Deusto* 66 (1995): 173–206.
———. "Primera etapa de una generación. Notas para la definición de un espacio poético: 1977–1982." *Ínsula* 565 (1994): 3–6.
———. "La poesía española: ¿hacia un nuevo romanticismo?" *El Urogallo* 60 (1991): 36–45.
Lucy, Niall. *Postmodern Literary Theory*. Oxford: Blackwell, 1997.
Machado, Manuel. *Alma. Caprichos. El mal poema*. Madrid: Castalia, 2000.
Mainer, José-Carlos. "'Con los cuellos alzados y fumando': notas para una poética realista." *Antología (1980–1995)*. Ed. Luis García Montero. Madrid: Hiperión, 1999. 7–29.
———. *De Postguerra (1951–1990)*. Barcelona: Crítica, 1994.
Oleza, Joan. "Un realismo posmoderno." *Ínsula* 589–90 (1996): 39–42.
Ortiz-Osés, Andrés. "Románticos e ilustrados en nuestra cultura." *En torno a la posmodernidad*. Ed. Gianni Vattimo et al. Barcelona: Anthropos, 1994. 161–67.

Prieto de Paula, Ángel L. "Poetas del 68 . . . después de 1975." *Anales de Literatura Española* 17 (2004): 159–83.

———, and Luis Bagué Quílez. "De ríos que se van (y que regresan): una aproximación a la poesía española en 2002 y 2003." *Diablotexto* 7 (2003–2004): 441–61.

———. "Sobre la poesía y el estatuto de la poesía en el año 2000." *Diablotexto* 6 (2002): 373–90.

———. *Musa del 68. Claves de una generación poética*. Madrid: Hiperión, 1996.

Riechmann, Jorge. *Resistencia de materiales. Ensayos sobre el mundo y la poesía y el mundo (1998–2004)*. Barcelona: Montesinos, 2006.

———. *Canciones allende lo humano*. Madrid: Hiperión, 1998.

———. *Poesía practicable. Apuntes sobre poesía, 1984–1988*. Madrid: Hiperión, 1990.

———. *Cuaderno de Berlín*. Madrid: Hiperión, 1989.

Rodríguez, Juan Carlos. *Dichos y escritos (Sobre "La otra sentimentalidad" y otros textos fechados de poética)*. Madrid: Hiperión, 1999.

Salvador, Álvaro. *Letra pequeña*. Granada: Cuadernos del Vigía, 2003.

Savater, Fernando. "El pesimismo ilustrado." *En torno a la posmodernidad*. Ed. Gianni Vattimo *et al*. Barcelona: Anthropos, 1994. 111–30.

Scarano, Laura. *Luis García Montero: la escritura como interpelación*. Granada: Atrio, 2004.

———. "Políticas de la palabra en el debate poético español contemporáneo." *Anales de Literatura Española* 17 (2004): 201–12.

Sontag, Susan. *Against Interpretation and Other Essays*. New York: Farrar, Straus & Giroux, 1966.

Soria Olmedo, Andrés. *Literatura en Granada (1898–1998). II. Poesía*. Granada: Diputación, 2000.

Vattimo, Gianni, and Pier Aldo Rovatti (eds.). *Il pensiero debole*. Milano: Feltrinelli, 1983.

Villena, Luis Antonio de. *Teorías y Poetas. Panorama de una generación completa en la última poesía española*. Valencia: Pre-Textos, 2000.

Wolfe, Roger. *Mensajes en botellas rotas*. Sevilla: Renacimiento, 1996.

Part II
Interrogating Memories

◆ 5

Testimonial Narratives in the Argentine Post-Dictatorship: Survivors, Witnesses, and the Reconstruction of the Past[1]

Ana Forcinito

> *No existen en la historia paréntesis inexplicables. Y es precisamente en los períodos de "excepción" en esos momentos molestos y desagradables que las sociedades pretenden olvidar, colocar entre paréntesis donde aparecen sin mediaciones ni atenuantes los secretos y las vergüenzas del poder cotidiano.*
> —Pilar Calveiro, *Poder y desaparición*

(There are no unexplainable parentheses in History. And it is precisely in these periods of "exception," in the annoying and unpleasant moments that societies seek to forget, put in parenthesis, that the secrets and the shames of daily power appear, without any mediation nor extenuating circumstance.)

> *El asunto es ése: no acallar las voces discordantes con la propia sino sumarlas para ir armando, en lugar de un puzzle en que cada pieza tiene un solo lugar, una especie de calidoscopio que reconoce distintas figuras posibles.*
> —Pilar Calveiro, *Política y/o violencia*

(This is what it's about: not to silence discordant voices with our own voice, but to add them in order to put together, instead of a puzzle in which each piece has only one place, a sort of kaleidoscope which recognizes different possible figures.)[2]

Former detainees have, without any doubt, a central place in the Argentine redemocratization process that started in 1983. Their testimonies have been essential in determining the existence and location of Clandestine Camps, in identifying repressors, in making visible methods of torture, living conditions in the Camps, and especially in providing information about the *desaparecidos*, when and where they were held captives, and other information pertaining to them. Their presence in the public reconstruction of the past is also connected with the constitution of the disappeared as a figure that could no longer be ignored in the redemocratization process. Nevertheless, this central role of the survivors seems to be conditioned by the marginalization of some memories, meanings and interpretations. Adriana Calvo, a survivor of the Clandestine Detention Camp "Pozo de Banfield," says about the silence that surrounds the figure of the former detainee: "A todos les pasó lo mismo. No había orejas dispuestas a escuchar, no querían saber, no podían soportarlo. No querían sentirse responsables de lo que estaba pasando" (Gelman 112) (It happened to everyone. There were no ears prepared to listen, no one wanted to know, they could not bear it. They did not want to feel responsible for what was going on). And later on, she ads: "Para esta sociedad existen las Madres y los HIJOS. Los detenidos-desaparecidos no existimos" (113) (In this society only Mothers and HIJOS exist. The *detenidos-desaparecidos* do not). Are the survivors—as those *desaparecidos* who can testify for those who did not survived—inside those parentheses that Pilar Calveiro, also a former detainee, proposes as what—and who—"societies seek to forget?" Even though their juridical role is widely accepted and unquestioned, are there other memories or senses attached to the very idea of becoming a witness that are not being listened to, as Calvo suggests? Or is this displacement a dispute about the meanings of multiple memories that cannot form a single perfect figure of the past but instead the kaleidoscope in which Calveiro locates the various possible figures of the exercise of remembering?

Memory as a social practice in the Argentine post-dictatorship continues to be open to new meanings, new questions, new recollections, sometimes conflictive, or even irreconcilable. Even though the recent commemoration of the 30th anniversary of the coup on March 24, 2006 took 100,000 citizens to the Plaza de Mayo (*Página 12*, March 25, 2006), the meaning assigned to memory, or better, to the plural memories of the past is still under construction. Once again, the concept of collective memory proposed by Maurice Halbwachs is challenged by approaches that privilege marginalized voices, individual stories and, as Michael Pollak suggests "underground memories" (4). The last years of democratic government in Argentina brought a number of changes in relation to the official politics in Human Rights. This official call for a politics of memory in the new millennium, thirty years after the last coup, is also opening new channels of debate that prove that memory, as Elizabeth Jelin points out, is a political struggle "not only over the meaning of what took place in the past but over the meaning of memory itself"(xviii). What at the beginning of the transition was thought of as a binary opposition between memory and oblivion has been more recently understood as a struggle that opposes "memory against memory":

> A basic fact must be established. In any given moment and place, it is impossible to find *one* memory, or a single vision and interpretation of the past shared throughout society. There may be moments or historical periods when a consensus is more pervasive, when a single script of the past is widely accepted, or even hegemonic. Normally the dominant story will be told by the winners of historical conflicts and battles. Yet there will always be other stories, other memories, and alternative interpretations. (xviii)

Those events, those subjects, those places, those meanings, and the will or desire to remember or forget them play an important role in the battle for the signification of memory. Memory is not just one but a set of recollections attached to oftentimes irreconcilable meanings, conditioned by—but also conditioning—the interpretations available in the present. Hugo Vezzetti uses the concept "labor of memory," as Jelin does too, to refer to the process of "working through the painful memories and recollections instead of reliving them and acting them out" (Jelin 6). The labors of memory, as the labors of mourning in psychoanalytic theory implies, for Vezzetti, an "implantation," a practice that aims to accommodate the past into the present not only against the meanings imposed by the dictatorship but also against the lack of meaning produced by the exhibition and repetition of the horrors in the media (33). In this task of reworking the past and the present, the memories of those who survived did not only reflect the attempt of reconstructing the past but also of problematizing memory, its blanks, its irrecoverable spaces, and the fact that the past—or that part of the past that remained in prisons and concentration camps—was to be remembered by former detainees, now witnesses but also suspects (of trauma, of unreliability). As Vezzetti puts it: "La memoria testimonial, viene a decir Primo Levi, es a la vez la 'fuente esencial para la reconstrucción' y una herramienta insegura" (182) (Testimonial memory, says Primo Levi, is at the same time, a 'source essential to the reconstruction' and an insecure tool).

One of the first steps in the redemocratization process that started in 1983 has to do—at least in the first years, before the impunity laws—with the official invitation extended by the State to the former victims, in the Commission of Investigation and then in the Trials of the Military Junta. That is the moment in which the official role of the witnesses is born and, with that, the mark of the Argentine "transition." This mark only stays as such, it can be argued, since then this gesture is superimposed by the history of impunity that starts in 1986 with the Full Stop and Due Obedience Laws and the Laws of Pardon of 1989 and 1990. It is, nevertheless a gesture that impunity cannot completely erase, especially if we are aware that today, after the recent annulment of *Punto final* (Full Stop) and *Obediencia debida* (Due Obedience), new trials with charges of repression and torture are taking place in Argentina. It is through the restitution of the citizenship of the survivor that comes hand in hand with the very act of bearing witness, Vezzetti argues, that the State legitimates the voices of the former detainees (187). The act of witnessing is then constitutive of the new meaning of citizenship that emerges with the democratization process in 1983.

It is relevant to note that the juridical role of the witnesses is not limited to the first years of democracy. Almost thirty years after the *coup*, survivors of military repression continue their practices as witnesses in Argentina and abroad in order to bring justice to those responsible for the violations of human rights during the military regime. After 1990, human rights organizations have been able to succeed in the prosecution of military personnel who were already pardoned or who were not charged in 1985. Their role was also crucial in the demand for the derogation of the Full Stop and Due Obedience Laws, and in the transformation of Clandestine Detention Centers into sites of memory (ESMA, Mansión Seré, Olimpo, Club Atlético). New trials have been taking place since the Supreme Court annulled the Full Stop and Due Obedience Laws in 2005. Therefore, the role of the witnesses is still very active in Argentina today in the prosecution of military personnel who was involved in forced disappearances.[3]

Beside their juridical testimonies in Argentina and abroad various types of testimonial practices have served to explore and reconstruct memory. The continuing role of the survivors is not to be circumscribed solely to juridical instances but also concerns a broad range of cultural practices, that not only serve to position witnesses as citizens in the official interpellation that was supposed to lead to justice, but also to affirm their role as cultural and political agents. An important number of testimonial accounts in Argentina have served a central role in the exploration of the past dictatorship and of the effects of that past in the present. Just to mention some of them, *Preso sin nombre, celda sin número* by Jacobo Timerman (1981), *Recuerdo de la muerte* by Miguel Bonasso (1984), *Historias de vida* by Hebe de Bonafini (1985), *The Little School*, by Alicia Partnoy (1986), *El vuelo* by Horacio Verbitsky (1995), *ESMA trasladados: testimonios de tres liberadas* by Ana María Martí, María Milia de Pirles and Sara Solars de Osatinsky (1995), *Ni el flaco perdón* de Dios by Juan Gelman y Mara La Madrid and more recently, *Sueños sobrevientes de una montonera* by Susana Jorgelina Ramus (2001), *Ese infierno* by Actis, Munu, Cristina Aldini, Liliana Gardella, Miriam Lewin and Elisa Tokar (2001), *Pase libre* by Claudio Tamburrini (2002), *179 días entre El Banco y el Olimpo y una vida para contar* by Celina Benfield (2003), *El tren de la Victoria* by Cristina Zuker (2003) and *Nosotras, presas políticas* by Viviana Beguan et alia (2006).

Also the role of human rights organizations is crucial in the reconstruction of social memory. In 2001, for example, the organization *Memoria abierta* (Open Memory) launched a project that gave birth to the first Oral Archive in Argentina that gathers testimonies about the last military dictatorship, including narratives of survivors of political repression. This project opened up a new space in which memories are being told, in relation to what is said and to whom –that is the audiences who could have access to the survivors' testimonies as well as to the objectives of the testimonial practice. Mario Villani, one of the *testimoniantes* who was also a witness in the Trial of the Military Junta, reminds us once again of the suspicion that surrounds the survivor and his narrative.[4] His example draws our attention to the language used by one of the defense lawyers of the military during the Trials of the Junta when he attempted to say "accused" to refer to the victim: 'Que le pregunten al acusa . . .' Y se corrige" (Ask the accused . . . And he corrects himself). Villani is pointing out that his position, as a witness in a Trial of the Junta, was still being perceived as the position of the accused—at least for the defense using the language of the prosecutor (246 A, September 14, 2002).[5] These considerations about testimonial accounts show that the status of the witness is that of the witness "in process," to borrow the concept that Julia Kristeva attributes to the subject, that is permanently being put into question, or under suspicion, but also is constantly trying to redefine himself or herself.

Testimonial literature serves as a privileged space—especially if compared with juridical testimonies—to discuss the transformations of the identity of the survivor and the way in which plural positionalities are negotiated in the past and the present: prisoner, illegal detainee, victim of torture, captive, militant, witness, citizen, and survivor. In the Argentine transition, testimonial writing concerns not only the accusation about the crimes against humanity that have been committed, but also the double movement of memory: "recuperar la historicidad de lo que se recuerda, reconociendo el sentido que en su momento tuvo para los protagonistas, a la vez que revisitar el pasado como algo cargado de sentido para el presente" (Calveiro *Política*, 11) (to recuperate the historicity of what is remembered recognizing the meaning that it had, in that moment, for the protagonists while revisiting the past as something charged with meaning for the present).

This movement from past to present and present to past concerns the reconstruction of the events that took place inside the prison or Camp, as well as the construction of the subject of memory—and also of witnessing, interpretation and narration—and the unavoidable questioning of her/his viability to remember, interpret, and reconstruct that past. In her recent approach to "the culture of memory" Beatriz Sarlo has underlined Susan Sontag's words when she states that "[p]erhaps too much value is assigned to memory, not enough to thinking" (Sontag 115). Sarlo's attempt is not to dismiss memory as a practice but to argue that the act of remembering should be intertwined with thinking and understanding because "es más importante entender que recordar, aunque para entender, sea preciso también, recordar" (26) (it is more important to understand than to remember, although for understanding it is necessary also to remember).

Two texts will serve in these pages to discuss some of the considerations that I have been posing so far: *Steps Under Water* (*Pasos bajo el agua,* 1987) by Alicia Kozameh and *A Single, Numberless Death* (*Una sola muerte numerosa,* 1997) by Nora Strejilevich.[6] Both texts, whose publication is separated by ten years, were written by victims of repression: as a former political prisoner (Kozameh) and as a former *detenida-desaparecida* (Strejilevich). The narration not only deals with an account of the witness/es but also with an interpretation of the past represented. In an attempt to make sense of the act of remembering, Kozameh and Strejilevich explore memory through its absences, lacks and incomplete zones. More than completing a lineal story of the experience of kidnapping, detention and liberation, these texts focus on the interruptions, the fragmentations and the fissures of recollection, presenting—and representing—an experience of pieces that puts knowledge—or at least complete knowledge—into question.

Testimonio, Memory, Fiction

The testimonial novel *Steps under Water,* published in Spanish in 1987 as *Pasos bajo el agua,* narrates the experience of a political prisoner while affirming and problematizing simultaneously the constitution of the testimonial subject. The text assumes the pose of fiction while claiming that fictional stories are not, cannot be completely fictional. Kozameh highlights not only the experience of the prisoner but also her life after the release and, with that, the novel explores the process in which the *former* political prisoner remembers, makes sense of, and represents the past.[7] When Nora Strejilevich (1991) studies *The Little School*, by Alicia Partnoy—one of the best known testimonial accounts, at least in the United States—she suggests that it is located in "an ambiguous zone between history and fiction" and that it actually represents "an effort to overcome the dichotomy between the two" (468). In the same way in which other testimonials seem to argue that there are fictionalized parts of any witness account, Kozameh seems to be proposing that there is no witness literature that can be completely fictional. As Kozameh herself points out in the English version of *Steps under Water*, after the publication of the book in Argentina, she was threatened by the Buenos Aires police. Therefore, the effect that the book has had as far as exposing police and military repression can be understood as the effect that testimony triggers in a juridical sense (as public accusation).[8]

The role of the witnesses in the Argentine post-dictatorship entails a process of interpretation of the past and present, and of the very notion of the act of witnessing and its reliability in the resignification of social memory. Calveiro poses this dilemma:

> Todo acto de memoria se interroga por su fidelidad, sin hallar jamás respuestas definitivas. Lejos de la idea de un archivo, que fija de una vez y para siempre su contenido, la memoria se encarga de deshacer y rehacer sin tregua aquello que evoca. Y, sin embargo, no deja de inquietarse, con razón, por la fidelidad de su recuerdo. (*Política* 11)

> (Every act of memory questions its own accuracy, without ever finding definite answers. Far from the idea of an archive that fixes, once and for ever, its contents, memory is in charge of undoing and redoing, without a truce, that which is evoked. And, nevertheless, it does not stop worrying, rightly, about the accuracy of the recollection.)

The juridical role of the witnesses in the postdictatorship was and is still linked to the notion of truth and justice and to the accusation of Human Rights violations in prisons and clandestine camps. The cultural role of the survivors—in interviews, documentaries, testimonial writing—has been, somehow different, in the sense that while acting as witnesses (the writer in Kozameh's case, the social scientist in Calveiro's case) they put into evidence the complex mechanisms of memory and forgetting, fiction and truth, and their overlapping zones. Kozameh re-signifies and interprets the past through the representation of truth as non-necessarily transparent, but on the contrary opaque and blurred. Vezzetti has also suggested that: "los acontecimientos del pasado son opacos y más aún cuando se trata de cernir su impacto en el presente" (46) (the events of the past are opaque and even more so when we are trying to measure their impact in the present). In Kozameh's text, this opacity is expressed with the fragmentation of stories, the jumps in time (as a prisoner and after the release) and most importantly with the emphasis on the difficulty to remember and on the gaps in former prisoner's recollections.

The chapters "Letters of Aubervilliers" in *Pasos bajo el agua* can be used to discuss the way in which Kozameh, in the eighties, explores the gaps, not only between past and present but also between truth and fiction. Let's remember that the novel *Steps under water* starts with Sara, the protagonist, after her release and then it goes back to the day of her detention, her first days in the Rosario Police Station and later on in Villa Devoto, her writing, the defense of her writing while in prison, and her release with "freedom under surveillance." It also includes stories of other detainees, claiming that the reconstruction of the past implies the fundamentally collective task of witnessing and, on the other hand, the unavoidable conflictive nature of collective reconstruction.[9]

The two letters between Sara and Juliana concern to the rethinking of their experience as prisoners in Rosario and in Devoto. These are letters that from their exile in Santa Barbara and Aubervilliers reflect on the life of these two and other women, and, most importantly, about the impact of those experiences after their release. The first of these two letters is Sara's letter to Juliana, also a former political prisoner. Sara is writing a novel and she asks herself (and Juliana) questions about the past, a past that remains in her present in 1984 during her pregnancy, almost six years after her release. Her experience in exile is also—and this is very clear in *259 saltos, uno inmortal* (2001)—about dealing with her experience as a former prisoner, who keeps listening to the voices of other victims of repression, and trying to make sense of that experience and, in Sara's case, writing about it, making it public. In her search for memories Sara asks many questions and even refers to past questions implying that the incompleteness of recollection is a central part of her narration: her experience as a prisoner cannot be recovered without these gaps. In this sense the exercise of memory that Kozameh proposes through Sara is about the present: a question about the remains of the past in the present. At the same time, memory cannot be fully located in the present nor in the past but precisely in the "in between": an unstable zone of contact and separation.

Sara is trying to remember one particular event of the past: the transfer from the prison of Rosario to Villa Devoto. She remembers parts of the transfer, but she needs to fill in the gaps in her story and she asks Juliana some questions about those gaps: "Who were you cuffed to?" (92), "Tell me, what was it that made us bid farewell as if we were going to die?" (96). The emphasis in the letter is on what Sara cannot remember and on the impossibility of perfect recollection; and even when memory seems posible, it might not necessarily be clear and transparent but blurred and vague. At the same time, there is an emphasis on what Sara has forgotten:

> I know we landed in Aeroparque because someone told me later on; I don't know when. But I can't, I can't get that part of the movie. I got from mid-flight to the prison trucks that transported us to Villa Devoto. The landing got cut out. What followed [. . .] also was erased." (97)

And later she adds: "[T]here are great, unbridgeable gaps" (97).[10] These gaps are pointing to the fact that the exercise of memory must inevitably go through areas that cannot be recovered. As Vezzetti suggests "no hay memoria plena ni olvido logrado sino más bien diversas formaciones que suponen un compromiso entre la memoria y el olvido" (33) (there is not complete memory nor an achieved forgetting but diverse formations that suppose a compromise of memory and forgetting). This compromise is located, for Kozameh, in the possibility of the reconstruction or "reinvention" that memory offers to the bridge between past and present, and between experience and narration. In *259 saltos, uno inmortal* (2003) Kozameh returns back to Juliana's story and to the role that the letters played in the reconstruction of the former prisoners' selves, their identity, and their memory after the release[11]:

> ¿Qué sería el pasado sin los audaces que se animan a reinventarlo? Re-inventarlo. Volver a inventar lo que ya es: una fantasía. Una mentira, una historia creada para dar alegría, diversión, a la omnipotencia de ciertos niños que nos habitan. Pero nada más. Porque, ¿qué de cualquier pasado, puede estar tan muerto que no se retome en cada gota del presente? ¿Qué puede estar tan enterrado? ¿Qué puede haberse desintegrado tanto en qué vacío? ¿Qué puede haber desaparecido hasta tal punto? (*259 Saltos*, 93)

> (What would the past be without those with the courage to reinvent it? To re-invent it. To invent again what already is: a fantasy. A lie, a story created to bring joy, amusement to the omnipotence of certain children that inhabit us. But nothing more. Because, what of any past could be so dead, that is not carried in every drop of the present? What could be so buried? What could have disintegrated so much in which void? What could have disappeared up to such extent?)

In contrast with the juridical testimonies of witnesses, Kozameh's testimonial novel explores memory as a construction and the opacity of what is remembered and forgotten while posing the impossibility of knowing the complete story as a central part of the witness' account. At the same time, the text affirms memory, with the transformations, the gaps, and the "reinventions." In this way her narrative moves away, even in the eighties, from the legal notion of testimony and the notion of truth, and it goes beyond them to explore the figure of the witness, and the expectations built around it through an unanswered question: How does one provide a clear and transparent account of what feels gray and opaque in the labor of memory? Through Sara's struggles, this testimonial novel suggests that no narration is bearing witness to the clarity of the experience recounted but to the impossibility of a complete and perfect account of the past, and to the complex process in which memories survive (or not) in the present.

Collective Memories, Suspicions, and Gaps

A Single, Numberless Death by Nora Strejilevich, a testimony of the late nineties (1997), also deals with these questions and limits, especially in relation to the difficulties of having access to a *one single* memory. The book is dedicated to "those who told me their lives far into the night and offered me the gift of stories in moments long as years" and therefore unfolds the intention of writing not only from one perspective but from numberless points of view. This text can be described as a collage of testimonies (some of them anonymous), quotes from newspapers, depositions in the *Nunca Más*, victims accounts, perpetrator's recorded words, personal stories, and fictionalized segments. The voices are collective but also fragmentary. *A Single, Numberless Death* does not attempt to represent a coherent life story but the very impossibility of recounting the experience of kidnapping and detention with anything but segments that claim to be collective—numberless—but also irrecoverable.[12] The shifting of testimonial voices and the multiple, though fragmentary and sometimes anonymous, perspectives addresses the question about the identification of those voices. Who is talking, who is remembering, who is after all composing this collage of voices? Where are we, the readers, located within the fragments? What is the effect of those segments in our own expectations of what testimonial narrative is or should be, or should accomplish?

Nunca Más, a text that does mention the first and last manes of the *testimoniantes,* also produces a fragmentation in the depositions according to the subjects being discussed in each section: detention centers, torture, anti-semitism, pregnant women, families who disappeared, among other topics. For example, Strejilevich's testimony is included in the description of the detention center "Club Atlético" with specific references to torture: "During the interrogation session I could hear the screams of my brother and his girlfriend whose voices I could make out perfectly" (*Nunca más* 145 [file 2535], Strejilevich 30). In the book published by the Commission of Investigation a multiplicity of depositions serve to "reconstruct" spaces, practices of violence, living conditions and information about the *desaparecidos*. Fragmentation, then, has a trajectory as a methodology that was used to present the information available about the Human Rights violations during the last dictatorship and therefore it serves as a paradigmatic example of "public" and official investigation. Strejilevich uses fragmentation as a strategy that affirms, at the same time, the possibility of reconstruction of truth—following the *Nunca más*—and its very impossibility, since the fragments are pointing to the incompleteness of testimonial narrative.[13]

The narrative structure of *A single, numberless death*, as I mentioned before, consists on fragments that interrupt the narrative of kidnapping and detention of Strejelivich herself. Even if we could argue that there is a main story (Strejilevich's detention) the continuity of her story is very difficult to follow: there are other voices that complete, dispute, increase and dilute her narration, so her own narration is only one among many others as the title indicates. The testimonial voice is articulated precisely through its dismantling as if the text would be reiterating the impossibility of giving a complete testimony and at the same time proposing that giving a testimony should be understood as a practice that implies confusion and disorder in its attempt to represent the multiplicity of voices capable of reconstructing the past. The text is affirming not only clear and distinct voices of the survivors, but also their polyphony.

When in "Men quick to unzip" (14–17) Strejilevich rethinks the specific violence received by women in detention camps she incorporates different testimonies that recount single stories that are also plural. This part starts with the anonymous narration of a woman who was pregnant during her detention and continues with the account of a rape and after that with a testimonial account from *Nunca Más* where another survivor bears witness to the violence received in a Clandestine Camp by a female detainee. After another anonymous testimony about a rape the narration focuses on a girl who was sexually assaulted in an elevator: "A hand gropes eagerly among the pleats of my smock, fondling, pinching, cornering me. I smell something blue. A glove covers my mouth" (16). The narration is now blurred and we cannot identify the agent of violence, as there are many of them: "During the history class I envision armies of rapists, in geography I imagine continents of flesh, mountains of fat like that belly" (16–17). And, in the following section "Good-bye cruel world" the testimonial voice continues with the narration of her own detention: "They drag me into a cell to think it over. The guard says in a soft, intimate and paternal voice, 'Calm down, sweetheart, relax'" (17). Through this fragmentation not only reading and understanding the literal stories become more difficult but also the meanings that we, as readers, can assign to all the ruptures in the narrative and all the different voices that create a polyphonic confusion. As in the introductory images of *Spoils of War* (2000), the documentary directed by David Blaustein, where the voices of the Grandmothers of Plaza de Mayo are superimposed and it is almost impossible to follow the single stories that are being narrated, it seems that the fragments in Strejilevich's text make difficult the task of recomposing the events of the past. All the witnesses have something to say. But the text is not pointing just to what needs to be said but to what remains unsaid. By rethinking the way in which these oral voices become writing, this narrative is exposing all that is lost in language. "¿Qué relato de la experiencia está en condiciones de evadir la contradicción entre la *fijeza* de la puesta en discurso y la *movilidad* de lo vivido?" (27) (What account of the experience is in conditions of evading the contradiction between the *fixity* of discourse and the *mobility* of life), asks Sarlo, pointing to the failure of representation and to the gaps that cannot be translated from the experiential to the narration. By focusing on these contradictions, Strejilevich is putting into question not only memory itself as plural and irreconcilable but also the representation of those memories through a grammar that seems insufficient to depict simultaneous voices and images, their voids and their jumps.

Voices are not just the voices of other survivors. We also have popular sayings ("Bring the knife / ring the bell / you die / you'll go to hell") (6) and protest songs ("Milicos, we have no fear / what did you do / with the ones who disappeared") (10).[14] The existence and recording of some voices is contrasted with the disappearance of other voices, as with her brother's:

> Gerardo is taking part in a relay race for first graders. The spectators are clapping. On your marks, get set, . . . go! Gerardito sprints to the front of the pack. Suddenly he stops, turns his head 180 degrees, and waves: Mama is there. He takes off again at top speed but comes in last. He burst into tears. (8)

And then:

Gerardo is being watched. He does not sleep at home. Gerardo supports violence from below and challenges violence from above. Gerardo lives in fear because he's being followed.

Gerardo reflects:

Suddenly it is clear to you: a flash of awareness that you are not forever. As if they'd casually taken a chunk out of you and then scornfully warned you, "Watch out kid," hinting that like it or not, slowly but surely, they'd continue chipping away at you until there was nothing left but ashes." (9)

The voice of her brother is incorporated into the narrative and as the voice of a *desaparecido* the claim of his juridical existence—and therefore the reconstruction of this voice—is bearing witness to the crime of his forced disappearance. This disappearance is represented with the memory of her surviving sister, also a *detenida-desaparecida*. At the beginning we read a poem: "When they stole my name / I was one I was hundreds I was thousands / I was no one." This obvious reference to her own experience is contrasted with some of the declarations of the military: starting with Emilio Massera "We shall not permit death to run rampant in Argentina" (3) or "Keep in mind that I have killed three or four people with my own hands" (4), and then going to Jorge Rafael Videla "In order for Argentina to achieve internal security, as many people as necessary will have to die" (6), and General Vilas "We conduct our operations between one and four in the morning when the subversives are sleep" (8). Her personal story gets lost again and again in the midst of official affirmations, popular songs, and the voices of those who were inside the Camp. Every time the narrative goes back to her own narrative we cannot but situate her narration within multiple and collective narrations, which are also highly conflictive because they imply the existence of contradictory memories, the effects of which explains the epigraph of the book (by Tomás Eloy Martinez): "From 1975 on, my entire country metamorphosed into a single, numberless death. At first this seemed intolerable, but later it was accepted with indifference and even relegated to oblivion."

The problematization of memory and the emphasis on its opacity have had an important place in the recent debates about memory in Argentina, where it has been underlined that recollection changes with time and with the cultural interpretation that accompanies the act of remembering. Vezzetti reminds us of a chilling example for the Argentine paradigm using a study undertaken by Guillermo O'Donnell. In the first years of the military regime O'Donnell interviewed a number of people who claimed to be in support of the military government. The interviewees used the dichotomy "order/subversion" to justify the coup and the repressive actions of the Junta. During the first years of democracy O'Donnell interviewed the same people and asked them to talk about the opinion that they had about the military regime during the dictatorship. The results were very different: the answers emphasized the repudiation of the Junta, and the interviewees denied to have justified the military regime in the past while arguing that they had rejected it during that time (Vezzetti 45). What we have here, Vezzetti suggests, is a new cultural interpretation that emerges with the accusations of human rights violations during the regime:

> Lo que me interesa—agrega Vezzetti—en todo caso es reconocer que esas formas de acomodar el pasado al presente constituyen el trabajo mismo de la memoria, en la medida en que se admita que la memoria es una construcción siempre retroactiva. (46)
>
> (What interests me here—Vezzetti adds—in any case, is to recognize that these ways of accommodating the past in the present constitute the very labor of memory, as long as one admits that memory is a construction that is always retroactive.)

The change in the understanding of Human Rights abuses gives shape to the repudiation of the Junta that the interviewees emphatically underlined in the eighties, once the mandatory understanding of the "order" linked to the military regime was displaced by the resignification of what that "order" really meant as a practice of kidnapping, torture, illegal detention and so forth. Nevertheless, it would be relevant to ask how much of that interpretation given to O'Donnell during the regime remains, unconsciously hidden, in the answer provided in the posdictatorship. This question would lead to rethinking the role of the witnesses and to understand it within the multiple—and conflictive—interpretations that surround survivors of military repression. I want to refer to two aspects that have undermined witnesses' accounts: First, the question about the truth of testimonial accounts and the reliability of the witnesses, and second, the depolitization of the witness as the condition of his/her official interpellation as a citizen in the Argentine redemocratization process.

Testimonio and Truth

In a now classic approach to testimony and witnessing in relation to the Holocaust, Dori Laub points out that it is important to remember the main objective of each testimonial narrative, that is, what it is that a certain narrative is testifying to (Felman and Laub 60). Laub is rethinking the discussion that a group of historians, psychoanalysts, and artists had about the discrepancies that one particular testimony seemed to show with narratives of other witnesses. This testimony "in trial" was considered "suspicious" and it was not judged a reliable account. Laub uses this discussion to suggest that this particular debate about the reliability of testimonial narratives was distorting testimonial accounts by condensing the truth in details that, after all, could be forgettable because forgetting them did not damage in the least the experience to which the survivor wanted to bear witness. Laub's approach—that has been recently discussed in the context of the post-Stoll debate on testimonial literature—is about having an understanding of testimony more concerned with the survivor than with the expectation of narrative authority. "[L]a historia nunca podrá contarse del todo y nunca tendrá un cierre, porque todas las posiciones no pueden ser recorridas y tampoco su acumulación resulta en una totalidad" (54–55) (The whole story cannot be told and will never have a closure because all the positions cannot be covered nor their accumulation results in a totality) says Sarlo in her reflections about the role of memory in the Argentine postdictatorship, having in mind the relationship between testimonial accounts and History, and proposing that a dialogue between the two can only be possible with the recognition of its incompleteness. When discussing the testimony of Holocaust survivors, Giorgio Agamben argues, that one must also consider its "lacunae":

> At a certain point, it becomes clear that testimony contained as its core an essential lacuna; in other words, the survivors bore witness to something it is impossible to bear witness to. As a consequence, commenting on survivor's testimony necessarily meant interrogating this lacuna or, more precisely, attempting to listen to it. (12)

Even if the survivor has an epistemological privilege (knowing what happened) this privilege implies a lack: "No one has told the destiny of the common prisoner since it was not materially possible for him to survive"(33). Agamben quotes Lyotard to affirm a sort of impossibility in the very act of bearing witness:

To "have really seen with his own eyes" a gas chamber would be the condition which gives one authority to say that it exists and to persuade the unbeliever. Yet it is still necessary to prove that the gas chamber was used to kill at the time it was seen. The only acceptable proof that it was used to kill is that one died from it. But if one is dead, one cannot testify that it is on account of the gas chamber." (Lyotard 3, in Agamben 35)

Testimonial writing is not, cannot be, a complete narration. But even with the exploration of this impossibility, texts like *Steps under Water* and *One Single, Numberless Death* are presenting fragments, bits and pieces of what is not possible to recuperate, those "traces of the real" to borrow René Jara's expression to refer to the images that testimonials narrate: "más que una interpretacion de la realidad esta imagen es ella misma, una huella de lo real, de esa historia que, en cuanto tal, es inexpresable" (2) (More than an interpretation of reality that image is itself a trace of the real, of that story that cannot be expressed as such). At the same time, those traces call for an interpretation that attempt to make sense of those same lacunae that the narratives are exposing.

Citizenship and Depolitization

The figure of the disappeared has had a central function in the reconstruction of the very meaning of democracy after 1983. Cultural redemocratization was linked to the respect of human rights and was established around the figure of the disappeared as victim, as Vezzetti suggests when he proposes: "[E]n este nuevo estatuto de la memoria, lo primero no eran los héroes sino las víctimas y la enormidad de los crímenes" (30) (In this new statute of memory, the priority was given not to the heroes but to the victims and to the immensity of the crimes). In this context, are the survivors of Camps and political imprisonment during the last dictatorship being silenced or marginalized? How and where are the meanings attached to the *detenidos-desaparecidos* articulated? What does survivor or *desaparecido* mean in the Argentine cultural democratization? It is not uncommon for the survivors to state that they were *desaparecidos* during their detention in Concentration Camps—that also call themselves "detainee-disappeared" at least in the name of the organization *Asociación detenidos-desaparecidos*. The former detainee Graciela Daleo uses, nevertheless, the name *aparecidos* (appeared) in an attempt to both detach and attach the figure of the survivors to the figures of the *desaparecidos* and also to resignify the figure of the survivors through their militancy:

Los *aparecidos* somos portadores de la memoria del horror. Y eso no es grato. También somos—como tantos otros que sobrevivieron, aun sin haber pasado por campos de concentración—portadores del recuerdo y sobre todo de una práctica real de militancia, compormiso y lucha que protagonizó un vasto sector de la sociedad argentina. (Vezzetti 209, emphasis mine)

(The *aparecidos* are the bearers of the memory of horror. And that is not gratifying. We are also—as many of those who survived, even without having being held in concentration camps—the bearers of the recollection and above all of a real practice of militancy, commitment and struggle that had as protagonists to vast sector of the society.)

These parentheses built around the *aparecidos* are, nevertheless, surrounded by an undeniable active role that survivors of prisons and clandestine detention camps have had in narrating their experiences in human rights' organizations, trials, commissions of investigation, literary texts, documentaries, and interviews. In particular, in the first decade of the democratic transition, the central role of the survivors in the National Commission for Investigation (CONADEP) and in the Trial of the Military Junta that took place in 1985 is marked by a process of de-politization that Vezzetti analyzes as the emptiness of meaning produced by the understanding of the *desaparecido* as a "purified victim" (119). This void of signification of the term "*disappeared*" is challenged, in the late nineties, by the three volumes of *La voluntad* by Martín Caparrós and Eduardo Anguita (1997, 1998) and their attempt to reconstruct the figure of the *militant* in the 1960s and 1970s.

Nevertheless, during the eighties, the figure of the disappeared, that served to resignify democratic practice in accordance with the respect of human rights, also marks the definition of citizenship deprived of the meaning of militancy, at least as it was understood during the years that preceded the last military regime. In part due to the lack of recording of the victim's political affiliation in the information gathered by the Commission of Investigation and therefore due to the de-politization of the figure of the detainee-disappeared, the first decade of the democratization process is characterized by an emphasis on the victim, which served in part to silence the former detainees and to limit their narration (of the portion of the account that was to be heard) to the story of their victimization (Vezzetti 119). The figure of the disappeared was then linked to those who were killed, especially if "they entered in the category of the innocents of all militancy" (119). This understanding, which characterizes the first decade of redemocratization differs from, for example, the approach that Calveiro proposes in the late nineties (1998) where she states that the majority of the detainees in Concentration Camps where part of a political organization.

One of the main points in Vezzetti's argument is precisely to show the fissures that are constitutive to social memory in Argentina, where the role of the State in the truth and justice process that starts with the appointment of the Commission is accompanied by a theory that plays an important role in the process of signification of the *desaparecido*. Vezzetti argues that by equating the armed struggle and the military, the "theory of the two demons" (*teoría de los dos demonios*) invokes the figure of the disappeared as deprived of political identity. It is this de-politized figure the protagonist of the resignification of democracy through human rights in the Argentine postdictatorship. Even though the gesture was about creating a landmark in the construction of democracy, "the will of instituting an end to political violence and clandestine action" created a social memory of the past that displaced those memories that did include the popular participation that started in 1960s (121, 128).

Both Calveiro and Vezzetti refer to the depolitization of the victim as a betrayal: "Cuando la memoria de un pasado cuyo sentido fue eminentemente político se construye como memoria individual y privada, recupera este aspecto, pero de alguna manera traiciona por lo menos en parte el sentido de lo que fue" (*Política* 16) (When the memory of a past which sense was predominantly political is constituted as a individual and private memory, it recuperates this aspect but it somehow betrays at least in part the meaning of what it was). The operation is therefore double: it seems to be insufficient the idea of finding a place for the past in the present without the other movement that implies to build a bridge, Calveiro argues, between two different ways of looking relations: that of the sixties and seventies and that of the present (*Política* 16).

Sarlo also proposes to rethink the relationship between the subject of the narration (and the experience) and the listeners, especially from another generations. As I mentioned before, Sarlo underlines the practice of understanding the past, and not only exposing it. Following Walter Benjamin, she reminds us of the shock that triggers the silence around traumatic experiences but also—and here she quotes Jean Pierre Le Goff—its nontransferable nature: "los jóvenes pertenecen a una dimensión del presente donde las creencias de sus padres se revelan inútiles" (36) ("young people belong to a dimension of the present where the beliefs of their parents seem useless"). The practice of memory, then, could not only be about attempting to understand an experience of the past through the significational marks *of the present* but also about going back and attempting to understand the meaning of the past in relation to the cultural marks that gave meaning to those experiences *in the past*. Once again, the idea of the "unbridgeable gaps" comes to surface, as well as the will to reconstruct a past that, as Kozameh proposes, is not, cannot be, completely dead but "carried in every drop of the present."

Steps under Water and *A Single, Numberless Death* as many other testimonial narratives in the redemocratization period and the recent debates about memory and witnessing deal with "reinventing" the past and, consequently, the present, as Kozameh herself suggests in *259 saltos*. The re-invention of the narratives of the witnesses after thirty years of the military coup has to do precisely with the way in which the present interrogates those parentheses of the past that can no longer be ignored and with the way in which narratives, even testimonial narratives, are being transformed in an attempt to establish a dialogue with the interpretations that, in the present, will look at the past. The role of the survivors continues to redefine itself and to explore its significance, its limits and the new areas of a social memory that is constantly re-actualizing recollections and meanings. New voices, sometimes discordant, are added to former narrations and transform them, put them into question, and interrogate those parentheses and gaps from different places. The practice of re-narrating the past awakens new interpretations that add different lights and shades to the construction of collective memory. In this context, memory should be understood –and here I am borrowing again Calveiro's image—not as a puzzle where all the pieces match exactly and make a perfect picture of the past but as a kaleidoscope, where the pieces form different figures, different representations of a past that cannot be completely restored, and where the gaps as constitutive parts of those representations are pointing not only to what the survivors cannot bear witness of, but also to the parentheses that contribute to the depolitization of the figure of the survivors, their experiences, their involvement and their claim to continue to be agents of democratization and acting witnesses of the past and the present.

Notes

1. I thank the American Philosophical Society for the Franklin Research Grant that allowed me to conduct research in Argentina during the summer of 2006, and especially to get access to the Oral Archive gathered by the organization *Memoria Abierta*.
2. All translations of texts quoted from Spanish are mine, except indicated otherwise.
3. The *New York Times*, for example, states "Impunity Gone, Trials begin" referring to the trial of the former chief the Buenos Aires police charged with "illegal arrest, torture and murder in eight cases" (Friday, June 30, 2006). The Organization Human

Rights Watch refers to this trial as the "end of 20 years of impunity" (hrw.org/English/docs/2006/06/19/argent13580.htm)
4. Mario Villani was kidnapped in 1977 and held captive until 1981. He was held in five detention camps: El Olimpo, Malvinas, El Atlético, El Banco and ESMA.
5. To see a list of the interviews of the Oral Archive, see http://www.memoriaabierta.org.ar
6. Alicia Kozameh was kidnapped in 1975, before the military coup but when the methodology of the paramilitary forces was already in place. She was a political prisoner first in el Sótano in Rosario and then in Villa Devoto in Buenos Aires, until 1978. Nora Strejilevich was kidnapped in 1977 and held captive in the clandestine center "El Atlético." She was liberated five days after her kidnapping. Her testimony to the National Commission about the Disappearance of Persons, CONADEP (file 2535) can be read in *Nunca Más*.
7. The preface refers to Kozameh's detention and imprisonment, establishing, from the very first pages, the connections between experience and writing.
8. It is relevant to remember that the book was published in 1987, that is two years after the Trials to the Military Junta, when the beginning of the impunity laws were taking place, in part due to military rebellions and coup d'etat threats. *Pasos bajo el agua* not only invokes the urgency related to the narration of political repression but also the path that testimonial writing takes in Argentina in the context of impunity: the claim for a justice that already began to fade. As a narration of urgency, *Pasos bajo el agua* deals with "a problem of repression, poverty, subalternity, imprisonment, struggle of survival, and so on, implicated in the act of narration itself" as John Beverley proposes when he outlines one of the definitions for *testimonio* (26). Even if *Pasos bajo el agua* is a novel, the testimonial dimension of the text and the urgency of the narration cannot be overlooked.
9. Barbara Harlow uses the expression "literature of resistance" to refer to the literature written by political detainees, a resistance that has to do not only with the logic of the prison but also with the logic of autobiography, through the affirmation of a collective first person. We should consider also the resistance that these texts offer to the expectation that collective reconstructions of the past should be a single consensual memory. Through these two fictional characters (Juliana, Sara), Kozameh refers to some of the survivors positions in relation to their experiences as political prisoners and the violence that surrounded that experience: Sara wants to remember and wants to make public her story through her writing. Juliana—and this is mainly developed in *259 saltos, uno immortal*—takes the conscious decision to forget. Recognizing memory as conflictive involves that even if the affirmation of the collective implies, as Beverley suggests, a connection between the individual subject and "a group or class situation marked by marginalization, oppression, and struggle" (35), it also invokes, paradoxically the existence of different voices that are oftentimes discordant.
10. In *Nosotras, Presas políticas,* a recent compilation of testimonial accounts of female political prisoners in Argentina, Kozameh narrates her transfer from Rosario to Villa

Devoto with emphasis on the facts of the transfer and not on the gaps of the recollection (78). Again I want to underline that the questioning of memory and the acceptance of what she calls "unbridgeable gaps" does not erode the reliability of the witness account. On the contrary it affirms that the narration of facts can serve to the prosecution of repressors or to reconstruct the conditions of life and the violations of human rights suffered as by political prisoner but is never a complete narration.

11. *259 leaps* can be read as a continuation of *Steps under water* (the accounts of imprisonment and liberation). Now the emphasis is placed on the narration of the exile in U.S. and Mexico and the return back to Argentina in 1984, with the advent of the democratic rule).

12. In her review of the text, Ileana Rodríguez states: "[N]o hay uno singular en este relato sino uno colectivo, el nosotros de esa sola muerte, esa sola tortura, esa sola pena y ese solo afecto, uno solo todo" (203) ("There is not a singular one in this story but a collective one, the we of this single death, this single torture, this single pain and this single love, all of them one single").

13. Strejilevich's doctoral dissertation *Literatura testimonial en Chile, Uruguay y Argentina 1970–1990* (University of British Columbia, 1991)—and later her book *El arte de no olvidar: literature testimonial en Chile, Argentina y Uruguay entre los 80 y 90* (Buenos Aires: Catálogos, 2006) deal with testimonial writing in the Southern Cone and discuss most of the theories and debates about *testimonio*. Strejilevich's theoretical approach to testimonial narrative underlines that *testimonio* is a hybrid genre that blurs the frontiers among anthropology, literature, journalism, and history (1991, 17) and where "the search for truth undertaken by the *testimonialista* inspired in the trust of other (journalist, reader) is rather a joint search for truth by means of a tacit dialog between witness and listener" (17).

14. Even though I am quoting from the English version, I will also use the Spanish edition for these quotes: "Corto mano / corto fierro," "Pisa pisuela color de ciruela" and "Milicos, muy mal paridos / que es lo que han hecho con los desaparecidos."

Works Cited

Agamben, Giorgio. *Remnants of Auschwitz: The Witness and the Archive*. New York: Zone Books, 2000.

Beguan, Viviana, et al. *Nosotras, presas políticas: obra colectiva de 112 prisioneras políticas entre 1974 y 1983*. Buenos Aires: Nuestra América, 2006.

Beverley, John. "The Margin at the Center: On Testimonio (testimonial narrative)." *The Real Thing: Testimonial Discourse and Latin America*. Ed. Georg Gugelberger. Durham: Duke University Press, 1996.

Calveiro, Pilar. *Política y/o violencia: una aproximación a la guerrilla de los años setenta*. Buenos Aires: Norma, 2005.

———. *Poder y desaparición: los campos de concentración en Argentina.* Buenos Aires: Colihe, 1998.
Caparrós, Martín, and Eduardo Anguita, eds. *La voluntad: Una historia de la militancia revolucionaria en Argentina.* Buenos Aires: Norma, 1998.
Felman, Shoshanna, and Dori Laub. *Testimony: Crises of Witnessing in Literature, Psychoanalysis and History.* New York: Routledge, 1991.
Gelman, Juan, and Mara La Madrid. *Ni el flaco perdón de Dios: Hijos de desaparecidos.* Buenos Aires: Planeta, 1997.
Halbwachs, Maurice. *On Collective Memory.* New York: Harper &Row, 1980.
Harlow, Barbara. *Barred: Women, Writing, and Political Detention.* Hannover and London: Wesleyan University Press/University Press of New England, 1992.
———. *Resistance Literature.* New York: Methuen, 1987.
Jara, René. "Prólogo." *Testimonio y literatura.* Ed. René Jara and Hernán Vidal. Minneapolis: Institute for the Study of Ideologies and Literature, 1986.
Jelin, Elizabeth. *State Repression and the Labors of Memory.* Minneapolis: University of Minnesota Press, 2003.
Kozameh, Alicia. *259 saltos, uno inmortal.* Unquillo, Córdoba: Narvaja, 2001.
———. *Steps under Water.* Berkeley: University of California Press, 1996.
———. *Pasos bajo el agua.* Buenos Aires: Contrapunto, 1987.
Lyotard, Jean Fancois. *The Differend: Phrases in Dispute.* Minneapolis: University of Minnesota Press, 1988.
Nunca más: The report of the Argentine National Commission on the Disappeared. New York: Farrar, Straus, Giroux, 1986.
Pollak, Michael. "Memória, Esquecimento, Silencio." *Estudos Históricos* 2 (1989): 3–15.
Rodríguez, Ileana. "Quedarme conmigo: No dejarme sola ni por casualidad. Memoria, Historia." Rev. of Nora Strejilevich. *Una sola muerte numerosa. Letras Femeninas* Vol. 24. No. 1–2 (Spring-Fall 1998): 203–6.
Sarlo, Beatriz. *Tiempo pasado. Cultura de la memoria y giro subjetivo.* Buenos Aires: Siglo XXI Editores, 2005.
Sontag, Susan. *Regarding the Pain of Others.* New York: Farrar, Straus, Giroux, 2003.
Strejilevich, Nora. *A Single, Numberless Death.* Charlottesville and London: University of Virginia Press, 2002.
———. *Una sola muerte numerosa.* Miami: North-South Center Press, 1997.
———. *Literatura testimonial en Chile, Uruguay y Argentina 1970–1990.* Dissertation. University of British Columbia, 1991.
Todorov, Tzvetan. *Facing the Extreme: Moral Life in Concentration Camps.* New York: Metropolitan Books, 1996.
Tompkins, Cynthia. "Pasos bajo el agua y 'Bosquejo de alturas' de Alicia Kozameh: Tortura, resistencia y secuelas." *Chasqui* 27:1 (1998): 58–69.
Vezzetti, Hugo. *Pasado y Presente: Guerra, dictadura y sociedad en la Argentina.* Buenos Aires: Siglo Veintiuno Editores, 2002.

◆ **6**

Tejanos: The Uruguayan Transition Beyond

Gustavo A. Remedi

When I was invited to partake in this collection of essays about Post-Authoritarian Spain and the Southern Cone, the first thing that came to mind was how far behind us "the authoritarian period" was in so many respects, and even the post-authoritarian one, often referred to as the "transition to democracy." Indeed, in Uruguay—as in much of South America—this transition, which might better be called a period of return to, or restoration of, the democratic institutions and practices that existed prior to the *coup d'etat* of 1973, took place between 1980 and 1985, that is, more than 20 years ago.

Instead, today, we find ourselves in the midst of two other kinds of transitions: First, a transition into a dramatically transformed society and culture, in the aftermath of the financial collapse of 2002, one of the results of three decades of Neoliberal reforms. Second, a transition beyond Neoliberalism, in the form of an experimentation with a kind of democratic reformist socialism—a re-foundation of the Welfare State upon new basis—as a result of the rising hegemony of the vernacular Left from 1989 onwards.

The Broad Front—the Leftist coalition formed in 1971 which was harshly persecuted and repressed during the military dictatorship—succeeded in breaking up the two party de facto monopoly, and obtained its first victory in the municipal elections of 1989. As a result of four consecutive electoral victories, the Broad Front has been governing Montevideo since that time. More importantly, in 2004 the Broad Front also gained control of the national government, the majority of seats in parliament, as well as control of the governments in the main provinces—or departments.

In order not to get lost in an excessively abstract discussion devoid of texture, and to better capture key social and cultural facets of these various transitions, what I intend here is to discuss this historical period from the perspective of the local, and from the viewpoint of the play *Tejanos* (2006), a collective creation of the Community Theater Group[1] of the Vidplan Cultural Center of La Teja, under the direction of Enrique Permuy (of the company and school *Polizón Teatro*)[2]; that is, *their* viewpoint, albeit mediated, and hence, partially distorted, by my *own* depiction and interpretation of it.

Vidplan is the name of a glass factory located in La Teja that, like many factories, closed down[3] due to the so-called "free market" (or Neoliberal) reforms and policies of the Uruguayan economy. In 2005, Viplan's owner offered the empty factory to the community for use as a cultural center. Today, the Vidplan Cultural Center (CE.CU.VI.) is run by Gilda Gutiérrez and other dedicated social, political and cultural activists in the neighborhood.

La Teja (also called Pueblo Victoria) is an emblematic working class neighborhood in the northwest of Montevideo well known for its leftist leanings, high degree of social and political organization, activism, and wealth of "typically" Montevidean cultural institutions. Among the more outstanding of these are: the carnival troupes *Diablos Verdes* and *La Reina de la Teja*, the *hip hop* band *La Teja Pride,* the soccer team *Progreso Athletic Club*, the *policlínica* of CASMU, the club *Arbolito*, the *El Puente* community radio station; and on a somewhat different level, the local newspaper *El Tejano*, the *comparsa Zumbaé*, the various local *boliches* (or bars) of La Teja, where people convene, converse and organize. It is worth adding that President Tabaré Vázquez himself was born and raised in La Teja, and actively participated in many of its social and cultural clubs. He was, in fact, president of *Progreso* (founded in the emblematic year of 1917), when it obtained the Uruguayan cup in 1989 —that is, the very same year Vázquez became the first Socialist Mayor of Montevideo.

It is my hope that a discussion of, and about *Tejanos* will give us some insight into the nature of the aforementioned transitions—social, economic, political, cultural—and of the way common citizens experience and conceptualize the social dilemmas and challenges related to them. What are the themes and issues that have become more pressing in their minds? What symbolic and discursive responses have people devised to represent and make sense of their lives, and to overcome their anxieties, hesitations, and fears? How do they frame their assessments of reality, dreams, actions, and life plans?

This decision to approach the Uruguayan cultural transition from the perspective of an experience of community theater taking place in a working class neighborhood carries with it another underlying premise: a belief that the established theater, largely a middle class cultural institution, has failed to represent, reach, or engage with the severely fragmented social and cultural reality of post-2002 Uruguay.

By the crisis of 2002, I refer to the commercial, industrial and financial collapse that came to a head after three decades of the Neoliberal developmental model, first, by the military dictatorship, and later, by the four elected governments that followed it. In the case of Uruguay, with few exceptions, Neoliberalism failed to privatize the public enterprises (as people mobilized against it), but succeeded in dismantling the Welfare State. It also encouraged short-term financial speculation, the export of raw materials (products with no or little value added), and the consumption of manufactured goods and services from abroad. The inability to capitalize on the national economy resulted in indebtedness and financial dependence. The servicing of the debt, in turn, resulted in a dramatic reduction of public investment and social spending. This combination of factors led, in the end, to de-industrialization, unemployment, and a dramatic reduction in income (direct and indirect), and in the standard of life of the popular classes. The crisis of 2002—same as the one in Argentina in 2001—altered the very structure of society and culture, and it has since come to symbolize the failure of the Neoliberal developmental model. It ushered in an impoverished, dismembered and polarized national culture composed of five very distinct fragments: the diminished and weakened middle and working classes, the ever-growing populations of the fast proliferating slums (called *asentamientos*), the affluent classes that live in luxury in the costal residential areas, the rural population, and the Uruguayans in exile.

Tejanos is but one example of a new kind of socially engaged theater that I have elsewhere termed "frontier theater"[4] and that has led me into a larger fieldwork research project.[5] This theater of the (new) frontier is heir to the best tradition of the socially and politically committed "independent theater" of the twentieth century. Unlike the latter, however, it travels and brings the opportunity to do theater together to where people live and work—other cultural worlds—thus bringing separate and distant social and cultural realities together—realities that do not enter in contact otherwise.[6] By making use of the spatial and formal attributes and conventions of the art of theater it facilitates a true encounter, dialogue, and cultural exchanges between different subcultures and people with very different backgrounds, ideas, aesthetics, which in turn engender new social subjectivities and forms of agency. Indeed, this is possible when locals become actors and partake in the creative process, actors and spectators face each other in person, there is a special sense of conviviality and camaraderie that is required by the fact that the illusion is being performed in real time/space, all parts are invested and engaged in the performance with all their senses, and so on. Last but not least, this alternative form of theater is able to capture and to represent on stage new social and national realities and problems that might be otherwise invisible in the context of other cultural practices.

After briefly summarizing the premise and plot of *Tejanos*, I will then discuss a number of themes put forward by this play: 1) the transformation of Uruguay from a society of immigrants into one of emigrants; 2) the social need to revise and rewrite history, and to cultivate the social and political memory of La Teja; and 3) the representation of the recent past and the present, focusing on both, what this play does bring to the fore—for instance, the problem of exile—, as well as what it does not —that is, the many new and interesting episodes and debates that have become equally central in our recent past. The description and discussion of the play's text and its actual performance[7] will help us to take a closer look at the social context—the transitions referred to above—and the interpretative keys and culturally determined connotations that make the play meaningful and moving for the community of participants, as creators, performers, or spectators.

* * *

The homemade announcement placed at Carlos María Ramírez Ave. invited the public to attend the *avant premiere* of *Tejanos* on Saturday, October 28, 2006, at 8 p.m., at the intersection of Real St. and José Mármol St., where CE.CU. VI. is located. It promised to be a "Great street spectacle," with more than 35 artists, and free and open to the public, and revolving around "The history of the neighborhood." I attended some of the rehearsals, but missed the *avant premiere*. Instead, I attended the *premiere* that took place the following Saturday, November 4th , half a block from the Plaza 25 de Mayo, at the very heart of La Teja.

Inviting as it may be for the local public, the advertisement—not surprisingly—was somehow misleading, for *Tejanos* did not—and logically, could not—tell the whole history of La Teja (although it tells one story), nor is it only about it.

Tejanos is a one-act play divided in roughly ten scenes, some of them further subdivided or consisting of parallel representations. Far from being formally naive or realistic in conception and treatment, *Tejanos* is a fast-moving play of relative complexity and ambition. Borrowing from a varied range of sources, codes and archives—theater, music, carnival, dance, social and political theatricalities, etc.—it attempts to handle various theatrical languages and forms, various historical periods and geographical locations, as well as scenes represented at various locations: up and down the street, on the main frontal stage, on both sides of the stage, in the middle of the street and amidst the public.

While cinematic and avant-gardist at times (for example, in terms of the assembling and editing of the scenes), the spectacle never retreats from the rules of "street theater"—which shares many features with the circus, the clown style, or the one-time and fleeting nature of performance—and of "community theater"—created and performed by amateur actors with an interest in theater (and other kinds of community artistic activities), but also with a social and political motivation and goal in mind.

The CE.CU.VI. Community Theater Group takes advantage of the many possibilities offered by street theater in terms of visibility, space, and movement, and also of the fact that the community is mobilized and interested in the spectacle. Yet, it is also aware that it needs to provide occasions for the broader public to engage and actively participate in the action, that it needs to speak the many-tongued and multi-form language of the popular, and that it needs to be agile, clear, and mesmerizing (for example, in terms of characterization, presentation of themes and conflicts, structure) in order to captivate and maintain the attention of a heterogeneous, timidly curious, but largely unaccustomed and undisciplined public.

The themes, characters, and scenes as well as the overall play were conceived and developed collectively under the guidance of Enrique Permuy, although some of these elements were based on the ideas of Xosé Enríquez, in consultation with local historian Carlos Pilo. It includes a myriad of characters, mostly archetypical and anonymous, requiring the participation of dozens of actors as well as of the public itself. Its representation requires a large and fluid space—a street, a plaza—where several stages or performing stations can be placed, enabling movement of both the characters and the public back and forth in between stations and performances.

The plot of *Tejanos* can be summed up as follows: a young man presently in exile in Hamburg (on a small improvised stage at the right side of the main stage) communicates with his mother back home, on the opposite side of the world—standing at street level, but on the opposite side of the stage (Scene II). He wishes to learn more of the history of his neighborhood because his new friends—including other immigrants—ask about him and his story, and he does not know enough about it. This makes him uncomfortable and miserable, something which itself is worthy of further exploration.

In Scene III another character, "Lafone," appears on the central frontal stage, accompanied by "His Assistant," much in the manner of carnivalesque theater, that is, each speaking to the public frontally, standing in front of their corresponding microphone. This triggers a historical narrative or flashback that recounts the story of the foundation of the neighborhood by Samuel Fisher Lafone, a local businessman born in England and who was, among many other things, owner of a highly profitable meat processing plant (or *saladero*) that functioned in the 1840s at the north shore of the Bay of Montevideo, and that employed mainly Afro-Uruguayan slaves and former slaves. To house the families that lived off this and other economic activities in the zone, Lafone developed Pueblo Victoria, presumably named after Queen Victoria. For this reason—or perhaps, because of having forgotten this—one of La Teja's main plazas carries Lafone's name and celebrates his memory.

In Scene IV, the simultaneous representation of parts of "La pobre gente" (1904), a two-act comedy by Florencio Sánchez, and of "Mustafá," a piece of *grotesco criollo* by Armando Discépolo and Rafael José De Rosa, which premiered in 1921, and of "Don Chicho," a *sainete* by Alberto Novión, which debuted in 1933, is the means used to represent the story of the arrival of a large number of immigrants that populated La Teja (mainly from Southern and Central Europe, from the Near East, and also from the countryside), between the second half of the nineteenth century and up to the 1930s. These acts also point to the dreams, problems and miseries of the *conventillo* (tenements) and of life in the working class quarters of the city.

The acts are performed in parallel in three different locations along the street turned into temporary stages by means of the deployment of the characters and the acting, some illumination, and the use of a minimum amount of objects and furniture—a table, a broom, a chair, little else.

This process of immigration and the subsequent urbanization and industrialization of peripheral neighborhoods such as La Teja were associated to a number of economic activities and industries: the port activity, the slaughterhouses, the meat processing plants (first the *saladeros*, and later the *frigoríficos*), the *curtiembres* (hide processing plants), the roof tiles (*tejas*) factories, the construction of houses, the *canteras de piedra* (stone-cutting) that provided the stones for building the Port of Montevideo, the railroad, the *lavaderos*, the soap-factory BAO, the state-owned oil refinery ANCAP inaugurated in 1934, and more.

Scene V takes us back to the mid-nineteenth century and it shows a different face of Lafone. Now playing the part of the archetypical and timeless bourgeois entrepreneur, he prides himself in bringing industry and "progress" to the town, yet he also warns that he does not want workers to create any problems. The sound of drums—of *a comparsa de candombe*—can be heard *in crescendo*, metonymically pointing to the mobilization of the slaves, and a more contemporary sentiment of working class mobilization. His assistant informs him that while there were "minor inconveniences," the situation was "under control."

Scene VI, bring us back to the "modern times." Amidst the sounds of "the siren of ANCAP" and "the whistle of BAO," both signaling the beginning of the working day, hiring officials from various factories loudly advertise the many job opportunities awaiting the people who wish to work, the money they could earn, and all they could buy as a consequence. At last, the promised progress and days of abundance had arrived to La Teja, or so it seemed.

Moments later, a long line of workers slowly appear from behind the main stage and move toward the middle of the street. Surrounded by the public, they move absent-mindedly and mechanically to the beat of a loud drum giving shape to an imaginary oval assembly line. Some wear white masks, vaguely resembling somber human facial features; others simply carry the masks in their hands, as if trying to convey the dehumanizing nature of their work. The scene is markedly expressionistic, and also reminiscent of such film classics like Fritz Lang's *Metropolis* and Charles Chaplin's *Modern Times*.

They only stop when a young worker—now treated in a more realistic or even *agit-prop* manner—stands on top of an oil container and reenacts a fragment of a pro-union speech that denounces their long days, low pay and exploitative working conditions. The scene reenacts the actual speech delivered during the strike of the stone factory of La Teja of 1901 registered by a chronicle of the Anarchist newspaper *Tribuna Libertaria*. The workers then march silently with their red handkerchiefs in their fists up high.

But the epic mood then rapidly evolves and leads to a lighter and more comic parenthesis or *entremés*. As the story of *Tejanos* proceeds, the long days and weeks of alienating work find their counterpart in the recreational activities such as card games, cock fights, music, dance that also took place in the neighborhood's streets and canteens.

Scene VII also includes a joyful, sexy and comical act of *varieté* or cabaret theater performed by "the flowers" of the newly opened brothel—"Violet," "Daisy," "Jazmin," "Rose" and "Lily"—under the direction of the "Matrona." Once again, the show draws vaguely from contemporary carnivalesque theatrical practices such as the vernacular *revista*, followed by an act of tango music and dance—a typical scene of the *orilla*—which is violently interrupted by a knife fight between *cafishios* and *compadritos*—*por cosas de mujeres*.

Up the street—figuratively and literally—Scene VIII recreates other facets of everyday life in the barrio: children playing in the street, and the all too common *vecinas* that sweep the side walks, enjoy gossiping, and who, like the two men in the preceding act, also end up arguing and fighting. These two gendered instances of broken harmony are punctuated by yet another instance of reunion, camaraderie and joy, when a wedding banquet is celebrated down the street to the sound of a joyful and sensuous *cumbia*, one of the rhythms most preferred by the popular classes. As the celebration fades away, in a premonition typical of tragedy, the pregnant bride tells the baby in her belly that is going to be born amidst of "a storm" and "darkness."

In a rather compact fashion, scene IX attempts to represent a number of diverse processes: the political polarization and social mobilization of the sixties and early seventies, the increasingly authoritarian and repressive behavior of the elected governments of Jorge Pacheco Areco and Juan María Bordaberry, and the arrival of the dictatorship in 1973. While the former are represented by a faceless multitude of small acts of disobedience, sabotage, and graffiti painting, the latter is embodied by the appearance on stage of an impeccably uniformed general. While we hear the actual recording of the speech of General Gregorio Álvarez on the 10th anniversary of the *coup d'etat*, the sinister character slowly descends from the stage and walks up the street parting the public in two halves in an attitude of confident defiance and vigilance.

The story ends abruptly in Scene X, which opens with a now legendary act of pan beating (or *caceroleada*) as a form of a massive disapproval and protest against the dictatorship and call for a return to democracy.

This is followed by the triumphant and exuberant appearance on stage of a *murga*, by now an established symbol of the triumph and coronation of the people. As the lyrics of the murga *La Reina de La Teja* goes: "*murga del pueblo reina / si reina el pueblo / que es su esperanza.*" (Murga, the people's queen / if the people reigns / which it is hope). Borrowing from this other form of carnivalesque theater, *Tejanos* ends with a farewell song (or *Retirada*) written by Martín Gurlekián, a local shoe-maker and poet (who makes a cameo appearance at the end), and interpreted by a murga chorus, titled: "In the old Plaza, winds are blowing" (*En la vieja plaza soplan vientos*).

"*[E]n la hora gris de la partida*," as it is customary, the *Retirada* mirrors the entire play and recounts the story of La Teja once more, by means of a long list of evocations of, and references to places, episodes, trades, characters, sufferings, dark hours and historical struggles in La Teja. It also speaks of the present challenges, of those who are still searching for their children, or who are not around any longer. Yet, it also reaffirms the militant spirit of this working class neighborhood, their dreams and hopes that are still alive and move the inhabitants of La Teja, all of which, in turn, "explains" why La Teja "will survive":

> Del alma, los sueños
> van forjando anhelos
> en el duro yunque
> de la vida
>
> Y ante la miseria
> gris de sus botijas
> marcha el obrero
> a su labor
> (*Levanta su puño con razón*)
> ...
>
> Y en el adiós su canto elevará
> bajo la luna de un cielo en esplendor,
> una utopía, un pueblo, una razón,
> que aquí en La Teja ¡Nunca morirá!

(Out of the soul and the hardships of life dreams give shape to desires. Confronting their children in misery workers face yet another day at the factory. They are right in raising their fists. (...) Under the moonlight that bathes the splendorous sky this farewell song reaffirms a utopia, a people, a reason, that survives in La Teja.)

Although figuratively, this epilogue also alludes to the political changes that took place in 2005, symbolized as a story of the defeat "of greed and haughtiness" ("*Eché por tierra la ambición y la soberbia*") and the arrival of a new "spring"—that is, the changes brought about by the Broad Front in the first two years of government—which explains why "[...] *en La Teja Flamea una bandera*" (The flag is up high in La Teja).

While during these two first years the leftist government has been rather cautious and moderate in terms of managing the economy and the pace of reform, there have been a series of changes that while they fall short of being "spectacular," they nevertheless signify quite a departure from the past. Some of these are: the creation of a progressive income tax system benefiting low income families; the prosecution of tax evasion and of large debtors that have historically abused the public credit system; the fight to stamp out under the table employment; the creation of a national health system and the revamping of the network of first aid neighborhood's clinics to provide health care to all; the creation of programs for sexual and reproductive education and health; the increase of the budget for public education; a significant salary increase for most public employees; guaranteeing of the right to strike and occupy the workplace; the protection of unionized workers from being arbitrarily fired; the creation of "salary councils" where workers' delegates and bosses negotiate the terms of salary increases and benefits under the supervision of the Ministry of Labor (one of the government offices given to the MLN-Tupamaros)—predictably on the side of the former—the reduction of unemployment to a single digit figure; the shortening of the sentences and the liberation of many persons that were incarcerated; the refinancing or outright pardoning of the debt of small farmers; the provision of credit for worker-run factories and small enterprises; the subordination of the military to the republican institutions; the support for anti-discriminatory mobilizations and the fight against racism, and more. All these acts have had an immediate positive impact in the lives of the people, in their social and economic material conditions of existence, as well as in psychological, ideological, and cultural terms.

As the play ends, actors, director, writers and other participants, all gather on stage to salute the public and receive, in turn, a warm applause by the attendants, who stay around the stage for quite some time as they approach, salute and congratulate friends and relatives participating in the play.

* * *

What appears to be simply a story about the Past and a piece of local history— "*la historia del barrio*," (the history of the neighborhood) as it was advertised—comes to be, understandably, more than that: a pretext or opportunity to stage and further explore, at the community level, other issues and questions.

Scene I, for instance, introduces an unexpected theme, which to a great extent sets the tone, and to a certain extent frames, the entire spectacle.

Indeed, the play begins when newspaper vendors (*canillitas*) typical of past times walk in between the public and "sell" (hand out) the program designed as a tabloid newspaper of the late nineteenth century. The front page contains the image of workers marching, and on the other side, a picture of a large transatlantic vessel filled with immigrants. So far, we are still led to believe that it is about the past. The reverse side of the paper/program, however, also contains a number of short monologues, talking about wanting to emigrate ("Jonathan"), about being tired and unhappy of moving around ("Noelia"), telling experiences of exile and of wanting to come back ("Silvana"), of resisting ("Claudio") and not wanting to leave ("Aurora"), and even one story of the child of a disappeared looking for her roots ("Daiana").

As the public reads the program, a multitude of characters or "statues"—fourteen of them—emerge in very slow motion from behind the stage, walk through the street-turned- proscenium, take various positions amidst the public, and begin to act out their monologues —written by the actors themselves— dealing mostly with the problem of emigration and exile. These sketchy characters—for they are not further developed or explored in any depth—move to another spot and repeat their act a couple of more times.

Other than causing, at first, a bit of perplexity among the incoming public, the resulting dramatic and aesthetic experience is also one of polyphony and relative confusion. Rather soon, spectators become aware that they cannot be everywhere and pay attention to everything that is happening. This, in turn, forces spectators to move around, and actively pursue the stories—somewhat uselessly, for it is all happening simultaneously.[8] This also sets the rules of spectatorship that the attending public will have to rapidly learn and adhere to throughout the play.

The monologues of Scene I, same as the transoceanic communication between mother and son in Scene II, both of them staging and bringing to the fore the problem of migration, exile and uprooting, work as stepping stones to tell (and represent) the history of La Teja. Yet, at the same time, the announcement and promise of telling the history of La Teja is what makes possible raising the question of exile. One of such monologues, written and performed by "Gilda" illustrates the content and mood of Scene I:

> Soy extranjera. Eternamente extranjera de mi Italia. Me quedan pocos borrosos recuerdos, a los que me aferro. Vine a este país pues mi esposo habría perdido su em-

presa: se fundió. Algunos me dijeron que fue porque era un jugador empedernido. Yo no les creí. Llegué a Montevideo en un viaje muy largo, en barco. Creí que en las noches de tormenta iba a perder mi embarazo, pero jamás a Dios y a la Virgen María, a quien tanto les ofrecí mis rezos, mis plegarias y promesas. Ya instalados, al mes nació Marco, mi único hijo. Mi esposo comenzó a trabajar y yo a criar a mi Marco, y a los quehaceres de la casa. No pudimos amasar ni siquiera una pequeña fortuna ya que lo que me decían era lamentablemente verdad: mi marido no sólo era jugador sino que de tanto extrañar comenzó a beber. A pesar de todo, cuando lo despidieron de su trabajo, yo tuve que salir a trabajar en un taller de bordados. Era lo único que sabía hacer. Con eso logré que finalizara los estudios —se recibió de abogado. Ahora me vino a decir que se va del país porque aquí no encuentra trabajo. Me desgarra el corazón. GILDA

(I am a foreigner. Eternally foreign of my Italy. I keep a handful of memories, to which I attach myself with all my strength. I came to this land because my husband had lost his business: he went bankrupt. Some said that he was an unredeemable gambler. I did not believe them. I came to Montevideo by ship. It was a very long trip. Those stormy nights in the high seas, I thought I was going to lose the baby inside my belly, but nor God neither the Virgin Mary, to whom I offered many prayers and promises. A month after our arrival Marco was born—my only child. My husband got a job; I raised Marco and took care of the house chores. We could not save any money at all, however. Unfortunately, what they had told me was true. On top of gambling, he began to drink—he missed Italy too much. When he was fired I got a job at a sewing workshop—the only thing I knew. With my earnings I financed Marco's studies and he graduated as a lawyer. Now he comes to tell me that he is leaving because in this country he cannot find a job. This breaks my heart. Gilda.)

Thus, right from the beginning, *Tejanos* points into the direction of two of the questions that have occupied and concerned Uruguayans in the past two decades: First, a concern for knowing, remembering, revisiting, and inscribing the past; the recent past in particular (the years of the dictatorship, the following 20 years of democracy), but also the national origins (as a way of rearticulating the national narrative so to make it correspond to the perspective and projects of the present) and the years preceding the dictatorship (to challenge accounts that sought to justify the turn to authoritarianism and the dictatorship). Second, the problem of exile and cultural uprooting (*desarraigo*) due mostly to economic necessity, the resulting political disenfranchisement, the broken families, the emotional and psychological costs, and the social consequences and costs of emigration to families in particular, and Uruguay as a whole.

Indeed, today Uruguayans living and working abroad comprise about half a million people in a population of 3.5 million—that is approximately 15% of its population. "Department Number 20," as it has been called (Uruguay is divided in 19 departments), is the second largest one after Montevideo. For obvious political reasons the peak of exile was reached during the dictatorship, most dramatically between 1974 and 1976. In 1974 alone, 70,000 persons went into exile. After the return to democracy exile had socio-economic causes and it reached its peak in 2002 (that year 29,000 persons went into exile)—mostly men, under 29 years of age, economically active, educated. After that, it is estimated that 20,000 persons emigrate yearly, mainly towards Spain and the United States.[9] Thus, if during most of its short history up until the 1950s, and mostly between 1850 and 1930s, Uruguay had been "a country of immigrants," from the 1960s and onwards, but mostly in the last two decades, became *"un país de emigración"* (a country of emigrants).

Uruguayans are slow to recognize the dimensions and relevance of this structural change, and of fully accepting and responding to this new reality. There is quite an ambivalent feeling about the diaspora. There is not a clear understanding of the extent and depth of this question, as it touches and affects almost every family—whether leaving or staying at home. Political rights are suspended. There are no clear public policies to prevent emigration or to revert it. If anything, the diaspora has begun to be of interest merely as a source of remittances, business opportunities and contacts (scientific, cultural, commercial, etc.). Interestingly enough, it seems surprising that in a culture with so much theater, there are not more plays focusing and exploring this theme, or attempting to intervene and respond to it. In this context, *Tejanos* is an exception, in part because this phenomenon has become particularly severe in impoverished La Teja. Since this is something that affects Montevideo and Uruguay as a whole, and indeed one can safely say that it is a feature of globalization and the times, it gives *Tejanos* an almost universal character.

The question of exile is perhaps the theme most explored and developed dramatically in that it confronts the audience with a true and unresolved—perhaps irresolvable—conflict or dilemma. With few exceptions—one dealing with gender issues, other with life at the old meat-processing factory, another that speaks to the question of the disappeared, another one of children in poverty and begging in the streets—most of the characters in Scene I and II talk of exile:

"Gabriela" does not want to leave; she can't find a good reason or a good place to go, yet she confesses that she is merely surviving in a world of oppressors and oppressed.

"Claudio" talks of having played a very risky game with much to lose but with a utopia to gain; what sustains him alive and "here"—he claims—is "the dream of a new sun that shines the same for everyone."

"Brenda" is 10 years old and does not want to leave because she loves her parents and it would mean saying goodbye to those who love her, and care for her, and helped her.

"Johana" is a child too, and talks of being having to beg in the streets to help her parents, but stresses that her parents love her a lot.

"Gilda," an Italian immigrant, laments that after all her sacrifices, his son, who graduated from Law School cannot find a job and is going away.

"Silvana" explains that she went abroad because she is young and wants to pursue her dreams, but then seems to suggest that she is working as a maid or prostitute, or both.

"Noelia" is tired of following her family around from town to town. Her father is a doctor, her mother a housewife, and she "comes and goes"; this disorients her and makes her unhappy.

An anonymous character, apparently living abroad, states that "the one who lives in two places only has half a life." While "here" he dreams of being "there". He shares his life with people taken apart by reality but brought together by a dream. Yes, he kept his culture and customs intact—that makes him feel free—and acquired new ones—which he appreciates and enjoys. But all in all, he longs for a lost harmony or sense of wholeness.

Another character (that signs "Pelícano") poetically speaks of the hard life in the leather processing plant (*El líquido viscoso / denunciaba el olor / la mezcla de sangre sal y carne / manchaba los cueros / los sonidos de los broches / apagaban los suspiros del vapor / que escapaban de la planchas / [...]*) (The viscous fluid denounced the strong smell / the mix of salt and blood that stains / the hides the deafening sound of the metallic buttons / silenced the sigh of the steam / that escaped from between the ironing press).

Another anonymous monologue meditates on his adventure abroad, clandestine; he enjoyed an experience that exposed him to other cultures and beliefs; there he had pleasures unavailable to him at home, yet his mind and heart were still at home—he longed for the *rambla*, the mate, the *murgas*, his friends. He asked himself if it was worthwhile, thought it was not, and decided to return.

"Jonathan" interprets a young man that moved to the Canary Islands (the actor's brother): "I have a job, enjoy a good life, am happy, women like me because of my colored skin." He came to persuade his family to join him— "people at home are passive and depressing," he complains.

"Aurora" was a maid and she had to go into exile in 1973 "because of political and ideological reasons."

"The young man living in Hamburg" talks of the many Uruguayans, Argentines, Colombians, all of whom also gather at a cultural center—like CE.CU.VI. perhaps?

All in all, however, the balance seems to be tilted towards favoring the decision to stay in La Teja, offering reasons, dreams and values for doing so, without necessarily condemning those who went abroad, but slightly pitying them, as exile is represented mostly under a negative light.

* * *

Being a working-class neighborhood, historically organized around industry and manufacturing, La Teja was one of the areas most affected by deindustrialization, unemployment and vanishing social benefits, all of which led to social disintegration, marginalization and polarization. This, in turn, led to indigence, the emergence of slums, drug consumption and trafficking, indeed, crimes of every kind. Logically, these changes have severely—and perhaps irreversibly—eroded the older codes of conduct, values and social pacts (such as respect, dignity, solidarity, sacrifice, austerity, etc.) that in the past had made possible and regulated conviviality and had brought people together in La Teja.

From day one, the Broad Front government launched an offensive to reverse this malaise by creating the Ministry of Social Development (the most important government office given to the Communist Party) with the charge of developing and implementing an ambitious and multifaceted "Emergency Plan" (*Plan de asistencia a la emergencia social*). Such plan was aimed, in the first instance, at assisting and reintegrating the most excluded and impoverished sectors by means of identifying who fell in this group, providing civil identification, paying them a social salary, creating temporary jobs, providing them with a package of basic food staples, constructing shelters for the homeless, making sure kids were attending schools, extending health services, providing other basic services (water, electricity, etc.), and more.

The Emergency Plan reached 750,000 people and has proved to be of great help for those in need. In 2007, the Equity Plan will replace the Emergency Plan, and will be aimed at providing even more opportunities for social reintegration, improving living conditions, and more importantly, making sure that they all have "equal access" to job opportunities, education, health care and housing.

This takes us to two other aspects of *Tejanos* which I wish to highlight: First, the aim of reuniting and bringing the community together—and of public-sphere building—by means of an experience of community theater to be represented for the community at the heart of the neighborhood, and by the telling and celebrating the history and idiosyncrasy of the neighborhood itself. Second, the aim of producing a narration of the local history and of history seen from the perspective of La Teja, as a means of maintaining and strengthening a sense of historical memory and working-class culture and identity, as a response to the cultural effects of social disintegration and marginalization, which has eroded conviviality and other values historically nourished—and needed—by the working class.

This concern for history, however, also needs to be read as a reaction to the dictatorship and the governments that followed, all of which wrote history in their terms, and called for neither revisiting nor questioning their account, and for forgetting, turning the page and stop looking back. In fact, all four previous governments, led by former president Julio María Sanguinetti, are said to have adhered to and followed "the Spanish model of transition."

In response to this, most Uruguayans—particularly on the Left, the workers unions, the social movements—have developed a natural obsession in the exact opposite, that is, to learn about and remember the Past and not to forget it. Not to forget those Uruguayans that in so many ways suffered under the dictatorship, or were jailed, tortured, or assassinated, the crimes that were committed between 1973 and 1985, the need to bring the criminals and their accomplices to justice. Also, not to forget the noble dreams of justice, freedom, solidarity, equality, and human dignity that historically inspired and mobilized Uruguayans during the turbulent years preceding the dictatorship (and for which they were incarcerated, died or were disappeared), or during the struggle against the military regime, or within the past 20 years, this time, in order to steer the country away from the destructive policies of Neoliberalism.

Such concern for "memory," "truth," and "justice," matches the goal and partial success stories of the very recent past with regards to the infamous Amnesty Law of 1986 (*Ley de caducidad de la pretensión punitiva del Estado*), due to a different interpretation of this law by President Vázquez. Strange as it may seem, the law itself empowers the President to decide which crimes are excluded in the Amnesty law. As for the guidelines, the law establishes that civilians are not protected by the law; top officials—those who gave the orders—are not included either; military officers that committed economically motivated or non-politically motivated crimes are not included; and crimes committed before the coup of 1973 or after the reestablishment of democracy in 1985 are also excluded. The recent international accord that ruled that the crime of secretly kidnapping and disappearing someone is committed *daily*—that is, in the present—as long as the person remains disappeared, added a new spin to the last exception, and it also prevents that those crimes are pardoned under the statute of limitations. President Vázquez has been the first president to restrict the reach of the law to its self-established limits.

As a result, in 2006, and for the first time ever since 1986, most of the more emblematic civilians and military officers still alive associated to the human rights violations—torture, assassinations, disappearances—committed during the dictatorship were brought to justice, out on trial, and imprisoned: former president and dictator Juan María Bordaberry, former Foreign Affairs Minister Juan Carlos Blanco, Lieutenant General José Gavazzo, Colonels Gilberto Vázquez, Jorge Silvera, Ernesto Ramas, Ricardo Arab, Ricardo Medina, Luis Maurente, Sande Lima, among others. Juan Antonio Rodríguez Buratti committed suicide when he was about to be detained. Colonel Manuel Cordero —who escaped to Brazil— was incarcerated and faces a request to be extradited. Ironically, only General Gregorio Álvarez —the very same one whose speech we hear in Scene IX—who led the dictatorship in its last years, is yet to be processed and incarcerated.

Archaeological excavations in military facilities encouraged by the new climate brought about by President Vázquez led to the discovery of the corpses of two disappeared political prisoners,[10] contradicting prior official accounts that denied their existence. These more active searches for the truth also led to the discovery of several other secret flights carrying political prisoners between Argentina and Uruguay as their respective dictatorial governments coordinated their actions within the parameters of the Condor Plan.

Suddenly, history is being challenged and rewritten daily, revisited from a myriad of other perspectives and experiences: that of the vanquished, of women, of oppressed ethnicities and sexualities, of the working class, youth or the marginalized, and also from the perspective of particular localities; all experiences, viewpoints and accounts which were rendered invisible, unrecorded, and always left out of the picture by the grand narratives of the official History.[11] (It is also quite telling that both, the Ministry of Defense and the Ministry of Interior [of Police] are now headed by women: Azucena Berrutti and Daisy Tourné, same as the Ministry of Public Health and the Ministry of Social Development).

In spite of this apparent interest in history, in local history, or in the point of view of heroic La Teja, *Tejanos,* however, falls short of being able to represent the recent historical past in terms that truly shed light on the factors and forces that led to the coup, or that sustained the dictatorship, that were capable of defeating the dictatorship. Also, it seems that the historical clock stopped after the return to democracy, even though the representation of the dictatorship is somewhat problematic.

Indeed, the dictatorship is excessively reduced to the character of the solitary and frightening "General" of Scene IX, a villain that seems to come out and belong to a graphic novel or a comic book more than anything else. To the contrary, we know that the military regime was fueled by powerful economic and corporative interests, led by two authoritarian and powerful elected civilian presidents (Jorge Pacheco Areco first, and Juan María Bordaberry later). Contrary to conventional wisdom, the dictatorship was a rather impersonal and banal bureaucratic authoritarian regime, run by military officers as much as by technocrats, mediocre bureaucrats and civil collaborators of all kinds and ranks. Further still, for complex and varied reasons, both the coup and the dictatorship had many sympathizers and supporters among the population.

In *Tejanos*' fast historical recount, the episode of the rise and fall of the dictatorship is important enough to be included. However, it comes and goes in a matter of seconds, almost as if it were enough to point to it—literally—"in passing" in order to awaken certain feelings—of outrage, or of complicity in its defeat. It is as if it was not necessary to offer a dramatic depiction geared towards illustrating its complexity, or able to produce a more profound understanding of it, in other words, an account that corresponds with the imperative of producing historical memory and remembering. A light or oversimplified treatment of the past it is not too different from forgetting. The whole idea behind rewriting history from a different perspective is that one problematizes and challenges all other preexisting accounts, adding new layers of complexity, and reaching deeper levels of understanding and truth, instrumental to transform social reality.

Assuming that the overall structure and concept of the play did not allow for a different—deeper, more complex, or enlightening—treatment of history, strangely enough *Tejanos*' story also mysteriously stops with the return to democracy—with the only exception of a couple of cryptic verses in the final *Retirada*—already pointed out.

To conclude, *Tejanos* managed to bring to the fore a local history and perspective of history traditionally ignored, and to stage a series of values, attitudes, and hopes that are alive and that define the culture of La Teja—or that are intended to redefine it. It also succeeded in raising and exploring such pressing matters like the question of exile, or in signaling the change in the political scenario. Yet, one cannot fail to notice that *Tejanos*' historical account falls short of stretching to the more recent past (the last decade or so), and of tackling many developments and debates[12] that are central in post-2002 Uruguay. Perhaps, this is due to the fact that "recent history" is often an elusive and slippery territory, as the current debate about teaching recent history in secondary education illustrates. In this sense, *Tejanos* is only partially able to deal with the various transitions Uruguay is going through, and in certain respects could not escape gravitating excessively around the period of the return to democracy that took place 20 years ago.

On the other hand, *Tejanos* is the product of merely a first stage in this experimentation with theater in the Vidplan Cultural Center of La Teja. Thus, away from what is being represented, the very existence of the CE.CU.VI., the creation of the Community Theater Group, their choice of using street theater as a mode of expression and intervention in the public sphere—and as a mode of public-sphere building—all indicates that we are before something entirely unedited, encouraging, and already gratifying. Since this experiment will be resumed and continued, one cannot but conclude—and hope—that they will venture into the exploration of other issues and conflicts that belong to, and are more clearly identified with, the more recent past, and to this open-ended and uncharted journey in which we find ourselves embarked today, that is, a transition beyond.

Notes

1. This experience is one of three financed by the "Esquinas" program established by the Department of Culture of the City Government of Montevideo to support emergent socio-cultural initiatives such as the one already taking place at the Vidplan Cultural Center. Two other similar experiences were supported by the "Esquinas" program: one in the Parque Posadas apartment complex (under the direction of Marcelino Duffau), and another in the locality of Villa García.
2. Graciela Abeledo, a custom and mask designer (also of *Polizón Teatro*), and composer and musician Daniel "Pollo" Píriz completed the team that led this experience of community theatre.
3. Cristalerías Unidas, another glass factory that also closed down, was reopened by its workers as Envidrio. Envidrio, same as Funsa (a factory that produces rubber manufactures) or Midovers (a leather factory), are examples of worker-run factories as their former owners declared bankruptcy. According to Raúl Zibechi (2007) there are more than 20 such worker-run factories or business in Uruguay, more than 100 in Brazil and more than 200 in Argentina. These factories have received financial assistance first by the Uruguayan government and now by the Venezuelan government.

4. I formulated and developed this idea in a paper titled "Teatro frontera: Espacios contaminados" (Frontier Theatre/Contaminated Spaces) presented at the II Coloquio Internacional de Teatro de Montevideo, in October 13–15, 2006, itself a byproduct of an earlier article: "La escena ubicua: Hacia un nuevo modelo del sistema teatral nacional," *Latin American Theater Review* Spring 2005 Vol. 38 No. 2 (University of Kansas, Lawrence), 51–71.
5. This paper is a part of a larger fieldwork research project whose aim is that of identifying, documenting and discussing experiences that would match the definition of frontier theatre and which this far includes: (1) *Tejanos* (2006), an experience of community theatre and street theatre by the Community Theater Group of the Vidplan Cultural Center of La Teja/Pueblo Victoria, under the direction of Enrique Permuy, of *Polizón Teatro*, (2) *Que no nos pase, que no le pase a nadie* (2003) a simulacrum of the bombing of downtown Montevideo conceptualized and staged by Ignacio Seimanas, as a form of protest against the bombing of Bagdad, (3) *Ubu* (2006), an adaptation by *Polizón Teatro* of Alfred Jarry's text translated into a clown grotesque form to be performed in open spaces, squares and cultural fairs, and performed in front of Teatro Solís (February 2006), at the Flor de Maroñas square (September 2006) and in other neighborhoods,(4) *Chicas de la noche* (2001), *Vo' Populi* (2002), *Qué se yo* (2003) and other plays created and performed between 2001 and 2006 by the interns of the Female Minors Intern Center (Centro de Ingreso de Adolescentes Femeninos "in conflict with the law" [CIAF-INAU]), under the direction of Ileana López and Federica Folco; (5) *Titanes* (2004) by Marcel Sawchik and Adriana Ardoguein, a mix of wrestling, comic, and tragedy staged at the Palermo Boxing Club, and (6) the work of the *Grupo de teatro ¡Eh-Che-pare!* (1991–1999) formed by patients of the Colonia Etchepare (a psychiatric hospital), under the direction of Ariel Gold and Ana Cabezas.
6. Title of the paper to be presented at the 6th Encounter of the Hemispheric Institute of Performance and Politics, Buenos Aires, June 8–17, 2007.
7. This discussion is based on documents produced and information collected in the course of my fieldwork while in Montevideo in 2006.
8. Here it is hard not to recognize in this respect the influence of the *Théâtre du Soleil* and the way in which Ariane Mnouchkine represented the French revolution in *1789*, as well as earlier forms of religious drama and spectacle, like the medieval celebrations of Corpus Christi, by means of a series of parallel short acts or *tableaux* placed one next to, or across from each other around a square or along a street.
9. Historically Uruguayans migrated to neighboring Argentina and Brazil. In the 60s and 70s there was a pattern of migration towards Australia, Canada and the United States—mostly for economical reasons. Australia and Canada had policies for recruiting Uruguayan immigrants—Quebec is still very active in this regard. During the dictatorship political exiles went to Argentina (up until 1976), Mexico, Venezuela, Holland, Sweden and France, all countries that generously hosted and aided Uruguay-

ans that were persecuted for political reasons and were forced into exile. In the 80s and 90s many Uruguayans became Spanish and Italian citizens and migrated to Europe, mostly to Spain, due to cultural factors. Emigration to the United States increased greatly in the last decade, in part because earlier in the decade, no visa was required for Uruguayan nationals to travel to the United States as tourists—although they used this opportunity to stay in the country and work without papers. While this is a tragedy of cosmic proportions for Uruguayan society and culture, seen from the perspective of the host countries, the number of Uruguayan exiles remains insignificant.

10. These were the cases of union leader Ubagesner Chávez Sosa and Law School professor Fernando Miranda, both associated with the Communist Party. The excavations, though, failed to find the remains of José Arpino Vega and María Claudia García Irureta de Gelman, also suspected of being buried in these military facilities, and of many other disappeared citizens.

11. This trend is also manifested in a substantial corpus of historical narrations produced in the past 20 years, both in the forms of historical novels—many of them revisionist—and testimonies, as well as in the form of history books, documentaries, courses, seminaries, conferences, and manuals.

12. To name a few: a series of emblematic and much debated episodes involving the closing of factories, or their relocation, and their occupation by workers; the tragedy of the indebted farmers forced to sell their lands, and the debate about pardoning their debts; the odyssey of emigrants that returned, or of those who are living abroad without papers; the debate about emigrants' rights to vote (*voto epistolar*); the situation and reform of the penitentiary system (*ley de humanización de las cárceles*) and the liberation of a number of convicts; the changes in the family, or the debate around abortion and its legalization (*ley de salud reproductiva*); the many realities and challenges uncovered and brought to the fore in the process of developing and implementing the Emergency plan, including the question of the *salario social* and the debates that surround it.

Works Cited

Achugar, Hugo. "De una cultura nacional a un país fragmentado." *20 años de democracia. Uruguay 1985–2005: Miradas múltiples*. Ed. Gerardo Caetano. Montevideo: Taurus, 2005.

Ballvé, Teo, and Vijay Prashad. *Dispatches From Latin America*. New Delhi: Left Word Books, 2006.

Bianchi, Adhemar. "Teatro comunitario: El Galpón de las Catalinas en la Boca de Buenos Aires." *II Coloquio Internacional de Montevideo*, octubre 2006.

Brando, Oscar, ed. *Uruguay Hoy. Paisaje después del 31 de octubre*. Montevideo: Ediciones del caballo perdido, 2004.

Caetano, Gerardo, ed. *20 años de democracia. Uruguay 1985–2005: Miradas múltiples.* Montevideo: Taurus, 2005.
Calvo, Juan José, and Adela Pellegrino. "Veinte años no es nada." *20 años de democracia. Uruguay 1985–2005: Miradas múltiples.* Ed. Gerardo Caetano. Montevideo: Taurus, 2005.
Cancela, Walter. "La economía. Los problemas pendientes." *Uruguay Hoy. Paisaje después del 31 de octubre.* Ed. Oscar Brando. Montevideo: Ediciones del caballo perdido, 2004.
Chartier, Roger. *El mundo como representación.* Barcelona: Gedisa, 1999.
De Armas, Gustavo. "De la sociedad hiperintegrada al país fragmentado." *20 años de democracia. Uruguay 1985–2005: Miradas múltiples.* Ed. Gerardo Caetano. Montevideo: Taurus, 2005.
Dubatti, Jorge. *El convivio teatral.* Buenos Aires: Atuel, 2003.
Ganduglia, Néstor. *15 años de teatro barrial y una canción desesperada.* Montevideo: YOEA—Multiversidad Franciscana de América Latina, 1996.
Garcé, Adolfo, and Jaime Yaffé. *La era progresista.* Montevideo: Fin de Siglo, 2004.
Hernández, Diego, and Paulo Ravecca. "Emigration, social capital and welfare access in vulnerable environments." *Cuadernos del CLAEH* (Montevideo) Vol. 2 (2006).
Katzman, Ruben (Coord.), and Fernando Filgueira. *Informe del desarrollo humano en Uruguay.* Montevideo: PNUD, 2000.
Marchesi, Aldo, Vania Markarián, Aldo Rico, and Jaime Yaffé, eds. *El presente de la dictadura. Estudios y reflexiones a 30 años del golpe de Estado en Uruguay.* Montevideo: Trilce, 2004.
Moreira, Constanza. "A mitad de camino." *La izquierda a media máquina.* Special issue of *Brecha* Año 22, No. 1110 (March 2, 2007): 7.
———. *Final del juego. Del bipartidismo tradicional al triunfo de la izquierda en Uruguay.* Montevideo: Trilce, 2004.
Pellarolo, Silvia, and Lola Proaño Gómez. "Somos los sobrevivientes de una utopía: Entrevista a Adhemar Bianchi." *Latin American Theater Review* 35: 1 (2001): 117–26.
Pellegrino, Adela. "La emigración en el Uruguay actual. ¿El último que apague la luz?" UNESCO Conference at the Cabildo de Montevideo, July 15, 2003.
Remedi, Gustavo. "La escena ubicua: hacia un nuevo modelo de "sistema teatral nacional." *Latin American Theater Review* (Spring 2005).
———. "The Production of Local Public Spheres: Community Radio Stations." *The Latin American Cultural Studies Reader.* Ed. Ana Del Sarto, Alicia Ríos and Abril Trigo. Durham and London: Duke University Press, 2004.
Rico, Aldo, ed. *Uruguay: Cuentas pendientes. Dictadura, memorias y desmemorias.* Montevideo: Trilce, 1995.
Sapriza, Graciela. "Cambios en la situación de las mujeres y las familias en Uruguay 1960–1990." *El Uruguay de la dictadura.* Montevideo: Ediciones de la Banda Oriental, 2004.

Sempol, Diego. "Historia local: Entre la aldea y la globalización." *Brecha* (March 5, 1999).
———. "Microhistoria: ¿Una alternativa a la totalización?" *Brecha*, October 16, 1998.
Vidal, Hernán. *La literatura en la historia de las emancipaciones latinoamericanas.* Santiago de Chile: Mosquito Editores, 2004.
———. *Política cultural de la memoria histórica.* Santiago de Chile: Mosquito Editores, 1997.
Vidal, Luis. "La memoria del teatro." *II Coloquio Internacional de Montevideo*, octubre 2006.
Villegas, Juan. *Ideología y discurso crítico sobre el teatro de España y América Latina.* Minneapolis: Institute for the Study of Ideologies and Literature, 1988.
Yaffé, Jaime. *Al centro y adentro. La renovación de la izquierda y el triunfo del Frente Amplio en Uruguay.* Montevideo: Linardi y Risso, 2005.
Zibechi, Raúl. "The Uruguayan Left and the Construction of Hegemony." *Dispatches From Latin America.* Ed. Teo Ballvé and Vijay Prashad. New Delhi: Left Word Books, 2006.
———. "Worker-Run Factories: From Survival to Economic Solidarity." *Dispatches From Latin America.* Ed. Teo Ballvé and Vijay Prashad. New Delhi: Left Word Books, 2006.

7

Dancing with Destruction: Pop Music during the Spanish Transition

Antonio Méndez-Rubio

> defeat was never as beautiful
> as some want to paint it
> —Sabino Méndez

Producing Historical Unmemory

Within any memory there may be, laying in silence, the inextinguishable remains of the forgotten. Thinking about it does not contribute to giving it a voice, nor does it help us acknowledge it. Furthermore, when the collective imaginary, for one reason or another, brings on a series of changes in the public discourse to try and define this strong nucleus, or keep it in its place, then, predictably, a spiral of noise rises up into the air. This rumor points to its own emptiness and, at the same time, it frees from the passing of time the impossibility of saying something, of mentioning the unsaid again. Current debates about the need and even the legal necessity for *historical memory* can be an example of this: a considerable effort is made to open up spaces for shared memories, whose visibility delays the pulsation of that which, within memory, is only forgetfulness or mere amnesia, the backdrop of denial.

At this crossroads, there is a well-known passage by Walter Benjamin in his *Theses on the Philosophy of History* which should be remembered here:

> To articulate the past historically does not mean to recognize it "the way it really was." It means to seize hold of a memory as it flashes up at a moment of danger.

(...) The danger affects both the content of the tradition and its receivers. (...) In every era the attempt must be made anew to wrest tradition away from a conformism that is about to overpower it. (*Illuminations* 180)

During the period known in Spain as the Transition (1977–1987), there was an unprecedented revival of what had been said and erased about the Spanish Civil War (1936–1939). It was, by definition, a moment of *danger*, in Benjaminian terms, which official culture and public opinion can only recuperate by placing it under the sign (naturalized on account of its inertia) of *subjugating conformism*. When memory is produced in terms of nostalgia, what happens (among other things) is what should be avoided: a celebratory complacency, in contrast with the precariousness of normal life, becomes symptomatic of the latency of a debt, of an open wound, of a wish, and of an outstanding balance, which is still looking towards the future.

Among the flurry of articles and media presentations which try, on a massive scale, to remember the years when Spain made the transition from Franco's regime to a democracy, those which want to conjure up a certain musical memory of Spanish society imply a special and seductive opacity. Two films from the year 2005 could serve as examples of the wounds and suturing that this memory causes. I am referring to *El Calentito*, by Chus Gutiérrez (2005), and *Los dos lados de la cama* (The Two Sides of the Bed), by Emilio Martínez-Lázaro (2005). Both films point to a moment and place of crisis, of subjectivity and sociality, as well as to a way of facing that crisis; therefore, a series of agreements and disagreements emerge between these two films that are not without a hermeneutic and explicative value.

In both films the story embraces, from the beginning, the crisis of linear narrative through the inclusion of music videos which mark the rhythm for the plot's resolution, and bore through the diegesis towards an area where the experience (of time) is suspended. In *El Calentito* the crisis in the world is especially apparent in the upset of authority within the traditional model of the couple and the family where, in turn, the generation gap between young people and adults takes center stage. This crisis is shown alongside, and is intensified by, the deterioration of the collective political framework: a State that is tainted by social constraints, police corruption, and the clandestine, though widespread, contempt for the dictatorship. The action takes place in 1981, and the outcome of the story is determined by the historical tension brought on by the attempted coup d'état of February 23 of that year. The "2/23" is used as the catalyst for danger, as the epicenter of the lack of social and personal safety, as if all hopes and conflicts were concentrated on that date. Also, as if that date demanded its materiality, its challenge as a real entity, file footage is edited into the film and songs from the time are used in the soundtrack. Among the latter, the quoting of the anthem-like song by Parálisis Permanente ("Quiero ser santa," 'I want to be a saint') stands out, which helps strengthen the Punk option chosen by the protagonist all-girl group, whose *nom de guerre* is Las Siux. In this way, Gutiérrez's film tries to resist the erasure of women's place in History, which is why she situates the action of the leading character, Sara, within a realm where that erasure has been privileged: the realm of cultural history, and more specifically, the history of pop music. The history of contemporary popular music is indeed one of the areas where the premise of the divide between the active, expressive power of masculinity and the passive, repressed experience of femininity has been most effective. In this sense, "the male rock performance turns the woman into a silent object of exchange among men" (Bradby 345).

But the critical resistance to the erasure of the female experience in *El Calentito* would appear somewhat mutilated if attention was not given to how this criticism is linked in the film to a new crisis: gender identity, which, in the end, leads to an *identity crisis*, plain and simple. The script emphasizes the central importance of the transvestite character, whose irresolvable ambiguity thoroughly affects the root of his own name: Antonia/o—the epitomic name, the synecdoche par excellence for all things Spanish. Antonia's character is presented as nothing less than a "gender terrorist." The political and existential tensions that affected society at that time are concentrated and intensified in this character—for example, when Antonia defiantly declares that "Our thing is really what you'd call a transition." She is also the character whose bravery unties the knot of suspense, thus reopening the vital, narrative flow. This flow of liberty and independence is emblematized in the sequence of Sara's race to Las Siux's night-time concert during the coup d'état, where she experiences a combination of fear and rage. The point at which Neo-fascist pressure is at its height is also the moment when the dialogue takes on a combative decisiveness: "—Where is the fight?—On stage." Therefore, the fact that the concert takes place does not annul the conflict framed by the decision of autonomy, nor the *bad vibes* caused by the ties that are broken when the decision is made. Rather, the conflict becomes the driving force of a fight that is festively and convulsively dramatized in the final sequence.

As for *Los dos lados de la cama*, it was conceived as a sort of sequel to *El otro lado de la cama* (The Other Side of the Bed, 2002), also directed by Emilio Martínez-Lázaro. The latter had been a remarkable box office success, reaching an audience of three million in cinemas alone. Set in a contemporary context, and featuring a cast of thirty-something, middle-class couples and their friends, *Los dos lados de la cama* brings the eighties to life through Roque Baños's adaptation of a select repertoire of pop songs from those years (by Alaska, Loquillo, Los Secretos, Mecano, etc.) which were decisive in the characters' personal development (and for the shaping of the collective framework in which their lives have evolved). The opening scene already features a slow adaptation of "Bailando" ("Dancing"), a hit by Alaska y los Pegamoides, performed here by Raquel who seductively writhes on top of the piano. Her gaze into the camera summons the scopic desire of Javier and Pedro's masculine gaze, but also the feminine gaze of Marta (Javier's fiancée), who is sitting with them among the crowd and who, we soon find out, is Raquel's (Pedro's girlfriend) secret lover. The discovery of her lesbian infidelity triggers comic effects in the film and recalls the climate of sexual freedom which was inherited precisely from the years of the Spanish Transition.

However, references to the collective and social world are relegated here to the outlandish appearances and grammatical nonsense of Rafa, the uncouth, working-class taxi driver friend who is dumped by Pilar, and is responsible for the distanced, ironic introduction of the two "trendy couples," as well as the humorous cheer: "Cheer up! We are in Spain!" From beginning to end, (when, after all that's happened, he grumbles, "It's all going down the tubes. Spain's washed up"), Rafa's character is in charge of the dirty work; he is the one who conceptualizes the action—with a wink to the aesthetics of Pedro Almodóvar by way of Santiago Segura—in the embarrassing territory of *Dark Spain*: the land of macho traditionalism, domestic violence and ignorance. Rafa is also responsible for widening the critical scope of the story: whereas in the primary circle the story focuses on the crisis of commitment within couples and on gender identity (introduced by the *leitmotiv* of *El otro lado de la cama*: "Some studies say everybody is bisexual"), in the second concentric circle, wider than the first, the crisis is extended to a crisis of trust, a crisis regarding the ties involving friendship and society in a broader sense (Rafa's girl leaves him for Carlos, his best friend, "the only person I can trust"). The fact that commitment (within the couple) is stripped of its meaning implies an irreversible deterioration of the most traditional marital and family ties, but it also affects to some extent a certain obliteration of the trust that is necessary for cohesion within couples and within society. Therefore, the climate of complicity and light humor that the film suggests cannot be separated from a somewhat bitterer background: the reference to an individualist and disoriented world, where, as Zygmunt Bauman has stated, "*dependence* has become a bad word: it refers to something that decent people should be ashamed of" (88).

In contrast to *El Calentito*, Martínez-Lázaro expresses the crisis of a male perspective, where men are openly in the hands of women and male decisions are continually presented in the form of self-parodies. In the middle of this amusing fall from grace, a new woman bursts in almost anonymously, who catalyses the crisis between Javier and Pedro by suggesting the possibility of a new arrangement: a *ménage à trois*. She is the one who offers an illuminating comment during the depressive ranting of the two friends: "I'm not much into talking. I have a better solution: dancing." The happy new threesome goes to a dance academy to cure their most immediate ills. Dancing, at this point, is obviously a lure for seduction and the possibility of a new sexual conquest, while it simultaneously becomes, no less obviously, a substitute for what is missing: not only their respective partners, Marta and Raquel, but also the communication that would allow them to get their girlfriends back or build new ties. Communication, as a pre-requirement not only for the couple, but for life with other people, is pleasantly depicted as an inopportune desert–"I don't like talking much . . ." Dancing is thus presented as the epitome of failure, of personal and social defeat. It is not by accident that, at this point, the soundtrack features songs from the end of the 1980s (by Los Ronaldos and Los Rodríguez), enabling a political interpretation of the film in terms of disillusionment, of a cynical Post-Transition hangover.

In *Los dos lados de la cama*, the dancing in the musical numbers is the time set aside for choral action, similar to the harmonic idealization of the community which is characteristic of classic Hollywood musicals. The lyrics of the songs and the body movements of the dance establish a self-reflective dialectic, which nonetheless sympathizes with the most conservative brand of nostalgia, along the lines of later musical films. The hugely successful musicals of the 1980s, such as *Flashdance* (A. Lyne, 1983) or *Dirty Dancing* (E. Ardoline, 1987) represent, in fact, an attempt to strike an accord between the caustic revisionism of the 1970s and the classic model of subjugating identification, and they do it by virtue of an auratic story of individual (and couple) learning, which moves, by the way, increasingly closer to the gay sensibility (Feuer). Is it deconstruction or a pastiche? Perhaps somewhere in between, the two films by Martínez-Lázaro, regarded from the point of view of repertory musicals, seem to agree with Jane Feuer's statement:

> Instead of a process of creation and neglect, what we really have here in the historic sense is a process of citation and preterition, since nothing entirely new is really ever *created*. Through time, the synthesis of past and present forms of shows eliminates the distinction between one form and another, so that the musical appears at

the same time innovative and traditional. Therefore, the show is put on in a perpetual present, which is also a perpetual past. (166)

In a kind of delirious, post-modern apotheosis, isn't the denial of temporality also a denial of memory, in spite of the fact that at first glance it may seem quite the contrary? To make a comparison, it would be like asking if listening to the music of the 1980s, which in Spain is known as *Remember music,* in mega-discos is, paradoxically, a collective celebration of not remembering, a catharsis of pain that causes oblivion. In the end, as Barthes stated, "without forgetting, life itself is not possible" (51).

To sum up, if we compare *El Calentito* with *Los dos lados de la cama,* we will find something more than a similarity in subject matter (the sexual and musical history of young people in recent Spain) and a striking coincidence in the roles of Sara/Marta, both played by Verónica Sánchez, the young actress who catapulted to fame thanks to her role as the perfect daughter in the television comedy *Los Serrano* (Tele 5), which relates the ups and downs of a large, well-adjusted family. Between the two cinematic texts, however, there is a double difference that could be resolved through a new interpretive convergence: the first one presents a story of sexual and political initiation, whereas the second proposes a comedy based on sexual and social disorientation (where the absence of politics is only comparable to the absence of drugs); the first takes on a constructive female point of view while the second depicts the masculine perspective that falls apart on its own. If one could judge from a historical point of view, which would be correct? What kind of (un)memory does each film produce? Or do they perhaps compliment one another, as if they had the same origin, and could both be *true,* in the sense that they respectively make an interpretation of the common history through an episode of relative autonomy for women, of masculine disorientation and depoliticization, and so on?

If we suppose that the two films could be read in a time sequence, as the cultural references in both indeed allow us to do, we would then also have a proto-sequential relationship between them: *as if El Calentito* took place first (at the beginning of the 1980s) and *Los dos lados de la cama* afterwards (in the no-time of the late 1980s and early 1990s). If this were true, wouldn't we find a transition between cheerful celebration and skeptical disappointment, wouldn't we read into it the story of a common defeat? The critical point of inflection between the two episodes could lie in the climate of irreversible threat and desperate reproach outlined in a song from 1984 entitled "77," by Loquillo y Trogloditas. "77" lent its title to the extended play version called *¿Dónde estabas tú en el 77?* ("Where were you in '77?"). In "77," the basic elements of

Country and Western music are crossed with Punk rage, resulting in a cry that pierces the solitude of the place of the statement, with no hope of company, a hope that can no longer be returned, that stems from a loss, from a questioning accusation: "si las calles ya no arden / ¿quién ha sido el culpable?" ("if the streets are no longer burning / who is to blame?").

The Mythification of a Hole

The hegemonization of nostalgia began within the field of recent popular music and, in fact, is part of the official agenda of the cultural industry. For example, in *Historia del Pop Español*, José Ramón Pardo documents a remarkable boom of nostalgia in the year 1985, whose most specific and superficial manifestation was the launching of cover bands specializing in revival, such as La Década Prodigiosa ("The Phenomenal Decade"). Therefore, already in 1985, one can see to what extent the collective memory was not going to be able to feed off of what had been done, off of the fact(s), since that illusion of change, at least for the youngest generations, was abandoned somewhere along the way. As for this point, the undone does not consolidate; it can never be consolidated in memory, since it never became a reality: what was experienced in the late seventies and the early eighties was as much of an experience as it was a wish. The inertia of time made it increasingly clear that this wish had not been exhausted; what had been exhausted were the channels of experience that made that wish into something more than a mere wish for the impossible. The unlivable erosion of the utopian project, which has been referred to as the craving for disillusion (Vilarós), not only resulted in the deadly nightmare of hard drugs, but it also opened a kind of undercurrent in the popular unconscious dominated by the feeling that the time experienced was no longer real, that everything had the fleetingness of a dream, that all that was left were embers exposed to the wilderness. Like many others, Sabino Méndez, the guitar player and composer of the band Los Trogloditas, crossed that desert of what was real, and made observations about the consistency of the common void, such as: "a human being who no longer has an idea of meaning or purpose for his acts becomes a zombie" (169). This "extreme weakness," this "feeling of absolute contingency" that Méndez speaks of in his book *Corre, rocker* ("Run, Rocker"), is related to the certainty of living within an empty space, within a distancing of historical time, which is perceived in the free form of a niche of air, a hole: "all of us heterodoxes profited, very fortunately, from a monumental hole in the historical time of the Transition" (63).

It is necessary to insist on the fact that the "withdrawal symptoms" do not only refer to the pathology derived from a drug addiction, but also the idea of resorting to drugs as one way (among others) to face up to the despair of an unexpected, irreparable wilderness—and live. Getting back to the course of events, for Méndez or for Vilarós the hyper-discourse about the *Movida* is the clearest symptom of its tangible decline, starting in 1987. As Vilarós metaphorically said, "the practical poetry of the *Movida* is, deep down, a methadone treatment" (35). And, indeed, within that climate, nostalgia appears like a therapy, as premature as it is efficient. The nostalgic reaction permitted (and permits) people to hold on to a few, albeit precarious, snapshots of a fascinating time, whose basic historical signs were its historical acceleration and its ephemeral character. The paradoxical and controversial period of the Transition establishes the imminence of a change that, however, is continually put off, unfinished, projected towards a future that does not exist, and this dose of non-existence has been opening up spaces within the continuity of experience and memory. Gérard Imbert explains this with exceptional skill:

> What is therefore saved from oblivion is not so much the history, but its writing. (. . .) All writing phantasmagorically refers to its origin, that which *originates*, makes up its story—structure—to a (primitive) form of the *un-said*. It is, in the collective unconscious, the image of Franco, the "Pére-sévère" (Lacan): the Father-who-is-still-there, who no one has killed (symbolically speaking). This murky origin, which is an obstacle in the construction of a new symbolic universe, is at the same time a lost object, and consequently, an object of nostalgia (the paternal realm), but also an object of abomination (subjugation, dependence); it is likewise an object left undone (rupture) that refers to a non-consummated death. (20–21)

In other words, the unfulfilled nature of the rupture makes it survive, persevere like a death wish, like a voracious, destructive pulse, though not so much in reality but in the desire of reality that the Transition activated among a great number of young people in Spain. Naturally, this pulse can only be the silent, invisible, phantasmatic threat of what in the end may break up (with) life. That is the unconscious threat that nostalgia promises to exorcise—albeit at the price of erasing all memory.

The main mechanism of nostalgia that has been put into play by the public opinion and by the common Post-Transition culture has been the ancient myth of the Golden Age. A good illustration of this is the fact that "La Edad de Oro" ("The Golden Age") became the name of an influential music program on Televisión Española, hosted by Paloma Chamorro, between 1983 and 1985, that is, immediately after the end of what Méndez calls the "unrepeatable lustrum," 1977–1982. In 1987, the record company Ariola, already part of the multi-national group BMG, launched a triple compilation album called *La Edad de Oro del Pop Español*, with the participation of iconic bands of the New Wave period: from Kaka de Luxe to Radio Futura, including Golpes Bajos, Aviador Dro, Los Toreros Muertos, La Mode, Alaska y Dinarama, Mamá, Los Secretos and many others. The all-encompassing aspiration of this record launching was again taken up in a later book with the same title, published by Luca Editorial in 1992. With the passing of time, far from losing momentum, this mythic coinage, as is befitting its very nature and function (Barthes), has spread and become naturalized in various, more recent launchings, such as the double DVD *La Edad de Oro del Pop Español (60 artistas / canciones)*, compiled by BMG/Dro East West in 2004, or the DVD+CD pack *La Edad de Oro del Pop Español (concierto sinfónico)* (2006), produced by Sony-BMG, in collaboration with the Orquesta Sinfónica *de Radiotelevisión Española*. In 2006, there was also Sony's massive launching of the karaoke *La Edad de Oro del Pop Español*, designed for use with video-game consoles (SingStar–Play Station2), following the success of the Japanese Famicom by Nintendo. The Playstation website announced the new product on the market with the headlines: "Those wonderful years: The Nostalgia of Madrid's *Movida* bursts out in the Play2." And it continued: "30 super hits which try to cover all the years and styles ..."

The myth's desire for totality is not completely innocent. As is well-known, the definition of *mythos* in Greek etymology alludes to the knowledge and expression of a reality that exceeds the limits of experience and reason. This expression is always a narrative, a story, a construction, and is ambivalent by nature: it points to a primordial, original time in the past which is the seed of the present that is being celebrated; at the same time it symptomatizes a historicity in crisis. The historical reality, as Barthes explains (*Mythologies*), is depoliticized and immobilized by the mythic tale, whose main function is to naturalize societal life in the form of a non-social, non-historical reality. Barthes's quote remains provocative: "statistically, myth is right-wing" (257). However, just like two negatives make a positive, the recurrence of the newly established myth can expose its character as a construct, as an arbitrary and interested affectation. This trait of myth as an ideological construct is, in fact, the first characteristic that a myth must deny through a hypotaxis of the supernatural, and even the sacred, of what by definition is not touched upon: the mythicized event stands out as exemplary and, at the same time and for the same reason, it is not discussed, it stands outside of criticism and change.

The myth of the Golden Age comes from afar. In his Fourth Eclogue, Virgil already made the Golden Age into a prophetic vision and, since then, it has become a continual crossroads: "In that instant the Golden Age converges with the socio-political Utopia. Whereas the former was cast upon an immemorial past, the latter models an absent space and an unknown future." (Guillén 262).

Already by the end of the fourth century AD, Prudentius retook Virgil's golden myth in *Books Against Symmachus* (I), to legitimize the conquests of Rome and to praise the figure of the Emperor Theodosius as a doctor of souls who, after forbidding the pagan cult, was able to spiritualize his Empire and combat the illness of secular paralysis. In the beginning, however, the myth of the Golden Age was portrayed by Virgil as a mythification that was neither conscious nor mature regarding its ideological and political powers: it refers, in a germinal way, to the fantasy of a time, as Ovid says in the first book of his *Metamorphoses*, "without law or king." Throughout history, the anarchistic illusion of the myth, not driven by a libertarian character, but rather by its condition as a myth, would have to shape or set an ideal past as a means to justify a present in crisis. Along the lines of Claudio Guillén's words, one could say that the Golden Age idealizes the past as an efficient way of covering the lack of a present, a present that lacks historical projection and only contemplates the hole of an "unknown future," listless, as the well-known Punk motto had already predicted: NO FUTURE. In other words, the myth of the Golden Age can work as a post-authoritarian defense mechanism, but also as a post-libertarian one, as a pleasant antidote to punk despair, which is so important for understanding the transgressive aspect of Spanish pop music during the Transition, in cases like Parálisis Permanente, Los Nikis, Polansky y el Ardor, Las Vulpess, the early Siniestro Total, and also, indirectly, Golpes Bajos, Alaska y Pegamoides, Los Burros, and Trogloditas, among others.

From that perspective, the impossibility of memory favors the erasure of history which confirms the myth, and the other way around: both elements mutually refer to one another in an effective, but not necessarily deliberate, way. At this crossroads of strategic vectors, we should take a closer look at how the market and the state deal with pop music.

The evolution of the record industry in the mid-1980s was already a good example of this. The Rock'n'Roll industry emerged through the efforts of mainly American mega-companies, such as CBS, WEA and RCA. In the last third of the twentieth century, only two large European companies, Philips and EMI, participated in the divvying-up of the big commercial pie created by the surge of new popular music. As the 1980s went on, the international economy put into place the bases for a globalized market which implied a certain rebalance of power at a geostrategic level, in spite of the fact that the domination of the United States remained unquestionable. Above all, however, globalization implied a new logic on the productive world map, demanding new alliances between international and local agents, so that the flow of capital (and also of symbolic and cultural capital) would not collapse, but instead, would be revitalized within the new framework of the global transaction. As was optimistically explained by J. Mª Cámara, Vice-president and General Director of BMG-Ariola Spain:

> The big multinational companies, acting simultaneously in many different countries, no longer work in *a single direction*. Each unit, each country, tries to develop their local talent and incorporate it into the general flow of information through its international network. The *global village* seems possible, and the direction towards the *global brain*, inevitable. The key to self-satisfaction or frustration lies in the degree to which each creative country, each community, maintains the balance between what they give and what they receive from the global current. (594)

Only five years after Cámara's diagnosis, it was already relatively easy to find much less euphoric interpretations about the Spanish music industry in the 1980s, such as the one in the article "La industria del disco: diez años de reconversión" ("The Record Industry: Ten Years of Restructuring"), by journalist Darío Vico:

> The companies renovated their structures, reduced their personnel, and rejuvenated their artistic departments. And some changes were made in the capital. CBS regrouped with Epic, as did Fonogram with Polydor, which became Polygram. Later, EMI and Hispavox merged, as did RCA (following external instructions)—which had been bought out by Columbia—and Arbola in the BMG group. On the other hand, veteran companies like Belter and Movieplay disappeared, while Virgin and WEA established themselves in Spain. (74–75)

Only the careful attention given to the national product, according to Vico, explains the resurrection of sales in the second half of the 1980s. In 1993, the report on the state of the music market prepared by the Ministry of Culture stated that

> the progressive commercial concentration and internationalization that took place during the 1980s caused most of the medium-sized Spanish companies, such as Hispavox, Columbia, Belter and EDIGSA, to disappear. In the early nineties, the only significant Spanish company is DRO/GASA/Twins, with a market share in 1989 of approximately 2.4% of the total. (104)

This means that the Spanish music industry was responding to the structural guidelines that the record industry was undergoing on an international scale, which had begun in the English-speaking world in the previous decade. This transformation had been described in terms of trends, like a combination of oligopolisation, conservatism, and standardization (Straw 98). In Spain, WEA arrived in 1981 and Virgin in 1983; EDIGSA closed in 1983 (although its funds were then exploited by PDI) and Belter, in 1984. Odeón went on to become part of EMI, which took over Hispavox; Columbia was acquired by RCA. It was a "convulsive context" (Fouce 106) which, at the beginning, was able to promote a large number of independent firms (Dro, Tres Cipreses, GASA, Lollipop, Twins, Nuevos Medios, etc.) but which, given the structural tendency of the industry, resulted in the pressure for standardization and risk minimization so common in the late 1980s and early 1990s. The crisis in the global growth of cultural industries was thus resolved through a process of oligopolistic re-concentration which, nonetheless, required intensive attention towards integrated local production.

In short, two factors resulted from this industrial adjustment which had a direct influence on post-1980s Spanish music culture: one, "the lack of diversity and of intelligence" (Alcanda) in radio programs, and in the media in general; and two, a simultaneous creative paralysis caused by the suffocating atmosphere imposed by the context of mass media and production. The explosive moment of the early 1980s was thus neutralized and channeled on a large scale. The sensation described by Silva in 1984 became a thing of the past: "The independent labels, envisioning a self-managed, self-sufficient dynamic, have made businessmen of young music lovers, thus turning record company executives into old arteriosclerotic folks who haven't a clue about music" (13).

The commercial insecurities in the period 1977–1984 opened a conflictive space which the supranational reconfiguration of the record industry would eventually neutralize. Already in 1987, as Pardo points out, the international economic crisis demanded adjustments on the mass culture circuit that were associated with a noticeable musical decline. That is why the flamboyant launch of the collection *Historia del Rock* by the newspaper *El País* in 1987 was something more, or something less, than a mere celebratory gesture: in fact, it can be interpreted as the moment in which the cadaver is being readied for embalming. It is not strange that the CD "Los alegres 80" (The Happy 1980s), also put out by *El País* in its CD collection *Un país de música 2* (A Country of Music 2, 2002), acknowledged in its liner notes that, in that decade, "the normalization of pop [music] in Spanish" had been achieved. The normalizing sanction was working there like in any other cultural and political discourses and practices, along the lines of what Foucault would call "the means of correct training." The pop songs from the Transition could already be seen (and this began to happen in the late eighties) as the country's music, like the soundtrack for a State which was finally democratic and modern.

In brief, from all the above, we can see how the fact that pop music during the Transition became Hispanized responds (perhaps not exclusively, but undeniably) to the convergence of two lines of interest: a *market interest* which requires a strategic insistence on the local identities as a precondition for global industrial rebalance; and an *interest of State*, that suffers from a foreseeable anxiety to renovate its coherence—of politics and of identity—at the end of one historical period and at the beginning of a new one. In this way, it seems unarguable that the mythification of *Spanish rock*, which includes the construction of the marketing label "rock español," paradoxically (or logically, given the compensating character of all myths) accelerates the creative and critical decline of this music.

Perhaps it is precisely the musical nature of this series of cultural practices (*Spanish pop-rock*, New Wave, "Movida" music. . .) which, comparatively speaking (in contrast, for example, with cinema, comics or literature), makes it easier for them to undergo a process of accelerated mythification. The myth relocates the non-place, which music, as a social practice, opens in the common culture, channeling it towards a way of circulation which fits within the Puritanism inherited by official culture in capitalist modernity (Gilbert and Pearson). The invisibility of popular energy at the moment of its emergence becomes, then, a massive, inoffensive, soothing hyper-visibility. To the extent that changes in music and changes in society go hand in hand (Small), the Neoconservatism of the 1990s demanded an acritical restructuring of musical practices which might be related to effects that are not so reassuring. Among these effects (and affections), corporal demonstration, through dance, holds a privileged place; it was already a reason for political concern for Plato. The popular and commercial success of *Bailando* (Dancing), by Alaska y Pegamoides (1982) shows the power of this ambivalent and decisive recourse: dance, as a libertarian form of pleasure and encounter, as a sexual experience, and as the *art of the weak*, was a defining element of this new music, in comparison with the folksinger style from the last years of Franco's regime, which was music for listening. *Bailando* had to be more than a song: it had to be an anthem. Its casual, naïve momentum distinguished this piece from the oblique and ironic treatment of other songs of the same vein in the early eighties, such as the *reggae* piece called *Divina* (*Los bailes de Marte*) and the delightful *Dance Vd*, both by Radio Futura, or the caustic, destructive treatment that is pushed to the extreme in *Branquias bajo el agua,* by Derribos Arias. Likewise, the openly *pop* approach of *Bailando* did not resemble other, less gentle songs by Alaska y Pegamoides (such as, *Odio* 'Hate,' *Quiero salir* 'I Want Out,' *Vértigo, Redrum,* etc.), which made it, almost unwittingly, into a precedent to the emblematic (and again, politically illustrative) hit by Olé Olé in 1986: *Bailando sin salir de casa* (Dancing without leaving home).

The Destruction of Form: A Question of State

The consideration of music as a social practice opens a tinderbox. The traditional and elitist bias which sees music as an autonomous aesthetic realm, purified from all worldly contamination, has been critically revised by musical anthropology, ethnomusicology and cultural criticism. This critical reformulation of the links between music, society and power may still be in an early developmental stage, but this does not render the question any less relevant. And this explicative relevance becomes even more necessary and opportune in the case of pop music, where the link between music and everyday life is quite clear at all different levels, from mass-media to street culture, from the noise and sex involved in partying to the laws of marketing and the concept of style as seen by young people, from the new artistic trends to the mutating nature of the most diverse sub- and counter-cultures, and so on.

A passage by Jacques Attali summarizes the necessary point of departure to continue on this critical path: "Yet music is a credible metaphor of the real. It is neither an autonomous activity nor an automatic indicator of the economic infrastructure. It is a herald, for change is inscribed in noise faster than it transforms society" (54). Of course, what Attali calls "change" can be productively applied to the dynamic of social and institutional power at the time of the Spanish Transition, from Franco's dictatorship to a democracy of the masses. Attali explains in detail how music in history has been a tool for control as well as a threat to the established power: "music is like the masses, at the same time threatening and a necessary source of legitimacy, a risk that each power must take, and try to channel"(29). Therefore, the transversal strength of music implies the imminence of cultural and political analysis in a broad sense, like "a call to theoretical indiscipline" (64) which is consistent with the off-centered and asystematic workings of the practices of popular music.

Precisely, pop music with urban and contemporary roots is a perfect area, though not the only one, for understanding how the illusion of classical harmony turns into conflict, into the proliferation of noise, and into bodily and social disturbance. In the words of Attali:

> Noise has always been perceived as destruction, disorder, filth, pollution, aggression against the code that organizes messages. It conveys, in all cultures, the idea of weapons, blasphemy, plague. . . . In its biological reality, noise is a means of injury. (54)

It is not strange, then, that noise is perceived as a "mortal threat" by authoritarian regimes, which do not only include state-run communism or classic fascism, but also post-modern fascism, market-run fascism, or *low-grade fascism*, which today's global model of (neo)liberal democracy keeps coming up against. In the case of Spain's Transition to democracy, fascism was too present, too inertially alive to just disappear overnight, and capitalism was too powerful to hide its leading role in the collective change. Fascism and capitalism, therefore, are crossed with different libertarian tactics of resistance and subversion, which are often preconscious, finding in popular culture a new arena for struggle and conflict.

The Spanish case, which is seen as exemplary among important sectors of the public opinion and by international diplomacy, not only had the peculiarity of the fascism/capitalism combination, which was already present in the context of Nazi Germany, but it also made the step towards a peculiar organization of capitalism, democracy and monarchy. In 1933, the young Georges Bataille wrote an essay entitled "The State and the Problem of Fascism," which is not often quoted, but useful on this point because of the way it articulates fascism and capitalism and resolves the differential and relational game between democracy and monarchy. According to Bataille, the capitalist State presents homogenization as normalization, finding a space of consensus between (despotic) authority and (democratic) adaptation. All heterogeneity or alterity are then perceived as a left-over, as unproductive waste. Within the capitalist State, fascism would find an optimal outlet in the religious/military and inter-class condensation of power as a massive form of power. For Bataille, this means that through the naturalization/institutionalization of (democratic) normality, even freedom and movement are turned into "an imperative form" (41). Therefore, democracy invests itself with the power to block radical social change, to the extent that such change must be regulated within an ideologically repressive and institutional framework. This is, obviously, an unstable dynamic that is open to conflict. What seems peculiar is that this conflict, which could even become intensified to the point of interrupting the institutional or systemic inertia, should be softened by the establishment of a monarchic axis within the democratic framework, because in a typical monarchic society:

> the need for change is only represented internally by a conscious minority: the grouping of *homogenous* elements and the immediate beginnings of *homogeneity* remain tied to the maintenance of legal forms and of the existing administrative framework, guaranteed by the king's authority; reciprocally, the king's authority becomes confused with the maintenance of these forms and frameworks. (40)

From this point of view, the homogenizing or normalizing imperative becomes the guarantor of stability in times of change for a fascist political system which needs to be democratic and capitalist, and finds in the monarchy a sufficiently solid and secure framework for legitimacy. However, is normalization as efficient as a clockwork mechanism? Is it not true, as Attali points out, that "a network can be destroyed by noises that assail and transform it, if the codes that are in effect cannot normalize and repress such noises" (67)? Within this context, how does the noise (of pop music) act, being aware of its participation in a situation of conflict and social change? What positions, for example, does Rock'n'Roll lean to, with its tendency towards do-it-yourself and popular inclusiveness (Berio 58), within conditions of macro-social normalization? The answer must undoubtedly be complex, heteromorphic and heterological. I will now offer a few suggestions which may enable us to find answers to these questions.

The Benjaminian notion of *destruction of form* could be used as an aid to tackle the corrosive capacity of certain musical discourses and practices. For Benjamin, Schlegel's concept of irony is linked to the "exteriorization of an opposition that is always alive against dominant ideas" ("Concept of Criticism" 125). This gesture of resistance and opposition offers an irony that does not remain within the statement, but affects the placement of the statement, undermining the possibility of unity in the form. In terms akin to Bertolt Brecht's concept of epic drama, the ironization of the shape produces a distance within the space of the gaze or the hearing, which would prevent the naïve absolutization of the representative illusion. Benjamin dialogues with Schlegel as follows:

> "We must rise above our own pride and be able to annihilate, in our thoughts, those things we adore, that is, if we do not lack ... the sense of the infinite." In these statements, Schlegel was clearly discussing the destructive element in criticism, its disintegrating effect on the artistic form. Therefore, very far from representing a

subjective fickleness on the author's part, this destruction of form is the task of the objective capacity in art, it is the critic's task. (125)

The *destruction of form* is supported in an effect of "irritation" (124) which would undermine the classic transparency and would send into the abyss the work of art, the musical form in this case, in an experience of extinction, which, as Theodor Adorno said, would be at the same time a trace of the experience of extinction. On this point, poetic writing necessarily becomes self-reflective.

My hypothesis is that self-reflection is what lies beneath the work of a musical group that called themselves Derribos Arias (Arias Demolitions). Their recordings, especially those made between 1982 and 1983, compiled in *Branquias bajo el agua* and in the LP *En la guía, en el listín*, are signs of a delirious and transgressive drifting. This drifting is embraced as an interruption in the order of the discourse, like an agonized collapse, in moments of extreme intensity such as "A flúor," "Lo que hay" and "Introducción." But, beyond those sudden heart attacks, the sound and noise of Derribos Arias is deployed in a convulsive, dislocated collage which, from the beginning, destroys the alleged logophonocentric authority (Derrida) of the lead voice through inexpressive, anti-canonical, often illegible rhythms. As for the lyrics, they confronted in turn, from this corrosive angle, current political topics, as in "Europa," "Misiles hacia Cuba" (Missiles towards Cuba) and "Dios salve al Lehendakari" (God Save the President of the Basque Country). The destruction of form, in Derribos Arias, shows its disturbing, self-aware edge, ironically challenging the fascist view of the world through broken references to Nazism and the holocaust ("Aprenda alemán en 7 días" [Learn German in 7 Days], "Lili Marlen," "Crematorio" [Crematorium], etc.). This wounding persistence of Fascism illustrates in itself the subconscious relationship between music and society at this specific socio-historic moment.

Apart from that, if the search for destructive noise in the soundtrack of the Spanish Transition were to begin with song titles, then "Mensajeros de la destrucción" ("Messengers of destruction," by Barón Rojo, off the live album *Al rojo vivo*, 1984) would surely hold a prominent place. As happens in heavy metal style, the transgression of Barón Rojo lies in the new rawness of what was said: "hablan los jerarcas de negociación: / farsantes sin pudor / que siembran el terror" (the leaders speak of negotiation: / shameless frauds / who instill terror). The frontal attack on the political class is approached in terms of an us vs. them dialectic, common in the denunciation rhetoric of hard rock that is not necessarily immersed in heavy-metal paraphernalia. An example of this would be Leño, whose song "Corre, corre" (Run, run; the title track from the album *Corre, corre*, which came out in 1982) proclaimed "sabemos lo que quieren y aunque no nos convenció / estamos en el juego y somos su preocupación" (we know what they want and though we were not convinced / we are in the game and we are their problem). Along the same lines, and on the same Leño album, is the song "Que tire la toalla" (Let him throw in the towel). Leño's skid-row rock and their singer, Rosendo Mercado, who appeared in the 1982 concerts dressed in sleeveless white overalls, worked with an effect of camaraderie, of fraternity which was not reducible to the parameters of *fan* behavior, and went for a verbal and musical rawness that earned them a comparatively large following at a time when "the street belonged to the people again" (Lechado 37). As for heavy-metal bands, such as Barón Rojo or Obús, they shared with the hard rockers this demonstration of alternative counter-power whose unity went beyond the limits of the clan. However, heavy-metal takes to the extreme a pattern which was already active in hard rock: the need to scream, to amplify the sound of the guitar, the violent percussion, etc. To sum up, we can say that the politics of heavy-metal are not so much a strategy of destruction (the "messengers of destruction" in the song by Barón Rojo were "they," the others) but an expository transgression based on the need to be heard.

The techno genre belonged to a different kind of musical poetics, as it was understood, for example, by El Aviador Dro y sus Obreros Especializados (Aviator Dro and his Specialized Workers), whose first long-play album (*Alas sobre el mundo*, 1982—'Wings over the World') strategically opened up with the track "Brigada de demolición" (Demolition brigade). Rosendo's proletarian clothes in Leño and Poch's destructive eagerness in Derribos Arias came together in the futuristic and anti-Utopian fiction of Aviador Dro: "los obreros cantan sobre el ruido / la ciudad de las máquinas despierta // brigada de demolición / derribar para construir . . ." (the workers sing above the noise / the city of the machines awakes // Demolition brigade / demolish in order to build . . .). Far from producing an automated or merely mechanical effect, Aviador Dro was able to put technology at the service of danceable eroticism (especially in tracks like "Ondina" and "Cita en el asteroide" 'Date on the Asteroid'). In the case of the techno music introduced by bands such as the German group, Kraftwerk, or the American band Devo, the destruction of form was staged as a post-industrial universe presented in terms of a collective hangover, where the machine element dissolved the aura of naturalness and authority found in folk music, as well as the genuineness and originality of rock. The sound production of Aviador Dro retook the connection between technology, body and dance in the blasphemous approach of the *cyborg*, as Donna Haraway has stated: "The cyborg skips the step of original unity, of identification with nature in the Western sense. This is its illegitimate promise that might lead to subversion of its teleology as star wars" (255).

The advanced sound technology (the use of synthesizers, drum machines, programmers . . .) seeped into other groups of the time, and rapidly became a massive new *doxa*, thanks to the success of groups like Azul y Negro. However, the techno component was not always associated with a euphoric or aseptic vision; sometimes it allied with more embittered codes, as was the case of the combination of techno sound and post-punk vocals in Golpes Bajos. In spite of its brief career, this group formed by Germán Coppini (formerly of Siniestro Total) and Teo Cardalda was the only one, perhaps together with the after-effects of Parálisis Permanente, which delimited katabatic tonalities and atmospheres of fear, sickness and relentless malaise, in the wake of expressionist avant-garde theatre and art. In Golpes Bajos, the destruction of form is achieved through a voice conceived as a lament, whose phrasing overwhelms the pre-established boundaries of a basic melody. It is channeled through imbalances, not between the voice and the melody ("Ayes"), but between the song and the rhythmic model (such as the crazy samba "La reclusa" or the schizoid salsa "Colecciono moscas" 'I Collect Flies'). Or it is specified as the destruction of childhood ("Hansel y Gretel"), of interpersonal relations ("Desconocido" 'Stranger') or of imposed, repressive religiosity ("La virgen loca" 'The Crazy Virgin'). Madness and childhood, abandonment, and isolation make up parts of the same poetics of rejection in Golpes Bajos, who reached an agonizing, but again danceable (as if it were an anguished, absurd dance) moment with "Fiesta de los maniquíes" (Mannequin Party) (*A Santa Compaña*, 1984), whose perception of social phenomena as a void was in tune with an experience of subjectivity which was becoming more and more extended, more desert-like, and less recognizable by the euphemistic levels of institutional politics. It was no accident that this perspective of a society in its death throes was anticipated in the band's debut song in 1983 "No mires a los ojos de la gente" ("Don't look people in the eyes"—from the EP *Golpes Bajos*, 1983).

But, if somewhere in the soundscape, a fateful combination took place between music, dance and the disruption of authenticity (and its adjacent meanings: originality, naturalness, identity, reality . . .), it was in Tino Casal's approach to music. With the experimental collaboration of Julián Ruiz's studio, Casal embarked upon an unprecedented intersection in the Spanish tradition between technological exploration (using samplers, rhythm, sequencers, synthesized sounds and voices, a vocoder, etc.) and the *glam* style, inherited from Bolan, Bowie, and The Human League. The result is an experience of sonic instability and tension, shared with other projects associated at the time with techno research and *cold wave* (such as Claustrofobia), but which also incorporated a liminar supplement through melodic forcing and a voice threatened by its own echo, rushed into the vicinity of an excitation understood as an imposture.

It is not surprising that Casal opened his set on the 1983 tour with "Legal, illegal." This song became an emblem of the crisis of Reality and Meaning promoted by the digitalization of popular music (Goodwin). And it achieved this status, not only because of the sophistication of the technical or playing devices, or the erotic, desiring confidence in the funk-inspired bass line that causes a physical urge to dance, but because this crisis was translated into a verbal syntax through an interplay of opposites organized around an ellipsis, a vacuum of meaning. As the chorus insists on reminding us, "Es legal, es ilegal. / Es sólo un truco y nada más. / Es legal, es ilegal. / Tan sólo tú lo entenderás" (It's legal, it's illegal. / It's just a gimmick and nothing more. / It's legal, it's illegal. / Only you will understand). However, we must insist that the undermining of meaning, the centrality of the message, is pursued through the articulation of the ellipsis in the lyrics and the syncopated treatment of rhythm and melodic phrasings. "Legal, ilegal" thus presented a kind of deconstruction through the seduction of the ideological notion of "reasonable realism" (García San Miguel 17) which was becoming the cornerstone for the large-scale construction of a new public consensus naturalized in terms of democracy. The dividing line between normal and abnormal, between real and unreal, between possible and impossible . . . remains in question, overwhelmed by the rhythmic interplay that makes us jump from one side to another, like slipping off the slash (/) that separates what is legal from what is illegal—with all of the impacts this interplay conjures up in the realm of sexual practices, drugs, professional politics, the business world, etc. Imbert makes it clear:

> The great debates of the Transition, asides from the ones affecting strictly institutional changes, followed a double impulse: a need to socialize the activity of the subjects (the adaptation of the more or less brutal practices of some more or less normalized behaviors); and a need to confirm, to formalize this activity, that is, to sanction it in accordance with the law; in legal terms: *prohibit / decriminalize / legalize.* (42)

As in other pop music songs from the time, Casal's music reminds us that, in this environment of new disciplinary rules, the body is in the center of these physical and cultural battles, and that within the possibility of moving the body in another way, there is more at stake than a style, an image or a form of government. The study of these and other manifestations of pop music could, in short, contribute to the understanding that a historical period, whether past or present, does not only refer to the "strictly institutional changes," and that even these changes in official culture can be reformulated and diverted by the common culture toward another place.

Works Cited

Alcanda, Santiago. "Los nuevos medios musicales." *Un año de rock '91*. Ed. Santiago Alcanda *et al.* Madrid: Luca Editorial, 1991.
Attali, Jacques. *Noise: The Political Economy of Music*. Trans. Brian Massumi. Minneapolis: University of Minnesota Press, 1985.
Barthes, Roland. *A Lover's Discourse: Fragments*. Trans. Richard Howard. New York: Hill and Wang, 1984.
———. *Mythologies*. Trans. Annette Lavers. London: Paladin, 1972.
Bataille, Georges. *El estado y el problema del fascismo*. Valencia: Pre-Textos / Universidad de Murcia, 1993.
Bauman, Zygmunt. *The Individualised Society*. Cambridge: Polity Press, 2001.
Benjamin, Walter. "The Concept of Criticism in German Romanticism." *Selected Writings, Vol 1. 1913–1926*. Cambridge, MA.: Harvard University Press, 1995.
———. *Discursos interrumpidos I*. Madrid: Taurus, 1990.
———. *Illuminations*. Trans. Harry Zohn. Ed. Hannah Arendt. New York: Schocken, 1978.
Berio, Luciano. "Commentaires au rock." *Musique en Jeu* 2 (1971): 56–65.
Bradby, Barbara. "Do-Talk and Don't Talk (The Division of the Subject in Girl-Group Music)." *On Record (Rock, Pop, & The Written Word)*. Ed Simon Frith and Andrew Goodwin. London: Routledge, 1990. 341–68.
Cámara, José María. "Las claves de la música grabada." *Historia del Rock*. Madrid: El País, 1987. 593–94.
Feuer, Jane. *The Hollywood Musical*. Bloomington, IN: University of Indiana Press, 1982.
Foucault, Michel. *Discipline and Punish: The Birth of the Prison*. Trans. Alan Sheridan. New York: Pantheon Books, 1977.
Fouce, Héctor. *El futuro ya está aquí: Música pop y cambio cultural en España 1978–1985*. Madrid: Universidad Complutense, 2002.
García San Miguel, Luis. *Teoría de la transición (Un análisis del modelo español 1973–1978)*. Madrid: Editora Nacional, 1981.
Gilbert, Jeremy, and Ewan Pearson. *Discographies: Dance, Music and the Politics of Sound*. London: Routledge, 1999.

Goodwin, Andrew. "Simple and Hold (Pop Music in the Digital Age of Reproduction)." *On Record (Rock, Pop, & The Written Word)*. Ed Simon Frith and Andrew Goodwin. London: Routledge, 1990. 258–73.
Guillén, Claudio. *Entre lo uno y lo diverso*. Barcelona: Tusquets, 2005.
Haraway, Donna. *Simians, Cyborgs, and Women: The Reinvention of Nature*. New York: Routledge, 1991.
Imbert, Gérard. *Los discursos del cambio (Imágenes e imaginarios sociales en la España de la Transición 1976–1982)*. Madrid: Akal, 1990.
Lechado, José Manuel. *La movida (Una crónica de los 80)*. Madrid: Algaba, 2005.
Méndez, Sabino. *Corre, rocker (Crónica personal de los 80)*. Madrid: Espasa-Calpe, 2000.
Ministerio de Cultura. *La cultura en España y su integración en Europa*. Madrid: Ministerio de Cultura, 1993.
Ovid. *Metamorphoses*. New York: Oxford University Press, 2004.
Pardo, José Ramón. *Historia del pop español*. Madrid: Rama Lama, 2005.
Silva, Diego. *El pop español*. Barcelona: Teorema, 1984.
Small, Christopher. *Music, Society, Education*. Hanover, NH: Wesleyan University Press/ University Press of New England, 1996.
Vico, Dario. "La industria del disco: diez años de reconversión." *La Edad de Oro del Pop Español*. Madrid: Luca Editorial, 1992. 74–75.
Vilarós, Teresa. *El mono del desencanto: Una crítica cultural de la transición española (1973–1993)*. Madrid: Siglo XXI, 1998.

8

Popular Filmic Narratives and the Spanish Transition

Germán Labrador Méndez

Is There Something Really Missing?

It is commonplace for contemporary Cultural Studies to address the Spanish transition to democracy's public representation and visibility in terms of memory and amnesia. Teresa Vilarós has explained in psychoanalytical terms the possibility of the emergence of a *mono* culture which would assure the repression of any representation of the period; were there to be any, it would have an "ill" symbolic form. This follows a tendency according to which "repressed elements turn out to be implemented." Moreover, this Lacanian formulation conceives of any anomaly in discursive logics in the form of a lack-existence of references to Franco's regime which are embodied in the person of Franco himself—taken to be the expression of a superior metonymy.

The above-mentioned formulation, characterized by its powerful conceptual nature, prevailed in much of the criticism following the one by Vilarós. These works, written according to different theoretical approaches, aimed at placing the issue of amnesia at the centre of their analyses—to the extent that some of them include this idea in their titles. Alberto Medina's book, which deals with the "exorcism exerted upon memory," with the idea of an unhealed mourning and with an ill rite of passage, is a good example; his work corrupts both the young democracy's aesthetics and its politics. In this case, the metaphor is taken from the crypt in the Valle de los Caídos (Valley of the Fallen), a place where the essence of Franco's regime is still preserved. Even if the regime has fallen into oblivion, this does not mean that its symbolism has disappeared. There are other works which stress the need to build a theory of amnesia in order to interpret Spain's contemporary culture: for example, Cristina Moreiras's and J. Francisco Colmeiro's, both of which place "historical memory" at the center of the issue of "collective identity."

It should be noticed that this conception is highly linked to certain types of political discourses and citizens: those who champion "historical memory." It is them who, in the last decade, have highlighted the need to revise in a critical way (i.e. in terms of political violence and social costs) the relations among history, institutions and society. These discourses aim at demanding the creation of new institutional stories about the past. These kinds of stories should judge in democratic terms the two most significant periods of Franco's regime (the Civil War and the transition to democracy). In this way, stories about the Civil War and the repression would be involved with stories about the transition to democracy. This is linked to the aspiration of establishing a republican family tree about democratic institutions that can be used so as to put an end to the notion of a transitional space that counts as zero in time. The reason is that the lack of previous history gives way *ex-nihilo* to a completely new political culture which is free of moral or political implications with regard to its own past. The abovementioned academic discourses—be they built on the same wavelength or rather on a dialectical opposition, be they subordinated to each other or rather correlated—favor, due to their conceptual formulations, the emergence of such kind of historical languages.

The advantage of these kinds of historical narratives is that they provide a satisfying response to certain discursive anomalies created during the transition and during the first part of the democracy. They offer an explanation for the interruptions and dysfunctions that arise between these two periods. The above mentioned scholars have dealt with this issue according to a series of interpretative theories which provide a more or less political, conscious and aesthetic response to an initial forgetfulness; an amnesia which short-circuits any representation about Franco's regime and about the democracy.

However, the construction of an omnipresent amnesia, to which these scholars refer constantly, may be objectified in relation to the linguistic and iconographic forms used in the documents of the period. It is necessary to highlight that there exist discursive continuities that emerge from the very historical framework on which these narratives are based. Having said this, it is possible to state that these kinds of "narratives about amnesia" (linked to a discourse dealing with a "fear to forget") arise directly from the transition to democracy period, to which we owe an intertextual debt. The period shaped and expressed the meaning of this discourse according to different expository levels: aesthetic formulations, political discourses or filmic representations.

Although at the time when they emerged these narratives did not have hegemonic nature, to reconstruct them may provide us with a map of continuities. Such continuities are useful in order to show that in the last three decades, academic discourses, and even a learned type of discourse (hereby referred to as critical or aimed at preserving memory, as opposed to an Adanist discourse), have pictured the transition to democracy in a supportive way. As a matter of fact, we can mention a great number of essays, journal reports or articles carried out by scholars that belong to the first part of the transition to democracy period. For instance, Vázquez Montalbán was one of the first authors who declared overtly that amnesia could turn up becoming a reality (*Cómo liquidaron el Franquismo*). He claimed this on the basis that it was possible to verify a rapid structural change which had led to write in a collective way about the relations between people, their past and identity patterns. The fact that the mentioned scholars used Montalban's texts as a primary source of documentation shows that those texts were characterized by a continuous nature.

Eduardo Subirats's critical essay on Spanish modern culture is another example of narrative continuity. In all of his works concerning this issue, Subirats has reflected on the relation that exists between collective identities, on discourses about the past and on awareness about the present. He analyses these issues on the basis of postmodern discursive logics and of the notion of entertainment. Moreover, he claims overtly that democracy was built on the basis of an agreement aimed at instilling amnesia. Faced with this situation, it is only possible to grow aware of the transformations that have taken place and to denounce the way in which these changes have taken place. It should be noticed that this is a constructive type of story because it places us in a historical logic in relation to the past.

Gregorio Morán outlines in an organized way the idea of an agreement aimed at instilling amnesia or silence. His book, which was received favorably, conceives the establishment of the basis for a democratic coexistence as a negotiation that resulted in the need to forget the past. Indeed, a series of discursive and legal consequences derived from this situation. It had an impact on institutional left-wing parties, an effect which became manifest in a collective amnesia. Moreover, from the political power, amnesia was instilled in the public opinion by means of the so-called "speeches on change" (Imbert).

I could go on quoting other works. However, I believe that the abovementioned examples are enough to prove that there is an obvious memory about an alleged amnesia, the existence of which must, thus, be doubted. The tributary nature of these narratives (they include references to some of the first narrations) shows that there exists a kind of narration that can be placed somewhere in between the scholarly and the public type. It is a *learned* type of narration and, during some thirty years, it has drawn attention to the fact that the transition from a dictatorial regime to a democratic system (a transition full of sacrifices, victims and costs) has not been narrated as a continuum. In this way, it protected from oblivion, even in small hermeneutic communities, the "awareness" of such continuity. Narratives which favor continuity are also common in genres that deal with a similar kind of writing. As a result, this discourse spreads significantly. For instance, it is apparent in the analytical language used in the political science employed in the media (by Ramón Chao, Haro Tecglen, Josep Ramoneda, etc.) and in some of the memoirs, chronicles and biographies written by politicians, activists, and important figures of the left-wing of Spain's transition to democracy.

This applies, likewise, to the novel. From the very beginning, this genre gave way to a critical narrative about the memories of this period. It should be noticed that this kind of narrative was not only practiced during the transition itself; rather, it has continued to be practiced right into the present moment, as proved by Vázquez Montalbán in an excellent essay in which he links the maintenance of certain types of narrative in modern Spanish novels with "the construction of a democratic city." For example, Rafael Chirbes' works—notably *La larga marcha*—are characterized by narrating the past as if it were a continuum where there is no interruption whatsoever in between the Spanish Civil War and the present moment. Were we to expound at length on this issue, we should focus on present-day narratives dealing with the theme of memory—or more precisely with *this memory*—in a variety of forms and formats (theatre, comic strips, poetry, art, etc.). In this way, it would be possible to find lineages explaining the atmosphere of *disagreement* that reigned in Spain during the last part of the millennium.

The fact that continuity narratives have not occupied a dominant position (as compared to the wider diffusion given to the "official narratives" of the transition period) does not account for a model of "critical epiphany"; a pattern aimed at providing a more "authentic" portrayal of the historical period on which modern Spain is built. By contrast, it is intended to produce a model in which different types of narratives come together. This pattern combines two kinds of narratives (both of which focus on the transition to democracy) that have rivaled each other during thirty years and continue to do so in an attempt to gain social supremacy. It should be noticed that these two narratives are surrounded by other narratives and formulations. These narratives seek, first of all, to dominate their intended sphere of reception (the discursive communities where they arise) and, later, to expand all over the society so as to attain an encompassing nature.

The first one, which is accepted at an institutional level (at least until 2004) with various degrees of enthusiasm, creates an idea of national reconciliation. According to this idea, Spain's conflicting brothers (represented, in Antonio Machado's terms, as Cain and Abel) go beyond the biblical story so as to allow their access into a new level of narration. By this means, History is re-established or rather a new History begins. Since it is characterized by a different discursive model—a (post)modern discourse—it can no longer be linked to the past; i.e. to the time of myths. The second one deals with the existing *décalage* among two levels of reality. As a matter of fact, it focuses on a continuous reality and a discontinuous reality or, in other words, on a transition period characterized by change and a transition period characterized by use. Reality, it should be noticed, is analyzed by using the language employed in the theatre, economic politics or psychology and by placing disappointment at the centre of the hermeneutic study.

In this way, we can think about such rhetoric (and in some cases poetics) in persuasive terms. This would prove that amnesia does not arise from a lack of awareness about previous discourses, which are in fact included in the form of works cited, but rather from a communicative strategy. Indeed, it is one of its most powerful means of persuasion: it attempts to make strange the dominant discourse about the past, and it does so by incorporating new narrative logics in a sudden way. It is interesting to notice that these logics enlighten in a different way a unique spatial reference.

In civic terms, these two kinds of narratives are, without any doubt, significantly different. The second type of narrative aims at paying tribute to forms of political repression, of historical injustice, of civil alienation which have been addressed to an important group of people. It does so by agreeing, in large terms, on the existence of "people who have gained something" and "people who have lost out" during Franco's regime. However, the narrative itself leaves out naming them one by one or giving an individual portrayal of each of them. Moreover, this narrative offers the possibility of providing "moral satisfaction" for those who had to face, because of political reasons, painful vital experiences owing to their being identified with "History's losers."

The second type of narrative, by contrast, claims that it is not viable to go back to the past. It defends that it is metaphysically impossible to write narratives dealing with a period prior to the dictator's death. This gives way to the creation of a zero time that divides into two the past, history, handbooks on history, literary historiography, university curricula, the legislation in force. We live in one of these two divisions, whereas the other one spreads away into the darkness of time. The latter represents the part of history in relation to which we have or are starting to have enough "historical distance" so as to be able to objectivize it and to reach a consensus on a common narrative. At least, this was the case until not long ago. However, as I shall comment on later, the reactivation of a critical discourse about memory has had as a consequence a crisis concerning the foundations of an "objective narration" about the Spanish Civil War, as studied by Sánchez León and Izquierdo, whose reflections have been very useful for the writing of this essay.

We can, therefore, think about an apparent amnesia not in absolute terms but rather in relative terms. This implies taking into account that there are competing discourses and that they are not innocent; rather, they were used and continue to be used as political tools. Moreover, the public acceptance of one over the other means enhancing a particular kind of democratic individual. The existence of citizens who are aware of the situation, who participate in political activities and who are implicated in the discursive construction of their society is linked, in this type of language, with a profound historical awareness concerning narratives about the past. Likewise, a model which is merely representative seems to be more easily associated to a flat history amidst a similarly flat citizenry.

It is then possible to understand the way in which these critical narratives link the issue of "amnesia" during the transition to democracy period with an ongoing process characterized by the dissolution of politicization in Spanish society. From this perspective, to leave out a political outlook about reality (which, by the way, would never encompass society as a whole, but rather large groups of the middle class; i.e. the so-called "sociological left-wing") would come hand in hand with an overlook about memories concerning the period, notably in places where there is a great political implication. This would ultimately be substituted by a process of disappointment-oblivion. Did it really occur in such a way? As far as Jordá's films are concerned, there are reasons to doubt about an interpretation of this kind. Despite a gradual dissolution of politicization—in terms of commitment to democratic institutions and to political organizations—this has not had an impact on the survival of an individual memory about the transition to democracy period. The latter is understood both in macro and micro terms and it is close to a critical stance about memory: it transforms memories into alleged universal experiences, into alleged histories.

When speaking about amnesia in relation with history (the starting point), it actually seems that we are referring not to the memory of the events themselves or to a sophisticated and generalizing narrative about them, but rather to political commitment. This represents a conceptual difference which, in certain authors, is simply an identification of a historical awareness linked to a political vision. In other authors, however, it takes the form of an intertextual heritage that encompasses the contradiction of the discourse itself. Moreover, there are others who use rhetoric strategies.

What Is, Thus, Missing?

Were we to think about the continuity of discourses not in terms of the immanence of ideas or languages but rather as an eventuality linked strictly to the materiality of the mediums (i.e. to open our analysis to genre theories and to reception theory), we should mention an area in which discontinuity manifests overtly: the world of films (narratives for the big screen and for television). This is probably the reason why we think about amnesia in relation to the transition to democracy as something ordinary. It is interesting to notice that this is almost the only field where amnesia occurs. Be that as it may, the fact is that there is amnesia about the transition to democracy period or, in other words, a lack of narratives. This has probably affected in a significant way our perspective of this historical period.

The fact that during the last twenty years of the twentieth century there are (almost) no films (nor television series, documentaries, etc.) about the transition to democracy period does not necessarily mean that the cinema industry has forgotten about it; lack of films does not mean amnesia. It does not imply either that society has forgotten, encoded, excluded or repressed the transition to democracy. However, it may help us to adopt a particular stance in relation to this evident void. Insofar as they create a massive number of narratives, both the cinema and television industries play an important role in the visibility of public discourses and in the ability to influence society (Camarero; Parenti). To recognize that there is a lack of films about the Spanish transition to democracy is essential in order to understand the uneven correlation of forces that exists in between institutional discourses and critical discourses about memory. To admit this allows for the creation of narratives that are set apart from the political memory (a plausible situation taking into account that these films are usually based on personal experiences). As a consequence, the scales of narrations are altered. In this way, narratives have the power to spread social languages effectively and to highlight curiosity, demand or, at least, the consumption of narratives about the transition to democracy. To sum up, this denies the possibility of oblivion.

From this perspective, there was no amnesia during the Spanish transition to democracy period; rather, there were no films about this period (i.e. no visibility and no filmic products). This does not mean that the Spanish transition disappeared, but rather that it tended to relate collective and popular narratives by means of images. It is possible that the discontinuous nature of media narratives altered the learned perception about amnesia. It should be noticed that this was only apparent in the lack of certain kind of discourses. It did not imply, however, that individuals suffered from a mental or psychological void. Individuals certainly told each other narratives about the transition to democracy. Moreover, in other cases, "lack of politisation" was included in the category of historical awareness.

In this essay, I focus on films of the type which, in Rosenstone's opinion, give rise to historical knowledge; films which create a complex view of the past or, in other words, establish a complex relation with the past—an authentic relation. At the same time, due to their specific circumstances, they offer an ampler space which allows for identification and which creates a greater impact on society. Furthermore, because of its means of producing stories, the film industry has the capacity to establish a link between anonymous lives and social and historical plots, in a similar way to nineteenth-century novels. Therefore, it gives way to a narrative about everyday life in which fiction projects, in a natural manner, a historical curtain.

The facts expounded above place filmic discourses in a privileged position as they recognize that the lives of concrete individuals must occupy *an important place*: they must be located amidst the impulsive framework of history. Moreover, they play freely with verification procedures: fiction is pictured as an honorable mechanism for transmitting historical issues. In other words, fiction allows narrating events that are not related in previous documents (events which are said "not to have taken place"). Therefore, by asking themselves "What would have happened if . . .?" these discourses allow a historical exploration which was not possible before. In fact, they place readers in a completely different reading sphere, which is not the least historical nor does it create in a lesser degree awareness about history.

It is widely admitted that films (and other kinds of audiovisual discourses) are capable of producing public narratives which attain a massive distribution and which offer the possibility for collective identification. This ends up producing, in specific socio-historical circumstances, a type of identity and awareness that can operate in different political directions. It should be noticed that the nature of the links created between social cohesion and public values and the representation of the past in popular filmic formats cannot be easily ascribed to the concept of collective historical memory or even to the notion of history itself (Ferro).

As opposed to the adhesion demanded by official narratives and the need for updating them in epic narratives, films which follow a popular pattern and which add a view about an individual history offer material for a complex reception of discourses about the past. This depends on the genre used to narrate history, on the possibility or not of choosing a particular kind of genre and on the degree of tolerance permitted in relation to historical *material*. By contrast, choral and collective plots (epic, tragedy, etc.) tend to dissolve the possibility of individualization. In other words, they dissolve the possibility of perceiving nuances and the specificities with which individuals live their lives on a given moment. Moreover, such plots demand total commitment and the withdrawal of personal values so as confer them to a sharing of values (emotions, memories, memoirs, etc.). This allows narrating reduced experiences (individualized experiences in relation to the past) and identification not with the community as a whole, but rather with other individual experiences or with certain community groups. In this way, it offers a series of options, alternatives, questions and it does so by building a moral panorama in which the reader must be placed on an individual scale. Therefore, s/he shall identify in a varying degree (depending on the receptive agreement) with the approach of each film. In this sense, these discourses offer interesting materials for constructing an autonomous and conscious public opinion and even narratives about the past.

If there had been films following this popular model, our current view about Spanish history might be spectacularly different. Leaving aside the above-mentioned facts, the most outstanding feature is that filmic narratives were lacking during some twenty years (1984–2002) and that they were totally absent during ten years (1986–1996). The cause of this absence is usually explained by arguing that there was no audience, that Spanish citizenry had lost interest in filmic narratives, that Spanish films were second-rate (the so-called "crisis" of Spain's cinema industry), that politicians and production companies showed no interest, that there was need for comedy and films about local customs instead of reflection, etc.

Despite a general absence of films (except for some documentaries and tapes of limited distribution), nowadays it is possible to watch a wide range of products both in cinema and television. These products use different genres to portray the transition to democracy: from fiction to documentaries, from comedies to drama, and through varying perspectives and styles. Moreover, they organize this portrayal according to a wide variety of discourses. The only worth-mentioning instances belong either to a minority sphere, which can be classified as learned critical discourses about memory, or to a group of films which propound a social space removed far away from the type of popular narrative on which I am focusing on here. I deal with the creation of collective identities based on visual languages and which aim at negotiating publicly the different meanings of history.

Fragments of Another Discourse

Historical films have been scarce in the last twenty years. It seems as if the existing material was reduced to Victoria Prego's documentary *Historia de la transición* (History of the Transition) (1993). This work, which was produced for television, displays a wide range of institutional and academic elements. Firstly, it has regal approval. Secondly, it proposes a narrative about the transition to democracy which is diametrically opposed to the parameters expounded in this paper up to this point. Because of its focalization (it is centered almost exclusively in the political space) and because of its temporal limitation (it encompasses merely the period in between President Luis Carrero Blanco's death and the celebration of the first democratic elections), it has been interpreted (and sold) as the filmic version of official history. It has, thus, been interpreted as the legitimate narrative of a new dynasty, placing the King as a metaphor for the reestablishment of Spain and as the model for Spanish citizenry. It is even suggested that he is a drawing done to scale of Spain's citizens (Abril).

The situation did not always coincide with the one described above. There was a time when there were the necessary elements so as to organize a discourse according to the creation of collective identities based on visual languages and aimed at publicly negotiating the different meanings of history). However, this favorable situation was interrupted for complex reasons. Be that as it may, there is a model based on continuities and discontinuities which, as far as the production of popular narratives about the transition period is concerned, can be divided into two periods. One of them corresponds with the historical moment in which events took place and the other one with the present.

As a result, in between these two periods there is a void lapse. Taking this into account, it is possible to deal with films about the transition to democracy (or at least with some of them) from a new perspective. These narratives aimed at offering a sophisticated discourse about the transition. They emerged at the beginning of the period and, from that precise moment onwards, they analyzed history with a kind of language based on the one used by the politics of the time (Hernández and Pérez). The most important elements of the so-called "exposing" narratives are present in these films. It is interesting to notice that they were proposed overtly in contrast to hegemonic narratives.

Documentaries were an essential genre. By using their own representation strategies, they offered material that was extremely useful for the concurrence of narratives even in its own aesthetics reception. Hernández and Pérez, Cerdán and Díaz López have pointed out that this genre played an important role in relation to the transition to democracy. It has the capacity to represent reality without delay; a reality which, in many cases, was disguised. For instance, the narration of social conflicts in the *media* contrasted with its urban visibility (in terms of its prominence in space). Politics in the transition to democracy period could be described as a double level of representation: visible narratives, produced by the public sphere amidst an age of video-politics (Muraro), as opposed to performative discourses which narrated reality in terms of spatial presence and emphasized visible, urban and everyday life elements. In this context, documentaries served to cover the distance between these two political theaters because they gave way, in media terms, to what occurred in performative circumstances.

Strange though it may seem, commemorative discourses in the 1980s were based almost exclusively on the information that appeared in the media or that was filed in newspaper and periodicals libraries. As a result, they used both their material and their ideological stance to deny the possibility of portraying reality in a different way, or even the possibility of rebuilding it. To domesticate these documents and to accept them as a coherent narration was a way of denying the possibility for representing that which was not said during the transition period. Moreover, it implied assuming a priori that these documents did not exist or else to condemn them to a marginal position (they were merely used by official narratives, which used them as a basis to produce their inflections and plots).

Documentaries, therefore, did not contribute, by means of their reception, to create dozens of differing narratives about current events. Due to their specific circumstances of production and diffusion they were part of small hermeneutic communities. However, because they were capable of objectivizing certain areas of reality that had still not been represented, they were extremely useful in order to criticize official discourses, as Medina or Vilarós interpret them. Furthermore, they are an extremely valuable material due to the fact that they present a genealogy which is rather different from the present one. They crystallized narratives and at the same time they encompass sophisticated narratives which contravened and complicated the narratives of the transition to democracy. They proved, therefore, that there were people working in order to put forth a project aimed at creating popular film narratives, though this does not mean that it was successful.

In that sense it is necessary to mention the works of the Bartolomé brothers, compiled in *Después de...* (1981): *Todo atado y bien atado* and *No se os puede dejar solos*. These are documentary narratives about the tensions of the period, shown in the filming of dozens of demonstrations, concentrations, protests, strikes, gatherings and political meetings which took place during the years encompassing 1978 and 1981. At this historical period, the conflicts created by anonymous citizens, who expressed in a vehement manner their opinions, views and concerns, became outstanding, as opposed to the *artifices* of parliamentarian politics, which were pushed into the background.

There are more documentaries worth mentioning: for example, Carlos Morales's *Noche de curas* (1977); Gonzalo García Pelayo's *Vivir en Sevilla* (1978); and Ventura Pons's *Ocaña retrato intermitente* (1978). However, because of space limitations, I shall only comment on one more work: *Numax presenta*, directed by Joaquín Jordá. In 1979, the strike committee of Numax's factory in Barcelona suggested that Jordá film a documentary dealing with a three-year period of labor conflicts and libertarian utopia. With 500,000 pesetas left over from the strike fund, the assembly in Numax decided to produce, in a retrospective way, a narration about its history. The aim was to provide a testimony projected towards the future; i.e. to offer future generations a different view of this historical period.

Many of the films that were shot during the period itself were based on the actual events that were occurring in that very moment. Even if their purposes and views are very different, it is useful to refer to them as a unit. In this way, it can be proved that at that time there were filmic narratives that dealt with the transition to democracy. Indeed, there were many historical films and some of them were successful. In general terms, they contributed to shape a view about that period at the very moment when it was taking place. This view was dense, and, in some occasions, diametrically opposed to the narrative logics produced by a politics which was aimed at neutralizing historical contradictions by means of linguistic transformations held in consensus.

Other filmic productions go beyond mere documentation. They put forth a minor degree of "historical truth" by offering a range of attitudes which go from docudramas to historical fiction. For example, we can mention the following: *La fuga de Segovia* (Uribe, 1978), *Siete días de enero* (Bardem, 1978), *El proceso de Burgos* (Uribe, 1979), *El crimen de Cuenca* (Rey, 1979), *Operación Ogro* (Pontecorvo, 1978). In these films, history—especially its tensions and troubled periods—is presented as the centre of a continuous reflection about identity and reality. History is likewise presented through intrigue or through a kind of plot aimed at undertaking a penetrating look into the period itself. It is indeed symptomatic that scholars representing discourses characterized by amnesia with regard to the transition to democracy used many of these productions as a source of inspiration. They looked for metaphors and other tools which could help them to reflect upon their own age. It should be noticed that in the majority of the cases they were domesticated by treating them as if they were isolated manifestations. Moreover, they were not considered as interrelated narratives.

There are some other films; yet, mentioning all of them exceeds the goals of this essay. I simply wish to create awareness about their existence. Having said that, my aim is to demand a rightful place for "popular films," similar to the one occupied by Eloy de la Iglesia's film *El Pico* (1983). *El Pico*, which was a box-office hit, proved that these types of films can produce successful public narratives and, at the same time, they may serve as a basis for the continuity of social memory in national terms. In his effort to create popular, documentary films capable of posing and analyzing social problems from the bottom, De la Iglesia managed to produce the most popular film about the Spanish transition to democracy. In the film, he portrays with sensitivity and skill a central problem which historical memory has ignored: a high mortality rate because of heroine among this period's youth.

A rhetorical analysis of these filmic texts may allow us to conclude that these narratives were organized in such a way as to assure their success in the market of collective narrations during the decade of the 1980s. This is so because they offered a sophisticated analysis of history, they were efficient from the point of view of communication, they were easily comprehensible for the audience, they were visible (in fact, they are a prominent part among the group of films which could be seen in Spain at that moment) and, last but not least, they were seen by a large audience.

Historical Memory and Political Logics

It is difficult to explain the reason why there has been silence on these narratives. It is usually argued that when dealing with narrations concerning collective processes there is a need for a distancing period. In other words, there is a need for a period of oblivion, of concealment. This is considered as a necessary step before entering into a second phase: the period of testimonies and narratives. In this case, it is possible to argue that the reason why there was so little interest in the narration about the transition to democracy was that historical events were too close in time. However, the fact that there exist films about this period which were shot while the events were taking place proves that this explanation is not valid. There are also explanations of a structural type: lack of means, of directors, of talented people, of scriptwriters, etc. It should be noticed, however, that this did not prevent the apparition of narratives some years before, when conditions were worse. It is, likewise, argued that during the 1980s there was a change in mentality, with a need to seek for more entertainment, to conceive life from a different perspective, etc. These are vague, psychological, socially restricted explanations which, if taken as a whole, seem to describe a society that was hardly interested in the narratives about its own period.

Be that as it may, many Spanish films shot in the 1980s portray the present in a continuous manner. They picture the present as if it were an everyday life history riddled with problems. They present the working class as striving to survive in a historical context which is divided into two worlds: on the one hand, the political, economical, cultural elites and, on the other hand, the popular sector which have to make an effort in order to survive among them. However, the fact that there were realist films does not necessarily mean that there were historical films. In any case, in this context the ellipsis of a transitional thematic carries with it almost automatically a set of narrative consequences: basically the absence of a historical dimension in all of the narratives that describe the present and the subsequent creation of a *flat* outlook, an outlook that lacks a temporal fable.

A suggestive hypothesis can be provided by focusing on its realistic nature. It is interesting to notice that the creation of this popular narrative coincided with the creation of a narrative about the present. Present time, indeed, was not referred to any period whatsoever but rather to a period of public transformations and metamorphoses and to the redefinition of the social agreement, which was now intended to encompass a wider collective-public individual. Insofar as present time was no longer felt as present time, it stopped existing.

In other words, once the transition to democracy period was over, present time moved towards a different temporal space; yet, the kind of popular and powerful narrative films that had arisen did not remain isolated in time. These narratives were not swallowed up by this temporal moment, but rather moved along in time in order to keep producing the same kind of films: realistic films about a present which had once been the future. As typical examples, it is possible to mention Eloy de la Iglesia's *La estanquera de Vallecas* (1987) and Ferando Colomo's *Bajarse al moro* (1989).

It is possible, thus, to explain discontinuity on the basis that not all periods react in the same way with regard to the density of events, and that the pace at which events show up and influence the lives of people is likewise different. These films, which usually portray the latest current affairs, moved little by little towards a less outstanding period; indeed, they show up less frequently during the 1980s. As a result, they lost their capacity to establish a link between important aspects; i.e. they were unable to deal with a narration about everyday life. They began portraying a more banal reality due to the fact that from a historical point of view their contemporary moment was less significant. Since films could no longer establish a relation with their origins, they stopped referring to the transition to democracy.

Those directors who involved in a greater degree in this narrative project, who were disappointed with the fact that the political project that was at the basis of these kinds of visual languages had lost importance or who were involved in creative crisis, stopped asking themselves about this kind of formats. Both Eloy de la Iglesia's and Joaquín Jordá's evolution are prototypical examples. Were we to add the lack of a generational heritage model and the differing concerns and works of young filmmakers, it is possible to understand why there are no discourses following that pattern. This should be considered without regard to the existence or not of an ample audience prepared to take in this kind of narrative about the recent past.

It is not my aim to give the impression that between the years 1986 and 1995 there was a total lack of films about the transition to democracy. Even if it is possible to find missing links, transitional issues survived in other genres, especially in film noir. This genre, which is characterized by its critical discourse on memory, is especially appropriate for this task. In fact, its own conventions give way to efficient narrative solutions when it comes to relate alternative narratives (hidden, secret, repressed) about the past. Because it implies a contemporary narration and because it projects historical periods as superimposing on top of each other, it can be argued that film noir allows for historical recreations.

In any case, it is easier to provide an explanation about the resurgence of this complex network of popular narrations than about its disappearance. One should take into account that, from the end of the 1990s until the present, filmic discourses have been being produced increasingly. They look at the transition to democracy from a new point of view aimed at reestablishing the connections between the past and our own time. As I noticed above, this should be done by establishing a direct connection with the debate about historical memory.

There are numerous works which have already considered and defended social movements connected to the recovery of memory. In fact, in no more than a decade, they have reconsidered the discussion about Franco's regime (Silva *et al.*). Their basis is the pioneering work of Asociación para la Recuperación de la Memoria Histórica (Association for Restoring Historical Memory), whose main goal is to open Spanish Civil War's communal graves. The work carried out by this association has encouraged other individuals to organize themselves in groups and associations. There are two reasons why they wish to open communal graves. Firstly, to look for members of their families who suffered reprisals at the hands of the regime and to investigate the circumstances surrounding their murder—be it either during Franco's rearguard or during the repression period that followed the war. Secondly, to initiate a public debate aimed at involving institutions and highlighting the need to recuperate memory and to arrange a moral compensation for the victims (Silva and Macías). From the very beginning, left-wing political organizations followed this trail. They gave voice and visibility to these groups by linking this phenomenon to their political programs.

This movement had a great impact in the media. It did not take long before it aroused interest in opinion columns and in well-known newspapers' editorials. As a result, in the last five years "historical memory" was dealt with from all existing points of view and was linked to other issues. Moreover, relatives, associations or individuals expressed their views on this debate in letters to the editor. From then on, numerous publications about the Spanish Civil War and Franco's regime arose. This gave way to the apparition of interesting testimony instances of literature, which had been scarce until that moment; yet, they also gave way to the publication of second-rate material. In other words, there appeared rehashes and texts lacking historical rigor which could be found (and can still be found) in the display stands of libraries and in the pages of literary supplements. There was, thus, as stated by Colmeiro, a "commercial exploitation of historical memory." The most important publishing companies exploited this market, in which a whole range of nostalgic outlooks were included.

Three heterogeneous elements are involved in the phenomenon of historical memory: firstly, associations' commitment; secondly, politicians' language use and verbal clashes; thirdly, the emergence of a market of cultural products involving books and also films that defended historical memory. As a result of the interaction of these three elements there came into being a public context aimed at rewriting the collective narrative about the Spanish Civil War from the perspective of citizens (Sánchez León and Izquierdo). In other words, there was a favorable context for the narrations about the recent past to be redefined. It should be highlighted that the rewriting of the Civil War brought with it the rewriting of the Spanish transition to democracy.

There is still one more issue that must be mentioned before ending this explanation about the process and about the impact it had on popular narratives about the past. The explanation is relevant because it allows understanding the way in which these two memories are related to each other. Moreover, it has to do in a direct way with the logics of parliamentarian political competence. Rafael Chirbes established the relation in between the latter and amnesia (lack of institutional interest in promoting works, writers and languages) about the Republic in institutional narrations. It is interesting to notice that in the 1980s the left-wing party could have added historical memory to its "triumphs, yet it did not do so" because it was interested in obtaining the votes of the "middle classes." Chirbes analyses in a protest text written by Max Aub the reception of historical memory in contemporary Spain or, more accurately, its lack of reception. Chirbes also establishes a connection between the right-left's seizure of power in the 1990s (accompanied by the left-wing's loss of public space) and the demand of historical memory, which had been missing in the language of politics and institutions during the rule of the PSOE (Partido Socialista Obrero Español):

> Hasta que sonó la alarma. Y se descubrió que el socialismo no era eterno y que policías, militares y banqueros podían votar también por el pepé, y entonces, se tocó a rebato, y empezaron a conmemorarse los sesenta años de la rebelión fascista y de la llegada y despedida de las brigadas internacionales (los cincuentenarios habían pasado desapercibidos), y se descubrió que había fosas de fusilados que tenían nombre, apellido y, desde hacía unos años, hasta ADN, y se puso de moda la memoria. La memoria se puso de moda, porque se convirtió en la guarida en la que se escondía el lobo que quería volver a comerse a Caperucita, y, porque, en su nombre, podía pedírsele al Parlamento que condenara un franquismo que, cuando se tenía mayoría absoluta, no se había condenado; que se condecorara a los héroes populares de la guerra a quienes se les había dicho que callaran; y se habló del exilio, de las torturas franquistas. Empezaron a aparecer los intelectuales orgánicos que reclamaban memoria, los novelistas y cineastas orgánicos que pedían a gritos

memoria, porque sólo en el mercado de la memoria podía volver a comprarse la legitimidad malgastada. (2003)

(One day the alarm went off: left-wing parties were not eternal. People found out that policemen, soldiers and bankers could also vote for the PP (conservative party). The alarm went off and, as a result, the sixty-year period involving fascist rebellion and the arrival and farewell of international brigades (whose fiftieth anniversary had gone unnoticed) was commemorated. People found out that the graves of the victims who had been shot had names and surnames—and even DNA. Then, memory started to be fashionable. Memory became fashionable because it was the hideout where the wolf, which wanted to eat up Little Red Riding Hood, was hidden. Parliament was, thus, asked to condemn Franco's regime. However, when the government had been ruled by absolute majority (by the left), Franco's regime had not been condemned. Parliament was also asked to honor popular heroes of the war who had been up to then silenced. At that time, there started to be references to life in exile, to the tortures carried out by Franco. Organic intellectuals started to come into the scene demanding memory. These were organic novelists and filmmakers who shouted for memory because the market of memory was the only place were it was possible to buy squandered legitimacy.)

Chirbes's perspective is even more interesting if it is considered from a wider point of view: a perspective from which it is possible to incorporate what has just been argued to an added and important tension. This view surrounds previous initiatives; i.e. other projects which are not assumed and combined by the noise made by the media. Thus, to assume such a partisan interest may be a good hypothesis in order to explain how and why there was a change in the primacy of the different available narratives at the end of the 1990s.

In this way, both the PSOE and the left-wing media implicitly assumed a critical discourse about memory and looked at the transition to democracy as a scenario based on continuities. As a result, they brought about, in a direct way, a movement of forces in relation to narrative concurrence. In fact, these narratives were suddenly placed in a central position. Since there began to be new spheres for reception, this encouraged an increase in the number of rewritings in all fields. Furthermore, in that game, the Transition to Democracy, the Second Republic, the Spanish Civil War and Franco's Regime were united in the same historical sphere. Moreover, their logics got involved in a double claim (citizenry and partisan) aimed at establishing a difference between the social groups of the past, human rights and the ideals of Spanish citizenry. This affected the present-past period which, in its most selfless version, gave rise to a series of roles which can be directly identified in current political agents.

The balance of forces was upset and, therefore, the possibility of creating an official narrative agreed by consensus came to an end. As a result, there were possibilities for an ideological rearmament not involved in the scholarly sphere. A third narrative in concurrence, rebuilt taking into account fascist discourses and some memories about the war, emerged. A further analysis about the so-called "Moa phenomenon" is provided in Sánchez León and Izquierdo. (Pío Moa is the reactionary and revisionist author of several books on the Civil War and its aftermath).

This highlights once again the difficulty of creating institutional historical narratives agreed by consensus and based on narratives of universal values in Spain. The tension about the responsibilities of the past is present: it is manifest in the existence of identification logics which intervene in such a way that amnesia seems to be the only possible agreement. This implies the exclusion of groups and the negation of both experiences and identities, which, because of their connection with democratic values, should be taken on by an institutional discourse. Revisionist outlooks such as the ones used in Germany or France can imply penal crimes; hence, it is inconceivable to give them political protection. The survival of busts and equestrian statues built in the memory of the dictatorship (present in certain places of the Iberian Peninsula) is likewise a democratic anomaly. Beyond the inevitable political meanings that result from giving priority to some narratives about the past over others and beyond there being or not accepted publicly or institutionally, it should be noticed that a non-Adanist narrative about Spain's current affairs poses a serious problem in relation to political and civic sensibility. Films, indeed, have a lot to say (and are probably trying to do so) in connection with this issue.

Popular Current Narratives about the Spanish Transition to Democracy in Cinema and TV

Taking into account the ideas exposed above, it is possible to state that during the transition to democracy period there was no amnesia; i.e. the war and what came afterwards was only allegedly forgotten during twenty years of democracy. It was films recounting the transition to democracy which were missing and, also, certain political logics. That is the reason why it was not possible to take on such a narrative from an institutional stance. As I mentioned before, this situation has resulted in a complex process that poses analytical problems because of its open nature and because it is still taking shape.

Numax presenta ended with an invitation towards the future, an invitation which Joaquín Jordá tried to return back by looking at the past in *Veinte años no es nada* (2000). He interviewed the people who had played a leading role in the strike held in Numax some twenty years before; i.e. he gave them the opportunity to talk so as to provide a documentary in which a group of people tell their lives in relation to the transition to democracy period. Jordá shows that there has been no amnesia. He proves that narrating history is a constituent part of those individuals and because they are anonymous citizens they give way to experiences of a universal nature. The equation established between transition narrative, identity and life is indissoluble. It presents a narrative about the existence of a firm historical narrative at the level of Spanish citizenry which is opposed to the lack of a critical discourse about memory at an institutional level.

Historical contemporary films—or at least most of them—aim at transferring the value of individual memories to collective narrations. Their goal is to transform them into a type of narrative which, due to its generality and to its discursive competence, is implicitly institutional. Insofar as a kind of narrative succeeds in asserting itself among other filmic narrations, it has a greater capacity to influence society. In this situation and beyond the considerable political awareness and public will of many of its producers (i.e., beyond their awareness of working in this field), it is necessary to mention that the development of a business structure with regard to films is growing stronger. This allows the diversification of genres and narratives. It is also necessary to state that in the context of "commercial exploitation" and "fashion" of "historical memory," there is public demand concerning these scenes. The reason for this sudden explosion is that these films are commercially interesting.

The first examples of commercially interesting films about the Spanish Civil War, were those based on best-sellers. We should mention the works by Manuel Rivas, an outstanding figure in this field. José Luis Cuerda did a screen adaptation of his work in *La lengua de las mariposas* (1999) and Antón Reixa in *El lápiz del carpintero* (2002). In these narratives, a moral scenario is portrayed in the foreground. In this way, representations about justice, kindness, truth, authenticity are opposed to cruelty, violence and selfishness in a scenario where there are victims and tyrants and where the community stands motionless; they are stock-still because of a natural and human fear. However, everyday life gestures, determination, action and identification maintain victims alive and, as a result, their memory. In this way, the community takes them to be for what they are: victims amidst a scenario of resurrection where the dead in the war leave their seeds (Castelao *dixit*) and where ideals remain and are reconsidered.

The most important film in this scenario is the screen adaptation of Javier

Cercas's novel *Soldados de Salamina* (Trueba, 2002). This film creates a problem in relation with narratives about the past. It proves the difficulty of rebuilding a true memory about the events and it creates awareness about the fact that all historical narrations are only historical in contemporary terms. On this basis, the film builds a notion of anonymous heroism which can be assumed by institutions and which deals simply with the commitment of anyone (holding democratic and human values) in any place.

In this context, it is possible to mention films that have considered such an approach in relation to the transition to democracy. There are many titles, though they are not equally remarkable. In any case, all of them are capable of establishing a relation with the events that took place during that period by portraying moral conflicts within fairly ample frameworks. These films show that in a corrupt world there is room for communitarian cohesion by relying on freedom and positive values. Some good examples are *El Calentito* (Chus Gutiérrez, 2004), *Vida y color* (Santiago Tabernero, 2005) or *Pasos* (Federico Lupi, 2005), all of which differ in their approach.

Lobo (Miguel Courtois, 2004), which fictionalizes the story of Mikel Lejarza, takes a similar approach. Lobo is a young man from the Basque Country who, in order to protect his family, collaborates with the Civil Guard by infiltrating into the armed separatist group ETA. As a result, he immerses into a game of complicity involving elements of Franco's regime and ETA activists and where he discovers that both authoritarianisms need each other. Amidst a film noir plot involving treacheries and double agents, Lobo is the only character who acts in an ethical way: he opposes himself simultaneously to two evil power networks. The film is, therefore, the story of a traitor who in reality never betrays himself. This applies to the film itself: it does not betray the audience. Lobo is neither faithful to his armed fellow partners nor to the political system for which he works as a spy; rather, he is faithful to the future political system. He works not for his own period but rather for future democracy. It should be noticed that in order to maintain his dignity he must hide his face. He is an anonymous hero, who lives nowadays among Spaniards, among citizens and who has a face which is not his own face; it could be anyone's face.

Gerardo Herrero's *Heroína* (2005) deals with a particular drama: the problems caused by hard drugs among young people at the end of the 70s and at the beginning of the 1980s. Indeed, the epidemic of heroine at the beginning of the 80s resulted in a very high mortality rate. Despite families' confusion, institutions kept a passive attitude and the state acted in complicity. This dramatic social reality was dealt with in an interesting documentary entitled *Marea Blanca* (1999). It was directed by Julio Azcárate and it was broadcasted in Spain's national television channel. In *Heroína*, however, the problem is dealt with from a different perspective. The film is based on the experiences of a series of women from Galicia whose sons and daughters are drug addicts. Through an association called *Érguete*, these women—almost appointed *Las Madres de la droga* (Mothers of drug)—denounced drug traffickers in a systematic way. As a result, they managed to make the problem visible and they demanded political commitment. *Heroína* is a dialogical title: a single word points out both to the problem (heroin) and to the process towards its solution (being heroic). The title, thus, refers to an important social drama and, at the same time, it is a praise aimed at *ordinary* individuals who at a certain time in history accomplished a heroic act by demanding justice and freedom on a collective scale. In this way, the film pays public homage to those individuals, who, by means of their commitment, shaped civil society; they provided it with a moral superego that represents true democracy. In other words, amidst a corrupt and miserable milieu, these people embody the potential wellbeing of society.

Manuel Huerga's film *Salvador* (2006) occupies a privileged place among these films. *Salvador* narrates the life and death of Salvador Puig Antich—one of the last men who died shot during Franco's regime. Being a member of MIR (a Catalan revolutionary group), he is arrested following a confusing situation and is judged around the time of the terrorist attack in which Carrero Blanco died. Thus, he is condemned to die. His execution, which occurs amidst unanimous protest, can be interpreted as a desperate gesture to implement power by a dying dictatorship. The film was shot in the context of Puig Antich's family legal claims, who demanded to officially overturn the death penalty, and coinciding with the demands of groups in favor of historical memory. This drama goes back to the scenario of the transition to democracy so as to revive the feelings, tensions and fears of that time. *Salvador* is also a dialogical title: it is the name of its main character and at the same time it means "savior"; i.e. it refers to this young man as if he were the country's savior. The film invites the audience to live his experience and it establishes a relation in between his life and Christ's. His desire of universal justice, kindness and freedom leads him to devote his life to fight against the authorities of Franco's regime and in favor of the oppressed, which in the end leads him to an unfair death. Throughout his never-ending ordeal, he seems to be surrounded by a Christian aura which illuminates the life of the jailer who is watching him. Finally, he dies; yet, his sacrifice, even if it is not what he wished, is not useless. It causes reactions. Therefore, through his heroism, Salvador embodies collective democratic values. Democracy, indeed, will be built thanks to his commitment. This is why remembering him as a collective hero is, from this point of view, an act of justice. At the same time, it is a way of proving that this is an identification narrative built through sacrifice and by rejecting injustice, cruelty, violence and suffering directly. Moreover, the film suggests a wide range of attitudes and of characters that embody emotions, fears and different moral values. The audience feels compelled to take a stand on these moral conflicts.

The list of films would be incomplete without the inclusion of a popular television series *Cuéntame cómo pasó* (2000–2007). Because it has been broadcasted on television, its impact on society has been even greater. This series narrates the story of the members of the Alcántaras, a Spanish family living in a known neighborhood in Madrid between 1968 and 1975. The characters of the series represent internal conflicts—of a moral type—which are related to the specific period on which the series is set: the point in history in which History embodies the lives of individuals. Development policies, rural life, consumer society, protest movements, and hippy cults are only some of the patterns related to the scenario of the transition to democracy. A series of attitudes, behaviors, and adventures arise in this framework in which the characters, who hope to achieve happiness, have both faults and virtues. The undeniable success of *Cuéntame cómo pasó* (followed by more than four million spectators each week) is due to its capacity to blend history. It is meticulously documented and, according to Rosenstone, it includes a great deal of historical knowledge. Likewise, it is perfectionist with regard to atmosphere: it is possible to see many of the cultural and consumer products that arose during the 60s, including tins of cocoa and picture cards. Moreover, its dramatic plots include anecdotes and personal stories of people who lived in that period, which are now told as a result of a great work of oral documentation.

There is another reason that explains *Cuéntame*'s success: it places nostalgia at the center of its expository narrative. Taking the American *The Wonder Years* as a model, history is narrated from the point of view of an adult who, thirty years after the events, remembers the transition to democracy period. Since this period is part of his childhood, he has idealized it, reviving it in a happy mood. Moreover, the use of a persuasive rhetoric moves the spectator to feel nostalgia even if s/he has not experienced the historical period. Identifying emotions with the narrative discourse used in *Cuéntame* is a means of transforming individual memories, which is, by the way, this series' major skill and power.

The most common attack on the series is that its portrayal of history is false (in the sense that it is far too happy). In this sense, it should be noticed that creating discourses that foster historical knowledge poses an important problem. *Cuéntame* is a narrative about the transition to democracy period; yet, it is also a work within a particular genre: melodrama. Its characters must face problems which they manage to solve in the limits of their community. Their family, their friends and their neighborhood are part of the milieu in which they put forth their conflicts. In fact, they form a mutual sense of solidarity based on defending and following a series of collective values which are of a universal and democratic nature.

Cuéntame's characters are not heroes; they are kind, ordinary and respectable people who try to survive amidst a hostile, corrupt, decrepit system: the public and political milieu of the last part of Franco's regime. Although they are not important figures in the transition to democracy, they are part of it. That is the reason why they have a right to narrate events from a melodramatic stance. In this way, their insignificant commitment and their minor role in the process of the political construction of a democratic state—limited to social involvement—can be analyzed from a different genealogy. It is a collective stance on account of which very different kinds of spectators may identify with this family and with the way in which its members look at the present (our past which is, at the same time, our present thanks to the effective use of anachronisms). It should be noticed that their outlook towards the past is disillusioned; yet, implicated in individual freedom and decency.

Is it possible to narrate the Spanish transition to democracy as if it were a melodrama? If so, what consequences does it have from the point of view of history and narrative? Be that as it may, narratives of this kind allow identification with a great deal of values at a popular level. These values coordinate each other in a complex way, so that they establish a difference in regard to structural problems and they rebuild politics at an intimate level, as if it were morality. This allows for collective and unitary popular narratives about our recent past. By looking for a scenario with which we cannot disagree, these narratives displace history's prominence; it is the lives of anonymous and individual ordinary Spanish people who are placed at the center. *Cuéntame*, therefore, pictures democratic main characters that are part of a popular story which can be seen by a wide range of spectators. The fact that several million spectators watch this narrative means that they identify to a certain extent with it. It also implies that they identify with a new past-present which deals with the necessity of a moral change in Spain's politics, with a lack of contemporary interest in the things that are going on in institutions and with the decision to use a social solution of an ethical kind (surprisingly enough, it coincides with the one put forth by Chirbes).

Conclusions

The transition to democracy still provides very different kinds of materials and it is visited constantly so as to shape our narratives. Indeed, this store has not been exhausted yet; there are many chapters which can still be narrated.

It is symptomatic that the great majority of films mentioned throughout this essay shape a type of narrative which may fit into the same approach. History is portrayed as the opposition between selfishness, violent attitudes, institutions' interests and people in power and the community's goodness, justice and truthfulness—which pretends to be part of history. Thanks to the sacrifice of its collective heroes and to an epic based on everyday life, this community—identified simultaneously as civil society, citizenry and Spaniards—manages to continue living in a legitimate and happy way, without aiming at great goals, transformations nor cataclysms. Be that as it may, they show a moral superiority with regard to their surrounding world that is based in the fulfillment of social values. This is the basis of their communitarian identity, an identity aimed at going through history with dignity and which carries with it the promise of doing so in the future.

It would be rather easy to apply these concepts to other documents about the period, and thus highlight their historical falseness. However, to provide a positive view about the morality of the Spanish working classes of that period or about the complicity, silence and acceptance of contemporary Spanish history with regard to power and violence does not provide further information about these types of narratives. We mean that it has no impact in narrative terms. Since it is always possible to find ordinary men who satisfy those prospects, there is always room for identification. This assumption serves as a starting point: it socializes that experience and, thus, it makes it universal. This is what these filmic and television narratives do: they allow the community as a whole to occupy a good place (the only possibly positive place) with regard to historical narratives; this should be interpreted as an exchange for subscribing to democratic and humanitarian values. In most cases, it takes place both at a public and a private level, in terms of personal awareness with regard to oneself and in terms of political awareness with regard to the rest of the people.

In conclusion, films lay the foundations for a historical debate of a different nature: a debate which does not arise only from the academic or political world and which is not spread institutionally among the population. Its aim is to incorporate ordinary people and to make them characters in the narration of their own history. In the context of political and intellectual disputes with regard to a particular pattern about the transition to democracy, films have gone for a comprehensive narrative; this must be taken into account. In fact, films might manage to do what institutions have not been able to do: to create a historical narrative that disavows Franco's regime socially and that takes as a model democratic individuals (individuals which become universal). To a certain extent this has already been achieved; insofar as this narrative has had social diffusion, it has spread and disseminated. Moreover, certain current legal initiatives have aimed at institutionalizing these narratives. However, it is likewise possible to consider that we are merely at a specific moment in a long process of subsequent narrative concurrences which might never end. There may come a time when they are not so prominent because of personal determination, hard-bargain between interests and lack of interests, the establishment of non-historical memory (a memory based on personal memories), or the creation of confusion in the temporal dimension of collective identities.

Works Cited

Abril, Gonzalo. "¿De qué informan las imágenes? Patucos para el capitán general." Unpublished talk. University of Seville, January 28, 2000.
Azcárate, Julio. *Marea Blanca*. Documentos TV, 1999.
Bardem, Antonio. *Siete días de enero*, 1978.
Bartolomé, Cecilia, and José Juan Bartolomé. *Después de . . . (Todo atado y bien atado y No se os puede dejar solos)*. 1981.
Camarero, G., ed. *La mirada que habla (cine e ideologías)*. Madrid: Akal, 2002.
Cercas, Javier. *Soldados de Salamina*. Barcelona: Tusquets, 2001.
Cerdán, Josetxo, and Marina Díaz López, eds. *Cecilia Bartolomé. El encanto de la lógica*. Barcelona: La Fábrica de Cinéma Alternatiu-Ocho y Medio, 2001.
Chirbes, Rafael. "Max Aub: desmemoria y creatividad. ¿Quién se come a Max Aub?" *Babelia, El País*, 06–31–2003.
———. *La larga marcha*. Barcelona: Anagrama, 1996.
Colmeiro, José Francisco. *Memoria histórica e identidad cultural. De la postguerra a la postmodernidad*. Barcelona: Anthropos, 2005.
Colomo, Fernando. *Bajarse al moro*, 1989.
Courtois, Miguel. *Lobo*, 2004.
Cuerda, José Luis. *La lengua de las mariposas*, 1999.
De la Iglesia, Eloy. *La estanquera de Vallecas*, 1987.
———. *El Pico*, 1983.
Desacuerdos (1,2,3). Sobre arte, políticas y esfera pública en el Estado español. VVAA. Granada: Diputación de Granada, 2005.
Ferro, Marc. *Historia contemporánea y cine*. Barcelona: Ariel, 1995.

García Pelayo, Gonzalo. *Vivir en Sevilla*, 1978.
Gutiérrez, Chus. *El Calentito*, 2004.
Hernández, Javier, and Pablo Pérez. *Voces en la niebla. El cine durante la transición española (1973–1982)*. Barcelona: Paidós, 2004.
Herrero, Gerardo. *Heroína*, 2005.
Huerga, Manuel. *Salvador*, 2006.
Imbert, Gérard. *Los discursos del cambio. Imágenes e imaginarios sociales en la España de la Transición (1976–1982)*. Madrid: Akal, 1990.
Jordá, Joaquín. *Veinte años no es nada*, 2000.
———. *Numax presenta*, 1979.
Lupi, Federico. *Pasos*, 2005.
Medina, Alberto. *Exorcismos de la memoria. Políticas poéticas de la melancolía en la España de la Transición*. Madrid: Ediciones Libertarias, 2002.
Morales, Carlos. *Noche de curas*, 1977.
Morán, Gregorio. *El precio de la transición*. Barcelona: Planeta, 2001.
Moreiras, Cristina. *Cultura herida. Literatura y cine en la España democrática*. Madrid: Ediciones Libertarias, 2002.
Muraro, H. *Políticos, periodistas y ciudadanos. De la videopolítica al periodismo de investigación*. México: FCE, 1997.
Parenti, M. *Make-Believe Media. The Politics of Entertainment*. New York: St. Martin's Press, 1992.
Pons, Ventura. *Ocaña, retrato intermitente*, 1978.
Pontecorvo, Gillo. *Operación Ogro*, 1978.
Prego, Victoria. *Historia de la Transición*. Madrid: Televisión Española, 1993.
Reixa, Antón. *El lápiz del carpintero*, 2002.
Rey, Fernando. *El Crimen de Cuenca*, 1979.
Rivas, Manuel. *O Lápis do Carpinteiro*. Vigo: Xerais, 2003.
———. *¿Qué me queres amor?* A Coruña: Galaxia, 1995.
Rosenstone, Robert A. *El pasado en imágenes. El desafío del cine a nuestra idea de la historia*. Barcelona: Ariel Historia, 1997.
Sánchez León, Pablo, and Jesús Izquierdo. *La guerra que nos han contado. 1936 y nosotros*. Madrid: Alianza Editorial, 2006.
Silva, Emilio et al. *La memoria de los olvidados. Un debate sobre el silencio de la represión franquista*. Valladolid: Ámbito/ARMH, 2003.
Silva, Emilio, and Santiago Macías. *Las fosas de Franco*. Madrid: Temas de Hoy, 2003.
Subirats, Eduardo, ed. *Intransiciones. Crítica de la cultura española*. Madrid: Biblioteca Nueva, 2002.
———. *Después de la lluvia: sobre la ambigua modernidad española*. Madrid: Temas de Hoy, 1993.
———. *El alma y la muerte*. Madrid: Anthropos, 1983.
Tabernero, Santiago. *Vida y color*. 2005.
Trueba, David. *Soldados de Salamina*, 2002.

Tusell, Javier, and Álvaro Soto, eds. *Historia de la transición (1975–1986)*. Madrid: Alianza Editorial, 1996.
Uribe, Imanol. *El proceso de Burgos*, 1979.
———. *La fuga de Segovia*, 1978.
Vázquez Montalbán, Manuel. *La literatura en la construcción de la ciudad democrática*. Barcelona: Crítica, 1998.
Vilarós, Teresa. *El mono del desencanto. Una crítica cultural de la Transición Española (1973–1993)*. Madrid: Siglo XXI, 1998.
———. *Cómo liquidaron el Franquismo en dieciséis meses y un día*. Barcelona: Fábula, 1977.

PART III
Looking In/Looking Out: Negotiating Identities

◆ **9**

Staged Ethnicity, Acted Modernity: Identity and Gender Representations in Spanish Visual Culture (1968–2005)

Estrella de Diego

What Do You Mean "We"?

In 1990, Spain chose Azúcar Moreno—a couple of gypsy women who sang so-called "flamenco pop"—to represent the country in the Eurofestival, a pop music event, that for some obscure reason has had a strong, even out of proportion, significance for the country in its own cultural representations. The title of the song they presented at the Zagreb edition, *Bandido* (brigand), was cliché enough to fit into the most predictable narrative about "Spanishness": gypsies, Carmen, bullfighters, bandits, and so forth. But of course, one should maybe start by explaining what the Eurofestival was meant to be as a cultural product and how it was perceived in Spain during Franco's years, soon after it was "designed" in the mid-1950s, right after the standardization of television.

The event was presented as a neutral territory for European countries to meet and get acquainted with each other in a ludicrous non-problematic common space: pop music. Nevertheless, the strategy behind the whole *mise-en-scene* was no doubt a clear commercial intention, which found its best ally in the newly explored power of a implacable medium such as television. Not only that, a quite strong undercover political aim was hiding backstage: in fact, voting for a song was voting for a country. As with any cultural representation, power was the name of the game.

Therefore, at least in those first years the Eurofestival seemed to be a place *to see* and *to be seen*. It was the perfect stage to materialize the visibility Spain desperately sought during the late 60s and early 70s, while the need to open Spain to foreign tourism seemed to be crucial for the apparatus's political and economic plans at a time when the dictatorship kept the country isolated internationally.

This is why in 1968, Spain overcelebrated the first and only time a Spanish song won the contest.[1] Returning from London, Massiel, a female singer who became a kind of cultural icon after the festival and from then on never did much more than enjoy her success in the contest, was received as a "national heroine" by official sectors. At last, Madrid would have the opportunity to organize an edition of the Eurofestival and show the world that new and modern image the regime was then eager to export, due to its mentioned tourism development plans. Paradoxically, Massiel´s song "La, La, La" was meant to be sung by Joan Manuel Serrat, an antifrancoist Catalan singer and composer who was finally banned from representing Spain in the Eurofestival: he would sing in Catalan or would not sing at all, Serrat claimed. Needless to say, Serrat never went to London and Massiel took his place. In fact, all local newspapers criticized his gesture.[2]

What seemed interesting about the whole story was how Serrat's gesture opened some kind of a debate—or at least the closest thing to a debate that Franco's newspapers could allow themselves. In 1968 it was already clear that politics were everywhere, especially when censorship controlled life and culture. The Eurofestival was no exception. The Barcelona daily *La Vanguardia*—at that time *La Vanguardia Española*—published a most ambiguous note entitled "El 'caso' Serrat" that openly defended the use of Catalan language.[3] Nonetheless, the article stated that Serrat lacked "*seny*" (common sense, responsibility), possibly the worst accusation in Catalan terms.[4] He should have decided he wanted to sing in Catalan before accepting the invitation.

Apart from that related to the redefinition of "Spanishness" as a shy political debate, when the great day came and Madrid hosted the event, the efforts to (re)present the country as a "modern" and "wealthy" one were as obsessive as pathetic. The flamboyant chinchilla coat Massiel was wearing for the festival opening was so pretentious, that far from being modern and elegant it represented the essence of a *nouveau rich* extravaganza, an interesting example of a kind of "flaunting modernity" that peripheries sometimes adopt, in order to keep up with the so-called center—whatever "periphery" and "center" may mean in this as in other contexts.

But of course, the often clumsy strategies of Franco's Minister of Information and Tourism in order to generate visibility for Spain, are not the my main concern here, although they offer a number of useful hints to interpret the image which was launched from officiality a few years before the Dictator's death and its impact in the construction of "Spanishness." What seems worth noting here is the way the Eurofestival was perceived (and still seems to be, to certain extent[5]) as an effective spot to stage identity, one of the most controversial issues in Spanish history.

That may explain why the artists chosen to represent Spain in the musical event along the years have fluctuated between "ethnic" (flamenco, gypsy style and so forth) and "modern" (closer to international pop trends) singers and songs. One could say that the tension between both choices materializes the inner contradiction that constitutes Spanish cultural identity and all the conflicts within. It is a contradiction that survived Franco as Azúcar Moreno's *Bandido* would prove: times had radically changed, but the conflict within (re)presentations of Spanish identity remained almost identical. As it often happens in minority and peripheral contexts, the use of stereotypes becomes the only possibility to present and represent oneself, since minorities and peripheries are never subtly written, read or narrated, but perceived as a homogeneous entity (Bhahba 66–84). How could Spain become visible, if the signs used were not historically associated with the repeated stereotypes everybody could immediately identify with "Spain?"

So, at the 1990 Eurofestival, Spain decided—once again—to (re)present itself through racialized women. Or, to be more precise, Spain "designed" an old/new easy-to-pin-down image of the country in which Stein's "oriental" Spain (Stein 30) fulfilled the most stereotypical mainstream desire. As Reina Lewis has pointed out when arguing that Edward Said omitted women's role in the formation of "Orientalism," "oriental women" end up being the ultimate representative of the center's desire, both as women and as "oriental." It is the "exotic as erotic," as many descriptions of Spanish women could testify, from the sweetest Andalusian characters Edmondo de Amicis pictured in his late nineteenth-century travels in Spain,[6] to the sexy and contemporary impersonation performed by Azúcar Moreno in the promotional videoclip for *Bandido*.

At a first glance, the viewer is confronted with an appalling visual artifact that summarizes all possible clichés about racial Spain and racial Spanish women . . . and men. Yet, a closer look uncovers quite a different reality. The

Bandido videoclip is a perverse product that eloquently pins down a certain image Spain wanted to export in 1990, two years prior to the big events that were going to take place in 1992 and which were perceived in the country as the "big chance" to once and for all change the eternally "ethnic" image the world had about Spain. The Quincentennial of America's "discovery," the Barcelona Olympics, the Seville Universal Exhibition and the Cultural European Capitality of Madrid (miles away in mediatic impact), were already regarded in 1990—and years before—as a crucial moment for that transformation and projection of Spain's new image. No doubt, 1990 was the right moment to establish the modern image the country had been working on since the early 80s, just when democracy finally took the lead in Spain. It was high time to replace traditional ethnicity with new modernity.

The Azúcar Moreno video clip could be read in this light, since, as it has been noticed, the Eurofestival did mean much more than one could think politically speaking. Besides, it has already been pointed out that the product was from a visual point of view, a rather perverse, even if appalling, artifact. Then, assuming the *Bandido* video was part of the change of image operation in the country *circa* 1992, why would it emphasize the Andalusian corporate fake image of plural Spain performed here as collectively "oriental?" Was Spain perceiving itself as periphery, no matter the efforts "to become part of it (the center)," and, therefore, was it representing itself through its well-established stereotypes? Or quite on the contrary, was Spain exploiting its "oriental" side, in order to join the Latino fashion—"The Coming (of Age) of Latino Lover," as mentioned in *The Village Voice* in 1988—that was gaining momentum even in New York (Tubert 227)?

And not only that, assuming, once again, we were in front of a perverse artifact (no matter how badly executed), one could try and contextualize it in the mid 80s/early 90 video production. As most video clips during those years (Kaplan), *Bandido*'s primary function was promotional, only that in this case "promoting" went beyond a specific song or singer. As most of those produced for the Eurofestival, *Bandido* promoted a corporate image of a specific country. In fact, other videos created for the same reason often showed landscapes or historical venues of a precise city. On the other hand, as it happened with all musical videos, *Bandido* subverted an important parameter one should take into consideration when confronting low culture, as described by Bufwack and Oermann: "The study of popular culture must be rooted in a careful analysis of the social relations and social environments of the people who make it, buy it, and identify with it" (91–92). Like in all videoclips of the 1990s, the audience that *Bandido* was made for became distorted by the means to publicize the product. Video-clips were shown on TV like advertising, and thus everybody would be exposed to the product, want it or not (Kaplan 9). So, the theoretically unsophisticated audience that would enjoy the Eurofestival—and eventually this tacky item—opened up in an unexpected way: anybody could be a victim of the propaganda by simply watching TV. However, one thing looked quite different in *Bandido*. Compared to other videos produced around this time (with music by Madonna and Michael Jackson, for instance) confronting race and gender identity issues, *Bandido* was disturbingly obvious.[7]

But let us briefly analyze the various constitutive elements of the *Bandido* video. The first image to appear on the TV screen was Velazquez's self-portrait from *Las Meninas*. It quickly vanished from sight consumed by some fire which seemed to burn the whole scene. The fire matched the unusual *camp* lyrics: "Mi pecho ardió" (my chest burnt). That image was soon followed by a number of other paintings by the same artist, that were finally substituted by the singing and dancing Azúcar Moreno couple dressed in elegant black outfits. The only dissonant "exotic" element for such an impeccable elegance was a short jacket, similar to those worn by bullfighters. Velazquez's *Venus* appeared for a few seconds and after that, Azúcar Moreno was back in action. This time they were wearing sexy flashy clothes.

The two representations of Azúcar Moreno—the elegant and "the exotic as erotic" ones—were alternatively used during the rest of the video, as well as various Velazquez's works. Yet, two other elements seemed worth noting. The first one was the image of the "bandido," who appeared three times: smiling, riding a horse with a Méliès sky and moon as a background, and then saying goodbye (abandoning his mistresses, one assumed). The second element was an out-of-the-blue picture of Groucho Marx, whose eyebrows rose in a kind of surprised fashion. Yet, the final image was, no doubt, the most eccentric one. The same Velázquez self-portrait closed the video, but this time his eyes moved to watch the two dancing women, who appeared reflected on the mirror present at the famous *Meninas*.

Leaving the terrible technical execution aside, the interest of the artifact can be found in its bricolage strategy—so typical for video-clips (Kaplan 33)—which in this specific example combines apparently antagonistic and otherwise impossible to match elements. Low and high culture, old and new signs constitute the narrative of *Bandido* and its paradoxical search for a "Spanish image." Nevertheless, all paradoxes in the video are nothing but the usually implied contradictions in all revisited stereotypes. What to keep and what to exclude in order to be different and yet recognizable by the outside world could be the imperative question to ask in these kinds of processes.

That could maybe explain the inclusion of a high culture representative (Velázquez) in the video. Besides, during those months the painter had become very popular, due to a colossal exhibition at the Prado Museum, the first mediatic exhibit in Spain, one may say,[8] with long queues and a strong impact in a wide segment of the population: presented like a "national hero," Velázquez, the truly Spanish tradition one could be proud of, was simply made into a commodity, a low-brow product ready to be consumed. And it could also explain the use of undoubtedly low-brow icons: the "exotic as erotic" women became "civilized" by their supermodel looks. The video presented a rather sophisticated *mise-en-scene*: it created a fusion of the race and gender stereotypes that had traditionally (re)presented Spain and dressed them up in an unusual masquerade, which conformed a perfect *ensemble* of everlasting Spanish "passion"[9] and "modern elegance."

In any case, simply by looking at the magazines and newspapers during those years, the audience was often confronted with the same two-way phenomenon. The racialized Azúcar Moreno took part of their new impersonation from the "moda de España" ("fashion of/from Spain"), a slogan promoted that time to define Spanish fashion that tried to find new international markets. But, on the other hand, "la moda de España" seemed related to the traditional racial Spanish image, both in the insistence of black and red and in the performance of "passion" for some advertising campaigns. A flagrant example of the above-mentioned staged ethnicity-sharing territory with acted modernity, was a piece on fashion published in *El País's* weekly supplement. The session took place in a gypsy village, with "real gypsy people" and a very well known top model, Inés Sastre (López de Haro 14–23). It was called "Olé, tu gracia," an almost impossible to translate Andalusian expression: "You're the best."

Finally, the staged ethniticy had found a territory to share with the acted modernity. Both were masquerades, none was more "real" than the other. The two were a consequence of the peripheral perception Spain had about itself, even after democracy was well established in the country. One could even think both were related to some ethnic autobiography problems, as understood by Huggan: "Ethnic autobiography, like ethnicity itself, flourishes under the watchful eye of the dominant culture; both are caught in the dual processes of commodification and surveillance" (155).

Then, the question to ask here would be: who was the dominant culture by which "ethnic Spain" was watched? Who was that dominant culture for which the community as a whole was ready to perform all different necessary roles, in order to be taken into consideration, internationally speaking?

Indeed, it does not seem an easy question to answer. One could of course say that the "dominant culture" was the "outside world." It was the "world" that had long lived in a democracy and had not then been excluded from all different modernity processes. So, in this specific discourse the dominant culture could be anyone who looked and sounded "modern," taking into consideration the ambiguity of the term from Spanish contexts where "modern" was often related to "political," as I will discuss later.

Anyway, if the dominant culture could be anybody surveying, during those late 80s/early 90s everybody was indeed closely watching the "young democracy." Even the New York art world—always thirsty for new discoveries—looked at Spain in search of no matter how small of a sign to make the country into the celebrity of the party. So, in September 1988, Jamey Gambrell spoke about the new art scene in Madrid, Barcelona and Valencia explaining how things (and prices) were rapidly changing. The ten-page article, published in *Art in America,* spoke about the Socialist Government, the Arco art fair in Madrid, the Centro de Arte Reina Sofía, the new galleries, and the 1992 Olympic Village, "all contemporary art institutions [that were] still in an embryonic state" (Gambrell 37–47).

Three years later, Robin Cembalest spoke about Spain again and things did not seem to have changed much: still too many stereotypes and hopes about "the young democracy" fighting for modernity through all kinds of perils (Cembalest 127–29). That very year, *Newsweek* published another article full of clichés (McGuigan 66–68) and full of hope, too. Much hope . . . too much hope and maybe even too much pressure. The romantic image of nineteenth-century travelers in Spain—an "oriental," but not too "oriental" tourist site—were replaced by the romantic Republican Spain and finally by the romantic image of the "new democracy" finding its way around history.

Needless to say, many of those hopes and historical clichés were coming from outside the country; the dominant culture was closely watching. In fact, I have taken three North American examples, but I could easily have chosen French or German ones, since at that time Spain was often on the international news. Perhaps that "young democracy," that modern Spain had hoped for, the finally "normal" Spain, was not very different than the old racial and Republican stereotypes. Modern Spain, as ethnic Spain before, was yet another commodity, some kind of an unexpected—and unwelcome—new stereotype.

One should admit that this new stereotype was fed from inside as much as from outside the country. So when 1992 finally arrived, the event was read in a bizarre messianic manner. It was read as the beginning of a new era, but to a certain extent it represented a kind of restoration of a more than dubious past. In fact, the choice of Seville to celebrate the Universal Exhibition was not made by chance. Seville had not only been very significant in Columbus' trip to America, but it had hosted an event that took place in 1929, the Iberian-American Exhibition. The 1929 Seville exhibition, which opened the same year as the Universal Exhibition of Barcelona—was presented as a way to celebrate centuries of common history between the continent and the former American colonies, but in fact it was—and as all universal exhibitions are—a colonialist display in which every Latin American country performed its own ethnicity the way it was expected in order to please the ever-dominant culture.

From many points of view, the *mise-en-scene* was not fundamentally different in 1992. In the first place, one could argue that the best way to face a different modern future was not choosing one of the most disgraceful years in Spain's history as a starting point. In fact, in Spanish history 1492 means much more than just the beginning of a controversial colonial expansion. It is also the year of the final victory over the "muslims" and the expulsion of the "jews." Therefore, 1492 was traditionally a celebrated and acclaimed year in Franco's rewriting of the history of Spain, when the "good ones" stayed and the "bad ones" left—or were christened. After all, 1492 implies the whole Reyes Católicos and Cid Campeador rhetoric that seemed to be so dear to Franco. Mixing this particular reading of Spanish history with the ethnomimesis[10] that Universal Exhibitions—in themselves nineteenth-century colonial artifacts—simply, one can easily image, the undeniable paradox Spain'92 meant in the construction of the nation's new image.

The progressive government that officially promoted the events, was no doubt conscious about the dangerous *Hispanidad*[11] rhetoric, but the whole set up functioned perfectly for the required performance: a pinch of ethnicity and a pinch of modernity. Some of the invited committee members contributing to the volume published on the occasion of the Expo'92 tried to rewrite history as best as they could, given the circumstances. Among others, Carlos Seco Serrano, who openly related the abovementioned two events, claimed the importance of the past in the whole celebration and tried to emphasize all positive things about "el descubrmiento del llamado Nuevo Mundo" (Seco Serrano 44) (the discovery of the so-called New World). What seems more interesting in his article, though, is the annoyance the author shows as a historian when noticing that the future is more relevant than past in this whole celebration.[12]

As it can be easily imaged, the book itself—except for a few contributions—was not critical at all. Those days nobody seemed to be openly and scholarly critical about "Spain'92," except for the usual newspaper articles which were written against the government and would have been written no matter what the result would have been. That is why it is worth remembering a most bizarre book called *El descubrimiento del 92. Expo, Olimpiadas . . . La otra cara del espectáculo* (The discovery of 92: Expo, Olympics . . . The other side of spectacle) by Colectivo Vírico, in which a number of people or dissident groups criticized the whole "España 92" events as a flagrant lie. An article by Antonio Peralta Morales went as far as calling the event "La refundación del Imperio español" (Peralta 13–18) (The Refounding of Spanish Empire").

How was this new image from Spain visible in the art world? A paradox became obvious here too. While the official policy had been trying to export artists from the National Exhibition Center at the Ministry of Culture during the 1980s—*New Images from Spain* at New York's Guggenheim Museum, or the 1985 *Five Spanish Artists* (Barceló, Campano, García Sevilla, Lamas and Sicilia) at Artists' Space, also in New York, among others—, the mentioned volume did not include any account about contemporary art. In fact, there was only an article related to art and culture. It was a short note that emphatically defended the role of art in a "better connected world" and that used words such as "universal," a term which was already very difficult to accept in the international context during the early 90s (Garín 68).

There were, of course, contemporary art exhibitions in Seville.[13] But if we take the Spanish Pavilion as the most representative example for Spanish contemporary art, the idea one got about Spanish artistic production from the 1960s on is quite accurate, but too traditional. Most important Spanish artists were represented at the show *Pasajes*—from Antonio López, Tàpies and Brossa, Pérez Villalta, Barceló and the rest of those who had been exported to the Guggenheim Museum to the younger generation—but none of them, or none of the works chosen, seemed to reflect the real innovation that had been taking place in the country from the 1970s on. For example, only a couple of photographers were included in the show, giving an idea about the restrictive old-fashioned curatorial approach the appointed committee had.[14]

Not only that, it was obvious that the show tried to avoid any political connotations, even in an undisputable case such as the one of Pepe Espaliú, whose work "Carrying" (1992), exhibited at the show, was referring to AIDS, an illness that killed the artist shortly after. His highly political works were presented as a mere esthetic exercise.[15] This appeared to be a contradiction in terms. Those official stances desperately looking for acquiring modernity and internationalization for Spanish art, ignored interesting cases like Espaliú, whose works and the problems they discussed did not differ much from other non-Spanish artists. In fact, internationally speaking, the art scene had been very political from the mid-1970s on. Works dealing with gender, masquerade, identity, autobiography, race issues, homosexuality, AIDS and so forth had been routine from the 1970s on outside Spain. Not to speak about photography, a more than well established medium in the art world during those years.

So, the significance of a show that opened at the Spanish Institute—therefore outside official influence—in New York in 1992, seems now more important than one could have then thought as far as exporting a "new image from Spain." *The Spanish Vision. Contemporary Art Photography, 1970–1990* showed some interesting examples of the photographs produced in Spain during the 1970s. They were photographs forgotten and disregarded for years by all promotional policies in the country. Alejandro Castellote, who wrote the opening essay for the catalogue, emphasized the role of *Nueva Lente*.[16]

It is very true that the exhibition at the Spanish Institute tended to generalize sometimes and that it pushed the "Spanish vision" a bit too far, like in the prolific selection of gypsy types, catholic scenes and even a mystic portrait of Almodóvar, but on the other hand the most relevant photographers were included—except for Cristina García Rodero—and ironical pictures about the Quintcentennial found also their place, like Falces's piece *V Centenario, Sevilla* (1985). One thing was obvious in the text: the tension between the national and the international seemed to be present. "It is now, after overcoming an inferiority complex and other imposed burdens, when there is no desperate need to be known and recognized, and when it is really possible to talk about a corpus of Spanish photography" (Castellote 12).

It should, then, be pointed out how those new artistic approaches were in the early 1990s more common than the *Pasajes* show would make one think. *El sueño imperativo* (The Imperative Dream), a show curated by Mar Villaespesa (Sueño), one of the most active people in the art field during that decade—also the curator of *Plus Ultra*, the Andalusian pavilion public art project at Seville'92—that opened in January 1991 at the Círculo de Bellas Artes in Madrid is a good study case. In this exhibit, Spanish young artists shared the exhibition space with international ones and the difference in both cases was not as remarkable as one would have thought looking at *Pasajes*. More politically oriented artists, like Pedro G. Romero and Rogelio López Cuenca, confronted issues related to cultural identity. And Juan Luis Moraza—later one of the most interesting gender-oriented artists—did look like a completely different artist than the conventional sculptor shown at the *Pasajes* less then a year later.

But leaving these petty things aside, 1992 was a missed opportunity to seriously revisit Spain's relationship with Latin America in the postcolonial terms the historical moment required. The country missed that chance and instead dreamed about being part of Europe, the center. Trapped in its own peripheral self-perception and obsessed with joining the center, Spain disregarded its old liaisons completely. Or even worse, it reproduced what in 1992 was, fortunately, a lost cause: the re-founding of the Spanish Empire. As before in Spanish history, once again it seemed enough to look modern, act modern, be modern in a somehow frivolous superficial–rhetorical—manner. Being modern was political enough, but if these terms could have been equivalent during the late 60s and early 70s, while Franco was still alive, in 1992 a bit more was expected from the country to seriously abolish traditional stereotypes. The impression one has looking back at Spanish history is that we were "post-modern"—whatever that definition could mean—without having been "modern" at all.

Political as Modern, Modern as International

Taking all this into consideration, it seems indispensable to redefine the notion of "modern" and "political" in Spain's late 1960s and early 1970s context. There seemed to exist an implicit *entente* about that new specific and rather peculiar perception of "modernity" as "politicalness," that was shared both by Franco's apparatus and progressive groups.

This way, the progressive groups who used Picasso's *Guernica* as a means to confront Franco, rarely thought of the image as a painting or as a homage to a bombed town. Those concepts had almost disappeared in a new meaning: they had vanished on the surface of the poster. During those years, one was "political" simply because one wanted to consume and explore images of "modernity," or at least images that belonged to what was understood as "modern" inside the country and which was often associated to internationality. Trying to be "modern" was in itself a militant act. Nevertheless, the interesting thing to emphasize is how the regime perceived *Guernica* in a very similar way: an icon, a poster, a polluting foreign image of "moderntiy" that arrived from the outer world. It is here, on this subtle split that the implicit paradox of the complex formation of "Spanishness" lies: both sides of the spectrum—progressive groups and reactionary officialdom—needed to be international, even if their motivations and means were radically divergent.

This precise coincidence could explain the curious phenomenon around *Informalismo* and other groups more or less associated with Abstract Expressionist painters. Progressive artists and art from Dau al Set and El Paso–basically, Tàpies, Saura and Millares—were exported by Franco's regime as a means to build a certain notion of a modern and liberal Spain through apolitical visual references. Just like it has been discussed for the Eurofestival, the exportation of Abstract Expressionism was seen by the apparatus as a chance to achieve some international status in a field that was not apparently too dangerous in itself, culture, and it demonstrates the eternal international / national issue, so tangible in the formation of "Spanishness" debate.

On the other hand, some of those "exported" painters often tried to defend the "national spirit" through rhetorical texts, which insisted on their artistic ties to Goya and the old (Spanish) masters[17] (even if looking at their works the visual impression seemed closer to American Abstract Expressionism). Once again, this showed the repetitious two-way road in the cultural *mise-en-scene* of the country: in order to survive inside and outside Spain, one had to be international, *ma non troppo*. Needless to say, most of the abovementioned painters really made it both inside and outside Spain, but their success was not only due to the high value of their production, as Gabriel Ureña has pointed out.[18]

As it could be explained in contemporary terms, artists like Tàpies—and to a certain extent Saura—were the required heroes for the narration of Spain during those years. One could even say, they were the kind of heroes that both groups mentioned needed in order to narrate the "new Spain"—a different "new Spain" in each case—, which was expected from abroad too. Following the old rhetoric line that linked Velázquez to Goya and Goya to Picasso,[19] the invented heroic and manufactured-for-exportation Spanish art of the 1960s had to be strong, even overwhelming, big, assertive. In other words, it has to be "virile,"[20] as the dominant discourse would say.

That is why the local conceptual production of the 1970s was never fully understood in Spain, and therefore never exported as a "national product." The ghosts from the past seemed too strong and they were perhaps more ancient than the members of the Catalan conceptual group thought.[21] Those ghosts' names were not Tàpies, Millares or Saura, but Picasso and Goya. They were the indisputable heroes that had always conformed the rhetoric of "Spanishness."

That could be one of the reasons why Conceptual art was never exported as a "national" logo. That art was too antiheroic, the opposite image that seemed to be required to perform "Spanishness." It was simply perceived as too international, too close to other countries' production. How could anybody understand it as "Spanish" if it did not *look* "Spanish?" As in all auto-ethnographic discourses, the invisible dominant culture was watching and looking for the commodification of the "exotic" as it needed it.

And here appears the main paradox in this discourse always infested by paradoxes: Spanish art aimed to become international—or, so to say, like any other art in any other country—but at the same time it had to be easily recognizable. Anyway, why should Spanish artists speak about their tradition or their specific problems? Was not that part of an imposed stereotype about Spain?

Doesn't this process show the *"mainstream* demand for ethnicity (minority) autobiography that is 'precipitated (in part) by voyeurism on the part of the dominant culture," (262) as Susan Hawthorne suggests

Nevertheless, the conceptual generation was the first one truly working on an international level, as far as their ideas and ways to express them were concerned. People like Juan Hidalgo and his gay iconography already in the early 1970s and Esther Ferrer and the use of her own image in a non-autobiographical fashion, like Sherman, during the same years, both belong to the group Zaj; or people like Carlos Pazos, masquerading in his series *Voy a hacer de mí una estrella* (1975) (I'm going to make myself a star); Toni Llena and his ambiguous use of the body in some of his earlier pictures, and even Nacho Criado and his somehow parodical use of "Spanishness" in works such as "¿Por qué no? Bésale en culo al mono?" (Why not? Kiss the monkey's ass)—a pun referring to Anís del Mono, a liquor rather popular in Spain during the 1960s[22]—can be quite representative examples of the internationality the country was looking for, even if manufactured in a new, unexpected way. So unexpected, that at this 70s generation it did not please anyone. They did not seem an appropriate "product to export," neither before Franco died, nor after his disappearance.

They were not even fully understood inside the country, perhaps because in order to fully appreciate their world view, the new theoretical approach that had been developing among art historians and critics in Great Britain and the U.S. and that to a certain extent created a new reading of the body and self— gender studies—was not fully established in Spain until the early 90s, and by that time the conceptual generation had been forgotten. In fact, all Spanish scholars interested in gender studies took mainly foreign examples as a starting point for their discussions, disregarding the production of Spanish artists who had been focusing on similar issues. But, of course, this could be yet another instance of Spain's low self-esteem.

Then, the 1980s soon arrived, and Spain was perceived as a sociological case study–the abovementioned "young democracy." The distorted Spanish "post-modern" logotype at that time, la *"movida,"*[23] was nothing but an easy to manufacture commodity that in a way was exported through some of the artists at the Guggenheim Museum and Artists's Space officially launched exhibits— mainly members of the so called *Nueva Figuración*. La "movida" was an easy-to-swallow product that made the staged ethnicity into acted modernity again, only in a yet different way. Is there, after all, anything more clearly "ethnic" than the Almodóvar phenomenon in Europe, New York and Hollywood? Would Almodóvar had had such a big success had he not played some of the auto-ethnography strategies as described before?

His *Women on the Verge of a Nervous Breakdown*,[24] for many the ultimate symbol of Spanish "postmodern" scene, was only a parody of "Spain." Just like the *Bandido* videoclip, the film was a succulent mixture of low and high culture, modern and traditional, national and international. Almodóvar's characters recreated an hyperbolic and hypertrophic Spanish reality as dubious as the one described in the TV serial *Dallas*.[25] One could even say his own performatic self is some kind of parody of "Spanishness," like his dedication of the Oscar Academy Award to his mother and a long list of Catholic saints or virgins. After all, isn't this *what Spain is all about*?

But, what do you mean "we" and, even more, who are "we" really, when the whole dynamics of the country has completely changed in the past ten or so years? The former emigrant and "exotic" Spain is now perceived as the door to Eden. A traditionally emigrant country, Spain has now become a popular destination for people from Africa, Latin America and the East, who come not to enjoy the sun and the beaches, as most retired foreign residents did before, but to look for better life opportunities. That has of course generated a new perception of Spain and Spanish people. What had been for centuries the only established race minority—the gypsy one—also used and abused as a commodity in the very construction of "Spanishness," has been replaced by a multiracial minorities cartography that has uncovered the real essence of Spain as a racist country (Soto 396). So, who are "they" really? How do "we" relate to "them"? And, even more important, can "Spanishness" be perceived the same way when some very basic things have changed in such a dramatic manner?

If a remarkable part of visual production in Spain has been about "(self) identity," how can identity representations remain unchanged while the everyday reality of the country is so radically different? Can Picasso be still presented as the national hero of "Spanishness" in the terms discussed here, when the whole concept of "Spanishness"—also as discussed here—is falling apart? How can one play "autoethinicy" when around oneself there are "more ethnic" people than oneself?

Some artists, curators and critics from the younger generation have of course understood this new conflict remarkably well. Among other, projects like *Nuevas cartografías de Madrid* (2003), cosponsored by Casa Encedida and Casa de América, focused on the everyday life of different emigrant communities in Madrid. The invited Spanish and non-Spanish artists living in town, mingled with the immigrant communities and described their lives, gathering places, problems, and so forth. No doubt, this project reflected a very deep change but not because the concept "we" had become some kind of mainstream gaze that looked at ethnic "exotic" "they." The point here was not an indulgent comment about how Spain had finally become international and to notice how new commodities were taking its place as shown in Javier Longobardo's works about Poland. Quite the contrary: the show confronted the deep inner conflict Spain has been experiencing about its own identity as it has tried to explore the conflict implied in this sudden change of status.

This was also the idea in the computer game work that Valeriano López designed in 2001, *Estrecho adventure*, in which he told the story and perils of a young Moroccan boy trying to make a living in Spain, a country only a few miles away from his native land even if miles away symbolically, much like Spain had been from France in Franco's time. That was also the idea of Pilar Albarracín's 2002 work *El viaje. Habibi*—the only Arab word known in Spain and meaning "beloved"—in which the visitors could get into a crowded old car clumsily moving and have a taste of what a trip from Morocco to Europe—or from Europe back to Morocco—was.

López and Albarracín and their critical approach are not exceptional cases among the new generation. All traditional values related to "Spanishness" are being subverted by younger artists. Gender issues are confronted in the works of Marina Núñez, Eulalia Valldosera or Juan Luis Moraza, among others. Carles Congost, Carmela García or Manu Arregi deal with gay issues in their works, while Mira Bernabeu and Enrique Marty subvert the notion of the family—Marty even put a physical fallus in his mother sculpture of 2003—a catholic symbol of Spanish identity for centuries.

The "dancing Spain" which appeared in the Azúcar Moreno video has radically changed. It has not only been subverted by Albarracín in the parodic work *Musical Dancing Spanish Dolls* (2001), but the Japanese artist living in Salamanca Kauro Kutuyama has erased the old stereotype about "dancing Spain" simply by creating a new unexpected one. Her *Technocharro* work—based on "charro," the traditional Salamanca dance—states clearly how Spain is not (only) Andalusia and how the "exotic" can be perceived and performed from many different angles. After all, are not ethnicities and dominant cultures mobile notions that vary depending on the performance chosen?

Acknowledgments

The author would like to thank the following people for their help and advice: José Guirao, Juan Andrés Rojo, Rafael Doctor, and Elodia Huelva. My special thanks to Miriam Basilio for her patient editing of the first English version of the text and her always intelligent comments on the text.

Notes

1. The following year Spain won the contest again with Salomé's song *Vivo cantando*, but it seemed to be a political vote, related to the fact that Spain was hosting the event. Besides, that year four countries won *ex aequo*, so the next edition of Eurofestival did not take place in Madrid.
2. It is interesting to note how things changed for Serrat as soon as he took the decision to sing in Catalan and how the very use of Catalan—or Galician—language was used in different contexts and with different meanings during those years. Simply by following the articles that appeared in *El Alcázar*, one of the most filofrancoist newspapers in Madrid, one could realize those changes. If on March 22, 1969, Miguel de los Santos was describing Serrat as "un joven poeta" (a young poet), "un estudiante" (a student) and "un muchacho español de hoy para triunfar en el mundo" (a young Spanish man of today ready to triumph in the world) (Santos 26), a day after José Luis Quintanilla was wondering why was he was booed in Valencia if he sang in Catalan most of the time (Quintanilla 15). Finally, on March 26 the news of Serrat's decision was on the first page, explaining that Massiel would take Serrat's place and calling his gesture "espantá" ("espantada," "bolting") (Molpeceres 2). The day after the same journalist would try to justify Spain's decision to substitute Serrat by quoting the BBC: Tom Jones never said he would sing in Welsh. Another Madrid newspaper, *Pueblo*, would be a bit more discreet in the whole polemics or at least it was less passionate, although not less critical. On March 25 the newspaper published Serrat's open letter explaining his motivation ("Sólo cantaré en catalán"), followed by the Spanish Television answer, in which it was explained that what they did disapprove of was the way and time to do it. In fact, the television answer explained that Serrat had sang in Catalan on different occasions—on May 6, 1967, he sang only in Catalan, they said—since Catalan was "una lengua que forma parte del patrimonio cultural de nuestra Patria" ("Sólo cantaré en catalán" 25) (a language that is part of our homeland's heritage).
3. The text said: "No hace muchos días publicamos un comentario editorial, abriendo nuestras páginas dedicadas a la ciudad, en el que preguntábamos, sin rodeos, por qué Joan Manuel Serrat no cantaba el dichoso "La, la, la" en catalán, lengua españolísima y tan ajena al entendimiento de los oyentes de un festival europeo como el propio castellano. Con esta pregunta no hacíamos otra cosa que continuar fielmente una actitud (...) de exaltación y defensa de nuestro idioma vernáculo, actitud que consideramos bastante coherente y lógica en un diario archicatalán, que se publica en Barcelona hace más de ochenta años, y que jamás ha dejado de ser, pese a sus hondas raíces regionales, espejo del más insobornable y limpio españolismo." In "El 'caso' Serrat." (Not many days ago, we published an editorial (opening our Local section) in which we asked directly why Joan Manuel Serrat would not sing the infamous "La, la, la" in Catalan, which is a most Spanish language and one which is as alien to the listeners of a European festival as Spanish itself. By asking that, we were faithfully continuing with our attitude of exaltation and defense of our own language. We consider that that

4. "Este volver sobre lo dicho, desdecirse, proceder de manera arbitraria e inconsecuente, demostrar tan poca firmeza de opiniones y criterios, es lo menos adecuado al sentido común, a la seriedad. En una palabra, al 'seny'" ("El 'caso' Serrat") (This coming back to what one has said, to correct himself, to act arbitrarily and inconsequently, to demonstrate such feeble opinions and criteria, is the furthest from common sense, of seriousness. In one word, of *seny*.)
5. In fact, in the last years a new TV program was designed in order to find the person to represent Spain in the Eurofestival: *Operación triunfo.* The mediatic impact of the program was amazing, and through it the whole mechanism of nostalgia of the "Massiel era" was rediscovered.
6. "No creo que en ningún país existan mujeres más capaces que las andaluzas para inducir a ser raptadas. No sólo porque despiertan la pasión que hace cometer tonterías, sino porque de verdad parecen estar hechas a medida para ser tomadas, recorridas y escondidas, tan pequeñas son y tan ligeras, rellenitas, flexibles, dulcísimas" (Amicis 227) (I do not believe that in any country there could be women who are more capable to provoke abduction than those of Andalusia. Not only because they awake the kind of passion which moves one to behave foolishly, but because they really seem to be made to be taken away and hidden, as they are so small and light, plump, flexible, most sweet.)
7. For a more complete discussion about foreign music videos and the issues of race and gender regarding Azúcar Moreno's *Bandido*, see Diego.
8. It seems interesting to notice how the success of the show was measured by the long queues waiting to get into the Prado Museum. An article appeared in the most important newspaper in Madrid, *El País,* and explained the phenomenon in the following terms, after the author of the article noticed that in the first week 60,000 people had visited the show: "la exposición de Velázquez" que ha motivado larguísimas colas (. . .) a las puertas del museo" (the Velázquez exhibit, which has provoked very long lines (. . .) at the museum's gates) (Jarque, Fietta. "Concluido y a punto de publicar el inventario general del patrimonio del Museo del Prado." *El País* 4 Feb. 1990: 24). Anyway, what seems more curious to point out is how more than 20 years after the event a very similar piece of news has been published on the occasion of Picasso's exhibiton at the Prado and the Reina Sofía museums. At the show, Picasso has been compared to Goya—by the way, an old project of the then Minister of Culture Jorge Semprún, as published in 1990 in *El País* ("Semprún anuncia una exposición que confrontará a Goya y Picasso." *El País* 1 Feb. 1990: 38). The title of the article about Picasso seems eloquent in itself: "Largas colas para disfrutar de Picasso." (Fernández-Santos 14). Just like Velázquez was in 1990, Picasso has been made into a Spanish "national hero," a truly representative of the genuine Spanish tradition made into a commodity.

9. The Spanish tourism campaign for France in the mid 1990s was in fact "Espagne, une passion: la vie."
10. I am referring here to the term as used by Robert Cantwell: a kind of "representation of culture."
11. For some issues related to "heroic touristic sites" and Franco's construction of reality, see Basilio.
12. "La exposición Universal de Sevilla 1992 se ha polarizado hacia el futuro y con acusada tendencia a volver la espalda a la Historia, como si ésta constituyese un lastre embarazoso. Sin embargo, el futuro sólo puede ser ambiciosa proyección del presente, y el presente es, consciente o no, consecuencia de un pasado que en él pervive condicionándolo. Basta con reparar en un pequeño detalle: la razón de ser de EXPO92 es el Quinto Centenario del Descubrimiento de América. Los historiadores—escasos—en el Comité de Expertos hemos tenido, sin anbargo, poco que decir ante las orientaciones—ponencias, cuestionarios, sugestiones—desarrolladas en las sesiones que han sido programadas hasta ahora" (Seco Serrano 44) (The Seville 1992 Exhibition has been polarized toward the future with a clear tendency to ignore History, as if it were an embarrassing burden. However, the future can only be an ambitious projection of the present, and the present is, consciously or not, the consequence of a past which lives within it, conditioning it. It should be enough to note a small detail: the Exhibition's *raison d'être* is the 500th Anniversary of the Discovery of America. But those of us in the Committee of Experts who are historians have had little to say regarding the orientations—presentations, questionnaires, suggestions—which have been developed in the sessions programmed up until now.)
13. In fact, the exhibitions were visited by many people. Statistics regarding Expo'92 from the Centro de Investigaciones Sociológicas showed that art exhibits were the most visited ones by for the general public (74%), after national pavilions (91%).
14. The show *Pasajes. Actualidad del arte español: Pabellón de España, Expo 92*. Toledo: Electa, 1992, showed the work of more than 60 artists, most of them painters and sculptors, except for a couple of photographers and a few installation works. The scientific committee members were: María Corral, María Teresa Blanch, José Luis Brea, Miguel Fernández-Cid and Rosa Queralt.
15. The text devoted to the artist in the catalogue explains his work in the following depolitized way: "Tres excelentes ejemplos de lo que no se conforma con quedarse en la obra plástica, que le tientan otras acciones aunque reconozca la dificultad de traspasar lenguajes y el valor final del silencio." (*Pasajes. Actualidad del arte español* 74).
16. In 1993 a *Nueva Lente* show opened at the Canal de Isabel II, an exhibiton space that belongs to the Comunidad de Madrid (*Nueva Lente*. Madrid: Comunidad de Madrid, 1993). The show was curated by Rafael Doctor and it started a very active photography exhibition policy at the Comunidad de Madrid, especially under the former General Director Dr. Miguel Angel Castillo Oreja. The Canal de Isabel II was one of the first spaces in Madrid to devote its activities to contemporary photography.
17. Some of these problems are discussed in the 1952 text of Boj reprinted in Ureña (364–65) and in the ideas of Saura in the "cuestionario" by Toussant (181).

18. Ureña explains the problems in these terms: "sino también, en buena medida, por la afortunada estrategia llevada a cabo por la Administración franquista, en concreto por la Dirección General de Relaciones Culturales y por el Comisario Luis González Robles" (174) (But also, considerably, due to the fortunate strategy carried out by the Franco Administration, especifically by the General Directorate for Cultural Relations and its Commissary, Luis González Robles).
19. See footnote 17.
20. It is interesting to note how even some of the most "international" women sculptresses in the 80s, like Solano herself, were working under the same kind of pressure, even if their production was confronting many of the traditional imposed ideas of women's art.
21. Tàpies' article "Arte conceptual aquí," which appeared in *La Vanguardia* in March, 1973 and where he discussed (and disapproved of) "nuestra versión local" generated polemics among a sector of the Catalan Conceptual artists, the Grup de Treball. But maybe the interesting thing was how the group answer was never published in *La Vanguardia*, except for a short version. The whole issue and the texts are discussed and reproduced in Marchán 279–89 and 426–32.
22. In the past months an exhibition about conceptual art has taken place at the Museo Reina Sofía, but it has not pleased many of the implied people. In any case, most of the artists have had solo shows in the country.
23. One of the first books concerning la "movida" is Gallero's *Sólo se vive una vez. Esplendor y ruina de la movida* madrileña. See also Martínez and Vilarós. In the past months two projects regarding "la movida" have taken place in Madrid: an exhibition by one of the photographers related to those years, Pablo Pérez-Mínguez, and a four-exhibition project undertaken by Comunidad de Madrid analyzing different issues related to "la movida" (music, painting, literature, etc).
24. As a review in *The New York Times* pointed out (11 Nov, 1988: 16) "Though feminist in its sympathies, "Women on the Verge" is far from being a tract of any sort. The characters Mr. Almodóvar has written and directed keep asserting idiosyncrasies that do not allow them, or the film, to be so humorlessly categorized."
25. Concerning Almodóvar and national identity, see Kinder 147 ff.

Works Cited

Amicis, Edmondo De. *España. Diario de viaje de un turista escritor*. Madrid: Cátedra, 2000.

Basilio, Miriam. "A Pilgrimage to the Alcázar de Toledo: Ritual, Tourism and Propaganda in Franco's Spain." *Architecture and Tourism. Perception, Performance and Place*. Ed. D. Medina Lasansky and Brian McLaren. Oxford: Berg. 93–107.

Bhabha, Homi. "The Other Question. Stereotype, discrimination and the discourse of colonialism." *The Location of Culture*. New York: Routledge, 1994. 66–84.

Bufwack, Mary, and Bob Oermann. "Women in Country Music." *Popular Culture in America*. Ed. Paul Buhle. Minneapolis: University of Minnesota Press, 1987. 91–92.
Cabañas, Miguel. *Artistas contra Franco: la oposición de los artistas mexicanos y españoles exilados a las bienales hispanoamericanas de arte*. México: Universidad Nacional Autónoma, 1996.
Cantwell, Robert. *Ethnomimesis. Folklife and the Representation of Culture*. Chapel Hill: University of North Carolina Press, 1993.
"El 'caso' Serrat." *La vanguardia española*. Barcelona 26 March 1968: 1.
Castellote, Alejandro. "Introduction." *The Spanish Vision. Contemporary Art Photography, 1970–1990*. New York: The Spanish Institute, 1992.
Cembalest, Robin. "I Love Flamenco." *Art News*. [New York] November 1990: 127–29.
Diego, Estrella de. "Videoalquimias: géneros vendidos, clases prestadas, razas adquiridas." *Abanicos excéntricos, 1995*. Ed. África Vidal. Salamanca: Universidad de Salamanca, 1995. 135–50
Fernández-Santos, Elsa. "Largas colas para disfrutar de Picasso. 6000 personas visitaron ayer la muestra 'Tradición y vanguardia' en el Prado y el Reina Sofía." *El País* 7 June 2006: 14
Gallero, José Luis. *Sólo se vive una vez. Esplendor y ruina de la movida madrileña*. Madrid: Ardora, 1991
Gambrell, Jamey. "Report from Spain. Gearing Up." *Art in America*. [New York] September 1988: 37–47.
Garín, Felipe. "Arte y cultura como elementos de integración universal." *En el umbral del tercer milenio*. Madrid: Tabacalera and Ministerio de Relaciones con las Cortes y de la Secretaria del Gobierno. Oficina del Comité General de la Exposición Universal de Sevilla 1992, 1992. 68.
Hawthorne, Suzan. "The Politics and the exotic: the Paradox of Cultural Voyeurism." *Meajin*, 1989.
Huggan, Graham. *The Post-Colonial Exotic. Marketing the Margins*. London: Routledge, 2001.
Jarque, Fietta. "Concluido y a punto de publicar el inventario general del patrimonio del Museo del Prado." *El País* 4 Feb. 1990: 24.
Kaplan, E. Ann. *Rocking around the Clock. Music, Television,& Consumer Culture*. New York: Methuen, 1987.
Kinder, Marsha. *Blood Cinema. The Reconstruction of National Identity in Spain*. Berkeley: University of California Press, 1995.
Lewis, Reina. *Gendering Orientalism. Race, Femininity and Representation*. London: Routledge, 1996.
López de Haro, Reneé. "¡Olé tu gracia!" *El País Semanal*. 13 Sep. 1992: 14–23.
Marchán, Simón. *Del arte conceptual al arte de concepto (1960–1974)*. Madrid: Akal, 1988.
Martínez, José Tono. "Contracultura y utopía en democracia. Once tesis sobre un malentendido llamado 'movida.'" *Revista de Occidente* (April, 2006): 99–128.

McGuigan, Cathleen. "Spain's Back on Track. The Post-Franco Generation Heats up the Art World." *Newsweek* February 1990: 66–68.
Molpeceres, Jesús G. "Serrat. 'Espantá' a destiempo." *El Alcázar* [Madrid] 26 March. 1968: 2.
Peralta Morales, Antonio. "La Refundación del Imperio Español." *El descubrimiento del 92. Expo, Olimpiadas . . . La otra cara del espectáculo*. Virus Editorial, 1992. 13–18.
Pérez-Mínguez, Pablo. *Mi movida. Pablo Pérez-Mínguez. Fotografías, 1979–1985*. Madrid: Museo Municipal de Arte Contemporáneo, July-Oct. 2006.
Quintanilla, José Luis. "Abucheo y ovación en Valencia." *El Alcázar* [Madrid] 23 March 1968: 15.
Santos, Miguel de los. "Pase lo que pase en Eurovisión . . . ¡Serrat, una explosión de vitalidad!" *El Alcázar* [Madrid] 22 March 1968: 26.
Seco Serrano, Carlos. "Reflexiones desde la Historia sobre lo que la Exposición Universal Sevilla 1992 ha conmemorado." *El umbral del tercer milenio*. Madrid: Tabacalera and Ministerio de Relaciones con las Cortes y de la Secretaria del Gobierno. Oficina del Comité General de la Exposición Universal de Sevilla 1992, 1992. 44.
"Semprún anuncia una exposición que confrontará a Goya y Picasso." *El País* 1 Feb. 1990: 38.
"Sólo cantaré en catalán." *Pueblo* [Madrid] 25 March 1968 : 25.
Soto, Álvaro. *Transición y cambio en España. 1975–1996*. Madrid: Alianza Editorial, 2005. 396.
Stein, Gertrude. *Ricasso. The Complete Writings*. Boston: Beacon Press, 1970. 30.
El sueño imperativo / The Imperative Dream. Madrid: Círculo de Bellas Artes, 1991.
Toussant, Laurence. *El Paso y el arte Abstracto en España*. Madrid: Cuadernos Cátedra, 1983.
Tubert, Carol. "The Coming (Of Age) of Latino Lover." *The Village Voice* 9 August 1988: 227.
Ureña, Gabriel. *Las vanguardias artísticas de la postguerra española. 1940–1959*. Madrid: Itsmo, 1982.
Vilarós, Teresa. *El mono del desencanto. Una crítica cultural de la transición española (1973–1993)*. Madrid: Editorial Siglo XXI, 1998.
Vírico, Colectivo. *El descubrimiento del 92. Expo, Olimpiadas . . . La otra cara del espectáculo*. Barcelona: Virus, D.L., 1992.

◆ **10**

Creating a New Cohesive National Discourse in Spain after Franco

Carsten Humlebæk

Every new democratic regime that comes after an authoritarian experience has to decide on how to face this episode and how to incorporate it into the national history in order to create a new cohesive national discourse. Countries that have experienced nationalist dictatorships face particular difficulties in doing this due to the monopolization of any discourse of nationalist affirmation by the dictatorship. But facing the authoritarian past remains an extremely delicate task in all post-dictatorial situations because it implies a reflection on the complicities of part of the national community with the dictatorship. All authoritarian experiences leave some sort of fratricidal memories in the nation, given that all dictatorships enjoy the support of part of the national community and their more or less active participation in the repression of the other part. This problematic legacy of national confrontation has to be dealt with by the new democracy, and the way in which it is handled will be very important in determining the character of the transition.

This process of integrating a democratic present with an authoritarian past in one way or the other could be termed coming to terms or coping with the past.[1] There exists a variety of ways in which this can be done which, said very simply, constitute a continuum from putting the former regime on trial for the injustices committed at one extreme to pardoning it completely at the other.[2] These different ways of relating to the past reflect the dilemma of choosing between rupture and continuity as guiding principle for a transition process. In most cases the solution chosen combines various ways of relating to the authoritarian past; elements of rupture are combined with elements of continuity, and most often the solution is subject to adjustment several times during the transition period as the correlation of forces change. These efforts of coming to terms with the past thus always constitute very dynamic processes. At stake is not just a series of perceptions of the past but active social (re-) construction, and the choices made during the transition process therefore also have real consequences for the society in question. Furthermore, these processes always happen in a specific historical context that sets a series of constraints on the process. To accomplish a democratic transition during the Cold War in the 1970s was, for example, subject to very different conditions from a transition taking place after the fall of the Berlin Wall both in terms of international support and demands as well as in terms of the range of possible solutions available.

The Spanish Transition as a Process of Coming to Terms with the Past

The Spanish transition to democracy is no exception from the rule that underlines the importance of managing the relationship with the immediate past. The character of the Spanish transition, and to a large extent also its success, was intimately related to specific ways of dealing with the traumatic past, which was part and parcel of an attempt to construct a coherent account of the nation, a new national discourse. This essay investigates the process of creation of this discourse of post-dictatorial order in Spain after the death of dictator Francisco Franco in 1975. My research focuses on the political and media discourse and on the writing of the new democratic constitution as the embodiment of the new post-dictatorial order. The principal focus is thus on the early transition years, but my intention is also to follow the development until more present times, albeit in a more superficial manner.

When Franco died, Spain was not only 'haunted' by the memory of the almost four decades of dictatorship, but also by the still vivid memory of the 1930s. The traumatic memory of the Second Republic (1931–1936) and the Civil War (1936–1939) had been carefully shaped and instrumentalized by the dictatorship. Victory in the Civil War constituted the principal source of legitimacy of the early Franco regime. But Francoist official discourse also insisted *ad nauseam* on the idea that Spaniards, in spite of all their many heroic virtues, were intrinsically unable to live under a democratic regime without resorting to violence. The political culture of the Spaniards was, in other words, unfit for democracy. The logical conclusion from this reasoning was that the Spaniards needed Franco and his regime to avoid internal confrontation and secure progress and prosperity. Elsewhere, I have called this the "myth of the ungovernable character of the Spaniards" because of the lessons that the Spaniards were supposed to learn from their historical experience (Humlebæk, "La construcción" 369–78, Humlebæk, "Collective Memory," and Aguilar Fernández & Humlebæk). From the early 1960s onwards, the discourse on victory was phased out in favor of a discourse on peace, stability, and economic development which stressed the achievements of the Franco regime. This discourse emphasized above all the importance of not repeating the Civil War, which, implicitly, meant to avoid any kind of take-over that had the character of rupture. It was thus also a very anti-revolutionist discourse. Significantly, the oppressed opposition, the losing side in the war, to a large extent also favored this interpretation of the historical experience.[3]

By establishing an official nationalism that excluded the losers of the Civil War, Franco's regime deprived approximately half the citizens of their identity as Spaniards. This explains the urgent necessity of reconstructing the nation on a basis of reconciliation after the death of Franco in November 1975. The post-Franco change of regime took the form of a smooth, gradual, and relatively rapid reform process, which was characterized by concord among most of the parties involved. It thus respected the anti-revolutionary imperative of the never again civil war-discourse of late Francoism. The formula employed was to dismantle the Francoist regime from within, using its legal and parliamentary structure against itself. In this way the sensation of rupture could be avoided and instead another perception of some kind of continuity could be favored. The culmination of this process was the consensual writing of a new democratic constitution and its approval in a referendum by ample majority in December 1978, just over three years after the death of the dictator.

The Consensual Transition and Its Relationship with the Past

The fear of a return of the pre-Civil War scenario of polarization and violence, was thus behind the decision of the political elites to avoid ruptures and strive for consensus. This anxiety was the result of a particular memory of the past fostered during the dictatorship, as shown above. Precisely the combination of a new political elite consisting of both former followers of the dictatorship as well as members of the former opposition and the urgent need of reaching a consensual solution to the post-dictatorial transition dictated a very specific way of relating to the immediate past. Despite agreeing in principle on a certain interpretation of the Civil War, as mentioned above, they, for obvious reasons, did not share the same memory of the dictatorship nor did they agree on any interpretation of that period. To achieve the longed-for consensus and reconciliation of the two sides, it was therefore believed to be necessary to fence out any direct dealing with the dictatorial past from the political realm in an attempt to avoid destabilizing ideas of revenge and collective guilt. In order to achieve this, the political elites abided by a tacit agreement not to instrumentalise the past politically, a solution which had the character of an informal pact.[4] The tacit agreement did not just remain an unspoken declaration of principles; it was translated into very tangible politics, for example, by a series of decrees and laws that gave amnesty to political prisoners from the opposition against the Franco regime. A democratic future for Spain and a profound political and public debate on the dictatorial past were perceived as antagonistic goals due to the fear of revenge and repetition of the civil conflict. Of the two, the achievement and consolidation of democracy was considered the most important.

This agreement was later disrespectfully called the "pact of silence," a point to which I shall return to below, but by the contemporary press it was often termed "placing Franco into history" or "Franco now belongs to history," which did not have the same negative ring and instead underlined a reassuring separation between the authoritarian past and the democratic present. An editorial in the leading Catholic newspaper, *Ya*, on the first anniversary of the death of Franco in 1976 stated: "(. . .) Franco already belongs to history; (. . .) Francoism ended with him; [and] (. . .) any attempt to continue it may have had its time, but that time passed" ("Primer aniversario").[5] The positive tone in this editorial is unmistakable. It is also important to remember that in its contemporary context the pact provided benefits for both parties. In return for letting the regime change towards democracy and parliamentary monarchy, thus giving up their power, the Francoists achieved legal amnesty against the possible penal consequences of their actions during the dictatorship and thereby avoided the revenge of those that they had oppressed. The opposition accepted to extend the amnesty to include the infringements committed during the Franco regime. In fact, borrowing the famous term used by the first Polish non-communist Prime Minister Tadeusz Mazowiecki, in a very real sense the amnesty law represented a "thick line" under the past for those who had committed injustices and human rights violations during the dictatorship.[6] On the occasion of the twenty-fifth anniversary of the first democratic elections in 2002, Alfonso Guerra, the second in command of the Spanish Socialist Workers Party (*Partido Socialista Obrero Español*, or PSOE) at the time of the transition, admitted that "in the transition, we forgot about what the rightwing had done on the condition that it did not repeat the same behavior" (Ibáñez). In return they gained a democratic system, their longed-for freedom, amnesty for their political prisoners, the granting of pensions to the republican soldiers and their widows, and restitution of part of the confiscated property, all of which were initiatives related to injustices committed by the Francoist side.

Celebrating the Peaceful Transition as a National Achievement: The Post-Dictatorial Order Begins to Take Shape

In much the same way as a particular memory of the Second Republic and the Civil War was functional to legitimize the dictatorship, the Francoist myth of the ungovernable character of the Spaniards was functional as a counter-narrative to the new democratic regime. As a commonly known narrative that denied the possibility of a peaceful transition to democracy, the fact that such a transition actually was taking place in itself enhanced its perceived value. The achievements of the transition increased their significance if it could be rendered probable that their genesis was threatened. After the first democratic elections, for example, it was underlined in practically all the media that the voting took place peacefully as if that could not be taken for granted, which is a good example of the way in which this mechanism worked. The day after the election, the editorial in the leading conservative newspaper, *ABC*, was entitled "A people votes in peace," containing a subtle allusion to precedent democratic experiences which did not connote peace ("Un pueblo"). The editorial of *Ya* on the same day explained it in detail: "The country has voted massively and it has done so pacifically, without any improper gestures. Those of us who recall the tumultuous elections of preceding epochs had to rub our eyes in disbelief to make sure that this is the same nation" ("La democracia").[7]

After an initial liminal phase of the transition in which the Spaniards could not refer to any independent foundational myth, the fact that the perceived threats against its success were now seen to be overcome by reason, peacefulness, and moderation was a first indication that a new common narrative was beginning to function. This narrative was the negation of the Francoist myth and with it the achievements of the transition could be celebrated, thereby legitimizing the process. Therefore, the oblivion or relegation of Franco and his regime "to history" was always only partial; the fabrication and maintenance of a certain, negatively charged memory of the past was necessary for the legitimacy of the democratic regime. But the generalized fear was on retreat, being replaced by a steadily increasing belief in the success of the democratization, and the remaining fear of outbursts of violence was becoming more and more instrumental.

Turning upside-down the Francoist legitimization discourse did not, however, result in a recuperation of the memory of the last democratic period, the Second Republic. The evaluation of the coming of the Second Republic as an overly revolutionary change of regime and of the resulting Civil War as a great national tragedy, which had been propagated by the Franco regime, was not altered substantially. The Republic remained inextricably linked to the outbreak of the Civil War, just like in the Francoist discourse. Consequently, the post-Franco change of regime was conceived of with the republican take-over as negative ideal.[8] The fact that the new democratic regime could not base itself on the rehabilitation of an old democratic tradition, or construct continuity with a previous period or regime, only enhanced the importance of the legitimacy constructed *ex negativo* from the Francoist legitimization discourse. The new master narrative that emerged during the early transition was thus quite influenced by the master narratives of the Franco regime.

The New Democratic Constitution as the Embodiment of the Post-Dictatorial Order

The most important embodiment of this new narrative of the peaceful and consensual transition was the writing and ratification of the new democratic constitution. The constitutional process still belonged to a second phase in which the new master narrative of the post-dictatorial order was taking shape. The generalized fear of a setback was on retreat and the Spaniards were slowly beginning to believe in the success of democratization, which happened concurrently with the formation of the narrative of the peaceful transition to democracy. Over time, the Constitution acquired a symbolic value in itself, but in the first instance it was the process of its coming into being that embodied the new way of *convivir* (living together) that was seen to characterize the transition. A special legitimacy was, and is, therefore attached to the new democratic Constitution, which was ratified firstly in a joint session of both chambers of Parliament on 31 October 1978 and secondly through a referendum on 6 December. The last act of the coming into being of the new Constitution took place on 27 December, when the King signed it. Especially the ratification through referendum, however, was felt as a historic moment as it was approaching. The editorials in the newspapers between 1 November and 6 December were replete with the notion of a turning point of enormous historical importance. Thus, the leading Catalan newspaper *La Vanguardia* in an editorial entitled "The collective destiny" stated that "today the Spaniards (. . .) will pronounce before themselves and before history" ("El destino colectivo").[9] The positive outcome of the referendum was interpreted as a definitive closure of both the dictatorship and the interim period that had lasted since the dictator's death in November 1975. It was the beginning of a new and unique era of democracy in Spain. This was of course amply reflected in editorials ("Manos," "Afirmación," "La Constitución de todos" [7 Dec. 1978], "Primera," "Y también," "Hoy").

The ratification of the Constitution was not the first important step in the transition. There had been other important historical moments since the death of Franco. Especially the referendum on political reform of 15 December 1976, by which the Francoist parliament agreed to dissolve itself and institute a democracy, and the first democratic elections of 15 June 1977 had been perceived in much the same way. But the importance of both dates faded away in comparison with the ratification of the new Constitution.

Immediately after the celebration of the first elections, it became clear that the newly elected Parliament would be a constituent assembly. According to the particular dynamics of continuity vs. rupture of the transition, the fact that the elections were to form a constituent assembly was not announced previously in order not to offend the sensibility of the Francoist hard-liners, because it would mean to announce the transition as characterized by rupture rather than by continuity.[10] Immediately after the elections, however, it was proclaimed as a *fait accompli*, and the elections were thus turned into the inaugural act of another interim period, more than the beginning of a new era. Democracy was still waiting to being definitively constituted. Almost from the day of the elections, the expectations of Spaniards were thus directed towards a future moment in which the new constitution would be finished, and this overshadowed the historical significance of these first democratic elections.

Even if a broad agreement on the need to elaborate a new constitution was soon reached, the way of accomplishing this task became the object of dispute from the very constitution of the first democratically elected Parliament. At first, the government headed by Prime Minister Adolfo Suárez considered writing a draft itself as a point of departure for later discussions. But the opposition rejected the idea and instead Suárez proposed to designate a commission of experts to elaborate a text which should serve as a basis for the future negotiations. This plan was also turned down by the opposition, which insisted that the new constitution should be elaborated only by the newly elected deputies. Finally, the government accepted to designate a parliamentary commission with the task of writing the draft Constitution, but this did not mean that the problems were over. Originally, the commission was to have nine members, but both Suárez's governing centre-right wing party, the Union of the Democratic Centre (*Unión Centro Democrático*, or UCD), and the PSOE rejected this option for various reasons. On the one hand, certain parties were not welcome, particularly the competing Socialist party, Popular Socialist Party (*Partido Socialista Popular*, or PSP) headed by the prominent and polemic socialist Enrique Tierno Galván.[11] On the other hand, both large parties were anxious to diminish the risk of loosing the internal elections inside the commission as much as possible. In the end, it was decided that the commission be composed of seven members of which three seats were assigned to the UCD, two to the Socialist block in Parliament, one to the ex-Francoists of the Popular Alliance (*Alianza Popular*, or AP), and one to the Spanish Communist Party (*Partido Comunista de España*, or PCE). This composition, however, left no place for representatives of the Catalan and Basque nationalists, but the PSOE willingly ceded one of Socialist block's two seats to the combined 'Catalan-Basque minority' since this impeded the presence of Tierno Galván. Since the Catalan deputies were more numerous than the Basques, the representative chosen, Miquel Roca, came from the moderate Catalan nationalists but he was supposed to represent the Basques as well.[12] That did not happen and the Basques felt marginalized, which they signaled very frequently.[13]

This situation was both a reflection of how the relationship between Spain and Catalonia and the Basque Country, respectively, had developed as well as an indication of future problems. From the very beginning of the nationalist movements in the late nineteenth century there was a noteworthy difference in the general attitude towards the Spanish nation of the Basque and Catalan nationalist movements. These different dynamics have very old roots, which concern the different relationship with Castile during the medieval period and the different processes of industrialization and economic development. Historically, the Catalan nationalists generally struggled to influence Spanish politics and saw themselves as partaking, at least to some degree, in Spain or the Spanish nation of nations. In this way they vindicated their part in the historical process that had led to the formation of Spain, and did not seek independence but rather a more or less extended form of autonomy. The Basque nationalists, on the contrary, generally denied belonging to Spain, and consequently they downplayed their role in the same historical process, vindicating instead a separate origin and historical development of the Basque nation. In their narrative, Spain was portrayed as the threatening 'other' and national enemy *par excellence*.[14] That the Basque nationalists were left outside the drafting commission fitted well into this self-conception despite the fact that intense negotiations were taking place with them to reach a satisfactory agreement.

The negotiations within the commission were followed intensely in the media, but the sessions initially went off rather quietly. After three months work, on 22 November 1977, however, an early draft of the first 39 articles was leaked to the press which occasioned a heated debate among and within the political parties and in the media. From then on it became clear that the political tension within the commission was enormous. Various times members of the commission warned (the UCD especially) about the danger of making ad-hoc alliances, and in March the PSOE member of the commission, Peces-Barba, actually resigned on this basis. Despite these problems, or perhaps because of the resolute action of Peces-Barba, the mantra of consensus finally prevailed, since none of the participants wanted to run the risk of leaving out any other significant political group. On 5 May 1978 the special commission handed in the draft to the Constitutional Commission of the Parliament and then began the lengthy and difficult discussions of the thousands of amendments and the successive passage of the draft through both chambers. Although the UCD and the PSOE had an ample majority in both chambers and therefore could have forced through everything that they agreed on, again the task was to achieve the broadest possible consensus. In the final vote on 31 October 1978, the positive ballots in both chambers were 551 against 11 negative. 22 parliamentarians abstained and 14 were absent. The negative votes and the abstentions came largely from the ex-Francoists of the AP and the Basque nationalists, who in the end had opted out of an agreement with the rest of the parties behind the Constitution. The consensus reached in Parliament was thus remarkably broad, although not complete.[15]

At the same time as the politics of consensus prevailed on all the most important issues, there was a clear conscience among those involved that the consensus around the Constitution and the whole project of creating a democratic system was a unique and temporary phenomenon. After the Constitution's ratification, it was feared, it would come a new period of 'normal' politics, although most people did not have a clear idea of what that would mean. The only preceding experience to draw on was the Second Republic, which did not constitute a positive image to imitate. The worst-case scenario was thus a return to the politics of confrontation, polarization, government by narrow margins and shifting coalitions that had characterized the Republic. This fear of a rupture of the consensus was deeply influenced by the Francoist myth of the ungovernable character of the Spaniards.

This historical inspiration was frequently used rhetorically. An editorial in *Ya* on the occasion of the 8th anniversary of the Constitution in 1986, for example, after having criticized the government for lacking consideration of the minorities stated that "We are not judging the work of the Socialist government, but exclusively its lack of respect for the spirit of the Constitution in the name of a hegemonic ambition whose similarities with Francoism are becoming steadily clearer" ("La aplicación"). The references to "the spirit of the Constitution" are rhetorically counterposed to a Francoist type of politics allegedly practiced by the Socialist administration. To strive for consensus was seen as a fundamental characteristic of a real democrat, whereas not to strive for consensus was equaled with being Francoist.

Initially, no symbolic value was attached to the Constitution itself or to the authors of the draft, only to the fact that they had been able to reach a broad, consensual agreement on the democratic future of Spain. As Miquel Roca, one of the authors of the draft expressed it in 1981: "the consensus was a fantastic effort—without precedent in the history of Spain—to coincide in the definition of a democratic way of structuring the State" (Roca i Junyent). Over time, the Constitution became a symbol of consensus, which is a sign that the new narrative of the peaceful transition had been definitively established. The Constitution had come to be seen as the foundational moment of the new democratic Spain. The consensus was often idealized by underlining that all political forces were behind it. An editorial in *La Vanguardia* on the occasion of the Constitution's 13th anniversary lauded it by stating: "The entire political spectrum, from Fraga to the Communists, participated in the writing of the Constitution of 1978" ("La Constitución del consenso"). In fact, the Basque nationalists had remained largely outside the negotiations and in the end recommended abstention in the referendum, as mentioned above. The assertion that "all the political forces" were behind the Constitution was thus not entirely true and this fact, of course, disturbed the idyllic picture and was usually not mentioned explicitly when the constitutional consensus was discussed. For example, in 1985, Jordi Solé Tura, also co-author of the draft, described the fusion of the demands for democracy and autonomy: "In the historic nationalities and other areas of Spain (. . .) the struggle for democracy became fused with the struggle for the lost autonomy and the recognition of their national or regional identity" (Solé Tura, "La forma"). This description was true for the Catalan case, but it did not take into account that in the Basque Country the identification between democracy, the Constitution, and self-government was not achieved in the same way as in Catalonia. On the contrary, there the Constitution was seen as an imposition from outside by a majority and the dominant feeling was that of dissatisfaction. The point here is not primarily to evaluate the truth value of these statements, but to show that the discourse of the peaceful and consensual transition was working behind them.

The slow conversion of the Constitution into the single most important symbol of the consensus behind the successful transition to democracy was mirrored by a parallel development of a tradition to celebrate the Constitution. In fact, there were no celebrations of the Constitution during its first anniversaries in December 1979 and 1980. But from around the second anniversary in 1980, and especially after the attempted military coup of 23 February 1981, the idea that the anniversary of the Constitution—that is, of the constitutional referendum of December 6—was to be made into an official celebration and possibly even a national holiday began to take shape. The parliamentary debate precisely centered on different perceptions of the Constitution's place in Spanish history. Those who wanted to turn the Day of the Constitution into the national holiday saw it as something radically new in the history of the nation, a view which implied a perception of the transition as primarily characterized by rupture. The other option in the discussions was the anniversary of Columbus' discovery of America; those who preferred this date as the national holiday explained that the Constitution to them was just another step in Spain's very long history and that, for the time being, it was more important to implement it than celebrating it. They did not conceive the transition and the Constitution in terms of total rupture and, furthermore, believed that the process of consolidating the democracy prevented its commemoration. In the end the constitutional anniversary eventually became a holiday in 1986, but not the national holiday of Spain, because a majority in Parliament preferred the anniversary of the discovery as the national holiday.[16]

Parallel to the process of converting the Constitution into a symbol, the view on the seven members of the drafting commission changed too. Initially they were simply considered "*ponentes de la Constitución*," which simply means members of the commission with the task of writing the draft of the constitution. But as they symbolized—in a very physical way—the ability to reach agreements across the political spectrum, over time they acquired a special status, being referred to as "*padres de la Constitución*" (Fathers of the Constitution). This term began to be used some time during the 1980s and became a standard expression. Whenever the Constitution was discussed—whether as a unique embodiment of broad political consensus or as an ambiguous text in the need of reform on certain points—the "Constitutional Fathers" would always be asked and special attention would be given to their opinion. On the 10th anniversary of the Constitution in 1988, the Catalan government organized a special event with the participation of 'fathers' of the Constitution. The event served both the purpose of lauding the seven authors as well as demonstrating the importance of Catalonia to Spain and its particular dedication to the Constitution, and the Catalan leader Jordi Pujol expressed pride in that "no other act, except those in Madrid, has had the greatness of this one. But the Generalitat wanted to underline the will of all of Catalonia to make an important contribution to the whole of Spain" ("Los 'padres'"). The fact that only Madrid produced commemorations of larger magnitude was a reason for feeling pride, which fitted well into the general conception of Catalonia as a very important part of Spain, second only to the central State. Another example of the particular esteem of the seven constitutional 'fathers' happened when in 1991 they were invested doctors *honoris causa* by the UNED university in a solemn act presided over by King Juan Carlos. The King pronounced a discourse in which he qualified the Constitution as appropriate, but he also insisted on the merits of its authors, and especially the general spirit of consensus which characterized their work in the drafting commission ("Los ponentes," "El Rey aboga," "El Rey califica," "El Rey insta").

The Consolidation of Democracy and of the Post-Dictatorial Order

Most analysts situate the end of the transition in late 1982, with the landslide victory of the Socialists in the general elections of October and their peaceful takeover of the government offices in December, because it demonstrated the regime's ability to handle alternation in power. By then, the fundamental characteristics of the democratic system's discourse of legitimacy were in place, but this does not mean that the process of consolidating democracy had been brought to an end. In the first half of the 1980s, the memory of the attempted coup of 1981 was still very vivid and democracy was felt to be in danger. This perceived threat urged the large political parties to continue the politics of consensus on certain important issues, particularly the constitution of the system of autonomous regions, which was one of the issues which had irritated conservative military circles the most. After the successful passing of the autonomy statutes of Catalonia and the Basque Country in late 1979, the early 1980s witnessed the negotiations of the autonomy statutes of the fifteen remaining regions which had resulted from the Constitution.

The effects of the coup attempt in terms of the perceived threat to democracy only reinforced the post-dictatorial order and urged politicians to respect the pact not to instrumentalize the past politically. As democracy was still seen to be fragile, it was considered more important to consolidate it rather than to open a profound debate on the past and questions of historical justice.

It is probably fair to say that sometime during the second half of the 1980s democracy had been consolidated. The ultra-rightwing never achieved any electoral success and its nostalgia for authoritarian times played no role in democratic Spain. The armed forces had been reformed and brought firmly under political control, and therefore no longer posed a threat to democracy. On the positive side also counted the fact that Spain had gained entry into the Economic European Community in 1986, which was perceived as an enormous national success that bore in it the overcoming of a historical problem. In spite of these positive developments, the post-dictatorial order was not altered substantially. As democracy was being consolidated a more profound debate on the uncomfortable past might have been possible, but it did not happen. In fact, Felipe González, socialist leader and prime minister from 1982–1996, recently lamented that he did not open a debate on the past when the moment was propitious. He therefore felt "responsible for not having caused a debate on our historical past, the Franco period and the Civil War (. . .) and therefore today I feel responsible for a part of the loss of our historical memory" (González & Cebrián 37–38). Whether he and the socialists in government continued to respect the pact not to instrumentalize the past politically out of prudence or for any other reason he did not explain.

The Reappearance of the Dictatorial Past and Questions of Historical Justice

It was only towards the mid- to late-1990s that discussions of the so-called "pact of silence" and the related political requests for moral and economic reparation of various victim groups began to appear. It seems that this kind of debate in Spain was less closely connected with the end of the Cold War in 1989–1990 than in many other European countries which experienced a veritable wave of dealings with the past in the wake of the fall of the Berlin wall. In Spain, the discussions were probably set off firstly by internal dynamics, among which generational change plays an important part. They marked the rupture of the pact not to instrumentalize the past politically. While this so-called "pact of silence" with regard to the Civil War was based on an equilibrium between the parties, since both sides had taken part in the atrocities of the war, the pact was not characterized by the same harmony concerning the Franco regime. The benefits of the accord were not equally distributed since those who had collaborated actively with the dictatorship had more to gain than others who had opposed it. By agreeing to not instrumentalize the past politically, the former opposition limited its own possibilities of obtaining political gains from their past, which helps to explain why the pact was broken.[17]

What often sparked off these reflections was a comparison with other European countries where a supposedly "rigorous" scrutiny of the recent past had taken place (Sartorius and Alfaya 21). These remarks usually referred to Germany and its active confrontation with the Nazi past, but also to France and its more recent discussion of the Vichy regime. Comparing these two countries with Spain is relevant as they also were deeply fractured national communities which were forced to reconstruct a national discourse after authoritarian experiences. This was, however, rarely the theme of the comparison. The purpose of comparing was usually to demand a more active—even if only symbolic—confrontation with the problematic legacies of the past. This phenomenon has been termed "politics of regret" by the sociologists Jeffrey K. Olick and Brenda Coughlin. According to these authors it is a major characteristic of our age, and in it they identify a new principle of legitimization which makes political legitimacy depend on collective memory (Olick & Coughlin). That the demands of the politics of regret are related to a new principle of legitimacy, or at least to attempts at instituting a new principle of legitimacy, fits the Spanish case well. For rhetorical purposes, the Spanish transition was compared with other cases which can be argued to have confronted the unpleasant past more actively, especially Germany and France. The transition, and in particular the pact not to instrumentalize the past politically, were criticized, arguing that Spanish society demonstrated a 'delay' or 'backwardness' vis-à-vis its European neighbors in terms of mastering the past.

These developments showed more similarities with the German process of coming to terms with the past of the 1970s and 1980s than the earlier Spanish process of mastering the authoritarian past that was characterized by the strategy of silencing. But there is a problem with such comparisons related to the different developmental stages of the process. If one compares transition Spain with contemporary Germany, the Spanish process of coming to terms with authoritarian past obviously falls short of the German, because Germany had a lead of thirty years over Spain. Comparing contemporary Spain and Germany will therefore necessarily give an erroneous picture, but this was never reflected on, which only underlines the fact that such comparisons are part of a political agenda to demand a different politics of the past.[18]

Conclusions

In the analysis above I have tried to illustrate how the transition to democracy in Spain and the development of a post-dictatorial order was—or rather is—a process which has had various phases characterized by a particular blend of continuity and rupture. Gradually, the historical master narrative changed, and the sense of rupture vis-à-vis the dictatorship increased, constructing it as a parenthesis. The first phase after the death of Franco was very influenced by the Francoist discourse of legitimization which connected democracy with a pre-civil war scenario. This period was characterized by a generalized fear of polarization and violence which made politicians opt for consensus politics and fence out any dealings with the authoritarian past. In this early liminal phase there was no autonomous foundational myth.

The absence of positively perceived historical antecedents with which to construct continuity made the democratic regime inherit the principal Francoist legitimization myth like a sort of curse which was necessary to turn upside-down in order to prove its predictions wrong. The legitimization discourse of post-Franco Spain therefore had to be constructed basically *ex-negativo* from the Francoist discourse, which nevertheless presupposed the continued existence of the *negativo*. Without keeping alive in some form the threat contained in the Francoist myth of the ungovernable character of the Spaniards, the reasoning of the new legitimization myth would fall apart. It thereby became self-referential; the democratic regime was legitimized simply by the fact that it was a democracy. The ultimate goal of the process was the establishment and consolidation of a democratic regime. At the same time, the transformation had to appear gradual so as not to awaken fears of repeating the history of revolution and Civil War.

In a second phase, which probably began around the time of the successful first elections, the new democratic regime was successfully proving the Francoist myth wrong. The elections demonstrated that the Spaniards had been able to create a democracy without polarization and violence. The fact that the Francoist instrumentalization of the memory of the Civil War focused on that period as a trauma, and that it was experienced as such by both victors and vanquished, determined that the sole fact of establishing a consensual democratic regime without violence was experienced as a true process of mastering the past. Being able to agree on the basic "rules of the game" was interpreted as the overcoming of a historical problem by both sides. In substitution of the old Francoist myth a new discourse of legitimacy of the peaceful transition was coming into existence, which was going to be the basis of the new post-dictatorial order. The writing of the Constitution, which was achieved with broad political consensus, was part of this phase. It was considered a big success and after its ratification intellectuals and politicians were beginning to believe in the success of democratization. But at the same time they were conscious that the consensus was a temporary phenomenon tied to the unique process which would end sooner or later, and the 'normal' politics, which supposedly would follow, was an unknown to most of them. Just as during the first phase, the change of regime still could not be seen in terms of rupture, since this would recall unpleasant historical experiences.

The discourse on the Spanish nation during the transition was thus caught between the two temporal principles contained in, on the one hand, reconciliation through silencing of the dictatorship and, on the other, regime change through reform. The reconciliation through silencing meant to forget about the past—at least for a time—and to begin anew, whereas the change through reform, on the contrary, presupposed a conscience about and even a certain respect for the immediate past that was being reformed. Initially, therefore, there was no clear historical dimension to the narrative that specified the exact locus of the transition in Spanish history and its specific relationships with the past. The past, and especially the Francoist past, was a controversial issue on which it would be difficult to reach any agreement. The first generalized historical narrative that appeared was a construction of distance with respect to the Franco regime. Gradually, the forty years of dictatorship were placed in a parenthesis and became an interim period, but without constructing any clear alternative continuities in the sense of identification with earlier periods. The largely negative evaluation of the preceding century of Spanish history in the Francoist historical master narrative continued to influence views on history in the democracy, thus making identification with earlier periods difficult.

After some time, however, the success of the peaceful transition became the foundational narrative of the democratic regime and the Constitution was converted into a symbol of consensus. Apart from being based on the mythification of certain aspects of the transition, this narrative—which is still fundamental to today's Spanish political system—also represents a democratic legitimacy based on popular satisfaction with the regime. The historical master narrative of the transition is essentially without a political stamp. The reference point is always the broad political consensus behind the most important decisions, and it is, for example, always emphasized that all the political parties from the Communists of the PCE to the ex-Francoists of the AP participated in the writing of the Constitution. This narrative is a narrative of the "coming of age of modern Spain" by means of which Spaniards can celebrate Spain as a modern, European, and developed nation. Thereby the Spaniards are perceived to have finally defeated their history of decline with respect to earlier periods of splendor and backwardness vis-à-vis European neighbors, a narrative which had dominated interpretations of Spanish history for over a century.

To see the successful transition and the ratification of the Constitution as a foundational period of the new regime implied seeing the transition more as rupture than as continuity. It is impossible to indicate a precise beginning of this third phase, since the development is a gradual process. Even when the discourse on the transition acquired enough self-referential power to refer to it as a success and extract legitimacy from its own existence, it still only referred basically to itself and implicitly to the Franco regime *ex-negativo*. The authoritarian past thus did not disappear and this dilemma marked the attempted normalization of the Spanish democracy. By and large the pact not to instrumentalize the past politically was respected during the 1980s and the larger part of the 1990s, and active confrontations with the authoritarian past in the political sphere were avoided.

It is precisely the progressive rupture of this pact from the mid- to late 1990s that possibly marked the beginning of a fourth phase. These most recent developments tend to regard the pact and the voluntary exclusion of any dealing with the authoritarian past as a price that the transition politicians had paid to achieve a successful transition. To most participants in the debate, that price was too high. Now that democracy has been consolidated and the transition to democracy is generally viewed more in terms of rupture than of continuity, the fact that the pact represents too much continuity with the previous regime constitutes a problem.

Notes

1. The issue of coming to terms with an authoritarian past has been described with the German term *Vergangenheitsbewältigung*, referring to the post-Second World War process of coming to terms with the past of German society. There is a large German literature on *Vergangenheitsbewältigung* in Germany or on similar processes in other countries. The classical texts by Hermann Lübbe from the early 1980s are still considered valid. For the current status of research on the subject, see, for example, König, Kohlstruck, & Wöll, eds. For a recent account of the politics of memory in Germany, see Camphausen.
2. For an interesting series of studies on the question of justice in democratic transitions, see Barahona de Brito, González-Enríquez, & Aguilar Fernández, eds.
3. For the principal study of the changes in the discourse of legitimacy during the Franco

period see Aguilar Fernández, *Memoria*. For a view that centres on developmentalism as a deliberate choice of the Franco regime, see Ucelay-Da Cal.
4. The term is taken from Aguilar Fernández, "Presencia," which is the best study of the reach of the pact. For a study of the political use of the past in Spain since 1975 and the rupture of the informal pact in the late 1990s, see Humlebæk, "Political."
5. For other examples, see "Franco, el hombre" or "Franco en el olvido."
6. In his first speech to the Parliament on 24 August 1989 he said: "The Government (. . .) assumes no responsibility for the mortgage that it inherits. (. . .) Below the past we will draw a thick line. We shall only be responsible for what we do to get Poland out of the present situation of collapse" (Mazowiecki, quoted in Grabowski 279).
7. See also "El decreto." In a somewhat anachronistic way, the media still often remarks that the elections happened "without incidents"; a phrase that one would have difficulty of finding in other democratic countries, but which in Spain is related to the way in which the transition took place.
8. Paloma Aguilar Fernández has shown how both the change of regime and the institutional set-up of post-Franco Spanish democracy were the antithesis of that of the Second Republic. Almost everything was done differently. The new regime was a Monarchy instead of a republic, the democracy was established by gradually changing the system from within instead of by revolutionary take-over, the Parliament was bicameral instead of unicameral, the electoral system was based on proportional instead of individual constituencies, and the national territory was divided into relatively uniform Autonomous Communities instead of an unsymmetrical territorial division (Aguilar Fernández *Memoria* 231–61).
9. Other editorials in the same vein: "El deber," "Acuerdo," "La Constitución de todos" [1 Nov. 1978], "Sí," "72 horas," "Tras el 'sí'."
10. An example of this delay in the recognition of the constituent quality of the Parliament elected in 1977 is that only in 1983 were the deputies of this first democratic legislature officially recognised with the title "deputies of the Constituent Assembly" (*parlamentarios de las Cortes constituyentes*) in a ceremony celebrated on the fifth anniversary of the constitutional referendum ("La semana").
11. Tierno Galván had held the chair of political law at the University of Murcia for over a decade under Franco and after his expulsion from the university in 1965 he had also taught at Princeton University in the United States. He therefore would have been an obvious choice as member of the commission, but his presence was unwanted by the PSOE due to his polemic nature and the fact that he was the leader of a competing Socialist party. As a kind of consolation and recognition he was asked to write the preamble of the Constitution. When after the first municipal elections in April 1979 Tierno Galván became the mayor of Madrid, PSP decided to fusion with the PSOE.
12. Apart from Miquel Roca i Junyent from the moderate Catalan nationalist party Democratic Pact for Catalonia (*Pacte Democratic per Catalunya*, or PDC), the other members of the commission were: Gabriel Cisneros Laborda, Miguel Herrero Rodríguez de Miñón, and José Pedro Pérez-Llorca from the UCD; Gregorio Peces-Barba from

the PSOE; Jordi Solé Tura from the PCE (actually the Catalan branch of the PCE, *Partido Socialista Unificado de Cataluña* or PSUC); and Manuel Fraga Iribarne from the AP.
13. For a description of the process from the point of view of the Government, see Suárez (103–85). See also Prego.
14. For a more detailed study of the relationship between Spain and its internal others, especially Catalonia and the Basque Country, during the transition, see Humlebæk, "The National." For good studies of the historically distinct developments of the nationalist movements in Catalonia and the Basque Country, see Díez Medrano and Conversi.
15. There exists a wealth of books on the constitutional process and the negotiations between the different parties. Practically all the members of the drafting commission have written one or more books on the process and their personal experience. One of the best ones remains Solé Tura, *Nacionalidades*.
16. For a detailed description of the conversion of the Constitution of 1978 into a symbol and of the 6th of December into a holiday, see Humlebæk, "La Constitución." See also Vernet.
17. For a more detailed discussion of the rupture of the pact, see Aguilar Fernández, "Presencia" and Humlebæk, "Political Uses."
18. The only article to seriously compare the Spanish and the German ways of coping with the past, written by the Spanish political scientist Ignacio Sotelo who is familiar with German circumstances, actually incurred in the same error. He stated that it would have been practically impossible to pull through a process of *Vergangenheitsbewältigung* following the German example during the Spanish transition. He thus obviously compared the Spanish transition with its contemporary Germany and not with the Germany of the immediate post-Second World War, which was not altogether different from transition Spain in terms of coping with the authoritarian past (Sotelo).

Works Cited

"72 horas para un futuro." Editorial. *Mundo Obrero* 3 Dec. 1978: 5.
"Acuerdo para el futuro." Editorial. *ABC* 1 Nov. 1978: 2.
"Afirmación mayoritaria." Editorial. *ABC* 7 Dec. 1978: 2.
Aguilar Fernández, Paloma. "Presencia y ausencia de la guerra civil y del franquismo en la democracia española. Reflexiones en torno a la articulación y ruptura del 'pacto de silencio.'" *Guerra Civil: mito y memoria*. Ed. Julio Aróstegui and François Godicheau. Madrid: Marcial Pons, 2006.
———. *Memoria y olvido de la Guerra Civil española*. Madrid: Alianza, 1996. In English: *Memory and Amnesia. The Role of the Spanish Civil War in the Transition to Democracy*. Oxford/New York: Berghahn, 2002.

Aguilar Fernández, Paloma, and Carsten Humlebæk. "Collective Memory and National Identity in the Spanish Democracy: The Legacies of Francoism and the Civil War." *History and Memory* 14.1–2 (2002): 121–65.
"La aplicación de la Constitución." Editorial. *Ya* 7 Dec. 1986: 5.
Barahona de Brito, Alexandra, Carmen González-Enríquez, and Paloma Aguilar Fernández, eds. *The politics of memory. Transitional Justice in Democratizing Societies*. Oxford: Oxford University Press, 2001.
Camphausen, Gabriele. "Diktaturbewältigung und Erinnerungspolitik in Deutschland und Österreich." Paper given at the conference "Remembering Dictatorship: Poland and Spain compared" held at University of Santiago de Compostela, March 2002.
"La Constitución de todos los españoles." Editorial. *Ya* 1 Nov. 1978: 5.
"La Constitución de todos los españoles." Editorial. *Ya* 7 Dec. 1978: 7.
"La Constitución del consenso." Editorial. *La Vanguardia* 6 Dec. 1991: 14.
Conversi, Daniele. *The Basques, the Catalans and Spain. Alternative Routes to Nationalist Mobilisation*. London: Hurst & Company, 1997.
"El deber de votar." Editorial. *El Correo Español—El Pueblo Vasco* 5 Dec. 1978: 32.
"El decreto de las urnas." Editorial. *El País* 16 June 1977: 6.
"La democracia empieza hoy." Editorial. *Ya* 16 June 1977: 7.
"El destino colectivo." Editorial. *La Vanguardia* 6 Dec. 1978: 5.
Díez Medrano, Juan. *Divided Nations. Class, Politics, and Nationalism in the Basque Country and Catalonia*. Ithaca NY/London: Cornell University Press, 1995.
"Franco, el hombre más olvidado del posfranquismo." Editorial. *El País Semanal* 21 Nov. 1976: 8.
"Franco en el olvido." Editorial. *El País Semanal* 20 Nov. 1977: 9.
González, Felipe, and Juan Luis Cebrián. *El futuro no es lo que era*. Madrid: Punto de Lectura, 2001.
Grabowski, Sabine. "Vergangenheitsbewältigung in Polen. Dossier und Analyse." König, Kohlstruck & Wöll. 261–90.
"Hoy somos ciudadanos." Editorial. *El Socialista* 10 Dec. 1978: 2.
Humlebæk, Carsten. "Remembering the Dictatorship. Commemorative Activity in the Spanish Press on the Anniversaries of the Civil War and the Death of Franco." *Totalitarian and Authoritarian Regimes in Europe. Legacies and Lessons from the Twentieth Century*. Ed. Jerzy Borejsza and Klaus Ziemer. Oxford/New York: Berghahn, 2006. 490–515.
———. "Political Uses of the Recent Past in the Spanish Post-Authoritarian Democracy." *Partisan Histories. The Past in Contemporary Global Politics*. Ed. Max Paul Friedman and Padraic Kenney. New York/Basingstoke: Palgrave-Macmillan, 2005. 75–88.
———. "La Constitución de 1978 como lugar de memoria en España." *Historia y Política. Ideas, procesos y movimientos sociales* 12 (2004): 187–210.
———. "La construcción de continuidad y la representación de la historia nacional en el discurso de la prensa en el aniversario de la muerte de Franco en 1976." *El siglo XX:*

balance y perspectivas. V congreso de La Asociación de Historia Contemporánea. Ed. Amparo Álvarez et al. Valencia: Fundación Cañada Blanch, 2000. 369–78.

———. "The National Question after Franco: Spain and Its Internal Others." *Postdiktatorische Geschichtskulturen in Europa. Bestandsaufnahme und Forschungsperspektiven.* Ed. Stefan Troebst. Wrocław: Wydawnictwo Uniwersytetu Wrocławskiego/ Wrocław University Press, forthcoming.

Ibáñez, Juan G. "'Eran más los riesgos que las dificultades.' Diputados elegidos en 1977 y que continúan en el Congreso hacen balance." *El País Digital* 15 June 2002.

König, Helmut, Michael Kohlstruck, and Andreas Wöll, eds. *Vergangenheitsbewältigung am Ende des zwanzigsten Jahrhunderts.* Opladen/Wiesbaden: Westdeutscher Verlag, 1998.

Lübbe, Hermann. "Der Nationalsozialismus im deutschen Nachkriegsbewusstsein." *Historische Zeitschrift* 236 (1983): 579–99.

———. "Der Nationalsozialismus im politischen Bewusstsein der Gegenwart." *Deutschlands Weg in die Diktatur. Internationale Konferenz zur nationalsozialistischen Machtübernahme.* Ed. Martin Broszat et al. Berlin: Siedler Verlag, 1983. 329–49.

"Manos a la obra." Editorial. *La Vanguardia* 7 Dec. 1978: 15.

Olick, Jeffrey K., and Brenda Coughlin. "The Politics of Regret. Analytical Frames." *Politics and the Past: On Repairing Historical injustices.* Ed. John Torpey. Lanham MD: Rowman and Littlefield, 2003. 37–62.

"Los 'padres' de la Constitución coinciden en la necesidad de restablecer el consenso para consolidar el Estado autonómico." *La Vanguardia* 8 Dec. 1988: 16.

"Los ponentes de la Constitución, salvo Fraga, rechazan su reforma a corto plazo." *El Correo Español—El Pueblo Vasco* 6 Dec. 1991: 22.

Prego, Victoria. "El largo camino hacia la concordia." *ABC* 6 Dec. 1998: 24–26.

"Primer aniversario." Editorial. *Ya* 20 Nov. 1976: 7.

"Primera reflexión." Editorial. *El País* 7 Dec. 1978: 8.

"Un pueblo vota en paz." Editorial. *ABC* 16 June 1977: 2.

"El Rey aboga por la práctica 'cada día' de los principios de la Constitución." *La Vanguardia* 6 Dec. 1991: 11.

"El Rey califica la Constitución de acertada combinación de realismo político y concordia." *ABC* 6 Dec. 1991: 23.

"El Rey insta a desarrollar al máximo los principios constitucionales y a aplicarlaos cada día." *El País* 6 Dec. 1991: 14.

Roca i Junyent, Miquel. "El pacto debe mantenerse." *El País* 6 Dec. 1981: 12.

Sartorius, Nicolás, and Javier Alfaya. *La memoria insumisa.* Madrid: Espasa-Calpe, 1999.

"La semana constitucional." *El País* 5 Dec. 1983: 13.

"Sí." Editorial. *El País* 5 Dec. 1978: 10.

Solé Tura, Jordi. "La forma de Estado." *El País* 6 Dec. 1985: 22.

———. *Nacionalidades y nacionalismos en España. Autonomías, federalismo, autodeterminación.* Madrid: Alianza, 1985.

Sotelo, Ignacio. "Vergangenheitsbewältigung: Spanien—ein unpassendes Beispiel." *Ver-*

gangenheitsbewältigung 1945 und 1989. Ein unmöglicher Vergleich? Ed Klaus Sühl. Berlin: Volk und Welt, 1994. 44–57.

Suárez, Adolfo [Abel Hernández]. *Fue Posible la Concordia.* Madrid: Espasa Calpe, 1996.

"Tras el "sí," que funcione la Constitución." Editorial. *El Socialista* 3 Dec. 1978: 2.

Ucelay-Da Cal, Enric. "Imagined Memory as the Weight of the Past: Political Transitions in Spain." *Spanish and Latin American Transitions to Democracy.* Ed. Carlos Waisman and Raanan Rein. Brighton: Sussex Academic Press, 2005.

Vernet, Jaume. "El debate parlamentario sobre el 12 de octubre." *Ayer* 51 (2003): 135–52.

"Y también la intendencia." Editorial. Mundo Obrero 8 Dec. 1978: 5.

◆ 11

Intellectuals, Queer Culture, and Post-Military Argentina

David William Foster

The return to constitutional democracy in Argentina in late 1983, seven years after the March 24, 1976, military coup, instituted a particularly draconian version of the neofascism of the period to that country. It also brought with it a call to pursue the injustices of the regime, put the leaders of the various Juntas on trial, and expose, as far as was possible the ideological principles and the practical dynamics of the so-called Dirty War against Subversion. This so-called war constituted undoubtedly one of the darkest periods of Argentine national history, rivaled only by the Terror of Juan Manuel de Rosas's regime in the early 1800s. It is perhaps unfair to all those who suffered the repression, and especially the presumed 30,000 (approximately 0.01% of the national population), to speak of a scale of persecution, with different weighting for different types of victims. Yet personal accounts and systematic scrutiny reveal that there were three categories of victims who were singled out for special attention: Jews, women, and alleged homosexuals.

The focus on Jews was the consequence of institutional anti-Semitism in Argentina that found its most undiluted form in the Officers Corps, and it reached ludicrous extremes in the persecution of those associated with the three allegedly modern Jewish plots against Christian Argentina: economics (because of Marx), physics (because of Einstein), and psychology (because of Freud). Semiotically, in addition to recognizing certain prisoners as Jews because of their names, Jewish men were quickly singled out because of the mark of circumcision, since that practice is widespread only among Jews (and Arabs) in Argentina. In addition to being the heirs of the crime of Christ-killing, Jews were claimed to be unpatriotic as well as subscribers in various ways to the modern Jewish plots against Argentina's rightful Catholic heritage.

Women—certainly those who were most easily identified semiotically—were, by virtue of being involved in guerilla activities or by being fellow travelers of subversives, viewed as violating the proper Christian role of nurturing the national family, and they were frequently the victims of systematic rape, which served as much to humiliate them for their transgressions of proper femininity as it did to affirm their status as the whores of subversion.

Homosexuals were also often raped, whether by their tormentors or by instruments of torture in the latter's arsenal. Semiotically, the agents of repression drew on an extensive inventory of signs putatively associated with homosexuality, such as particular forms of dress, long hair, bodily appearance and body display, forms of language use, and monikers of identity, such as nicknames, and transgendered pronouns along with appositive and predicate agreement. It was often assumed that all Jews were homosexuals because Jewish culture was held to be insufficiently masculine.

As a consequence of the special attention to these (often overlapping) three categories of social subjectivities, the redemocratization of Argentina involved a prominent recognition of individual rights associated with all three. I will be examining in this essay the contributions of some of the important voices in the post-1983 movement toward a set of democratic rights that include sexual preference/sexual identity/consenting sexual conduct. Some of these intellectuals are academics, and their contribution may come in the form both of public activist positions and as formal scholarly research. Yet, often such intellectuals are not academics. This is so because the Argentine university system is not broad enough to contain all reputable intellectual voices, many of which must seek other forums, such as journalism in its various forms. Moreover, because the Argentine university, with the exception of Catholic universities (themselves frequently allied with conservative or reactionary social positions) and a handful of private schools (often dependent for their support on elitist interests), represents statist interests, it is often an unpropitious forum for the sort of allegedly radical and deviant social positions represented by the lesbigay rights movement and the cultural production associated with it.[1]

Because of the nature of Argentine universities, it is important to begin with the work of Juan José Sebreli.[2] Born in 1930, Sebreli has never been associated with university appointments, and the majority of his intellectual formation occurred during the first Peronista period (1946–1955), which had a deleterious effect on Argentine education, with the defection of legendary scholars, and the bulk of Sebreli's publications have come during the round of deeply authoritarian (1966–1973) and neofascist (1976–1983) regimes. Yet it is important to note that one of his most famous treatises, *Buenos Aires, vida cotidiana y alienación* (1964), appeared during a period of relative democracy and, indeed, a high point in the development of the social sciences in Argentina. Although sexuality studies were hardly yet part of anyone's research agenda in Argentina, the idea of focusing on the everyday lives of common people was an important innovation. Sebreli does couch his exposition in terms of an ideological commitment to the existentialist views of the day concerning the profound alienation of the social subject induced by everyday urban capitalism, beyond this overarching interpretation typical of the middle-class leftist values in Argentina at the time. But the recovery of the social subject whose daily life is not characterized by the narratives of melodrama as seen, for example, in the highpoint of Argentine commercial filmmaking in the 1930s and 1940s (the "Golden Age"), but rather by the micro-dramas of the routine relations with other essentially ordinary people, opens the way for the consideration of interpersonal interactions that are not part of the narratives of melodrama. These interactions will include questions of sexuality that are hardly contemplated by said narratives of melodrama: the latter only contemplate them in terms of the master code of criminality and moral degradation. There is not yet available a registry of "homosexuality" in the Argentine films of the Golden Age, but it is not difficult to survey major noncomedic titles in order to find images of sexuality as a force of tragic destruction and images of homoeroticism as either corollaries of criminality or as an even more profound circumstance of moral corruption that heterosexual passion in general occasions.

There is nothing surprising about such characterizations, because they are repeated throughout Western culture, but at a time when, aside from social realism and romanticizing folklorism, there is scant attention to the routine of everyday life. Of course, this is part of the view that a cultural production-like film is, precisely, an escape from everyday life, as is quite evident in the view of film in Manuel Puig's *La traición de Rita Hayworth* (1967). If I am emphasizing film here as a paradigm of cultural production, it is only because Golden Age filmmaking (again, in particular noncomedic genres) provide such a vivid contrast to any interest in everyday urban lives. Thus, when Sebreli (and others), following the influential model of American movements in sociology, begin to concern themselves with everyday urban lives in Buenos Aires, it marks a transition to the possibility of not only dealing with the dynamics of previously unrecorded everyday lives, but also of raising topics that there were previously considered either undignified and inappropriate for analytical commentary or as simply non-existent.

Indeed, transcending the homophobia of the left of his day, Sebreli is able to recognize the falsity in the belief that homoerotic practices are absent from the honest working class and its revolutionary vanguard and existing as only part of the intractable decadence of the bourgeoisie and part of its corrupting influence on the working class. I have written elsewhere about Sebreli's interest in such a popular icon as Evita Perón and the queer dimensions of her character (Foster, "Evita"). The narrative voice of *Eva Perón, ¿aventurera o militante?* (1971) is neither that of the putatively objective historian or the political partisan, but rather of a common man who understands the complexity of Evita's allure and who is unabashedly gushing in a way that sounds very much like what an American audience is accustomed to hearing with reference to Maria Callas or Marilyn Monroe.

If Sebreli's interest in Evita Perón, an interest that mixes both shrewd sociological analysis and personalized interpretations, *Fútbol y masas* (1981; reissued with substantial revisions in 1998 as *La era del fútbol*[3]) represents a significantly different stance toward popular culture icons. If Sebreli is writing as a gay man viewing a (not unproblematical) gay icon in the case of Evita Perón, his attention to soccer, which is one of the defining images of the popular culture of mass society in Argentina, represents some substantial shifts.[4] In the first place, one could focus on soccer in terms of icons on a par with Evita, such as Diego Maradona, who has attracted a measure of homoerotic symbolism (not to be confused with accusations of homosexuality as part of a smear campaign, such as Maradona is recorded to have done against his archrival Pelé). However, Sebreli is uninterested in monumentalized icons. Moreover, in contrast to the business dimensions of soccer (which included using soccer as an ideological emblem of the Argentine envisioned by authoritarian and neofascist dictatorships), Sebreli's interest lies with soccer as part of the everyday life of Argentines, as seen in the after-school and weekend pick-up games in the city's parks and plazas. Indeed, in this regard Sebreli complains of the commercialization of soccer, which signals a certain degree of investment in the "natural" masculinity of soccer that may be displaced or restructured by the crass commercialization of big-time sports which is what, with globalized television, soccer has certainly become.

What Sebreli is interested in, however, is the homoerotic dimension of soccer as one more example of a tight-knit homosocial group where various degrees of male bonding, body-grounded rituals, and manifestations of deep affection are viewed as continuous with homoeroticism as it is conventionally understood. One can argue quite convincingly that soccer (and the same may be said of all single-sex sports) functions as a training ground, so to speak, for the yoked dynamics of heterosexual masculinity and machismo (which includes avowed homophobia). Nevertheless, Sebreli takes this proposal one step farther in seeing the soccer field as a site for the homoeroticism that is always the underanalyzed middle term between heterosexuality and homosociality (see the analysis of the use of soccer and other all male-based images in the photography of Marcos López: Foster, "Homosocialism"). Part of the public discourse over sexuality in Argentina since 1983 has included the uproar in the late 1980s over the suggestion that, like any social grouping, a soccer team was likely to sustain the Kinseyan statistic of ten-percent homosexuality, which occasioned both affirmations of the necessarily straight sexual orientation of all Argentine soccer players and outrageous combinations of phenomena such as the exuberant interpersonal physicality of scoring and shared showers and locker-room antics after the game.

In 2003 Sebreli published his long essay on "Cien años de homosexualidad en la Argentina," (One hundred years of homosexuality in Argentina) but it is rather a disappointment. Clearly the product of years of stuffing notes and clippings into a file, Sebreli provides a rather gossip-magazine account of various scandals and secret affairs that usually involved the rich and famous of the country. In this regard, the cast of characters is much like that of the aforementioned Golden Age films, and when common folk appear, as in the case of the cadets of the Colegio Militar who pick up pin money by posing for suggestive photographs and servicing well-healed and presumably aging homosexuals, there is the hint of the customary view regarding the corruption by the latter of the former: certainly none of the (often unnamed) protagonists of Sebreli's account are portrayed in the heroic terms that Osvaldo Bazán's 2004 more documentary history is sustained by.

Néstor Perlongher (1949–1992) was born in Avellaneda, an industrial city immediately across the Riachuelo from Buenos Aires, into the sort of working-class family that is part of the everyday panorama examined by Sebreli and monumentalized by the culture of Peronism. Perlongher was also the benefactor of the democratic principles of Argentine public education, in their various changing guises during Peronism and subsequent elected governments and military dictatorships, and he completed studies in sociology in Argentina and social anthropology in Brazil, where, because of the unpropitious political climate in Argentina, Perlongher remained as a professor until his death from AIDS in São Paulo. After the return to democracy in Argentina in 1983, Perlongher returned to Buenos Aires on several occasions, where he published various books of poetry in the late 1980s and early 1990s. However, it was only after his death that two major collections of prose pieces, both narratives and essays, were published: *La prostitución masculina* (1993) and *Prosa plebeya; ensayos 1980–1992* (1997).

La prostitución masculina is the Spanish translation of *O negócio do michê; a prostituição viril em São Paulo* (1987), which was based on his doctoral dissertation at the Universidade Estadual de Campinas. Although Perlongher conducted his professional life in Brazil, where he exercised considerable influence on the development of gay rights during the debates there both before and after the Brazilian return to constitutional democracy in 1985,[5] his influence in his native Argentina is unmistakable (particularly on Osvaldo Bazán and Flavio Rapisardi) both in his contributions to the burgeoning bibliography of homoerotic writing after 1983 and in his contributions to the theoretical bases of the gay rights movement. The transition to democracy was more gradual in Brazil and afforded much larger parameters of public and academic debate than had been possible in Argentina before the early 1980s, although the Comunidad Homosexual Argentina (Argentine Homosexual Community) was legalized in 1984 as an officially recognized "Asociación Civil," the culmination of a growing public profile that had its roots in clandestine groupings dating back at least to the 1970s.[6] Perlongher's works complements the pioneering publications—more manifestos than scholarly works—of Carlos Luis Jáuregui, Zelmar Acevedo, and Alejandro Jockl.

It is undeniable that *La prostitución masculina* is Perlongher's most influential work because of the broad social and cultural dimensions it implies. Perlongher conducted field work in areas of extensive and quite public male hustling in São Paulo, and it is hardly doubtable that his own working-class background and personal homosexual experiences afforded him a level of confidence with his subjects that had not previously been the case regarding discussions of the subject. That is, prior publications had been historical in nature (such as Luiz Mott's work in Bahia; an anthropologist, Mott was associated with the founding of the pioneer Grupo Gay de Bahia in 1980, while the dictatorship was still in force), celebratory (João Silvério Trevisan's 1986 *Devassos no paraíso*), or part of the long tradition in Brazil of moral condemnation, such as the social hygiene writing examined by Richard G. Parker in *Bodies, Pleasures, and Passions* (see also Foster on Peter Fry). However, Perlongher's research was, so to speak, down and dirty because of the degree of personal communication he was able to establish with the men (or, in many cases, boys) he interviewed.[7]

Thus, from one point of view Perlongher's work, in the best spirit of professional sociology, is local in its applications: it refers to a particular segment of São Paulo society and to a particular point in time, and such work is usually understood as not affording a reliable transference in either a chronological or spatial dimension. Indeed, the reliability of the research model and the inferences to be drawn from the data recorded is predicated on the assumption of a clearly identified and circumscribed segment/segmentation of society. Yet, Perlongher's conclusions had important implications, which explains how it ended up being published in Argentina in Spanish translation. These implications have to do with an interpretational move on Perlongher's part that shifts the significance of the male prostitutes he examines from the domain of sex work to that of gay culture.

First of all, Perlongher uses in the Portuguese original the colloquial word *michê*, which is equivalent in English to "taxi boy." The emphasis on youth, which is explicit in the English term, is implicit in the Portuguese word; indeed, the Library of Congress assigns to the book, in addition to the subject heading of male prostitution, that of child prostitution. This colloquiality is lost in the Spanish translation, which uses the neutral phrase *prostitución masculina*. However, in his use of such a colloquial term in the original, Perlongher is both humanizing his subjects and affording them the familiarity of a subaltern group. That is, he does not see them as disembodied subjects in an exercise of sociological inquiry, mere statistics to be calculated, say, on the basis of sober indicators such as their youth, geographical provenance, or class origins. Nor do they fit the conventional profile of alienated and often violently competitive individuals pitted against each other for the privilege of servicing the least demanding and most generous clients, always in the context of the mean streets where their are always fewer clients than there are bodies for sale. Quite literally, Perlongher sees them as members of an extended family that may involve seep-seated romantic liaisons between and among them. In this sense, Perlongher sees them as modeling a social constitution that is alternate to the heterosexist society from which they basically draw their clients. They are not just social outcasts and misfits, but rather members of a homoerotically banded clan that occupies a mostly unseen sphere of the urban landscape. It is this essentially revindicative image of the frequently despised male hustler that has made Perlongher's work so influential in first Brazil and then Argentina. If Perlongher is correct in his analysis, the *michê* is not a solitary heterosexual who happens to sell his body to homosexual or bisexual clients, but rather he is part of a clan that is joined by homoerotic commitments and thus is, in very important ways, continuous with a larger homosexual community that often regards the male prostitute as extraneous to it.

Secondly, Perlongher's original Portuguese title is more eloquent than the Spanish translation in the use of the word *viril* to qualify the head noun *prostituição*. Unlike English, *viril* in Portuguese is, in the first instance (*Dicionário Houaiss da língua portuguesa*), a synonym of "masculine." However, like its only meaning in English, *viril* has secondary meanings in Portuguese that are equivalent to English "manly," in the sense of the positive features associated with being a man, such as strength of character, energy, vigor, and the like. That is to say, what Perlongher is doing is characterizing his social subjects' men who are models of their masculinity, which involves their rhetorical transformation from social pariahs into social models. More conventional sociology may see Perlongher as stretching the boundaries of the putatively objective observer, but this sort of "activist interpretation" is what brought his work a far larger than merely academic audience.

Viviana Gorbato, who died suddenly in 2005 at the age of 54 (she was born in 1950), had an extensive career as an investigative journalist. In addition to her formal academic training, she taught at the Universidad de Belgrano and briefly did doctoral work in the international journalism program at Florida International University in Miami. Her published books were part of the vast enterprise analysis and commentary that has taken place in Argentina since the 1983 return to democracy and which includes several dozen names of prominent professional journalists, many of whom, like Gorbato, have come out of the rich Jewish cultural heritage of Buenos Aires.[8] Gorbato participated in this undertaking with her detailed and in-depth examinations of social and political phenomena that were as much a part of the chronicle of Argentine society in the process of rebuilding a democratic civil society as it was the characterization of the abiding specter of a generation of authoritarian and neofascist military dictatorship. Specifically and although not self-identified as a homosexual, Gorbato made several important contributions to the intellectual and political debates concerning gay rights.

Gorbato's most important intervention in these debates is *Fruta prohibida; un recorrido por lugares, costumbres, estilos, historias, testimonios y anécdotas de una sexualidad diferente: la cara oculta de la Argentina gay* (1999), whose main title is a trope of *Fruto prohibido* (1884), the founding novel by the Franco-Argentine writer Paul Groussac (1848–1929) and one of the first Argentine novels to deal with sexuality. Gorbato's textual plan is to bring together as much disparate information about gays and gay life in Argentina as she can, and the run-on list of her subtitle is certainly indicative of the miscellaneous nature of the contents. She begins with a very useful precis of "El heterosexual cliché"—that is, an account of the heterosexual imaginary as it relates to homosexuality and homosexual lives. The bulk of the cliche consists of unanalyzed assumptions, gross inaccuracies, wild speculations, and plain and simple blind hatred toward the perceived or alleged sexual other (the real quite appallingly "clever" thing about homophobia is that it rarely is challenged to prove its assumptions, define its terms, or analyze its discursive logic). As a consequence, there is little in this so-called heterosexual cliche that matches sociohistorical lived experience. The remaining fourteen chapters are dedicated to detailing what information is available to Gorbato in Argentina as regards to the actual lives of those social subjects, in the spirit of the globalized and neoliberal Argentine society of the 1990s, who are being called—because so they call themselves—gays and lesbians. Part of Gorbato's sources are fairly standard Homosexuality 101 historical materials (such as queen Victoria's famous take on the absence of homoerotic desire among women); a large measure of her sources are interviews with living people, some in the public eye (like the performers Tato Boris and Chris Miró), while some are not prominent public figures (I particularly liked the "confesiones de una sargento lesbiana" (Confessions of a lesbian sergeant) because of the crossing of the categories of grammatical gender that such identity necessitates, although more for reasons of feminism than lesbianism). There are also journalistic accounts of some of the scandals that the shift in the awareness and legitimation of homosexuality have brought, such as notorious cases of involving male hustlers and their high-profile male clients,[9] and there are interviews with peripheral individuals, such as the parents of queer folk: "'Gracias a mi hijo aprendí un mundo diferente y me convertí en militante' (Iris Fischer)" (130) (Thanks to my son, I learnt about a different world and I became a militant).

Also, there is an abundance of photographic and other graphic material relating to the enormous public face that gays and lesbians begin to assume following the early 1980s and, especially, with the "Argentina es Primer Mundo" (Argentina-is-part-of-the-First-World) mentality of Menem Argentina in the 1990s. And finally—and these two features are a shared distinguishing characteristic of Gorbato's journalism—there are lists, some of the best of which are vocabulary lists: "Breve glosario lésbico no ilustrado" (99) (Short Unillustrated Lesbian Glossary), "Enriquezca su vocabulario antes de ir a Miami" (220) (Improve your vocabulary before going to Miami), along with various "tests": "Conozca—si se atreve—su verdadera orientación sexual" (46–47) (Get to figure out—if you dare—your true sexual orientation) and "Test para saber si tu madre te acepta" (140–41) (Test to check if your mom accepts you), plus, of course, a "Mapa gay de Buenos Aires" (60–61) (Gay map of Buenos Aires).

Gorbato is particularly impelled to give considerable treatment to Lesbians, who are often ignored or written out of the homosexual matrix in Argentina studies (there is no lesbian equivalent for the work of Sebreli, Osvaldo Bazán, or Flavio Rapisardi), although Ilse Fuskova and Claudina Marek had published their groundbreaking manifesto *Amor de mujeres; el lesbianismo en la Argentina, hoy* in 1994.

Prior to *Fruto prohibida*, Gorbato had published *Noche tras noche; del cabaret y las milonguitas a la movida de fin de siglo: un viaje vertiginoso y revelador al corazón de la noche de Buenos Aires* (1997). As the subtitle suggests, *Noche tras noche* bears a generic relationship to *Fruto prohibido* as regards to a similar coverage and similar compositional strategies, the abundance of graphic material and, of course, lists, of which those relating to vocabulary are particular interesting for cultural studies: "El pequeño fashion ilustrado" (74) (Little illusrated fashion) (*fashion* in Buenos Aires means something like "hip") or "Glosario [de la droga]" (231). Material relating directly or indirectly to homosexuality runs throughout *Noche tras noche*, although it is significant to note that the very first chapter is titled "Cuando la noche cambia de sexo," (When the night changes sexes) which refers to drag and its related sexual/erotic parameters.

Finally, Gorbato's last major project before her death was *Montoneros: soldados de Menem. ¿Soldados de Duhalde?* (1999),[10] an investigation of the recycling of members of the Montonero guerilla movement of the 1970s as leaders and functionaries of Carlos Menem's government in the 1990s. Where this work is pertinent to the matters at hand is that Gorbato delves, for the first time as part of the public record, into the homophobia of the Montoneros and other guerrilla movements of the so-called revolutionary left and incorporates allegations of instances when members who were discovered to bear the "reactionary, bourgeois stain" of homosexuality were actually sentenced to death by their colleagues.[11] Gorbato pursues this aspect of the guerilla movements less out of any attempt to discredit them (that began as early as 1984 with Pablo Giussani's *Los montoneros; la soberbia armada*), but rather in establishing the degree to which the sociopolitical left was as homophobic as the right, such that we must understand the public and legal vindication of lesbian and gay rights in Argentina as something that wipes clean a whole slate of political options and not just those on the right.[12] In this sense, the legitimation of homosexuality in Argentina, culminating in the official protection of the rights of sexual difference recognized by the 1996 constitution of the city of Buenos Aires, goes far beyond the presumed triumph of democracy over fascism: the agents of democracy, especially those on the left, had their own accounts to balance (Foster, "Más allá" discusses contemporary gay visibility in Buenos Aires).

The three writers/intellectuals examined in this essay can essentially be characterized by Gramsci's concept of the "organic intellectual." This is certainly the case with both Sebreli and Perlongher, who are out gay men, deeply committed for personal reasons to the analyses they present, so much so in the case of Perlongher that the much touted professional objectivity of his academic base in sociology and social anthropology is threatened.[13] This is less of a case with Sebreli, not because he retains great objectivity, but because he has never written from a formal academic forum as did Perlongher. Although Gorbato was not a gay activist in the mold of Sebreli and Perlongher, nevertheless the organicity of her commitment to democratic culture and to recording its fault lines is clearly evident in the intense scope of her accounts—of considerably more interest, I would allege, to students of culture than more formal academic treatises—of the sea changes in Argentine life in the wake of neofascism and under the guise of democracy and neoliberalism.[14] Finally, the three individuals whom I have showcased here are part of the scholarly and professional wealth of Argentina undertaking to interpret the social life of that society and, of particular pertinence here, what is now a firmly entrenched gay and lesbian life with its attendant cultural production.[15]

Notes

1. There is too much information covered in these two paragraphs to document in a detailed fashion in such a short paper. However, the main points may be explored in greater detail in the studies by Hodges, Graziano, and Novaro and Palermo; the report of Argentina. Comisión Nacional sobre la Desaparición de Personas, *Nunca más* is an invaluable source of information. It is significant to note that neither Hodges nor Graziano address the fate of lesbians and gays at the hands of the agents of the Dirty War.
2. I have discussed Sebreli and Néstor Perlongher (see next section) as gay spokespersons in Foster, "Argentine Intellectuals," although none of the material from that earlier essay is reproduced here.
3. This edition has as its cover Claudio Bravo's very homoerotic 1983 painting *Before the Game*.
4. Sebreli's work is best read in conjunction with other more properly academic interpreters of the sport such a Osvaldo Bayer and Eduardo P. Archetti.
5. Two of the finest studies on queer issues in Brazil are those by James N. Green, who argues that, if it is true that carnival is a gay spectacle, one must go beyond that im-

age of homosexuality in Brazil to understand a complex national dynamic, and João Silvério Trevisan's widely reissued history of gay culture in Brazil.

6. Such as the Frente de Liberación Homosexual, which had been active in the reelection of Juan Domingo Perón in 1973 as part of the groups on the political left that—mistakenly as it turned out—hoped to benefit from that reelection.
7. The legal age of consent in Brazil is 14, although it is illegal for an older person to "corrupt" someone under the age of 18.
8. Indiviuals like Jacobo Timerman, Santiago Kovadloff, Sylvina Walger, Horacio Verbitsky, Silvia Sigal, Mario Diament, Héctor Timerman, Diego Melamed, José Eliaschev, Jorge Halperín, Alejandro Horowicz, Alfredo Leuco, Carlos Ulanovsky, Daniel Muchnik, to mention only a few.
9. Recall that prostitution is legal in Argentina, although organized houses are not: thus, the scandals mostly involved married men in the public eye frequenting illegal male brothels.
10. The hiatus between this book and the incomplete one on the presidency of Néstor Kirschner and her death is explained by her decision to pursue a doctoral degree in international journalism in Florida, a project she abandoned because of the serious health problems not unrelated to her untimely death in 2005.
11. See the chapter "Cristianismo, sexo y revolución." One of the rallying cries of the Montoneros was "No somos the entire left, but also a putos / ni somos faloperos" (We are neither fags nor do we do drugs), which was both a repudiation of right-wing accusations agaínt the alleged hippy quality of repudiation by the left of the alleged bourgeois decadence of being both a *puto* and a *falopero*.
12. The homophobia of Castro's social revolution in Cuba, leading to the UMAP camps in the 1960s, accompanied by legendary homophobic statements by as prominent a figure as Che Guevara (despite the Che Gay motifs available elsewhere, such as the one from a London gay ride march reproduced by Kunzle 95), is, to be sure, well known, not to mention in a wide array of other instances of the left.
13. In this sense Perlongher's work stands in stark contrast to Silva's recently reissued founding sociological study on the subject.
14. In a personal conversation she was asserted that she thought her health had been seriously damaged by the consumption of alcohol and the exposure to second-hand smoke (she did not herself smoke) during her nightly forays in the after-hours jungles of Buenos Aires: in this sense, the phrase "noche tras noche" is as much a suggestion of the vast continuity of Porteño nightlife as it is the intensity of her reportorial coverage.
15. See studies by Foster ("Argentina, Filmmaking" and "Argentina, Literature"), Gustavo Geirola ("Latin America, Filmmaking" and "Latin America, Literature"), and Gabriel Giorigi for diverse aspects of the cultural production of record.

Works Cited

Acevedo, Zelmar. *Homosexualidad: hacia la destrucción de los mitos.* Buenos Aires: Ediciones del Ser, 1985.

Archetti, Eduardo P. *Masculinidades; fútbol, tango y polo en la Argentina.* Buenos Aires: Editorial Antropofagia, 2003.

Argentina. "Comisión Nacional sobre la Desaparición de Personas." *Nunca más: informe de la Comisión Nacional sobre la Desaparición de Personas.* Buenos Aires: EUDEBA, 1984. Trans. into English as *Nunca más, the Report of the Argentine National Commission on the Disappeared.* With an introduction by Ronald Dworkin. New York: Farrar Straus Giroux, in association with Index on Censorship, London, 1986.

Bayer, Osvaldo. *Fútbol argentino.* Buenos Aires: Editorial Sudamericana, 1980.

Bazán, Osvaldo. *Historia de la homosexualidad en la Argentina: de la conquista de América al siglo XXI.* Buenos Aires: Marea, 2004.

Foster, David William. "Argentina, Filmmaking." *The Routledge International International Encyclopedia of Queer Culture.* London: Routledge, 2006. 47–48.

———. "Argentina, Literature." *The Routledge International Encyclopedia of Queer Culture.* London: Routledge, 2006. 48–49.

———. "Más allá de la visibilidad gay en Buenos Aires." *Las ciudades latinoamericanas en el nuevo [des]orden mundial.* Ed. Patricio Navia and Marc Zimmerman. Mexico, D.F.: Siglo XXI Editores, 2004. 125–32.

———. "Argentine Intellectuals and Homoeroticism: Néstor Perlongher and Juan José Sebreli." *Hispania* 84 (2001): 441–50.

———. "Evita, Juan José Sebreli y género." *Revista Canadiense de Estudios Hispánicos* 23.3 (1999): 529–37. It also appeared in English as "Evita Perón, Juan José Sebreli, and Gender." *Reading and Writing the Ambiente.* Ed. Susana Chávez-Silverman and Librada Hernández. Madison: University of Wisconsin Press, 2000. 218–38. A final version is to be found, with the same English title, in *Sexual Textualities; Essays on Queer/ing Latin American Writing.* Austin: University of Texas Press, 1997. 29–38, 149–52.

———. "Do 'Para inglês ver' ao 'Para brasileiro entender': escrevendo o socio-texto homoerótico brasileiro." *Mester* 24.1 (1995): 63–73.

———. "Homosocialism <---> Homoeroticism in the Photography of Marcos López." *Dissidence* 1 (205). on line http://dissidence/marcoslopez.html

Fuskova, Ilse, and Claudina Marek. *Amor de mujeres: el lesbianismo en la Argentina, hoy.* Buenos Aires: Planeta, 1994.

Geirola, Gustavo. "Latin America, Filmmaking." *The Routledge International International Encyclopedia of Queer Culture.* London: Routledge, 2006. 352–55.

———. "Latin America, Literature." *The Routledge International International Encyclopedia of Queer Culture.* London: Routledge, 2006. 355–61.

Giorgi, Rafael. *Sueños de exterminio: homosexualidad y representación en la literatura argentina contemporánea.* Rosario: Beatriz Viterbo Editora, 2004.

Giussani, Pablo. *Montoneros: la soberbia armada.* Buenos Aires: Sudamericana/Planeta, 1984.

Gorbato, Viviana. *Fruta prohibida: un recorrido por lugares, costumbres, estilos, historias, testimonios y anécdotas de una sexualidad diferente: la cara oculta de la Argentina gay.* Buenos Aires: Editorial Atlántida, 1999.

———. *Noche tras noche; del cabaret y las milonguitas a la movida de fin de siglo: un viaje vertiginoso y revelador al corazón de la noche de Buenos Aires.* Buenos Aires: Editorial Atlántida, 1997.

Graziano, Frank. *Divine Violence: Spectacle, Psychosexuality, and Radical Christianity in the Argentine "Dirty War."* Boulder: Westview Press, 1992.

Green, James N. *Beyond Carnival: Male Homosexuality in Twentieth-Century Brazil.* Chicago: University of Chicago Press, 1999.

Hodges, Donald C. *Argentina's "Dirty War."* Austin: University of Texas Press, 1991.

Jáuregui, Carlos Luis. *La homosexualidad en la Argentina.* Buenos Aires: Ediciones Tarso, 1978.

Jockl, Alejandro. *Ahora, los gay.* Buenos Aires: Ediciones de la Pluma, 1984.

Kunzle, David. *Che Guevara: Icon, Myth, and Message.* Los Angeles: UCLA Fowler Museum of Cultural History, in collaboration with the Center for the Study of Political Graphics, 1997.

Mott, Luiz. *Homossexuais da Bahia: dicionário biográfico (séculos XVI–XIX).* Savaldor: Editora Grupo Gay da Bahia, 1999.

Novaro, Marcos, and Vicente Palermo. *Historia argentina: la dictadura militar 1976/1983; del golpe de estado a la restauración democrática.* Buenos Aires: Paidós; Embajada de España en Buenos Aires; CAECI, Centro Cultural, 2003.

Parker, Richard G. *Bodies, Pleasures, and Passions: Sexual Culture in Contemporary Brazil.* Boston: Beacon Press, 1990.

Perlongher, Néstor. *Evita vive e outras prosas.* Seleção e prólogo; Adrian Cangi; tradução: Josely Vianna Baptista. São Paulo: Iluminuras, 2001.

———. *Prose plebeya; ensayos 1980–1992.* Ed. Christian Ferrer y Osvaldo Baigorri. Buenos Aires: Ediciones Colihue, 1997.

———. *O negócio do michê; a prostituição viril em São Paulo.* São Paulo: Editora Brasiliense, 1987. Reissued as *La prostitución masculina.* Buenos Aires: Ediciones de la Urraca, 1993.

Rapisardi, Flavio, and Alejandro Modarelli. *Fiestas, baños y exilios: los gays porteños en la última dictadura.* Buenos Aires: Editorial Sudamericana, 2001.

Sebreli, Juan José. "Historia secreta de los homosexuales en la Argentina." *Escritos sobre escritos, ciudades bajo ciudades.* Buenos Aires, 1997. 275–370.

———. *Fútbol y masas.* Buenos Aires: Editorial Galerna, 1981? Reissued in an expanded version as *La era del fútbol.* Buenos Aires: Editorial Sudamericana, 1983.

———. *Eva Perón, ¿aventurera o militante?* Buenos Aires: Editorial La Pleyade, 1971.

Silva, José Fábio Barbosa da Silva. "Homossexualismo em São Paulo: estudo de um grupo minoritário." *Homossexualismo em São Paulo e outros escritos*. Org. James N. Green and Ronaldo Trinidade. São Paulo: Editora UNESP, 2005. 39–212.

Trevisan, João Silvério. *Devassos no paraíso*. 1986. 5a ed. Rio de Janeiro: Editora Record, 2002. Trans. into English as *Perverts in Paradise*. Trans. Martin Foreman. London, GMP, 1986.

◆ **12**

Some Notes on International Influences on Transition Processes in the Southern Cone

Heinrich Sassenfeld

The transition processes in Argentina and Chile date from the 1980s. After more than two decades and having reached stable democracies, it is interesting to retake the subject and check if the international actors have learned some lessons from these experiences as they reflect the Argentinean and Chilean processes in another light. As someone who was an actor in these transitions and is still working in this field, my reflections will obviously also be influenced by the developments that have taken place since then.

I will use very general basic definitions, such as Garretón's concept of democracy (with its main elements of popular sovereignty, universal vote, separation of powers and validity of human rights and public liberties),[1] and Whitehead's notion of transition (Whitehead 3) which discerns three phases. The first one is defined by putting pressure on undemocratic governments; the second one refers to the support for fledging democracies; the third phase is characterized by policies to assist democratic consolidation. For the purposes of this essay, I would like to distinguish only two periods. A first phase of transition includes the preparative steps needed to organize elections. In a second phase, the basic transformations of the political system become the main objectives. In chronological terms, the first phase means basically the last period of dictatorship, while the second one would last at least from the first election until a new democratic government has ended its rule and a second round of elections has been successfully accomplished. In some cases, and this includes very clearly Chile, the transformation could last much longer. Some of the barriers, which Garretón calls "authoritarian enclaves" (3) such as institutionalized senators or other rules of the Pinochet constitution, have been eliminated just recently or are still in place. Considering that democracy is a living organism, which is constantly being modified and adjusted, I will limit my reflections to the preparative and the first post-election period.

International influences on democratization processes may stem from a series of intervention levels:

1. Governments may use boycotts, threats and pressure against authoritarian regimes. Guilhon Albuquerque points out that in some examples direct intervention and threats of retaliation had different probabilities of success in different countries as compared to warnings about the cost of isolation. In the second phase, fledging democracies can obtain important support by other government, in political as in economic terms.

2. International organizations and regional institutions have augmented their activities especially after the return to democracy in Latin America. The role of MERCOSUR as a model of open regionalism is an interesting case: two recently democratized governments in (Argentina and Brazil) would play a significant role in overcoming the 1996 coup attempt in Paraguay. The Presidential Declaration of Democratic Commitment in MERCOSUR introduced a democratic clause which allows suspending membership rights.

3. The "political level" of influences is basically channelled by parties and parliaments. While foreign policy is made by governments, parties have an indirect influence on the government's decision-making processes and on public opinion. Additionally, they can count on resources, trans-national linkages and contacts (Grugel).

4. International NGOs and similar development institutions often take development- oriented actions in order to assist transition processes, but can also influence public opinion considerably.

In this essay, I will concentrate my analysis on the last two levels of intervention. The European experience and its contribution to the transition processes will be in the foreground.

Reasons for International Presence in Democratization Processes

Why would a democratic system be the best solution for the countries and societies considered? Already in the 1960s and 1970s, there had been some efforts to find a "third way" for political systems, such as Yugoslavia's workers auto-administration or Peru's nationalistic revolution under General Velasco Alvarado. Chile's "Chilean way to socialism" (which Salvador Allende in a popular version defined as a socialist way that includes "vino tinto y empanadas" [red wine and *empanadas*]), can also be considered within this category. They all had in common their failure to offer a long-term political and economically stable alternative.

If democracy was then the best alternative, the question remains to be why international players took such a comprehensive and dedicated action in the Southern Cone. In the 1980s, the Cold War was still the main framework for international relations and the system competition was at stake. But until that moment this had not necessarily translated into a strategy of strengthening democracies, as some North American interventions in Latin America showed. It seems that in the 1980s, as in the decade before, the principal reasons for U.S. intervention were still order and stability, and the establishment of a pattern of growth (Grugel). Parallel to the decline of economic strength of socialism, the initially very attractive paradigm of neo-liberalism became the dominating force for economic development models also in Latin America.

Another reason is the fact that European nations tried to expand their international influences and Latin America was a good field of action due to the long existing cultural and political ties and contacts between parties. In this case, democratic strengthening was intended to go hand in hand with deeper economic ties. But while the U.S. maintained trade and other economic restrictions, political relations between the two continents became the cornerstone. Thus, European national parties played an important role. Especially active were German and Italian Christian democrats, and among the social democratic forces, those from Germany, Spain, UK and Sweden (Grugel).

From the European point of view, there were many political reasons for an engagement toward regaining, stabilizing and strengthening Southern Cone democracies. The strong relationship between democracy and international peace is one of the main aspects. It was Kant who showed the theoretical way to worldwide peace. Already in 1793, Kant distinguished "preliminary articles" or "laws" which should put war situations to an end. On this base, he pointed to the existence of three so-called "definitive articles" which would guarantee peace in the long run: civic constitutions in every state should be of a republican character; the Law of Nations should be based on the federalism of sovereign states; and, International Citizenship Law should be limited to general hospitality.[2] Kant develops the idea of a democratic peace: democracies do not fight against democracies, and wars are not compatible with a democratic value system. The less intensive participation of democracies in wars is also explainable because institutional controls and procedural hurdles, previous to a country's involvement in a war, are more strict than in other regimes (Merkel).

Europe has experienced many times that wars can be the definite impulse for democracies: such was the case of Cyprus in 1974 or Serbia in 1999. The most impressive case, however, was that of Germany after World War II. The Germans' conviction to end—once and forever—the terrible and bloody national-socialist nightmare existed, but the means and resources for the implementation of a democratic alternative were not sufficient. It was the combination of material help, intellectual inputs from abroad and reconciliation with Germany's European neighbours which made a substantial contribution to the process. A stable economic development path and growing wealth, together with the constructive interaction of the different interest groups, were the main domestic ingredients which allowed Germany to enter a long-term cycle of democratic political stability.

Spain, Greece and Portugal experienced long and painful processes of democratization, and enjoyed successful European support. Later on, and based on this experience, what we now call the European Union also felt a strong motivation and commitment for Latin America's democratization (Guilhon). Thus, there was an important international element in what Samuel Huntington calls the third wave of democratization. We can also assume that international presences in the process of recovery of democracy are normally implemented with full intention (Freres, "Defensa").

A debate on the justification of international interventions, possible violations of national sovereignty and related issues has existed for a long time. Although it cannot be repeated here in detail, it is worth mentioning that one of the more interesting positions was early developed by Damrosch. According to his analysis, one should not only look at legal documents, but at the common practice of states in influencing elections, and using economic pressure to shape politics. He proposes to use the concept of sovereignty in terms of integrity of the political institutions of a country. If the outside influences are integrated and made subject to the discipline of those institutions, the author would not define them as intervention. Consequently to this approach the limits of legal jurisdiction, i.e. the borders, are not as determining as are the limits of regular interactions.[3]

Black and White . . .

As we can see, international factors exist in practice and also can be justified politically in order to return to democratic systems. Now we should have a closer look at their importance. In the literature on the Southern Cone transition cases, one finds often very opposed points of view. A clearly domestic approach emphasizes exclusively the own political and societal forces which determine the process.[4] Garretón also puts strong emphasis on the internal factors. In the Chilean case, he compares the plebiscite to the death of Franco in Spain. His whole analysis is based on the isolation of the hardliners, the political defeat of the fascist sectors and the negotiation between the regime and the opposition. For him, it is confirmed that military regimes finish by political fight, not by "derrocamiento" (removal). If and how international actors intervene is not worked out in this part of his analysis.

On the other hand, an international approach puts heavy weight on the support from abroad. The main thesis is that without international solidarity return to democracy is nearly impossible. Of course, the main supporters of this point of view are the numerous institutions and persons related to what might be called the democratization industry. Interestingly enough, there are few serious academic studies backing this thesis, but a lot of self-portrayal publications.

. . . and the Truth Lies in Between

Probably, as often happens, both approaches have their *raison d'etre* (Blasier 219). Grugel observes that political systems are "penetrated" ones that are always open to influences. In key moments they could play a significant role. Chalmers talks about "Internationalized Domestic Politics" (8). For him, "foreign-linked businessmen, diplomats, political and labor organizers, religious proselytizers" are the important persons who "stay involved over a period of time" in a country, but are "still identified with international sources of power." Even simple migrants who become citizens also maintain some political identification with their roots. These fenomena have increased considerably after the end of the of Cold War, and still more since economic globalization is at stake. Apart from state-to-state relations, military advisory, official financial and technical aid, multinational corporations, political parties and many players entered the stage. Last but not least, academic influences are also to be considered.[5]

Unfortunately, we lack the appropriate instruments to quantify the impacts of international efforts because "the absence of adequate analytical tools and also problems of evidence deriving from the confidential nature of some political activity crossing the boundaries between countries limits our capacity to document empirically the impact of policies" (Pridham 2). As this analysis is still valid, I would like to present my own experiences on the transition processes in the Southern Cone in the form of some thesis.

Thesis 1: International Support for Democratization Requires a Sufficient Domestic Democratic Potential of Institutions and Personalities

The Inter-American Dialogue stated in 1992 that governments and citizens of each nation are responsible for strengthening and safeguarding their own democracy. Or putting it in a more popular version: each nation has the political system it deserves. Thus, it is nearly impossible to establish a democratic structure without counting with the main pillars on the domestic side. The concept of the domestic ownership of the ongoing processes, in which international actors are involved, has proved to be the major factor of success. In this sense, Freres even believes that international reactions towards Latin America have come up because of events that were already underway in the region (Freres, "Defensa" 4).The longer and more positive historical experience with this political system has been, the higher is the potential of democratic forces. And the longer the period of authoritarianism has been, the more complicated it is to get commitment for the success of a transition.

Which kind of national institutions and persons could act as leaders in the transition depends on every case. In Chile, some "democratic enclaves" existed even in the most repressive phase of Pinochet's authoritarian regime. They were principally located around political and academic elites [6] and formed a nucleus for the debates about the failed Unidad Popular government, common positions of all democratic forces and the possible ways to return to democracy. These were strong bases for an efficient preparation of the transition and assured important international support for the process. After the elections, many of those persons entered the government. On the one hand, this undermined the structure of strong NGOs that had been built up during the Pinochet regime, and many of them never recovered. On the other hand, their participation in the executive branch guaranteed a highly homogeneous government program as it had been agreed upon mostly by the same players during the preparative phase. By the inclusion of NGOs, the program also had sufficient adhesion to the needs of the broader population.

In Argentina, it was less the push of a democratic opposition than the sudden military weakness after the Falkland/Malvinas war that moved things forward quickly. The parallel economic crisis brought internal discontent, but not a decisive political opposition movement. In any case, the military regime lost the support of the United States (Malamud). Toward the end of the dictatorship, the international cooperation was not so intense, and concentrated on transferring the South European experiences and on those returning from exile. After elections took place, the international community immediately channelled their support institutionally through the new government of president Alfonsín, and not through parties, NGOs or think tanks.

Whenever it is possible, it is preferable to work with the democratic forces within the nation. Exiles are not always sufficiently informed about the ongoing processes in their own countries, where changes of structures and political thinking are sometimes quite radical and require new strategies to overcome authoritarian regimes. However, the experience of exile can be very helpful when looking into democratic systems.[7] Especially in the phase of consolidation of democracy, the combination of both experiences may be very stabilizing in order to define which kind of political structure the society wants to have in the future.

It is very helpful to have the good fortune of a return to democracy coinciding with a satisfactory economic development. This was already very obvious in post-war Germany. In Chile, the Concertación government took special care not to spoil the overall macro results and introduced wealth redistribution elements very cautiously. International support to such a policy, as it was seen in this case, can be very effective in order to reassure the political process. On the other hand, the combination of political and economic crises at the end of president Alfonsín's government was during some time a quite disturbing factor for the stabilization of Argentina's democracy.

Thesis 2: Long-term Engagement and in Situ Presence Are Fundamental for Successful International Support of Transition Processes

When there is a political crisis in a country, it often becomes "fashionable" for international actors of the democratization industry to be present. At home, those institutions want to show that they are engaged on the right spot at the right time. As media attention in this period is strong, their own image can be influenced positively. When a new focus of attention appears, activities are reduced quickly and the media caravan moves forward. This sort of "country hopping" is counterproductive for the transition and stabilization of the political system of any country.

Effective political cooperation requires a kind of trust which is impossible to build up in the short run. This trust capital can be achieved by different means, but always works in the longer run. If conditions allow so, even a physical personnel presence during the period of dictatorship would be of great help.[8] On the one hand, international contacts in their own country give political opponents a certain shelter against repressive measures. On the other, they are encouraged to continue with their political work in order to achieve democracy (Chalmers 11). If foreign institutions cannot be present, invitations for travelling abroad may partially substitute such presence. On these grounds, there is a growing net of organizational links with a new set of internationally based actors.

Presence is also a determinant factor, as observation of and participation in the considerations about domestic political strategies allow international actors to find out promising kinds of support for the democrats. In Chile, the building up of the "Concertación" out of the constitutional lawyers of the "Grupo de los 24" (Group of the 24) was a core element for bringing together the democratic oppositional forces of all political signs; this was initially criticized by the exiles. Living on the spot meant to understand the intentions and to be able to support this initiative. In a similar way, the establishment of an efficient network of NGOs that coordinated their work was facilitated through international cooperation. Instead of short-sighted competition, Chilean NGOs during the Pinochet regime found their specializations and complementarities. In Chile, cooperation of German social democrats with socialists during the Unidad Popular government had been nearly non existent, as the Europeans were considered too "reformists." Only the long-term relation both with exiled politicians and those inside Chile built up the necessary confidence for closer political ties.

The Argentinean case developed quite differently. As I have already mentioned, the pull factors dominated over the push for democratic reestablishment. The long tradition of nationalism in politics made it extremely difficult to enter into deeper relations with the parties in the preparatory phase of the transition. It is interesting enough that Argentinean exiles concentrated much more in Latin America than did the Chileans and did not search European contacts as intensively. These are the reasons why support for democracy in Argentina was not strong until Alfonsín assumed the government. His expectations from international players were basically economic ones, i.e. that Europe would reduce trade restrictions. In this regard, party and NGO contacts did not have a great impact. The economic crisis in the country mixed with a political one were responsible for the coup attempts. Also in this case, official international policies, and especially the threat of isolating Argentina again, were more important than party or NGO activities when avoiding a democratic backlash.

Finally, in both cases it became clear that money cannot substitute trust. Although the survival of institutions and persons within a country requires some material support, the biggest effort seems to lie in helping to organize the developing of a political strategy that could turn out to bring positive results. As the consolidation of democracy normally is being accomplished in a longer period, international actors should try to accompany the whole process. This means a permanent presence at least during the first election period, and if authoritarian enclaves are still active, go on for a longer time.[9]

Thesis 3: Instead of Exporting Models, International Actors Should Favor Domestic Debates

In the United States, there has been an ongoing debate about the export of its own democratic model, which nowadays with the experiences in the Middle East seems more current than ever. For Freres, there is a tendency to exaggerate the impact of U.S. actions, especially as former support was not only towards democracies but also for Military coups (2). Blasier points out that the United States should not intervene in domestic politics of other countries as that nation is not appropriate for this role and nearly always fails in its efforts. He therefore suggests limiting actions to denunciation of violations of human rights and facilitation of aid programs (219). Other authors propose an indirect policy which would present the North American democracy as an "inspiration" rather than as a "model" (Pastor 198).

It is frequent that international donors determine the main issues that should be dealt with by their counterpart organizations. In this sense, domestic NGOs often have to adapt their activities (Freres, "Latin American"). Fashionable topics or issues that are of high priority in developed countries may come too "early" in societies which are concentrating on a process of political transition. At least, the counterparts should have the opportunity to define on their own if such topics should form the center of attention. Again, the concept of domestic ownership, the own responsibility of domestic political forces of the processes is at stake.

The existence of very different democratic political systems which co-existed smoothly in the post-war decades might make it easier for Europeans to understand that every country and society should find their own specifications of the democratic system. In this sense, the Friedrich Ebert Stiftung also has not advocated for the "export of a German model," but rather has understood itself for a long time as a platform where different political and social organizations come together in order to debate their own problems and solutions. Domestic forces should prevail. If there are concrete demands or if the internal debates get stuck, specific international ingredients are offered as one of many other elements. Of course, with globalization tendencies it is ever more important to introduce international elements, although not necessarily to copy them, but to take them into consideration, when it comes time to define a nation's own strategies. It is necessary to adjust the democratic system and the pace to establish it according to the concrete conditions given in every case (Adam 24). German foundations' strength might be their flexibility to introduce new types of activities according to the circumstances.[10] Such possibility of innovation seems to be a major asset in their performance even today.[11]

In order to make this explicit, I would like to give some details of the cooperation of the Friedrich Ebert Foundation in the establishment of the "Asociación Chilena de Municipalidades" (Chilean Association of Municipalities). For Garretón, the consolidation of democracy in his country had to confront the problem of the new relations between politics and society. He advocated for major autonomy and higher participation of civil society organizations (9). For him, the only really important political reform during the first years of democratic government had been the introduction of municipal democracy and the local elections in 1992. In order to deepen the political importance of the municipalities, there was a strong domestic leadership of some elected mayors, especially the mayor of Santiago.[12] This referred not only to the local level as such but also to the role of local governments within the political system.

The Friedrich Ebert Foundation supported the idea of a national association of municipalities from the beginning. Its first activities tried to define the needs and perspectives for such an institution and mobilized the Chilean forces which would be willing to join the project. In a second phase, the Foundation helped to collect international experiences on local government associations, in Latin America and in Europe. This led to the most crucial phase, i.e. the definition of the principles which should guide this new institution. The result was a mixture of domestic ideas and international inputs. Chile opted for an association which would, among other activities:

1. Represent municipalities as a whole, and not be an association of mayors, city councils or local administrations only;
2. Rule itself by the principle of "one municipality, one vote;"
3. Not be a partisan institution;
4. Offer services according to the needs of their members; and
5. Avoid dependence on other state levels by auto-financing.

The Friedrich Ebert Foundation then helped to start working according to these principles by some initial organizational and financial support which was limited in time. Due to the strong leadership and this aid concept, within a few years the association managed to be an institution which gathered the immense majority of Chilean municipalities, and it became highly recognized by the central government and other national and international institutions.

Lessons Learned

The experiences with Southern Cone transitions and other cases were institutionally incorporated in different forms and speeds. The International Organisations had applied the concept of "Structural Adjustment" during the 1980s as a response to the failing development results in many third-world countries. They concentrated on the macro factors with measures like the adjustment of relative prices, the reduction of the public sector or the improvement of preconditions for economic growth. Explicit intervention in politics was avoided and thus reforms often would not be implemented rigorously enough. In 1989, the World Bank introduced the concept of "Good Governance," whose main characteristics were defined as accountability, transparency, predictability, openness and rule of law. This approach was still basically focussed on technical-instrumental aspects and not on political ones.[13] Even in the late 1990s, when the World Bank rediscovered the central role of the state in the development process,[14] such approach did not change in a fundamental way. It seems that multilateral institutions do not have sufficient margin to consider a more strict intervention in national politics.

The German case had a different dynamic. In 1989, one of the most prominent German development experts claimed a fundamental change: with the key slogan "Aid through Intervention" he asked for conscious political structural adjustments (Waller). In 1990, the scientific council of the German Ministry of Economic Cooperation presented a report on the framework conditions which would be necessary for the opting nations to have in order to obtain aid. It stated that the number of countries where the prerequisites for development exist is much lower than the number of countries which receive aid. After a long debate between official institutions, experts and other persons concerned, the Ministry of Economic Cooperation redefined the criteria of development cooperation. Since then, five major aspects would guide the decisions about aid: respect of human rights, participation of the population in political decisions, existence of rule and security of law, social market economy and state action oriented towards development. The number of receivers was nearly cut in half, resulting in a final count of 70 countries worldwide. Within the new conception of 1996, development aid was seen as a political task whose core was the creation of of a positive framework for development and the change of structures. Programs on descentralization of administration, local develoment and reforms of the finance and tax system gained more importance.

Perhaps the most innovative aspect in this reorientation refers to political participation. The direct relation between good governance and political participation was shared within the OECD. A DAC working group on this issue stated in 1994 that "it has become increasingly apparent that there is a vital connection between open, democratic and accountable systems of governance and respect for human rights, and the ability to achieve sustained economic and social development" (5). Civil society can be seen as a space where self-organized groups try to articulate their values and to assert their interests (Linz and Stepan 7). A strong civil society is able to initialize transitions, to bring them further and also to deepen democracy.[15] Sometimes, these forces of society had stronger impacts on transition processes than traditional political parties or trade unions. Likewise, NGOs get growing attention as counterparts in socio-political development activities. According to Freres e.g., EU cofinanced more than 4,000 projects of NGOs in Latin America in the period of 1992/95 (Freres "Latin American").

On the institutional side of implementation of development projects, the German Cooperation Ministry had acted in a broad sense as soon as in the 1970s. The philosophy developed then was that international cooperation should reflect the structure of the whole German society. Thus, since the very beginning, the ministry supported not only official technical and financial cooperation projects, but also gave incentives for NGOs, political foundations and churches to carry out international programs. The Friedrich Ebert Foundation, for example, considers its mayor international task to cooperate with partners in developing countries in the establishment of puralistic and democratic societies whith social justice.[16] The existence and experience of a whole range of non-official implementation agencies made it relatively easy that the official

German cooperation would take more into consideration the political participation and institutions of civil society in its new strategy in the 1990s.

With respect to the bilateral relations and their role in the region, democratization in Argentina and Chile was of the highest value. Alfonsín made the first steps to come to an agreement about the border conflicts with Chile, and after the ratification of the bilateral treaty in May 1985, that long lasting tension between the two countries finished (Malamud 9). With Aylwin being the democratic Chilean president, also the last smaller differences on the border lines were eliminated in cooperation with the Menem government. Democratic Argentina and Brasil, joined later by Chile, were the pillars for the MERCOSUR agreement which included commercial relations as well as aspects of democratic values. In 1996 their role was decisive in the failure of the military coup in Paraguay. Stabilized countries may thus retribute later on by supporting other crisis managements, as is the case currently with the participation of Southern Cone countries in Haiti, and in United Nations' peace missions in other parts of the world.

In order to achieve a successful cooperation in transition processes and in the deepening of fledging democracies, it is crucial to carry out a profound analysis of the history, cultural values and political forces of these societies. Only such understanding, together with the acceptance that the ownership and principal responsabality of the processes lie on the domestic side, allows international actors to make productive contributions.

Notes

1. It is about a regime that is "basado en los principios e instituciones que consagran la soberanía popular, la elección de los gobernantes y autoridades efectivos por voto universal, la vigencia de los derechos humanos y libertades públicas, la separación de los poderes, el pluralismo político, la alternancia en el poder." (Garretón 1).
2. This concept deals with the conditions of international visits and relations, and Kant is especially critical about the praxis of colonialism.
3. Chalmers calls the latter "Boundaries."
4. Boeninger, in his otherwise very clear and clarifying book, dedicates only one page to external factors related to the Chilean transition (Boeninger, 375).
5. The most spectacular case is probably the diffusion and impact of the economic neoliberal paradigm.
6. Such is the case of "Grupo de los 24" or some NGOs like CIEPLAN, VECTOR, and others.

7. Many Chilean socialists got reflexive about the political systems when they experienced concrete life in exile in socialist countries.
8. For instance, the Friedrich Ebert Foundation decided already in 1981 to reestablish an office in Chile, although initially it had to work in very precarious conditions.
9. The Friedrich Ebert Foundation even considers that there are enough reasons for maintaining more permanent activities after stabilization of democracy is reached, as new fields of cooperation arise, e.g. regional cooperation or dialogue about globalization.
10. Some possible cooperation options are developed in Sassenfeld, "Beziehungen."
11. A recent study on democratic promotion in Serbia by David Koschel comes to this conclusion.
12. Jaime Ravinet was accompanied by several other mayors from municipalities in Santiago and in provinces stemming from different political parties.
13. One of the weaknesses of implementation of macro economic consultancy in this time seemed to lie in the underestimation of reactions of the affected or befitted groups and persons. See Sassenfeld, "Die Bedeutung makropolitischer und makroökonomischer Beratung."
14. "The state is central to economic and social development, not as a direct provider of growth but as a partner, catalyst and facilitator." *World Development Report, The State In a Changing World*, 1997. 1.
15. The debate and the new concepts naturally also had their space in the U.S. The Ford Foundation e.g. in a brochure about their work in Latin America says: "Since the early 1990's the foundation has supported research institutes addressing issues central to the consolidation of democracy, such as transparency, citizen empowerment and public interest law." Ford Foundation: Democratization—Renewing the Promise of Just Society. p. 57.
16. (Es ist die Aufgabe) „mit Partnern in den Entwicklungslaendern bei der Herstellung sozial gerechter, pluralistischer und demokratischer Gesellschaften zusammenzuarbeiten." Friedrich Ebert Stiftung: Die FES In der Internationalen Entwicklungszusammenarbeit, Aufgaben, Ziele, Handlungsfelder, April 1993.

Works Cited

Adam, Erfried. "Gesellschaftliche Transformationsprozesse in unterentwickelten Laendern." *Das muehsame Geschaeft der Demokratisierung.* Bonn: Ed. Friedrich Ebert Stiftung. Konzepte und Erfahrungen, 1999. 13–67.

Blasier, Cole. "The United States and Democracy in Latin America." *Authoritarians and Democrats: Regime Transition in Latin America.* Ed. James M. Malloy and Mitchell A. Seligson. Pittsburgh: University of Pittsburgh Press, 1988. 219–34.

Boeninger, Edgardo. *Democracia en Chile.* Santiago: Editorial Andrés Bello, 1997.

Chalmers, Douglas. *Internationalized Domestic Politics in Latin America.* New York: Columbia University Press, 1993.

Damrosch, Lori Fisler. "Politics across Borders: Non Intervention and Non forcible Influence over Domestic Affairs." *American Journal of International Law* 83/1 (January 1989): 1–50.

Freres, Cristian. "Latin American Democratization and Development: The Role of European and Latin American Civil Societies." LASA, XXI International Conference, Guadalajara 1997.

———. "La defensa hemisférica de la democracia latinoamericana," *Estudios Interdisciplinarios de América Latina y el Caribe* Vol. 4 No.2 Julio/Diciembre 1993. http://www1.tau.ac.il/eial/index.php?option=com_wrapper&Itemid=134

Garretón, Manuel Antonio. "La redemocratización política en Chile: Transición, Inauguración y Evolución." *Revista de Estudios Interdisciplinarios de América Latina y el Caribe* Vol. 4 No. 1 (Enero/Junio 1993): 101–33. http://www1.tau.ac.il/eial/index.php?option=com_wrapper&Itemid=134

Grugel, Jean. "External Support for Democratization in Latin America: European Political Parties and the Southern Cone."*Estudios Interdisciplinarios de América Latina y el Caribe* Vol. 4 No. 2 Julio-Diciembre 1993. http://www1.tau.ac.il/eial/index.php?option=com_wrapper&Itemid=134

Guilhon Albuquerque, José Augusto. "Integration, Democratisation and External Influence." Workshop paper for *Dollars, Democracy and Trade: External Influences on Economic Integration*, Los Angeles, May 2000. 1–14.

Huntington, Samuel. *The Third Wave: Democratization In The Late Twentieth Century.* Norman and London: University of Oklahoma Press, 1991.

Kant, Immanuel. *Zum ewigen Frieden, Ein philosophischer Entwurf.* Bd. II Frankfurt:Theoriewerkausgabe, 1968.

Koschel, David. "Approaches and Instruments of the German Political Foundations and the US Party Institutes in Comparative Perspective." Unpublished essay. Berlin, 2005.

Linz, Juan, and Alfred Stepan. *Problems of Democratic Transition and Consolidation. Southern Europe, South America, and Post-Communist Europe.* Baltimore: Johns Hopkins University Press, 1996.

Malamud, Andrés. *The International Dimension of Democratization: the Case of Argentina.* Working Paper, Instituto Português de Relaçoes Internacionais.

Merkel, Wolfgang. "Im Zweifel fuer den Krieg." *Die ZEIT*. April 20, 2006: 5.

OECD. *Development Cooperation Guidelines Series.* Paris: Development Cooperation Guidelines Series, 1995.

Pastor, Robert. *Whirlpool: U.S. Foreign Policy towards Latin America and the Caribbean.* Princeton: Princeton University Press, 1992.

Pridham, Geoffrey. "International Influences and Democratic Transition: Problems of Theory and Practice in Linkage Politics." *Encouraging Democracy. The International Context of Regime Transition in Southern Europe.* Ed. Geoffrey Pridham. Leicester and London: Leicester University Press, 1991. 1–30.

Sassenfeld, Heinrich. "Beziehungen der politischen Parteien und Stiftungen." *Deutsche*

Beziehungen zu Lateinamerika. Ed. Achim Schrader. Muenster: Lit Verlag, 1991. 99–116.

———. "Die Bedeutung makropolitischer und makroökonomischer Beratung in der Zusammenarbeit mit Regierungen." *Neue Konzepte in der Entwicklungszusammenarbeit mit Lateinamerika? Ein Dialog zwischen Entwicklungspolitik und Wissenschaft.* Ed. Gleich, Albrecht et al. Hamburg, 1991. 119–24.

Waller, Peter. "Hilfe durch Einmischung." *Die ZEIT* 17. 11. 1989: 26.

Whitehead, Lawrence. *The International Dimensions of Democratization: Europe and the Americas.* Oxford: Oxford University Press 1991.

◆   Afterword

David William Foster

The editors of this volume state very precisely the important fact that the circumstances of the rise of authoritarian regimes in Spain and, subsequently, in Argentina, Uruguay, and Chile (to place them in chronological order) were owing to diverse internal and external historical circumstances, and they go on also to point out precisely the equally diverse factors that influenced the transition from authoritarianism to democracy and the variegated nature of institutional processes and cultural responses that must require one to bear very much in mind that an impulse to homologize the events of the four countries in question undermines any adequate historical perspective. Since internationally there is, in fact, a significant underdifferentiated perception of the nature of the various Latin American societies and their relationship to Spain, one does well always to articulate such considerations forcefully—especially in a society such as the United States where most people cannot even get the capitals of Latin America right.

Yet, there is a continuity between the four countries that goes beyond just the question of authoritarianism. That is, if only authoritarianism were at issue, one could question why these four countries. Or, why Spain and these three Latin American countries. What about the many faces of authoritarianism in other parts of the continent, from the pseudemocracy of the PRI era in Mexico, to the fossilized revolution in Cuba, to the long legacy of strongman dictatorships in Paraguay and other societies. One might also want to take into account how the 1964 coup in Brazil was something like a mid-twentieth century ur-tyranny for the Southern cone. The answer is an intriguing one, for it has to do with the way in which the neofascist regimes in Argentina, Uruguay, and Chile, despite singular textual differences between them (such as policies of detention, interrogation, torture, imprisonment, liquidation, and disappearance), all saw themselves as in some ways inspired by the fascist model of Francisco Franco. Franco's regime, well into its third decade by the time of the neofascist coups in the 1970s in the three countries in question,[1] was viewed as an inspiration, ideologically and executively, to the coup leaders of the respective countries. Franco's death in 1975, moreover, provided for the quite ironic situation that, whereas Spain's fascist legacy was renewed as an intellectual and political influence in Argentina, Uruguay, and Chile, the process whereby Spain was returning to democracy at the same time that these three countries were restaging the Franco experiment with renewed vigor and new technological resources, the mother country nevertheless became an important port of refuge for Latin American refugees from neofascism. While the latter played important roles in the consolidation of democracy in Spain and the revitalization of intellectual and artistic institutions (one must recall that Spanish literature was pretty moribund in the latter decades of Franquismo, which is why Spain provided important and welcoming publishing opportunities for Latin American authors and thus contributed materially to the so-called boom of the 1960s and early 1970s), these Latin Americans were not always welcome (especially academics who sought posts in the tight Spanish university market) and contributed to the emergence of the *sudaca* syndrome of Spanish mistrust of and often outright discrimination against the South Americans, the *sudamericanos*.[2] It is this privileged historical relationship between Spain and the southern cone military dictatorships, both in terms of Franco's legacy and the Spanish asylum, that lends particular weight to the conjugation of the four countries in this volume.

The issues raised in the twelve essays in this volume—and I count myself privileged to be among them—are magisterially introduced by the volume editors, Luis Martín-Estudillo and Roberto Ampuero, and they raise important overarching issues that give cohesion to the book as a whole: 1) The nature of institutional transition and the difficulties of charting its boundaries, particularly as regards cultural production; 2) The different emphases of that cultural production as it relates to the daunting task of making sense of lived social history, such as the microrécits that have predominated in Chile vs. the macrohistories that emerge more prominently in Argentina; 3) the complex question of the Spanish *Movida* and the degree to which it represented something profoundly "contestatorial" vs. an opportunistic, market-driven, individualist continuation of capitalist-based circumstances of late Franquismo; 4) the imperative for an inquiry into the degree to which a touted freedom of expression and the release from censorship in its many forms may have much of the chimera about it, to the degree that institutional forces, the neoliberalism of the postdictatorship period (the promise of whose imposition played an important role in Washington's "discovery" that military tyranny would not, could not ensure stable societies propitious for American investment and other interests), and the emergence of an aggressive globalization impacting profoundly on culture all presented challenges for the integrity, originality, and sociohistorical pertinence of that culture. This included serious debates relating to *Culture* as much as *culture* as valued ideologemes of the respective societies.

Indeed, one may even question the degree to which cultural production has delivered on the promise of a return to censorless freedom of speech, although would not want to overlook the ways in which some forms of censorship did continue, such as the right-wing Catholic opposition, successfully voiced, to the role of a Jew as Argentina's Secretary of Culture in the mid-1980s and the banning of Jean-Luc Godard's *Je vous salue, Marie* as immoral and injurious to Catholic institutions. And, while Spain remains relatively prosperous and has continued to capitalize on the decision by Franco's government to develop the book industry into one of the most extensive on the world, market forces have essentially exercised a form of censorship in the Latin American countries, where alternative publishing operations and minority-interest magazines have had a difficult time surviving. It does not mean all that much to have queer rights if few can afford access to queer culture: in many cases, foreign tourists are what keep some of the venues open, but foreign tourism is not always a reliable ally of cultural freedoms: the latter demand, for example, establishments (e.g., Hard Rock Café) that look like what they know from home and not historically verisimilar local ones. The way in which the Argentine and Uruguayan tango has had to adjust to international tourism is a case in point, and one wonders what will be left when the tourists are no longer interested in going to Buenos Aires or Montevideo.

Of particular interest to me is the issue of the horizons of transitionality, and only in part vis-à-vis the foregoing paragraph. Yet it is pertinent here: one of the major transitions that have been part of the record of redemocratization has been queer life and queer culture, and questions arise as to what extent the queer presence (very strong in Argentina, somewhat so in Uruguay, but still very retarded in Chile, although progress has been made with Bachelet: all three presidential candidates at the time of her election pledged themselves to protect gay rights) is for real. Sexual rights in general present aspects that are not really yet in transition, as may be witnessed by national conversations—or, often their virtual absence—over abortion. Certainly there were manifestations of a "gay rights movement" still under dictatorship, especially in Argentina, and, because of internal debates within queer culture (including questioning whether it is a useful concept), it is difficult to announce when a transition from heterosexism to the queer has/will have taken place. Obviously this is not just an issue within Spanish and the diverse Latin American societies.

What is more pertinent to the four societies under examination in this volume is the matter of transition to a definitive post-authoritarian society. I would venture to say that perhaps the transition will never be a closed matter and that the price of maintaining and preserving substantive democracy in Latin America, with a concomitant commitment to substantive cultural freedoms, will be the need for the transitional to be a permanent part of the sociohistorical record. Something like a Spanish/Latin American equivalent of the American bywords "The price of democracy is constant vigilance." The title, borrowed from Jewish/Israeli culture, that has been used in official and semiofficial reports on the disappeared as iconic of the period of tyranny, *Nunca más* (*Nunca mais* in Brazil), is meant deliberately to evoke the Holocaust. One is well aware of how certain Jewish interests lament—or, in fact, strenuously protest—against what they see as the hijacking (and, they fear, trivializing) of what, for something like the Holocaust Museum in Washington, D.C., is necessarily to be understood as a unique historical event, the Shoah, tied to the rise of fascism in Europe in general, but most directly to the Final Solution of Nazi Germany. In this sense, one cannot speak of other Holocaust, and the use of the term in Latin American societies to describe their experience with neofascism is vigorously to be refuted.

Nevertheless, holocaust, at least as a common noun, has been used to describe that experience, and like the writing on the Holocaust, which may be factored out into writing by deceased victims (i.e., Anne Frank), writing by the survivors, writing by the witnesses, writing by the descendents of the survivors, and writing by those who have developed an emotional involvement with the Holocaust, although their personal story is not that of the targets of the Final Solution, writing about the neofascist military regimes in Latin America and in Franco's Spain cannot neatly be grouped into a single transitional consciousness that will be superseded by other events. One might well ask why a

Mexican director, Guillermo del Toro, would produce, in 2006, a film dealing with Franco Spain in 1942, *El laberinto del Fauno* (*Pan's Labyrinth*). Leaving aside the argument that anyone has the right to produce culture on any available topic (yet a proposition, surely, not universally subscribed to), Del Toro's interest as a very now Mexican with events sixty years old is part a recognition that the thematic and ideological parameters of his story are still pertinent to both societies (and just as the history of all of the Latin American societies is reciprocally pertinent) and part recognition that one must not forget the role Mexico played in the 1930s and 1940s in receiving victims of the Civil War and Franco's subsequent regime, individuals who still figure prominently in Mexican cultural and academic history. In this sense, contemporary Argentine, Uruguayan, Chilean, and Spanish societies may never overcome the foundational trauma of the authoritarian/fascist/neofascist moment, just as they have never overcome other foundational traumas: for Spain, for example, the Moorish invasion and occupation; for Latin America, for example, the Spanish invasion and conquest. Has Argentina ever really transitioned from the Rosas period? I remember seeing back in the 1970s a graffiti that read "Vuelve Rosas" (Rosa's will return, a trope on the post-1955 Peronista slogan). Will Argentina ever really transition from Perón? Will Uruguay really ever transition from its symbiotic relationship with Argentina (Borges still always called the Uruguayans *orientales*, the term Argentines have customarily used to refer to Uruguay as the lost Argentine province). Will Paraguay ever really transition from the Guerra de la Triple Alianza (1865–1870)? I present these as rhetorical questions, but they could serve to organize a course on the respective national cultural productions, to the extent that one can refer to the ongoing return thematically to these foundational traumas and analyze the particular ways in which they are, yet again, ideologizing in a new fashion by a novel, a film, a play, an essay. Note how David Viñas has brilliantly insisted that the indigenous Argentines of the Pampa were, in the 1870s, Argentina's first disappeared, and that they prefigured the Dirty War massacres of the 1970s. And note how María Luisa Bemberg's film *Camila* (1984) is not a historical romance of something that occurred a century and a half ago, but rather a serious attempt to make that past history resonate in the presence and vice versa.

I have spoken too much of Argentine examples, but that is because it is the corpus that I have studied in depth for almost fifty years, a time span that has encompassed multiple transitions and a back-and-forth movement of culture among them. But given the sort of unity, with deep differences, between the four national cultural traditions examined here, that the editors have pointed out and that I have wished to complement, it will not be hard for others to offer parallel examples, which may, in turn, serve to illuminate Argentine ones that I have not immediately thought of: I close with one line of thought none of us here have pursued, which would involve the contrasting and comparative institutional history of the Spanish, Argentine, Uruguayan, and Chilean academy and its professorate.

Notes

1. Actually, in the case of Argentina, there had been a dress rehearsal in the form of the Revolución Argentina under the aegis of Lt. General Jorge Rafael Videla in 1967, which lasted (with other Junta leaders) until 1973; Lt. General Juan Carlos Onganía led the 1976 coup that imposed the Proceso de Reorganización Nacional, which lasted (with other Junta leaders) until the return to constitutional democracy in late 1983. The Argentine convention is to characterize the period inaugurated by Videla as authoritarian in nature and that inaugurated by Onganía as neofascist. It is in this sense that the authoritarian regimes of the previous decade are viewed as prelude to the neofascism that emerges in 1976.
2. The Argentines have been particularly stung by the *sudaca* syndrome, and not just because the Argentines are not wont to homologize themselves with other Latin Americans (with the exception of the historically fraternal Uruguayans). Argentina had an open door policy in the 1930s and early 1940s for victims of the Spanish Civil War and the creation of the Franco regime, one that particularly favored artists and intellectuals (one only need consult the extensive Spanish presence in the Museo del Teatro at the Teatro Nacional Cervantes in Buenos Aires), and it was disappointing for them to sense that Spanish society was not as welcoming of Argentine refugees of political repression as Argentina had been, forty years previously, of Spanish victims of political repression. Of course, all of this has as much to do with the material circumstances of history as it does with conflicting sociocultural imaginaries, but it does play out textually in the cultural production relating to the matter in the respective countries.

◆ Contributors

Roberto Ampuero is the author of nine novels, one volume of short stories, and one book about the narrative of Jorge Edwards. Born in Chile, he lived in Cuba, East Germany, West Germany, and Sweden before coming to the United States in 2000. He was an International Writers' Program fellow in 1996, and earned his master's and doctoral degrees at the University of Iowa, where he now teaches Latin American literature and creative writing. He also writes columns for the Chilean daily *La Tercera* and *The New York Times* Syndicate. His work has been published throughout Latin America as well as in Croatia, China, France, Germany, Italy, Portugal, Spain, and the U.S.

Luis Bagué Quílez is a postdoctoral fellow at the Universidad de Murcia, Spain. He is the author of several award-winning books of poetry and of the essays *La poesía de Víctor Botas; Poesía en pie de paz: modos del compromiso hacia el tercer milenio* (2006 Gerardo Diego Prize of Literary Criticism). He has also edited poetry by Ricardo E. Molinari, Julio Herrera y Reissig and Humberto Díaz-Casanueva. Since 1999 he co-directs the poetry review *Ex Libris*, published by the Universidad de Alicante, Spain. He is a regular contributor to the Arts section of the Spanish daily *Información*.

Estrella de Diego is Professor of Contemporary Art at the Universidad Complutense de Madrid and has been King Juan Carlos I of Spain Professor of Spanish Culture and Civilization at New York University. Her research deals with gender theory and postcolonial studies. Among other books, she is the author of *La mujer y la pintura en la España del siglo XIX*; *El andrógino sexuado. Eternos ideales, nuevas estrategias de género*; *Tristísimo Warhol* and *El filósofo y otros relatos sin personajes*. She has also curated a number of exhibitions, such as *Simbolismo ruso* (Madrid, Barcelona and Bourdeaux, 1999–2000) and Spain's representation at the 49th Venice Biennale (2001).

Hans-Otto Dill is Professor Emeritus of Latin American Literature at Humboldt University, Berlin and has been Visiting Professor at the Universities of Gottingen, Hamburg and São Paulo. His numerous essays include *El ideario literario y estético de José Martí* (Casa de las Américas Award); *Zwischen Humboldt und Carpentier: Essays zur kubanischen Literatur*; *Dante criollo. Ensayos euro-latinoamericanos*; a history of Latin American literature and books on Carpentier and García Márquez. He has also edited and translated several literary works from Spanish, Italian and French into German.

Jorge Edwards is considered a living classic of Latin American literature. Born in Chile, he has been awarded the National Prize for Literature and the Cervantes Prize, which is regarded as the highest honour for a Spanish-language writer. He studied law, and served as a diplomat until 1973, when General Pinochet overthrew Salvador Allende. Edwards resigned his post in Paris, and went into exile. In 1985 he returned to Chile, where he played a leading role in the anti-dictatorial movement. He was reinstated as an ambassador by the new democratic government in 1990. He has taught as a visiting professor in several American and European universities. He has published several award-winning novels, among them: *El peso de la noche* (1964); *El museo de cera* (1982); *El anfitrión* (1987); *La mujer imaginaria* (1989); *El origen del mundo* (1996); *El sueño de la historia* (2000) and *El inútil de la familia* (2004), as well as essays and memoirs. In 1973 he published *Persona non grata*, the first major critique of Fidel Castro's regime by a Latin American intellectual. Edwards is also a columnist for *La Segunda* (Santiago de Chile) and *El País* (Madrid).

Ana Forcinito is Associate Professor of Latin American Literature at the University of Minnesota, Twin Cities. Her research deals mainly with memory, human rights, film, and gender. She is the author of *Memorias y nomadías: gé-*

neros y cuerpos en los márgenes del posfeminismo and is currently co-editing a volume on human rights in Latin America.

David William Foster is Regents' Professor of Spanish and Gendeer and Women's Studies at Arizona State University. He served as Chair of the Department of Languages and Literatures from 1997–2001. His research interests focus on urban culture in Latin America, with an emphasis on issues of gender construction and sexual identity, as well as Jewish culture. He has written extensively on Argentine narrative and theater, and has held Fulbright teaching appointments in Argentina, Brazil, and Uruguay. He has also served as an Inter-American Development Bank Professor in Chile. His most recent publications include *Violence in Argentine Literature: Cultural Responses to Tyranny*; *Cultural Diversity in Latin American Literature*; *Contemporary Argentine*; *Gay and Lesbian Themes in Latin American Writing* and *Contemporary Brazilian Cinema*.

Carsten Humlebæk holds an M.A. in Spanish and a Ph.D. in History, and is an Assistant Professor in the Department of International Culture and Communication Studies of Copenhagen Business School. He has worked on the changes of the discourse on the nation and memory politics in Spain after the death of Franco. Recent publications include articles in the journals *Iberoamericana*, *Historia del presente* and *Historia y política*, and chapters in *Memoria de la Segunda República* edited by Ángeles Egido León (Biblioteca Nueva); *Totalitarian and Authoritarian Regimes in Europe* edited by Klaus Ziemer and Jerzy W. Borejsza (Berghahn) and *Partisan Histories* edited by Max Paul Friedman and Padraic Kenney (Palgrave Macmillan).

John Kimmich-Javier, who photographed the cover image, has exhibited extensively, participating in solo and group exhibitions in spaces such as the National Museum of Fine Art in Stockholm, Sweden; the Art Institute of Chicago; Harenberg Center in Dortmund, Germany; El Visor Centre Fotogràfic in Valencia, Spain; the Camera Club of New York, and many other institutions. His work has been published in venues such as *Stockholm New* (Sweden), *Architectural Record*, *Photography* (China), *Foto Profesional* (Spain), *Creative Camera* (England), *Chicago Tribune*, *The Los Angeles Times*, *Newsday*, and other North American and international publications. Between 1987 and 1988 IBM Corporation (White Plains, N. Y.) acquired 361 of his photographs for their collection. Kimmich-Javier's work is also included in the collections of the Art Institute of Chicago, the Canadian Centre for Architecture in Montreal, University of Texas at Austin, Harry Ransom Humanities Research Center, The

Polaroid Collections, Deloitte & Touche, Price Waterhouse & Co. and other corporate, public and private collections. He is Professor of Photography at the University of Iowa School of Journalism and Mass Communication. He is represented internationally by the picture agency, Bildhuset/Scanpix, Stockholm, and in the U.S. by ArchiTech Gallery, Chicago.

Germán Labrador Méndez is a researcher in the Department of Spanish and Spanish American Literatures at the University of Salamanca, Spain. His current focus is on the Spanish Transition and its counter-cultural movements. He is the author of the forthcoming book *Letras arrebatadas. Poesía y química en la transición española*. He co-directs a Seminar on "Discourse, Memory and Legitimation" at the University of Salamanca.

Juliet Lynd is Visiting Assistant Professor of Spanish at Carleton College. She studies contemporary Latin American literary and cultural production, specializing in the Southern Cone and Mexico. She has published articles on literature, film and cultural studies in Latin America and is currently at work on a book project that examines aesthetics, politics and performance in post-dictatorship Chile.

Luis Martín-Estudillo is Assistant Professor of Spanish Literature at the University of Iowa. His research deals with Spanish cultural and intellectual history, with an emphasis on early modern and contemporary aesthetics and epistemologies. His latest studies include *Hispanic Baroques: Reading Cultures in Context* (co-edited) and *La mirada elíptica: el trasfondo barroco de la poesía española contemporánea*. He is currently working on a book on the European ideal in Spain's transitional and democratic cultural discourses.

Antonio Méndez-Rubio is Associate Professor of Communications at the University of Valencia, Spain. His research deals with cultural criticism, popular music, poetics, and social movements. Among other books, he has authored *Encrucijadas: Elementos de crítica de la cultura*; *La apuesta invisible: Cultura, globalización y crítica social*; *Perspectivas sobre comunicación y sociedad* and *La destrucción de la forma*.

Gustavo A. Remedi is Associate Professor in the Department of Language and Culture Studies and the Latin American and Caribbean Studies Program, at Trinity College in Hartford, CT. He is the author of *Murgas: El teatro de los* *tablados* (Montevideo: Trilce, 1996), later translated and published as *Carnival Theatre: Uruguay's Popular Performers and National Culture* (Minneapolis: University of Minnesota Press, 2004). With historian Daniela Bouret, he co-authored the forthcoming *Escenas de la vida cotidiana (1910–1930). Hacia una sociedad de masas*. Remedi has translated Arjun Appadurai's *Modernity at Large*, and has published articles on popular culture, popular theater, cultural mediation, and urban life and the city as cultural discourse. He is currently writing on the discourse of property, and researching theatrical experiences taking place outside the theatrical establishment and as forms of social and political action.

Heinrich Sassenfeld holds a Ph.D. in Political Economy from the University of Bonn, and has been a Visiting Professor at Stanford University. Since 1977 he has worked for the Friedrich Ebert Foundation (a Germany-based political foundation) focusing especially on Latin American topics, and serving as the head of its Latin American department between 1984 and 1992. Since 2004 he has been the Director of the Belgrade office of the Friedrich Ebert Foundation, in charge of Serbia, Montenegro and Kosovo.

◆ Index

Compiled by Marcus S. Palmer

Abeledo, Graciela, 117
Abril, Gonzalo, 153, 169
Acevedo, Zelmar, 223, 230
Achugar, Hugo, 119
Adam, Erfied, 242, 246
Adorno, Theodor, 138
Agamben, Giorgio, 91, 97
Aguilar Fernández, Paloma, 198, 212–15
Aira, César, xxvi
Alaska, 125, 131, 134–35
Albarracín, Pilar, 189
Alcanda, Santiago, 133, 142
Aldini, Cristina, 81
Aleixandre, Vicente, 58
Alfaya, Javier, 209, 216
Alfonsín, Raúl, 239, 245
Almodóvar, Pedro, 59, 125, 187–88, 193
Alonso, Dámaso, 72
Alvarado, Velasco, 235
Álvarez, Gregorio, 106, 115
Allende, Isabel, 10
Allende, Salvador, 4, 5, 12, 235
Amnesia, 122, 144–47, 149, 160, 162; amnesiac society, 15; collective amnesia, 147; as a communicative strategy, 148; omnipresent amnesia, 145; with relation to history, 150; of the Transition, 150. *See also* Spain
Ampuero, Roberto, 250

Anderson, Perry, 72
Anguita, Eduardo, 93, 98
Aparecido, 92–93
Arab, Ricardo, 115
Aranguren, José Luis L., 58
Archetti, Eduardo P., 229–30
Ardoguein, Adriana, 118
Ardoline, Emile, 126
Art: conceptual, resistance, 15–16, 29; contemporary Spanish, 183; as cultural identity, 184; as cultural products, xvi, 186; and gender, 183; and homosexuality, 183; new Spanish images, 184
Arregi, Manu, 189
Asturias, Miguel Ángel, 35
Attali, Jacques, 135–36, 142
Aub, Max, 160
Auerbach, Erich, xii
Avaria, Antonio, 10
Avelar, Idelbar, 13, 22, 29, 31
Aviador Dro, 130, 139
Aylwin, Patricio, xv, 12, 245
Azcárate, Julio, 164, 169
Aznar, José María, 69
Azúa, Felix de, 59
Azúcar Moreno, 175, 177–91
Azul y Negro, 140

Bachelet, Michelle, 28, 252
Baeza, Mario, 6
Bagué Quílez, Luis, xvii, 70, 72
Bakhtin, Mikhail, 45
Balcells, Fernando, 30
Balderston, Daniel, 56
Ballvé, Teo, 119
Balmaceda, 3
Bamberg, María, 56
Baño, Roque, 125
Barceló, Miquel, 183
Bardem, Antonio, 169
Barella, Julia, 71–72
Barón Rojo, 138–39
Barra, María Josefa, 56
Barrentos, Mónica, 30–31
Barthes, Roland, 127, 130, 142
Bartolomé, Cecilia, 155
Bartolomé, José Juan, 155
Basilio, Miriam, 189, 192–93
Bataille, Georges, 136, 142
Bauman, Zygmunt, 125, 142
Bayer, Osvaldo, 40, 230
Bazán, Osvaldo, 222–23, 227, 229–30
Beguan, Viviana, 81, 97
Bejarano, Francisco, 60
Beltrán, Fernando, 70
Bemberg, María Luisa, 253
Benfield, Celina, 81
Benítez Reyes, Felipe, 60, 71–72
Benjamin, Walter, 63, 94, 122–23, 137, 142
Berg, Walter Bruno, 37, 56
Berio, Luciano, 137, 142
Bernabeu, Mira, 189
Berruti, Azucena, 115
Bessière, Bernard, 72
Beverley, John, 96–97
Bhabha, Homi, 177, 193
Bianchi, Adhemar, 119

Blanch, María Teresa, 192
Blanco, Juan Carlos, 115
Blasier, Cole, 237, 241, 246
Blaustein, David, 88
Bochino, Adriana, 38, 52, 56
Boeninger, Edgardo, 245–46
Boj, 192
Bolan, Marc, 140
Bolivar, Simón, 53
Bonafini, Hebe de, 80
Bonaso, Miguel, 80
Bonilla, Juan, 67, 72
Bordaberry, Juan María, 106, 115–16
Borello, Rodolfo, 34–35, 38, 56
Borges, Jorge Luis, 35, 52, 253
Boris, Tato, 227
Botas, Víctor, 60
Bowie, David, 140
Bradby, Barbara, 142
Brando, Oscar, 119
Bravo, Claudio, 229
Brea, José Luis, 192
Brecht, Bertolt, 64, 137
Breton, André, 63
Brito, Eugenia, 29–31
Broch, Hermann, 52
Brossa, Joan, 183
Buckley, Ramón, 58, 72
Bufwack, Mary, 178, 194
Bürger, Peter, 59, 72
Bush, George W., 69

Cabañas, Miguel, 194
Cabezas, Ana, 118
Caetano, Gerardo, 120
Callas, María, 221
Calveiro, Pilar, 77–78, 81, 83, 93–95, 97
Calvo, Adriana, 77
Calvo, Juan José, 120
Cámara, José María, 132, 142

Camarero, Gloria, 150, 169
Campano, Miguel Ángel, 183
Camphausen, Gabriele, 212, 215
Cañas, Dionisio, 66, 71, 72
Cancela, Walter, 120
Cánovas, Rodrigo, 31
Cantwell, Robert, 192, 194
Caparrós, Martín, 93, 98
Capote, Truman, 38
Cardalda, Teo, 140
Carpentier, Alejo, 35, 45
Carrero Blanco, Luis, 153, 165
Casado, Miguel, 71–72
Casal, Tino, 140–41
Castellote, Alejandro, 184, 194
Castillo, Juan, 30
Castillo Oreja, Miguel Ángel, 192
Castro, Fidel, 230
Castro-Klaren, Sara, 17, 31
Cebrián, Juan Luis, 208, 215
Celaya, Gabriel, xvii
Cembalest, Robin, 181, 194
Cercas, Javier, xxiv, 163–64, 169
Cerdán, Josetxo, 154, 169
Cernuda, Luis, 61–62
Chalmers, Douglas, 237, 240, 245–46
Chamorro, Paloma, 129
Chao, Ramón, 147
Chaplin, Charles, 104
Chartier, Roger, 120
Chirbes, Rafael, xxiv, 147, 160–61, 167, 169
Christ, Ronald, 31
Coetzee, J.M., xxiii, xxvii
Colectivo Vírico, 183, 195
Collective imaginary, 122
Collyer, Jaime, xxvi
Colmeiro, Francisco J., 145, 159, 169
Coloane, Francisco, 8
Colomo, Fernando, 158, 169
Commitment: "deep commitment" vs. "great objectivity," xxi; to democratic institutions, 149; of literature, 15; to political organizations, 149
Conti, Haraldo, 52
Contreras, Gonzalo, xxvi
Conversi, Daniele, 214–15
Coppini, Germán, 140
Cordero, Manuel, 115
Corral, María, 192
Cortázar, Julio, 35, 41, 52
Corvalán, Luis, 5
Coughlin, Brenda, 209, 216
Coup d'état: Argentine, 79–80, 95, 218; Brazilian, 250; in Chile, 3–4, 6, 13, 27; failed attempt in Spain, 59, 123–24, 206; *golpe*, 12; Uruguayan, 99, 106, 116
Courtouis, Miguel, 164, 169
Criado, Nacho, 187
Croce, Marcela, 35, 38, 56
Cuerda, José Luis, 163, 169

Da Silva Barbosa, José Fábio Silva, 230–31
Daleo, Graciela, 92
Damroch, Lori Fisler, 236, 247
Darío, Rubén, 9
de Amicis, Edmondo, 177, 191, 193
de Armas, Gustavo, 120
de Brito Barahona, Alexandra, 212, 214
de Diego, Estrella, xv–xvi, 194
de Gelman, Irureta, 119
de la Iglesia, Eloy, 156, 158, 169
de los Santos, Miguel, 190, 195
de Miñón Rodríguez, Miguel Herrero, 213
de Osatinsky Solars, Sara, 81
Décalage, 148
del Toro, Guillermo, 253

Deleuze, Gilles, 16, 31
Democracy: emerging in Spain, xiii; general definition, 233; and Kantian democratic peace, 236. *See also* Transition to democracy
Derribos Arias, 135, 138
Derrida, Jacques, 138
Desaparecido, 92–94
Devo, 139
Diament, Mario, 229
Díaz de Castro, Francisco, 71–72
Díaz López, Marina, 169
Dictatorship. *See* Franco, Francisco; Pinochet, Augusto; Videla, Jorge Rafael
Diderot, Denis, 63
Díez Medrano, Juan, 214–15
Dill, Hanso-Otto, xii, 56
Dinarama, 130
Dirty realism, 67, 70
Discépolo, Armando, 104
Discourse: Francoist, 210–11; media, 197, 200, 205; national, 196, 204, 207, 209, 211; "pact of silence," 199, 208; political, 197, 206
Doctor, Rafael, 189, 192
Documentary narratives, 155
Donoso, José, 10, 36
Drama: "community theater," 101, 103, 114; of fragmented realities, xxi–xxii; "frontier theater," 101; "independent theater," 101; "street theater," 103; *Tejanos*, 100–101, 103, 114–15, 117
du Gard Martin, Roger, 42
Dubatti, Jorge, 120
Duffau, Marcelino, 117
Dylan, Bob, xvii

Eagleton, Terry, 63, 69, 72
Echevarría, Esteban, 34, 37, 41

Edwards, Jorge, xviii–xix, xxv, 36
Egea, Javier, 60, 71
Einstein, Albert, 219
Eliaschev, José, 229
Eltit, Diamela, xv, xix, 12–17, 22–23, 27–32
Enríquez, Xosé, 103
Espaliú, Pepe, 183

Falcón, Enrique, 70
Falkland/Malvinas war, xiv, 54, 239
Feinmann, Pablo, 34, 37, 56
Felman, Shoshana, 91, 98
Fernández-Cid, Miguel, 192
Fernández-Santos, 191, 194
Ferro, Marc, 152, 169
Feuer, Jane, 126, 142, 241
Filgueira, Fernando, 120
Film, 59, 123–24, 162–63; Argentine Golden Age, contemporary, 163, 220; historical lack of during Transition, 150–52, 158; homosexual registers in, 220; Mexican, 253; of the 1980s, 157; of Transition, 151, 154
Fischer, Iris, 227
Folco, Federica, 118
Forcinito, Ana, xxii–xxiii
Foster, David William, xx, 221–24, 228, 230–31
Foster, Hal, 59, 63–64, 73
Foucault, Michel, 134, 142
Fouce, Hector, 142
Fraga Iribarne, Manuel, 214
Franco, Francisco, xii, xiv–xvii, xx, xxiv, 123, 129, 134, 144–45, 148, 159, 165, 167, 169, 176–77, 182, 185, 187, 189, 192–93, 196–205, 208–13, 237, 250–54
Franco, Jean, 17, 32
Frank, Anne, 252

Franz, Carlos, xv
Freres, Cristian, 236, 238, 241, 244, 247
Fresán, Rodrigo, xxvi
Freud, Sigmund, 219
Friedman, Milton, 28
Friedrich Ebert Stiftung, 242–43, 246
Fry, Peter, 223–24
Fuertes, Gloria, xvii
Fuguet, Alberto, xxvi
Fukuyama, Francis, 65, 73
Fusi, Juan Pablo, 73
Fuskova, Ilse, 227, 231

Gallero, José Luis, 193–94
Galsworthy, John, 42
Galtieri, Leopoldo, 44
Gambrell, Jamey, 181, 194
Gamoneda, Antonio, 71
Ganduglia, Néstor, 120
Garcé, Adolfo, 120
García, María Claudia, 119
García Calvo, Agustín, 58
García Corrales, Guillermo, 30, 32
García Lorca, Federico, 61
García Márquez, Gabriel, 35, 42
García Martín, José Luis, 60–61, 71, 73
García Montero, Luis, 60–62, 69–71
García Pelayo, Gonzalo, 170
García Rodero, Cristina, 184
García San Miguel, Luis, 142
García Sevilla, Ferrán, 183
Gardella, Liliana, 81
Garín, Felipe, 183, 194
Garretón, Manuel Antonio, 233–34, 237, 242, 245, 247
Gavazzo, José, 115
Geirola, Gustavo, 230–31
Geist, Anthony L., 71–73
Gelman, Juan, 78, 81, 98

Gender: identity, 124; persecution of women, xxi, 12, 23, 42, 218–19; representations, 124, 175; studies in Spain, 187
Gilbert, Jeremy, 134, 142
Gilman, Claudia, 35, 56
Gimferrer, Pere, 59
Giorgi, Gabriel, 230–31
Godard, Jean-Luc, 251
Gold, Ariel, 118
Golpes Bajos, 130–31, 140
Gómez, Lola Proaño, 120
Gómez, Teresa, 71
González, Felipe, 62, 208, 215
González-Enriquez, Carmen, 212, 214
González Robles, Luis, 193
Goodwin, Andrew, 141–42
Gorbato, Viviana, xxi, 226–27, 231
Goya, Francisco de, 186
Goytisolo, Juan, xviii, xx–xxi, xxvii, 59
Grabowski, Sabine, 213, 215
Gramsci, Antonio, 50, 228
Grandes, Almudena, xxiv
Graziano, Frank, 229, 231
Green, James N., 229, 231
Groussac, Paul, 226
Grugel, Jean, 234–35, 237, 247
Guattari, Felix, 16, 30
Guerra, Alfonso, 200
Guevara, Ernesto, 230
Guilhon Albuquerque, José Augusto, 234, 247
Guillén, Claudio, 131, 143
Guirao, José, 189
Guissani, Pablo, 228, 231
Gurlekián, Martín, 107
Gutiérrez, Chus, 123–24, 164, 170
Guttiérez, Gilda, 100
Gutiérrez, Menchu, 71

Gutiérrez Haces, María Teresa, 34, 38, 50, 53, 56
Guzmán, Delfina, 7

Habermas, Jürgen, 59, 73
Halbwachs, Maurice, 78, 98
Halerpín, Jorge, 229
Haraway, Donna, 139, 143
Harlow, Barbara, 96, 98
Haro Tecglen, Eduardo, 147
Havel, Vaclav, 7
Hawthorne, Suzan, 187, 194
Hemingway, Ernest, 38
Hernández, Diego, 120
Hernández, Javier, 154, 170
Herrero, Gerardo, 164, 170
Hidalgo, Juan, 187
Hodges, Donald, 229, 231
Horowicz, Alejandro, 229
Huelva, Elodia, 189
Huerga, Manuel, 165, 170
Huggan, Graham, 194
Human League, 140
Humlebaek, Carsten, xiii–xiv, 198, 213–15
Huneeus, Cristián, 10
Huntington, Samuel, 236, 247
Hutcheon, Linda, 22, 32
Huyssen, Andreas, 63, 73

Ibáñez, Carlos del Campo, 3
Ibáñez, Juan G., 200, 216
Identity: "collective," 145–46, 153; ethnicity, vi, 175, 177–78; "identity politics," 14, 19; marginalization, 14, 16; minority representation, 177; multi-indigenous cultures, 12; (re)representation, 180, 188; (self)identity, 188; Spanish orientalism, 178, 181; "Spanishness," xvi, 175–77, 185–89; subjugating identification, 126; transformations of, 81
Ilie, Pauel, 71, 73
Imbert, Gérard, 129, 143, 147, 170
Irigaray, Luce, 31
Izquierdo, Jesús, 149, 160, 162, 170

Jackson, Michael, 179
Jameson, Fredric, 63–64, 73
Jara, René, 92, 98
Jarque, Fietta, 191, 194
Jarry, Alfred, 118
Jaúregui, Carlos Luis, 223, 231
Jelin, Elizabeth, 78–79, 98
Jews: homophobia of, 219; persecution of, xxi, 218–19
Jockl, Alejandro, 223, 231
Jordá, Joaquín, 149, 155, 158, 163
José De Rosa, Rafael, 104
Joyce, James, 52
Juan Carlos (King), 207
Juaristi, Jon, 71
Junta, 34, 53–54, 81, 90, 93, 218

Kaka de Luxe, 130
Kant, Immanuel, 235–36, 245, 247
Kaplan, Ann E., 178–79, 194
Katzman, Ruben, 120
Kavadloff, Santiago, 229
Kinder, Marsha, 193–94
Kirschner, Néstor, 230
Kissenger, Henry, 5, 56
Kohlstruck, Michael, 212, 216
Kohut, Karl, 56
König, Helmut, 212, 216
Koschel, David, 246–47
Kozameh, Alicia, xxii, 82–86, 95–98
Kraftwork, 139
Kristeva, Julia, 81
Kundera, Milan, 7

Kunzle, David, 230–31
Kutuyama, Kauro, 189

La Madrid, María, 81, 98
La Mode, 130
Laborda, Gabriel Cisneros, 213
Labordeta, José Antonio, xvii
Labrador, Germán, xxiv
Lacan, Jacques, 129, 144
Laforcade, Enrique, 10
Lagos, María Inés, 32
Lamas, Menchu, 183
Lamillar, Juan, 60
Lang, Fritz, 105
Langbaum, Robert, 63
Lanz, Juan José, 59, 64, 73
Las Vulpess, 131
Laub, Dori, 91, 98
Le Goff, Jean Pierre, 94
Lechado, José Manuel, 139, 143
Lejarza, Mikel, 164
Leño, 138–39
León, Sánchez, 149
Leuco, Alfredo, 229
Levi, Primo, 79
Lewin, Miriam, 81
Lewis, Reina, 194
Lezama Lima, José, 41, 52
Létora, Juan Carlos, 30, 32
Lihn, Enrique, 9
Lima, Sande, 115
Linares, Abelardo, 60
Linz, Juan, 244, 247
Llach, Luís, xvii
Llena, Toni, 187
Lojo, María Rosa, 41
Longobardo, Javier, 189
López, Antonio, 183
López, Ileana, 118
López, Marcos, 222

López, Valeriano, 189
López Cuenca, Rogelio, 184
López de Haro, Reneé, 180, 194
Loquillo, 125
Los Burros, 131
Los Nikis, 131
Los Rodríguez, 126
Los Ronaldos, 126
Los Secretos, 125, 130
Los Toreros Muertos, 130
Los Trogloditas, 128, 131
Loubet, Jorgelina, 35
Lübbe, Hermann, 212, 216
Lucy, Nial, 73
Lupi, Federico, 164, 170
Luque, Aurora, 60
Lynd, Juliet, xix, xxii
Lyne, Adrian, 126
Lyotard, Françoise, 59, 98

Machado, Antonio, 63, 148
Machado, Manuel, 72–73
Madonna, 179
Mainer, José-Carlos, 38, 62
Makenna, Benjamín Vicuña, 4
Malamud, Andrés, 239, 245, 247
Mallarmé, Stéphane, 63
Mamá, 130
Mann, Thomas, 42
Mansilla, 41
Maradona, Diego, 221
Marchán, Simón, 194
Marchesi, Aldo, 120
Marcuse, Herbert, 50
Marechal, Leopoldo, 38, 41–42
Marek, Claudina, 227, 231
María, Ana del Río, xxvi
María, Javier, xxiv
Markarián, Vania, 120
Mármol, José, 34, 37

Marsé, Juan, 42
Martí, Ana María, 80
Martín-Estudillo, Luis, 250
Martínez, José Tono, 193–94
Martínez, Tomás Eloy, 89
Martínez-Lázaro, Emilio, 123–24, 126
Martínez Mesanza, Julio, 71
Marty, Enrique, 189
Marx, Groucho, 179
Marx, Karl, 50, 219
Marzal, Carlos, 72
Masiello, Francine, xiv, xxvii, 30, 32
Masowiecki, Tadeusz, 199, 213
Massera, Emilio, 89
Massiel, 176, 190
Mathei, Fernando, 9
Maurente, Luis, 115
McGuigan, Cathleen, 181, 195
Mecano, 125
Medina, Alberto, 144, 155, 170
Medina, Ricardo, 115
Melamed, Diego, 229
Memory, 79, 82, 84, 89, 91, 94–95, 114, 126–28, 144, 146, 150, 161, 163–64; arbitrary selection of, xxii; authoritarian control of, xii; collective, 15–16, 84, 86, 89, 128, 198; conscious oblivion, xiv; culture of, 82; denial of, 127; discordant, 198; and exile, xxiii; and experience, 129; fragmentation of, 86–88; historical, xi, 114, 145, 157, 159–60, 163; "Historical Memory Act," xxiii; historical unmemory, 122; impossibility of, 131; "labor of memory," 79, 88; learned discourse, 153; marginalization, 78; "memory and oblivion," xxi, 79; "musical memory," xvii, 123; as narrative theme, 148; non-historical, 169; political, 102; reconstruction of, 80–81, 85, 87, 92, 95; recovery of, xxii, 159; social, 83, 94–95, 110, 156; social amnesia, xxiii, xxvi, 78; in terms of nostalgia, 123, 128–29; (un)memory, 127
Méndez, Sabino, 122, 128–29, 143
Méndez Rubio, Antonio, xvi, 70
Mendoza, Eduardo, 59
Ménem, Carlos Saúl, 227–28, 245
Mengíbar, Inmaculada, 71
Mercado, Rosendo, 139
Merkel, Wolgang, 236, 247
Mestre, Juan Carlos, 70
Milia, Marí de Pirles, 80–81
Millán, Antonio Jiménez, 71
Millares, Manolo, 185
Miranda, Fernando, 53, 119
Miró, Chris, 227
Mitre, Bartolomé, 46–48, 53
Mnouchkine, Ariane, 118
Moa, Pío, 162
Modarelli, Alejandro, 231
Molpeceres, Jesús G., 190, 195
Monroe, Marilyn, 221
Monteforet Toledo, Mario, 42
Mora, Ángeles, 71
Morales, Carlos, 155, 170
Morales, Leonidas T., 31
Morán, Gregorio, 146, 170
Moraza, Juan Luis, 184
Moreira, Constanza, 120
Moreiras, Alberto, 29, 32
Moreiras, Cristina, 145, 170
Mott, Luiz, 223–24, 231
Moulián, Tomás, 30, 32
Movida, xiv, 59, 62, 129–30, 134, 250
Muchnich, Daniel, 229
Munu, Actis, 81

Muraro, H., 154, 170
Music: music videos, 123–24; political messages, xvii; self-reflection, 138; and social change, 137; as social practice, 135; spaces of freedom, xvi
Myth, 130–31, 134

Napoleon III, 48
Narrative: of amnesia, 146; of authoritarianism, 34–35; of dictatorship; 35, 37; economic critique, 16, 22–24, 27, 40; expository, 166; fragmented perspectives, xxvi; historical narratives, 145; historical novel, 41; magazines and newspapers, 7, 58, 176; of marginalized sectors, xix, 21–22; media narratives, 151; "micro-narratives," xiv; performance novel, 14, 23; perspective of the defeated, xxiv; political commitment, 16, 26–27; reception of dictatorship, 51–52; recovering memory, xxii; role of military, 37–38; of soldiers, 34–36, 40–42, 44–45, 50, 53, 55; of testimony, 38, 77, 81–83, 86–87, 91–92, 95; "totalizing story," xiv
Navarro, Vicenç, xiii, xvii, xxvii
Neruda, Pablo, 4–5
Neustadt, Robert, 30–32
Nixon, Richard, 5
Novaro, Marcos, 229, 231
Novión, Alberto, 104
Núñez, Aníbal, 71
Núñez, Marina, 189

Obús, 139
O'Donnell, Guillermo, 90
Oermann, Bob, 178, 194
O'Higgins, Bernardo, 7
Olea, Raquel, 32

Oleza, Joan, 69, 73
Olick, Jeffrey K., 209, 216
Olivares, Carlos, 29, 33
Onganía, Juan Carlos, 254
Ortiz, Fernando, 60
Ortiz-Osés, Andrés, 73
Otero, Blas de, xvii
Ovid, 130, 143

Pachecho Areco, Jorge, 106, 116
Padilla, Heberto, 6
Pagni, Andrea, 56
Palermo, Vicente, 229, 231
Parálisis Permanente, 131, 140
Pardo, José Ramón, 128, 133, 143
Parenti, Michael, 150, 170
Parker, Roger G., 223, 231
Parra, Marco Antonio de la, 30, 32
Parra, Nicanor, 6, 10
Parra, Violeta, xvii
Partnoy, Alicia, 80, 83
Pastor, Robert, 241, 247
Pazos, Carlos, 187
Pearson, Ewan, 134, 142
Peces-Barba, Gregorio, 204, 213
Pegamoides, 125, 131, 134–35
Pelayo, Gonzalo García, 155
Pelé, 221
Pellarolo, Silvia, 120
Pellegrino, Adela, 120
Peralta Morales, Antonio, 183, 195
Pérez-Llorca, José Pedro, 213
Pérez-Minguez, Pablo, 193, 195
Pérez, Pablo, 154, 170
Pérez Villalta, Guillermo, 183
Perlongher, xxi, 222–26, 228–31
Permuy, Enrique, 100, 103, 118
Perón, Eva, 221
Perón, Isabel, 46
Perón, Juan Domingo, 37, 42, 43, 229

Pessoa, Fernando, 70
Petisme, Ángel Muñoz, 71
Picasso, Pablo, 185–86, 191
Piglia, Ricardo, 52
Pilo, Carlos, 103
Piña, Juan Andrés, 31
Pino-Ojeda, Walescka, 29–30
Pinochet, Augusto, xi, xv, xviii–xix, 4, 7, 9–10, 12, 17–18, 28–30, 234, 238, 240
Píris, Daniel, 117
Plato, 134
Poch, 139
Poetry: "of experience," xvii, 62–63, 66, 70; figurative, 60, 70; generation of 1927, 59; Novísimos (generation of 1968), xvii, 59–60; poems and anti-poems, 6; *poesía del diálogo*, 63; *poesía del fragmento*, 63; *poesía metafísica*, 63; *poesía practicable*, 64, 129; *poesía social*, xvii, 62
Polansky y el Ardor, 131
Pollak, Michael, 78, 98
Pons, Ventura, 155, 170
Pontecorvo, Gillo, 156, 170
Post-authoritarian orders, xii, 200
Postmodernism, 59–60, 63, 65–66, 69, 185
Prado, Benjamín, 71
Prashad, Vijay, 119
Pratt, Mary Louise, 17, 33
Prego, Victoria, 153, 214, 216
Pridham, Geoffrey, 238, 247
Prieto de Paula, Ángel L., 59–60, 64, 74
Puig, Manuel, 220
Puig Antich, Salvador, 165
Pujol, Jordi, 207

Queralt, Rosa, 192
Quintanilla, José Luis, 190, 195

Radio Futura, 130, 134
Raimon, xvii
Ramas, Ernesto, 115
Ramoneda, Josep, 147
Ramos, Susana Jorgelina, 81
Rapisardi, Flavio, 223, 227, 231
Raveca, Paulo, 120
Ravinet, Jaime, 246
Reixa, Antón, 163, 170
Religion, role of, 8
Remedi, Gustavo, xxi–xxii
Retardierung, xii
Rey, Fernando, 156, 170
Ribas, José, xvii, xxvii
Richard, Nelly, 29–31, 33
Rico, Aldo, 120
Riechmann, Jorge, 64, 70, 71, 74
Rimbaud, Arthur, 63
Rivas, Manuel, 163, 170
Roa Bastos, Augusto, 35
Roca i Junyent, Miquel, 203, 205, 213, 216
Rodríguez, Ileana, 97–98
Rodríguez, Juan Carlos, 60, 74
Rodríguez Buratti, Juan Antonio, 115
Rodríguez Monegal, Emir, 56
Rojo, Juan Andrés, 189
Romero, Pedro G., 184
Rosas, Juan Manuel, 37, 41, 46, 218
Rosenfeld, Lotty, 30
Rosenstone, Robert, 151, 166, 170, 253
Rosseti, Ana, 60
Rovatti, Pier Aldo, 65–66, 74
Ruíz, Julián, 140

Said, Edward, xxiii, xxvii, 177
Saint-Jean, Manuel, 51
Salmoral, Lucena, 42
Salvador, Álvaro, 60, 71, 74

Salvago, Javier, 60
San Martín, José de, 3, 44
Sánchez, Florencio, 104
Sánchez, Verónica, 127
Sánchez Ferlosio, Rafael, 58
Sánchez León, Pablo, 160, 162, 170
Sánchez Robayna, Andrés, 60
Sánchez Rosillo, Eloy, 60
Sanguinetti, Julio María, 114
Sapriza, Graciela, 120
Sarlo, Beatriz, 82, 88, 91, 94, 98
Sarmiento, Domingo Faustino, 34, 36–37, 44, 48, 53, 56
Sartorius, Nicolás, 209, 216
Sartre, Jean Paul, xx
Sassenfeld, Heinrich, xix, 246–47
Saura, Carlos, 185–86, 192
Savater, Fernando, 58–59, 74
Sawchick, Marcel, 118
Scarano, Laura, 69–70, 74
Schlegel, Friedrich, 137
Schneider, René, 5
Sebreli, Juan José, xxi, 220–22, 227–29, 231
Seco Serrano, Carlos, 182, 192, 195
Segura, Santiago, 125
Seimanas, Ignacio, 118
Sempol, Diego, 121
Semprún, Jorge, 191
Sepúlveda, Luis, xv
Serrano, Marcelo, xxvi
Serrat, Joan Manuel, 176, 190
Sexuality, xvi, 115; bisexual, 125; gay iconography, 187; gay map, 227; homoerotics, 221–22, 227; homophobia, xxi, 43, 218, 221–22, 228; homosexuality, 226; lesbian, 125, 227; lesbigay rights movement, 219, 223, 226, 252; liberation, xxv; persecution of gays, 219; prostitutes, 17, 47, 49; queer, 227, 251–52; transvestites, 17, 124
Sharim, Nishim, 7
Sherman, 187
Sicilia, José María, 183
Sigal, Silvia, 229
Siles, Jaime, 59
Silva, Emilio, 133, 159, 170
Silvera, Jorge, 115
Siniestro Total, 131
Skármeta, Antonio, xv
Small, Christopher, 134
Solano, Susana, 193
Solé Tura, Jordi, 205, 214, 216
Sontag, Susan, 66, 74, 82, 98
Soria Olmedo, Andrés, 74
Sosa, Mercedes, xvii
Sotelo, Ignacio, 214, 216
Soto, Álvaro, 171, 188, 195
Sotomayor, Aurea María, 31, 33
Spain, xi–xii; concepts of "modern," 185; concepts of "political," 185; hole in transition, 128; as a "modern" nation, xiv; Post-Transition culture, 129
"Spanishness," xvi
Spiller, Roland, 35, 38, 56
Stefan, Alfred, 244, 247
Stein, Gertrude, 177, 195
Steinbeck, John, 38
Strejilevich, Nora, xxii, xxvii, 82–83, 86–88, 96–97
Suárez, Adolfo, 59, 202–3, 214, 216
Subirats, Eduardo, xviii, xxvii, 146, 170

Tabernero, Santiago, 164, 170
Tamburrini, Claudio, 81
Tàpies, Antoni, 183, 185–86, 193
Tarradellas, Josep, 58
Teitelboim, Volodia, 35, 41

Television, 163, 166, 175, 179
Tierno Galván, Enrique, 203, 213
Timerman, Hector, 229
Timerman, Jacobo, 80, 229
Todorov, Tzvetan, 98
Tokar, Elsa, 81
Tompkins, Cynthia, 33, 98
Tourné, Daisy, 115
Toussant, Laurence, 192, 195
Transition to democracy, 99; "accorded transition," xiv; aesthetics and politics, 8; character of, xii; of Chile, xiv–xv, 6, 13; Chilean intellectuals in, xviii; civilized transition, 58; double transition, 58; after Fascism, xiii; faulty transition, xxiv; "model transitions" of Argentina, xiv; musical scene of, xvii; official accounts, xvi; permanence of transitions, xxv; phases, 233; presence or absence in Spain, xxiv; pre-transition, 13; processes, xvi; question of, xi, 28; rhetoric of, 12; Southern Cone, 233; of Spain, xiii, xv, xvii; of Uruguay, xvii
Trapiello, Andrés, 60, 71
Trevisán, João Silvério, 223–24, 229, 231
Trueba, David, 164, 170
Tubert, Carol, 178, 195
Tusell, Javier, 171

Ucelay da Cal, Enric, 213, 216
Ulanovsky, Carlos, 229
United States: pentagon, xi; CIA, 4
Ureña, Gabriel, 186, 192–93, 195
Uribe, Imanol, 156, 171
Uribe, Olga, 33
Uriburu, José Evaristo, 37, 43–44
Urquiza, Justo José de, 46–47
Urrutia, Matilde, 8

Valle-Inclán, Ramón María del, 35
Vallejo, César, 41
Vargas Llosa, Mario, 35, 41
Vattimo, Gianni, 65–66, 74
Vázquez, Gilberto, 115
Vázquez, Tabaré, 100, 114–15
Vázquez Montalbán, Manuel, 146–47, 171
Vega, José Arpino, 119
Velazquez, Diego, 179–80, 186, 191
Verbitsky, Horacio, 80, 229
Vernet, Jaume, 214, 216
Vezzetti, Hugo, 79–80, 83, 85, 89–90, 92–94, 98
Vico, Darío, 132, 143
Vidal, Hernán, 121
Vidal, Luis, 121
Videla, Jorge Rafael, 35, 44, 89, 254
Viglietti, Daniel, xvii
Vilarós, Teresa, 128–29, 143–44, 155, 171, 193, 195
Vilas, Acdel, 89
Villaespesa, Mar, 184
Villani, Mario, 81, 96
Valldosera, Eulalia, 189
Villegas, Juan, 121
Villena, Luis Antonio de, 71, 74
Viñas, David, xii, 34–38, 40–46, 50–56, 253
Viola, Roberto Eduardo, 35
Virgil, 130–31
Visual media: debates on memory, xxv; Chilean television, 9

Walger, Sylvina, 229
Waller, Perter, 243, 248
Walsh, Rodolo, 34, 38, 52
Whitehead, Lawrence, 233, 248
Wittmán, Tibor, 57
Wolfe, Roger, 66, 70, 72, 74

Wöll, Andreas, 212, 216
Wright, Thomas, 33

Yaffé, Jaime, 120–21
Yrigoyen, Hipólito, 39–40, 43

Zibechi, Raúl, 117, 121
Zola, Émile, xx
Zuker, Cristina, 81
Zulueta, Iván, 59
Zurita, Raúl, 30

VOLUMES IN THE HISPANIC ISSUES SERIES

35 *Post-Authoritarian Cultures: Spain and Latin America's Southern Cone*
    edited by Luis Martín-Estudillo and Roberto Ampuero
34 *Spanish and Empire*
    edited by Nelsy Echávez-Solano and Kenya C. Dworkin y Méndez
33 *Generation X Rocks: Contemporary Peninsular Fiction, Film, and Rock Culture,* edited by Christine Henseler and Randolph D. Pope
32 *Reason and Its Others: Italy, Spain, and the New World*
    edited by David Castillo and Massimo Lollini
31 *Hispanic Baroques: Reading Cultures in Context,*
    edited by Nicholas Spadaccini and Luis Martín-Estudillo
30 *Ideologies of Hispanism,* edited by Mabel Moraña
29 *The State of Latino Theater in the United States: Hybridity, Transculturation, and Identity,* edited by Luis A. Ramos-García
28 *Latin America Writes Back: Postmodernity in the Periphery (An Interdisciplinary Perspective),* edited by Emil Volek
27 *Women's Narrative and Film in Twentieth-Century Spain: A World of Difference(s),* edited by Ofelia Ferrán and Kathleen M. Glenn
26 *Marriage and Sexuality in Medieval and Early Modern Iberia,*
    edited by Eukene Lacarra Lanz
25 *Pablo Neruda and the U.S. Culture Industry,* edited by Teresa Longo
24 *Iberian Cities,* edited by Joan Ramon Resina
23 *National Identities and Sociopolitical Changes in Latin America,*
    edited by Mercedes F. Durán-Cogan and Antonio Gómez-Moriana
22 *Latin American Literature and Mass Media,*
    edited by Edmundo Paz-Soldán and Debra A. Castillo
21 *Charting Memory: Recalling Medieval Spain,* edited by Stacy N. Beckwith
20 *Culture and the State in Spain: 1550–1850,*
    edited by Tom Lewis and Francisco J. Sánchez
19 *Modernism and Its Margins: Reinscribing Cultural Modernity from Spain and Latin America,* edited by Anthony L. Geist and José B. Monleón
18 *A Revisionary History of Portuguese Literature,*
    edited by Miguel Tamen and Helena C. Buescu
17 *Cervantes and His Postmodern Constituencies,*
    edited by Anne Cruz and Carroll B. Johnson

16 *Modes of Representation in Spanish Cinema*,
   edited by Jenaro Talens and Santos Zunzunegui
15 *Framing Latin American Cinema: Contemporary Critical Perspectives*, edited by Ann Marie Stock
14 *Rhetoric and Politics: Baltasar Gracián and the New World Order*,
   edited by Nicholas Spadaccini and Jenaro Talens
13 *Bodies and Biases: Sexualities in Hispanic Cultures and Literatures*,
   edited by David W. Foster and Roberto Reis
12 *The Picaresque: Tradition and Displacement*, edited by Giancarlo Maiorino
11 *Critical Practices in Post-Franco Spain*,
   edited by Silvia L. López, Jenaro Talens, and Dario Villanueva
10 *Latin American Identity and Constructions of Difference*,
   edited by Amaryll Chanady
9 *Amerindian Images and the Legacy of Columbus*,
   edited by René Jara and Nicholas Spadaccini
8 *The Politics of Editing*, edited by Nicholas Spadaccini and Jenaro Talens
7 *Culture and Control in Counter-Reformation Spain*,
   edited by Anne J. Cruz and Mary Elizabeth Perry
6 *Cervantes's Exemplary Novels and the Adventure of Writing*,
   edited by Michael Nerlich and Nicholas Spadaccini
5 *Ortega y Gasset and the Question of Modernity*, edited by Patrick H. Dust
4 *1492–1992: Re/Discovering Colonial Writing*,
   edited by René Jara and Nicholas Spadaccini
3 *The Crisis of Institutionalized Literature in Spain*,
   edited by Wlad Godzich and Nicholas Spadaccini
2 *Autobiography in Early Modern Spain*,
   edited by Nicholas Spadaccini and Jenaro Talens
1 *The Institutionalization of Literature in Spain*,
   edited by Wlad Godzich and Nicholas Spadaccini

www.ingramcontent.com/pod-product-compliance
Lightning Source LLC
Chambersburg PA
CBHW030107010526
44116CB00005B/139